A WORLD BANK COUNTRY STUDY

Belarus
Prices, Markets, and Enterprise Reform

The World Bank
Washington, D.C.

World Bank Country Studies are among the many reports originally prepared for internal use as part of the continuing analysis by the Bank of the economic and related conditions of its developing member countries and of its dialogues with the governments. Some of the reports are published in this series with the least possible delay for the use of governments and the academic, business and financial, and development communities. The typescript of this paper therefore has not been prepared in accordance with the procedures appropriate to formal printed texts, and the World Bank accepts no responsibility for errors. Some sources cited in this paper may be informal documents that are not readily available.

The World Bank does not guarantee the accuracy of the data included in this publication and accepts no responsibility whatsoever for any consequence of their use. The boundaries, colors, denominations, and other information shown on any map in this volume do not imply on the part of the World Bank Group any judgment on the legal status of any territory or the endorsement or acceptance of such boundaries.

The material in this publication is copyrighted. Requests for permission to reproduce portions of it should be sent to the Office of the Publisher at the address shown in the copyright notice above. The World Bank encourages dissemination of its work and will normally give permission promptly and, when the reproduction is for noncommercial purposes, without asking a fee. Permission to copy portions for classroom use is granted through the Copyright Clearance Center, Inc., Suite 910, 222 Rosewood Drive, Danvers, Massachusetts 01923, U.S.A.

ISSN: 0253-2123

Library of Congress Cataloging-in-Publication Data

Belarus: prices, markets, and enterprise reform.
     p.   cm. — (A World Bank country study)
    Includes bibliographical references.
    ISBN 0-8213-3976-1
    1. Belarus—Economic conditions—1991– 2. Belarus—Economic conditions—1991– —Statistics. 3. Economic stabilization—Belarus.
I. World Bank. II. Series.
HC340.17.B475 1997
338.9478—dc21

                                  97-13283
                                     CIP

CONTENTS

Text Figures

Text Tables

Text Boxes

ACKNOWLEDGMENTS

This report is based on the findings of a World Bank team that visited Belarus in April/May 1996. The team included John Hansen (Mission Leader and Principal Author), Elliott Hurwitz (Industrial Reforms), David Sewell (Divestiture of Social Assets), and Sudhee Sen Gupta (Agro-industrial Reforms). The work of the mission in the field was guided by a CEM Steering Group under the Chairmanship of the Minister of Economy, with representatives of key ministries and organizations including Agriculture, Anti-Monopoly, Cabinet of Ministers, Industry, Finance, Foreign Economic Relations, Labor Prices, Supreme Soviet, and Vneshekonombank. Staff from the Resident Mission in Minsk who prepared major written contributions to the report include Sergei Kritchevsky (Trade) and Nikolai Lisai (Competition and Public Finance). David Phillips prepared the chapter on enterprise reform.

The analysis in this report draws on a series of special studies that were prepared by Belarusian teams of experts headed by L.A. Khankevich (Taxation), V.V. Pinigin (Enterprise Debts), B. Shapiro (Agriculture), L. Zlotnikov (Trade), and G. Turban (Exports). Sergei Shatalov (IECIF) prepared a note on the external debt of Belarus. A list of the background documents used in preparing this report is in the References section at the end of the report. The report draws significantly on the macroeconomic analysis and data prepared by the IMF during a parallel mission, but the Bank is solely responsible for the analysis and recommendations presented here.

The team would also like to express its appreciation to Yuri Dikhanov for preparation of the macroeconomic modeling framework used for the report, to Konstantin Senyut for assistance with data collection and analysis in Minsk, to Ivan Kupchenko for his work on external debt, to Yuri Sobolev for preparing the macroeconomic projections, to Zhicheng Li and Yuliya Merkulova for preparing the statistical annex, and to Leigh Hammill for assistance with copy editing and document preparation. Special thanks are also due to Elena Klochan for interpretation and translation. This report was prepared under the guidance of Basil Kavalsky (Director), James Harrison (Division Chief), and Christopher Willoughby (Resident Representative). The peer reviewers are Joel Bergsman (FIAS) and William Easterly (PRDMG). Jack Baranson, previously of the World Bank and most recently of the International Executive Service Corps office in Minsk, was the external reviewer.

The report was discussed with the Government in early 1997. Special thanks are due to Prime Minister Sergei Ling and his colleagues for their excellent comments on the draft and for the opportunity to discuss the findings and policy recommendations of the report in detail. Although some statistical updating was done on the basis of these discussions, the report reflects primarily the situation in Belarus as of late 1996.

ABSTRACT

Belarus is in a major economic crisis. The trade deficit has become unsustainable. External reserves have fallen to negligible levels. The number of loss-making enterprises is increasing rapidly. Budget revenues are falling far short of targets, and the Government has announced its intention to pursue expansionary monetary and credit policies to support the loss-making enterprises in industry and agriculture, to pay workers, and to cover its own expenses.

Like all former Soviet republics, Belarus suffered the twin shocks of higher energy prices and the loss of traditional markets when the Soviet Union collapsed. The Belarusian response to these shocks, however, has been very cautious. This has seriously delayed the structural changes that are needed to increase efficiency and develop new export markets. At the same time, the Government sought to cushion the shock of the adjustment process through expansionary credit policies and lax financial discipline on enterprises. Further delays will make the transition increasingly difficult.

The adverse effects of high inflation on the investment climate were compounded by unpredictable tax enforcement and extensive government controls on pricing, business establishment, credit, and access to suitable business premises. The business environment was further degraded by slow privatization and continued widespread presence of large state enterprises with preferential access to credit, subsidies, and government purchase orders. Faced with this, private investors, both domestic and foreign, have stayed away, and the falling levels of real net investments in fixed capital formation have created further barriers to renewed economic growth.

The situation has become notably worse in the last 18 months because the Government, instead of focusing on monetary discipline and structural reforms, began to intervene actively in the foreign exchange market to maintain an artificially stable exchange rate. The three-fold real appreciation of the Belarusian rubel against the US dollar since the end of 1994 has been the major factor causing the unsustainable trade deficit. It has also led directly to the rising rate of financial failure among Belarusian enterprises.

Escaping the current crisis and restoring growth will require rapid creation of a stable, predictable business environment that will attract the domestic and foreign investment needed to improve productive efficiency and international competitiveness. Establishing a good investment climate will require the immediate implementation of policies that will assure the competitive market determination of prices (especially for foreign exchange), strict financial discipline enforced by the effective and immediate threat of bankruptcy, a competitive market structure dominated by independent, privately owned enterprises, a transparent and predictable legal framework (especially for taxes), even-handed administration of laws, access to critical infrastructure services, and an efficient, well-targeted social safety net to protect those who need help during the transition period.

BELARUS - SELECTED INDICATORS TABLE

Indicators	Actual				
	1991	1992	1993	1994	1995

Part A: Main Macro Aggregates

Annual growth rates, calculated from data in constant 1993 prices

	1991	1992	1993	1994	1995
GDP (mp) per capita	-1.3%	-10.0%	-11.0%	-12.6%	-10.0%
Total consumption per capita	-6.7%	-10.7%	-4.1%	-10.8%	-16.4%
GDP at market prices	-1.2%	-9.6%	-10.7%	-12.6%	-10.1%
Total consumption	-6.6%	-10.3%	-3.7%	-10.8%	-16.5%
Private consumption	-6.0%	-7.8%	-0.6%	-14.0%	-23.3%
Government consumption	-7.7%	-15.3%	-10.5%	-3.0%	-1.8%
Gross domestic investment (GDI)	15.3%	-15.7%	-11.6%	-33.5%	-26.1%
Gross dom. fixed investment (GDFI)	4.4%	-18.1%	-15.4%	-17.2%	-27.0%
Exports (GNFS)	-1.1%	-34.0%	-38.0%	-17.0%	-6.0%
of which Goods	..	..	..	7.3%	13.1%
Imports (GNFS)	0.2%	-43.0%	-31.9%	-39.0%	11.0%
of which Goods	..	..	..	-19.2%	14.4%

Cumulative Developments (1990=100)

	1991	1992	1993	1994	1995
GDP (market price)	98.8%	89.3%	79.8%	69.7%	62.7%
Investment	115.3%	97.2%	86.0%	57.2%	42.3%
Consumption	93.4%	83.8%	80.7%	72.0%	60.1%
Exports	99.0%	65.3%	39.2%	38.7%	38.2%
Imports	100.5%	57.1%	38.1%	31.7%	30.2%

Savings-investment balances, calculated as shares of GDP in current prices

	1991	1992	1993	1994	1995
Gross Domestic investment, of which	29.5%	32.3%	38.4%	28.9%	25.2%
Fixed capital formation	22.4%	25.7%	31.2%	29.2%	25.1%
Government investment	..	..	..	..	7.3%
Foreign savings (negative of cur.act.balance)	..	-4.5%	30.6%	12.5%	2.5%
Gross national savings	..	36.8%	7.8%	16.4%	22.7%
Government savings	..	0.0%	-0.6%	-0.2%	-0.3%
Non government savings	..	36.8%	8.4%	16.6%	22.9%
Gross domestic savings	32.9%	33.7%	21.4%	15.6%	20.4%

Other

	1991	1992	1993	1994	1995
GDP inflation	107%	1,078%	1,097%	1,967%	647%
Annual average exchange rate (LCU/US$) 1/	..	23	269	3,694	11,534
Index real average exchange rate (1993 =100)	..	..	100	192	257
Terms of trade index (1993=100)	..	..	100	74	87
Incremental capital-output ratio (GDI based)	-22.4	-3.3	-2.8	-2.3	-2.2
Import elasticity with respect to GDP	..	..	..	-0.58	-1.30
Money growth (% p.a.)		376%	956%	1931%	158%
Real credit growth in the monetary sector (% p.a.)	-3%	-7%	-73%	-33%	-20%

BELARUS - SELECTED INDICATORS TABLE

Indicators	Actual				
	1991	1992	1993	1994	1995

Part B: Government Finance Indicators

Shares of GDP (%)

Indicators	1991	1992	1993	1994	1995
Total revenues, of which	..	46%	55%	48%	43%
Tax revenues	..	40%	45%	42%	35%
Total expenditures, of which	..	46%	53%	51%	45%
Consumption	..	37%	38%	41%	39%
Deficit(-)/Surplus(+)	..	0.0%	-1.8%	-2.6%	-1.9%
Financing:	..	0.0%	1.8%	2.6%	1.9%
Foreign	..	..	0.9%	-0.9%	-0.5%
Monetary sector	..	..	0.8%	3.2%	2.1%
Other domestic	..	..	0.1%	0.3%	0.3%

Other

Indicators	1991	1992	1993	1994	1995
Total Debt/GDPmp	..	..	9.9%	57.6%	36.9%
Total interest payments/Tax revenues	..	..	18.0%	1.0%	2.3%

Part C: Debt & Liquidity Indicators

Total DOD and TDS

Indicators	1991	1992	1993	1994	1995
DOD (US$ millions)	0.0	189	969	1,273	1,648
DOD / GDPmp ratio	..	5%	27%	27%	16%
TDS (US$ millions)	0.0	0.6	14.7	118.6	180.0
TDS / exports (XGS) ratio	..	0.0%	0.5%	4.1%	3.6%
Total gross reserves (months' imports G&S)	..	..	0.3	0.3	0.8

Part D: External Financing Plan

US$, millions

Indicators	1991	1992	1993	1994	1995
Official capital grants	0.0	0.0	0.0	0.0	0.0
Private investment (net)	..	7.0	18.0	10.0	7.0
Net Long term borrowing excl IMF	..	181	320	193	78
Adjustments to scheduled debt service	0.0	0	7	143	0
All other capital flows	..	-365	974	390	161
Financing Requirements (incl IMF)	..	-177	1,319	736	246
of which current account deficit	..	-182	1,113	599	254

Note: 1/ Weighted average exchange rate.

LIST OF ABBREVIATIONS

CEE	Central and Eastern Europe
CIS	Commonwealth of Independent States
EBRD	European Bank for Reconstruction and Development
FDI	foreign direct investment
FSU	former Soviet Union
GDP	gross domestic product
IBCE	Inter-Bank Currency Exchange
IBRD	International Bank for Reconstruction and Development (The World Bank)
IMF	International Monetary Fund
MOE	Ministry of Economy
MOF	Ministry of Finance
NBB	National Bank of Belarus
RUR	Russian ruble
SOE	state-owned enterprise
VAT	value added tax
YOY	year on year

CURRENCY EQUIVALENTS

Belarusian Rubels (BYR) per one U.S. Dollar (USD)

Prevailing average rate in 1995	11,500
Top of Currency Corridor	
First half of 1996	13,100
Second half of 1996	15,500
April 2, 1997	24,650
Prevailing Free Market Rate	
1995	11,000 - 12,000
June, 1996	15,000
September, 1996	18,500

UNITS OF MEASURE

bls	=	billions
ha	=	hectares
km	=	kilometers
mls	=	millions
ths	=	thousands
trs	=	trillions

CONVENTIONS

"East," in the context of trade discussions refers to the former Soviet Union (mainly Russia), and "West" refers to all non-CIS countries.

Vice President	: Johannes Linn
Director	: Basil Kavalsky
Division Chief/Manager	: James Q. Harrison
Principal Economist	: John Hansen

Executive Summary

Belarus faces a serious economic crisis. Although the Government has managed to reduce the rate of inflation significantly and output is expanding in a few areas of the economy, the overall picture is unsatisfactory. Aggregate industrial output continues to fall. The number of loss-making enterprises is increasing sharply month by month. Enterprise non-payments are creating serious problems. The trade deficit has become unsustainable. Foreign exchange reserves have fallen to excessively low levels. The budget is seriously short of resources. The lack of adequate structural adjustments in the enterprise sector is creating pressures on the budget and the banking system that could easily rekindle high rates of inflation. And living standards continue to fall. But these problems can be overcome. The necessary policy changes do not require extensive research, nor are major capital investments required. The changes could be launched almost literally at the stroke of a pen.

Though simple in concept and easy to initiate, these policy changes will lead to other changes that will have a profound impact on the future prospects for Belarus. These policy measures will create an environment that stimulates investors—both foreign and domestic —to increase production in Belarus and to make it more efficient. New jobs, larger export volumes, a more stable balance of payments situation, and lower domestic inflation will soon follow. Despite these benefits, the reforms will be difficult to sustain because, in the short term, they will require adjustments such as closing or radically restructuring some failing enterprises with no future prospects for efficient, competitive production in their current lines of business.

The people of Belarus need to understand why a continuation of past policies would be ruinous, and therefore why the reforms must be completed despite the short run difficulties. They must understand what needs to be done to prevent Belarus from sliding deeper and deeper into a severe economic crisis. They must understand that distorted prices cannot be the basis for protecting people against poverty. They must understand the importance of allowing prices to be determined by the normal interaction of supply and demand. They need to understand that everyone—individuals as well as enterprises—must pay for what they consume. If this consensus of understanding and support can be developed, Belarus can quickly lay the foundation for restoring living standards.

Background

When Belarus became independent in 1991, it was the richest of the twelve republics of the Commonwealth of Independent States (CIS) in terms of per capita income—a status reflecting the republic's steady growth during the 1970s and early 1980s. It had developed an industrial sector that, in terms of share of total GDP, made it one of the most heavily industrialized countries in the world. The agriculture sector was modernized and came to depend not only on heavy equipment, much of which was manufactured in Belarus, but also on imported fuel and fertilizers. Industrial and agricultural development was based on oil and gas from Russia that was priced at less than 10 percent of world prices in 1990. Enterprises in Belarus also enjoyed access to material inputs for processing and final assembly at internal transfer prices, as well as heavy infusions of capital investment, and preferential access to the markets of the former Soviet Union (FSU) and Eastern Europe due to artificially low transport costs and no customs barriers. As a result, Belarus became one of the most trade-reliant nations in the world, with imports and exports each constituting 50 to 60 percent of GDP. It was also one of the FSU republics most deeply dependent on intra-regional trade, which was equivalent to 70 percent of total trade.

Belarus lost its privileged position with the breakup of the former Soviet Union. Traditional markets collapsed, and the cost of critical inputs (especially energy) increased sharply in real terms. The terms of trade loss in 1991-92 has been estimated at 11 percent of GDP. The resulting decline in production and increase in inflation were primary factors contributing to the current economic crisis. Other countries experienced similar problems in 1990-91, but have found it easier to control inflation, stabilize their economies, and begin to restructure enterprises.

In Belarus, the problems caused by the collapse of the Soviet system were compounded by economic policies that sought to cushion and delay the transition to a market economy. Rather than implementing policies that would encourage people to adjust their living standards to the new realities and encourage enterprises to restructure and become internationally efficient, the Government sought to maintain living standards and employment through expansionary monetary and credit policies. As a result, aggregate demand far exceeded domestic production, leading to serious macroeconomic imbalances. These problems were made even worse by the distortions that were introduced to compensate for these imbalances and sustain living standards. For example, the directed credits that were used to support failing enterprises led to high rates of inflation; efforts since early 1995 to control inflation by stabilizing the exchange rate have produced a serious overvaluation of the exchange rate. This has seriously eroded the competitiveness and profitability of the enterprise sector in this traditionally open and heavily trade-dependent country.

These policies were part of an attempt to find a third way, a system that would combine the best of planned and market economic systems. The attempt has failed. The output decline is now as severe in Belarus as for the average economy of the FSU. And while other economies are starting recover, the economy of Belarus is only beginning to stabilize and is at risk of further declines in the future. By postponing the necessary structural adjustments, Belarus has failed to establish the foundations of enterprise productivity needed for restored growth. The lack of structural adjustments in the enterprise sector now threatens even the modest price stability that has taken Belarus so long to achieve.

The failure of past policies to restore growth on a sustainable basis has hurt the people of Belarus. According to World Bank data the average poverty rate has risen from about 5 percent to about 25 percent. Only about five percentage points of this increase in poverty has been the result of higher income inequality. The rest has been the direct result of economic decline. This report discusses ways in which the Government can protect the very poor during the transition process, but most of the emphasis is on restoring satisfactory rates of economic growth, for this is the only way that Belarus will be able to afford to take the majority of today's poor above the poverty line.

Although the Belarusian people lived well under the Soviet system, a return to the past is not feasible because, as history has shown, the Soviet system of command and control has too many built-in inefficiencies. The Soviet system worked for many years because of the vast natural resources and limited population density of the FSU, but eventually the degradation of the region's environmental and physical capital, the low efficiency of enterprises, and the growing inability to meet the needs of consumers led to the system's collapse.[1]

The potential for restoring growth in Belarus is excellent. The nation has a highly educated population, a disciplined work force, close proximity not only to traditional Russian markets, but to the rich European markets as well, and a history of heavy reliance on external trade. In the late 1980s, it exported a higher percentage of its output to other FSU republics than any of the other republics. By Soviet standards, its manufactured products were highly sophisticated. Nostalgia about the Soviet regime, under which Belarusians lived well, has led many Belarusian citizens and leaders to seek an alternative to market reforms including continued state ownership of production facilities. But as this report demonstrates, a return to the past is impossible. Instead Belarus needs to implement the policy measures presented in this report; a measure will allow Belarus to move out of the current stagnation and decline associated with the collapse of the Soviet-era command economy and improve living standards for all.

Belarus now needs to press forward to transform its economy into an efficient, market-based economy. This will require (a) major improvements in the policy framework to provide incentives for efficient production; and (b) substantial investments to improve the energy efficiency, product quality and competitiveness of the existing industrial and agricultural infrastructure. This infrastructure was poorly suited for competition in world markets when the former Soviet Union collapsed in 1991, and it is in even worse condition today because of inadequate investment—even for maintenance in many cases—during the intervening years. The investment required vastly exceeds that which the Government could possibly mobilize. One of the top priorities of the Government today is therefore to attract private investors, both foreign and domestic. Current rates of net fixed capital formation are close to zero, and foreign direct investment is among the lowest in the FSU and Eastern Europe on a per capita basis, reflecting serious problems with the business and investment climate in Belarus today. One of the key objectives of this report is to identify these problems more clearly and to find feasible solutions that will allow Belarus to attract the investment required to restore growth, generate productive jobs, and improve the productivity of investment, thereby allowing the country to improve living standards.[2]

Among the most important tasks identified in this report for improving the investment climate are (a) establishing the legal and administrative structures needed to create a market-friendly environment; (b) establishing the ownership structures and hard budget constraints required to assure that producers seek to maximize profits, thereby optimizing the use of resources; and (c) protecting people from poverty, especially those who lose their jobs temporarily because of the industrial restructuring required for the transition to a market economy.

Establishing Market-Determined Prices

Until recently Belarus had made considerable progress in moving from administratively determined prices to prices determined by the interaction of competitive market forces. Price controls on manufactured goods were removed in 1992-93, and most of the remaining price controls on food and other "items of popular consumption" were officially removed in November 1994. However, the national Government still publishes "indicative" prices for various agricultural goods that tend to be treated at the local level as the allowable market prices. More importantly, local governments impose profit margin controls on certain socially sensitive goods such as dark bread and milk. Because the cost accounting systems of Belarusian enterprises do not make adequate allowance for the impact of inflation and, in some cases, do not allow certain production and marketing expenses to be counted as costs, profits are often seriously overstated, and controls on profit margins therefore result in a severe erosion of working capital. Such controls should be eliminated at all levels as soon as possible to help assure the financial viability of enterprises, and the efficient use of their goods and services. Concerns that monopolistic market structures will distort prices are legitimate. In such cases, the Government should use regulated prices as a last resort, working instead wherever possible to create competitive markets through demonopolization, privatization, and removal of barriers to trade and private sector development. This would also help reduce the de facto price distortions caused, for example, by government-owned trading enterprises that hold prices to artificially low levels for "social" reasons.

The Government has significantly reduced the number of "monopolistic" goods that are subject to price controls, and has sharply increased prices for many goods and services such as electricity and heating that are still subject to state control. But much remains to be done. For electricity and heating, the two largest elements in housing costs, charges still cover only about 70 percent of costs, and charges for gas and hot water, the next two most important items, cover only about 55 percent of costs. Furthermore, cross-subsidization is still a major problem, with commercial users being forced to pay energy prices well above costs—one of the factors contributing to the large number of loss-making enterprises in this sector. Price reforms are difficult but vitally important to efficient resource allocation, and thus to prospects for growth and improved living standards, as are efforts to increase the efficiency of energy production and consumption. Raising prices to allow efficient cost recovery will reduce poverty in the medium term by promoting efficiency and economic growth, and by increasing the resources available to the Government for targeted poverty reduction programs. While care must be taken to control fiscal costs, the adverse short-term social impacts of full cost recovery can be reduced with appropriate social safety net programs.

The most seriously distorted price today in Belarus is the price of foreign exchange. This happened because the Government attempted to control inflation by controlling the exchange rate. The focus of anti-inflation policies should instead be on controlling monetary emission, imposing strict financial discipline, maintaining tight fiscal restraint, and creating an environment that encourages investment and growth. The overvalued domestic currency has, during the past 18 months, been an increasingly important cause of continued decline in industrial output, the growing number of loss-making enterprises, the unsustainable trade deficit, the rising energy arrears with Russia, the continued reliance on administrative controls, and the loss of jobs. Establishing an exchange rate that restores the competitiveness of Belarusian enterprises is of highest priority.

An open external trade policy is also critically important in avoiding monopolistic pricing within the domestic market. As one of the most heavily industrialized and trade-dependent economies in the former Soviet Union, Belarus has factories designed to serve the entire FSU market as well as major markets in Central and Eastern Europe (CEE). Belarus has sold some products to international markets as well. These enterprises clearly have a monopolistic position within Belarus, and unless external trade policies assure that they are subject to potential competition from imported goods, these enterprises will almost certainly charge excessive, monopolistic prices to Belarusian consumers. Breaking up all of these large factories into competing units is not feasible because of the loss of economies of scale in production. Maintaining

open borders and the threat of competition from imports, on the other hand, would also provide local enterprises with incentives to improve design quality and production efficiency, making Belarusian products internationally competitive and providing more jobs to Belarusian workers. The improved performance would also assure lower prices and higher quality for goods sold to domestic consumers—for both final goods and intermediate inputs. The latter point is important, because if Belarusian factories are forced to buy high cost, low quality inputs from local sources, their products will become non-competitive in world markets, thus reducing the prospects for growth, employment, and improved living standards.

Establishing Profit-Oriented Producers

A market economy will not allocate resources efficiently unless producers generally seek to maximize profits. Otherwise, resources will be used inefficiently, slowing down economic growth and poverty reduction. Under the Soviet system, profit maximization was not explicitly an objective in most situations. If an enterprise was in a priority sector, the state would arrange for the banking system to transfer the necessary resources through directed credits to keep the enterprise in operation. The failure to set profit maximization as a primary objective is one of the most important factors in the collapse of the previous system. Overcoming this heritage is extremely difficult. Allowing prices to be set in competitive markets as noted in the previous section is of course a precondition; otherwise, profit maximization will become monopolistic exploitation. Well-functioning markets are necessary but not sufficient, however. If Belarus is to create an environment that attracts the level of foreign and domestic investment needed to attain the desired levels of growth, and if that investment is to be efficient, it will also need to make some fundamental structural changes to encourage the same kind of profit-maximizing behavior that is typical in the commercial environment of a normal market economy. Most importantly, it will need to: (a) impose hard budget constraints, using bankruptcy as an incentive for financial responsibility where necessary; (b) privatize a major share of state-owned enterprises to avoid the conflicting objectives that frequently prevent public enterprise managers from maximizing profits and thus using resources efficiently; and (c) encourage the establishment of new competing firms.

Hard Budget Constraints and Bankruptcy. One of the most urgent tasks for the Government of Belarus at this point is to impose and enforce hard budget constraints on all economic agents in the country—enterprises, individuals, and equally important, on the Government itself. A market-based system of allocating resources cannot work—and market-determined prices will be irrelevant—if enterprises and others do not pay their bills. The Government does not have to act as the nation's bill collector. However, it should establish a framework of laws and a system of tight fiscal and monetary discipline so that creditors, especially the banking system, will be able to take effective action against those who fail to pay their bills on time.

Non-payment has reached serious levels in Belarus. The lack of payments discipline creates a chain of debts that leads to widespread financial problems in the economy. Good enterprises in Belarus are being destroyed by other enterprises that do not pay for their purchases. This discourages serious investors from trying to do business in Belarus. Banks are facing liquidity and even solvency problems because of the overdues on loans, thus making capital excessively costly to investors, if it is available at all. Workers and their families are suffering because enterprises do not pay wages on time. And the Government is facing a severe shortage of revenues because enterprises are not paying their taxes. This in turn creates pressures on the Central Bank to make loans to the Government, creating inflationary pressures as the money supply expands. The excess of government expenditures over revenues also diverts resources that could otherwise be invested by the business community in economic recovery.

Rather than improving the situation, the Government is actually making it worse in at least three ways. First, it is subsidizing loss-making enterprises by allowing them to delay and reduce the amounts of tax owed. Second, it allows agricultural enterprises that supply food for government procurement to delay payments to input suppliers without penalty. Third, the Government itself is not paying its bills on time; because of policies such as the sequestration of funds, the Government's "expenditure arrears" or overdue bills have risen sharply in recent months.

Experience throughout the world indicates that the most effective means of imposing hard budget constraints is the credible threat of bankruptcy. Even if very few enterprises are taken into bankruptcy, the threat of losing ownership of one's assets, and control of one's enterprise is usually enough to assure that managers will do everything possible to pay their bills. Faced with the threat of bankruptcy, managers will spontaneously reform their enterprises to improve efficiency or they will go out of business, freeing resources for those who can manage them more efficiently. For example, they may lease or sell unused buildings and equipment, dismiss idle workers, seek new markets, develop new products, invest in new technologies, and seek new partners, both foreign and domestic, who can inject new capital and management expertise—all key ingredients of any successful strategy for enterprise reform. Without the threat of bankruptcy, however, such reforms, including privatization, will probably have to be imposed through administrative decree by the Government, and this is generally a very inefficient way to obtain economic efficiency. Therefore, an effective bankruptcy law, backed up with a judicial system that makes bankruptcy a credible threat, is essential for meaningful enterprise reform, an improved investment climate, and restored economic growth.

Privatization. Privatization should be seen not as an objective per se, but as one of the best possible ways to assure that enterprise managers try to maximize profits, thereby increasing economic efficiency and growth. Public enterprise managers could in theory attain the same levels of efficiency that managers of private manufacturing enterprises do.[3] However, several factors make such occurrences quite rare. First, because public enterprises are owned by government, they are far more subject to political pressures than are private enterprises. This is seen today in Belarus—the Government asks (often unofficially and indirectly) that enterprises retain excess employees and provide goods and services below cost for social reasons. This drain on their earnings reduces the incentives for public enterprise managers to maximize efficiency, increases incentives to seek subsidies from the Government, and distorts the prices of goods and services in the economy. Second, the benefits from efficient production in the form of extra profits generally go to the Government rather than to the public enterprise itself. Furthermore, profitable public enterprises commonly find themselves subject to pressures to take on various social responsibilities or to increase their payments of dividends to the Government so that these resources can be used to help ailing enterprises. In private enterprises, owners and managers have their own funds at risk, and what happens to these funds depends on their making good decisions. This, combined with the real threat of bankruptcy, is a powerful force for efficiency. Privatization also helps the Government, because once enterprises are privatized, it is much more difficult for them to pressure the Government into extending subsidies, concessional credits, tax relief, and other financial privileges.

Privatization in Belarus has gone very slowly, and this helps explain why it has been so hard to reverse the continuing economic decline. The 1995 privatization program was never approved by the President for implementation, and while the 1996 program has been approved, very limited progress was made during the first six months of the year. As a result, only about 6 percent of the republican enterprises and about 10 percent of the smaller communal enterprises have been privatized. Almost no enterprises have been "corporatized" (transformed into joint stock companies) during the past year. A large share of the enterprises that have been corporatized remain owned by the Government, leaving them subject to the various non-economic pressures and inefficiencies noted above. The voucher distribution phase of the privatization program was completed by mid-1996, but delays in preparing enterprises for privatization have created a serious shortage of enterprises that can be sold for vouchers.

In sum, to establish the preconditions needed for higher efficiency, increased investment, restored economic growth and improved living standards, the Government needs to move as quickly as possible to complete the liberalization of prices, impose hard budget constraints, and stimulate privatization.

Protecting the People

If implemented in a timely manner, the measures outlined here will make a major contribution to reducing poverty in Belarus by reversing the economic decline of the past five years. The transition to a market economy inevitably creates social problems, however. The most difficult problem from a social perspective is the short-term loss of jobs as workers move from failing enterprises to healthy ones. Good government policies can prevent or reduce these problems. In particular, the Government needs to create the best possible environment for the development of small-scale enterprises, for they offer the best prospects for expanding the availability of new jobs. Policies such as the abolition of the "propiska" (a residency/work permit system), the decontrol of wages, and improved access to rental housing in growth areas should also be implemented to improve the flexibility of the labor market. Finally, recognizing that some people will become poor for more than a short time during the transition process, the current system of social protection needs to be improved to assure that it can provide, in a fiscally sustainable manner, a cost-effective combination of means-tested social assistance, categorical assistance to certain groups (especially single-parent families with a large number of children), unemployment insurance, and insurance-based programs for health and old age.

The Government needs to make a radical change in its approach to providing a social safety net for the poor. In the past, the Government has sought to help the poor—and many other groups in society—by distorting prices. Food, housing, energy, and transport were all made available at artificially low prices that did not cover the costs of production. The Government has made it very difficult for enterprises to get rid of excess labor, thus distorting the normal functioning of the labor market. To compensate farming, manufacturing, and public transport enterprises for their losses due to the artificially low prices that they were able to charge consumers and the excess workers that they were forced to retain, the Government has distorted the prices and allocation of credit, energy, raw material inputs, and foreign exchange. These distortions in prices to the enterprise sector led to further economic problems. For example, the high levels of payments arrears to Russia for gas developed because the gas distribution companies did not receive enough money from the enterprises to buy the foreign exchange needed to pay Russia. This restricted the demand for foreign exchange, contributing to the overvaluation of the domestic currency and thereby inflicting further losses on exporters in the industrial and agricultural sectors. In short, although intended to help the people of Belarus, in many cases the Government's past policies created or prolonged serious economic problems. The damage can be repaired. But doing so will require a fundamental shift in the way the Government goes about protecting the poor.

The Government's draft economic plan, *The Major Trends of Social and Economic Development of the Republic of Belarus for 1996-2000,* stresses that Belarus wants to create a socially-oriented market economy. To the extent that this implies a concern for basic human rights and individual dignity, this is the objective of virtually every civilized nation in the world. People are very important. But the way in which governments help people is also very important. Belarus should be supported in its desire to create a market-based economy that creates a good living environment for people, but for this strategy to succeed, Belarus needs to use the approach normally followed in successful industrialized countries. *The Government needs to move from a social assistance strategy based largely on price distortions to one based on the taxation and redistribution of efficiently produced income.*

Past attempts to protect the poor of Belarus by distorting prices are a major source of the serious economic problems facing the country today. For example, artificially low prices for bread, milk and meat have helped to destroy the financial viability of farms and the agro-processing industries. To compensate, the Government provides excessive amounts of credit at artificially low interest rates. This creates inflation that eats away the value of the credit, resulting in shortages of real working capital and investment resources despite the credit expansion. To compensate, the Government provides subsidies, many of which go to the most inefficient enterprises because they have the most serious financial problems. To meet the fiscal burden, the Government raises tax rates to excessively high levels that discourage honest businessmen, then covers the remaining budgetary shortfall with inflationary borrowing from the Central Bank or with funds borrowed from the enterprise sector that would better be used by the enterprises for investments in more efficient equipment. Another example of the problems caused when the Government tries to help the poor by distorting prices is its efforts to hold down the price of energy, especially electricity and heating. This has been done by keeping the domestic currency overvalued and by charging consumers less than the full cost of energy. The overvalued currency destroys the competitiveness of Belarusian producers in both foreign and domestic markets, leading to enterprise failures and the loss of jobs. And the low cost recovery rates have led to financial problems for local utility companies and to unacceptably high levels of arrears in payments to Russia for imported gas and oil.

The poor need to be protected, but this should be done instead with revenues derived from modest levels of taxation on economic activity that has been maximized by allowing competitive markets to price all inputs and outputs at their true value. With undistorted prices for inputs and outputs, enterprise efficiency will increase and new investors will be attracted, thereby increasing output, tax revenues, and the ability to fund social protection programs.

The system for protecting the poor also needs to be redesigned so that it depends more heavily on means-tested social assistance programs. Given the administrative cost of means-testing, short-cut approaches will be required. For example, programs should be made "self-selective," placing the burden on those who want assistance to come forward and prove their eligibility. Claims from high risk groups such as families headed by a single parent and families with a large number of children could generally be accepted at face value with only limited random audits. Actual means testing, aside from reviewing the papers submitted to support such claims, could be limited to groups falling outside the high-risk categories, thus minimizing the administrative burden of introducing a means-tested income transfer program. Improvements are also needed in the efficiency and equity of the insurance programs for unemployment, health insurance, and old age.

Outline of Document

After a review of recent economic developments in Chapter 1, the report identifies the measures needed to create an efficient, productive market economy that will attract the investment necessary for increasing productivity and improving living standards in Belarus. Chapter 2 examines the measures that are needed to establish the market-determined prices required to guide the efficient allocation of resources. Chapter 3 outlines the actions required to establish profit-maximizing enterprises. Recognizing that these actions will involve major short-term dislocations for many Belarusian workers as they move from non-viable to viable jobs, Chapter 4 describes the actions needed to protect people, particularly the poor, during the transition process. Chapter 5 concludes the report with a discussion of three scenarios that illustrate the future prospects of the Belarusian economy under alternative policy strategies, and of the resources that will be required to finance the transition of Belarus to a market economy.

Key Themes and Conclusions

The analysis presented in this report leads to the following important conclusions, which are developed more fully in the following chapters:

- First, a return to the past is not feasible. The previous system, to which many people in Belarus would still like to return because of the many benefits they enjoyed, collapsed because the system was intrinsically inefficient. It tried to allocate resources based on decisions made by a relatively small group of government administrators based on a variety of economic, social and political considerations. This system, despite its high ideals, cannot compete in the real world with economic systems where resources are allocated to maximize profits, and consumer welfare is based on the individual decisions of those most directly affected.

- Second, the inefficiency by world standards of Belarusian enterprises today, particularly those in industry and agriculture, is the main source of the country's economic decline and poverty.

- Third, this inefficiency can only be overcome by creating the competitive, efficient product and factor markets and profit-maximizing production systems in Belarus that exist in Europe and elsewhere in the industrialized world.

- Fourth, substantial investments will be required to physically transform the production sector in Belarus, and this level of investment can only be attained if Belarus creates (a) an investment climate that attracts private investment from both domestic and foreign sources, and (b) a market-driven incentives framework that ensures efficient production and sales decisions.

- Fifth, these goals cannot be reached in a system where the majority of production activities are still controlled by the state. Attempting this would simply perpetuate the problems of the past. Consequently, privatization, which has moved very slowly to date, must be accelerated dramatically to assure appropriate incentives for profit-maximizing behavior of managers within a market-oriented environment such as exists in all successful industrialized countries.

- Sixth, hard budget constraints—rules that force enterprises to spend no more than they earn or can responsibly borrow—must be imposed to control inflation and to provide the incentives that will lead to spontaneous, efficiency-oriented privatization and production decisions.

- Seventh, the transition process will involve hardships for those who must leave their present jobs and look for new ones. The social safety net needs to be focused on protecting these workers and their families while, at the same time, maintaining their incentives to find new, more productive jobs. The social safety net should be provided through programs financed with tax revenues, not by distorting the prices of goods and services.

The Economic Crisis - Sources and Solutions

Belarus faces a serious economic crisis. GDP continues to fall; the trade deficit has become unsustainable; foreign exchange reserves have fallen sharply; the number of loss-making enterprises is increasing sharply month by month; the budget is seriously short of resources; and monetary pressures are building that could easily rekindle high inflation.

When Belarus became independent in 1991, it was the richest of the twelve republics of the Commonwealth of Independent States (CIS) in terms of per capita income, a status reflecting the republic's steady growth during the 1970s and early 1980s. It had developed an industrial sector that, in terms of share of total GDP, made it one of the most heavily industrialized countries in the world. The agricultural sector was modernized and came to depend not only on heavy equipment, much of which was manufactured in Belarus, but also on imported fuel and fertilizers. Industrial and agricultural development benefited from oil and gas from Russia that was priced at less than 10 percent of world prices in 1990. Enterprises in Belarus also enjoyed the benefits of access to material inputs for processing and final assembly at internal transfer prices, heavy infusions of capital investment, and preferential access to the markets of the former Soviet Union and Eastern Europe with artificially low transport costs and no customs barriers.[4] As a result, Belarus became one of the most trade-reliant nations in the world, with imports and exports each constituting 55 to 60 percent of GDP in 1992. It was also one of the FSU republics most deeply dependent on intra-regional trade, which was equivalent to 70 percent of total trade.

Belarus lost its privileged position with the breakup of FSU. Traditional markets collapsed, and the cost of critical inputs—especially energy—increased sharply in real terms. The terms of trade loss in 1991-92 has been estimated at 11 percent of GDP. The resulting decline in production and increase in inflation were primary factors in the current economic crisis. Other countries experienced similar problems in 1990-91, but have found it easier to control inflation, stabilize their economies, and begin to restructure enterprises.

In Belarus, however, the initial problems were compounded by suboptimal economic policies that sought to cushion if not avoid the transition to a market economy following the collapse of the Soviet system. Rather than implementing policies that would encourage people to adjust their living standards to the new realities, and encourage enterprises to restructure and become internationally efficient, the Government sought to maintain living standards and employment through expansionary monetary and credit policies. These policies were part of an attempt to find a third way, a system that would combine the best of planned and market economic systems. The attempt has failed. The output decline is now as severe in Belarus as for the average economy of the FSU. And while most of the other FSU economies are starting recover, the economy of Belarus continued to decline, until 1996 when, stimulated by factors that may not be sustainable, the economy reportedly grew by 2.6 percent. (These factors are outlined below in the section on GDP growth.) By postponing the necessary structural adjustments, Belarus has failed to establish the foundations of enterprise productivity needed for restored growth. The lack of structural adjustments in the enterprise sector now threatens even the price stability that has taken Belarus so long to achieve.

Based on an analysis of developments over the past five years, this report recommends policy actions that can help Belarus restore the international competitiveness of its production. The Government is very concerned about mobilizing the investment resources needed to improve production efficiency, reduce the use of energy, and raise product design and quality to international standards. Heavy investments will indeed be required. Much of the existing equipment did not meet international standards even when new, and the clearly inadequate levels of investment in fixed capital asset renewal since 1991 have left much of the current stock in a seriously depreciated condition.

Far more important than investment per se is to implement the policies needed to make Belarus attractive to investors and to create a climate in which investments, both old and new, can potentially operate with world-class efficiency and productivity. Such efficiency, which is essential to attract additional investment, requires that prices be determined by competitive market forces, not by administrative intervention, and that enterprises and consumers alike be obligated to pay for whatever they consume—that "hard budget constraints" be imposed on everyone to assure universal financial discipline. Privatization must play an important role in this process, for the Government cannot possibly afford to undertake this investment on its own account—nor should it attempt to do so. If

Belarus is to make a successful transition to a more market-oriented economy, much of the required investment will have to come from the private sector. The report therefore focuses on measures that can be taken to improve the investment climate in Belarus.

This report places heavy emphasis on growth-oriented policies because, as indicated in the Bank's recently completed poverty assessment for Belarus, economic growth is the only feasible way for Belarus to reduce poverty, which is caused primarily by the current low levels of output.

The next section analyzes the key developments since independence in major dimensions of the economy—inflation, fiscal and monetary policies, growth, and external trade. The concluding section outlines the policy initiatives that will be required to stimulate the structural reforms needed to restore growth and living standards.

A. ORIGINS OF THE ECONOMIC CRISIS

The current economic crisis in Belarus originated in large measure in the country's credit and banking policies, which led to high rates of inflation. High inflation and other lax monetary and fiscal policies excerbated problems in other areas of the economy including economic growth and expenditure patterns, external trade balances, the exchange rate, enterprise profitability, and fiscal performance.

Inflation, Credit, and Banking

The Level and Causes of Inflation. Inflation has been a more serious problem for Belarus than for most of the former republics of the Soviet Union. Of countries not severely affected by civil or military conflict following the breakup of the FSU, only Turkmenistan experienced significantly more inflation over this period than did Belarus and Ukraine, which both saw prices rise by 55,000-60,000 times between 1989 and the end of 1995 (Figure 1.1). Recent experience is not any more encouraging. In fact, Ukraine cut its rate of inflation in half between 1994 and 1995, and even the previously strife-torn countries had reduced their inflation sharply,

leaving Belarus second only to Turkmenistan in terms of record levels of inflation for 1995.

Figure 1.1: Inflation in Belarus has been well above average.

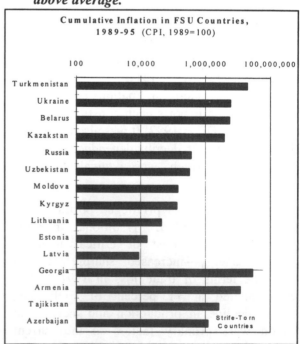

Source: World Bank data.

Part of Belarus' high rate of inflation was caused by the roughly ten-fold increase that was needed to move the prices for energy products to world levels. But this increase fails—by a large margin—to explain why prices in Belarus have increased by over 50,000 times since 1990. Energy had a very small weight in total expenditures in 1990-92, and even after a ten-fold increase, expenditures on energy today are only equivalent to 20 percent of GDP. Other factors clearly predominated.

The real source of inflation in Belarus has been the unwillingness of the Government to come to grips with the fact that living standards have had to be contracted significantly as a result of the loss of export markets and the higher energy prices that came with the collapse of the former Soviet Union. Some FSU countries immediately contracted expenditures in line with the terms of trade shock from higher energy prices. And by maintaining competitive exchange rates and stimulating private sector development and public enterprise restructuring, these countries were able to replace exports to the FSU with exports to Western markets based on skilled labor that was made highly competitive in dollar wage terms by the undervaluation of their domestic currencies. Rapid efforts in these countries to complete the unavoidable transition process enabled them to minimize total economic decline and to restore growth within two to three years.

Belarus chose a very different route, one that has already proven very costly for the people, and one that, by delaying the transition process, has placed Belarus in a difficult position as it now seeks to catch up with the other countries in transition. The delays in moving forward with the transition process have led to a serious deterioration of the nation's capital stock, the loss in value of whatever savings households had, an accumulation of substantial external debt, and the loss of export markets. As difficult as the current situation may be, Belarus has no choice but to tackle the problems one by one and move forward. Returning to the past is impossible. The Soviet system, which collapsed from its own internal inefficiencies, was propped up for years by the energy and natural resources of Russia. But

even Russia's massive wealth was not enough to save the fatally flawed centrally planned system. Belarus, with its meager natural resource base and its heavy dependency on imported energy, has no hope of recreating the Soviet system within its own borders. Neither private investors, nor Russia, nor the bilateral donors, nor the international financial institutions have the mandate, the interest, or the resources required to make this possible. The only way to restore living standards in Belarus is to establish a strong, internationally competitive market economy.

Past attempts to avoid the social and economic problems that are an unavoidable part of moving from one economic system to another lie at the root of the inflation in Belarus. The Government sought to cushion the transition to a market economy by printing money to maintain living standards. The consequent massive injection of credit into the economy was the primary cause of inflation. The process soon degenerated into a vicious cycle where the inflation generated by the last round of credit wiped out the value of that credit, leading to demands for new injections of credit—a classic hyperinflationary cycle.

The Government got into this problem with the best of intentions. It wanted to help enterprises avoid laying off workers, thereby easing the stress of the transition to a lower standard of living. Rather than force loss-making enterprises to restructure by imposing hard budget constraints, the Government has subsidized them, largely through the highly inflationary mechanism of having the central bank extend refinancing credits to the banking system that are then directed to end users in specific sectors. As seen in Figure 1.2, a high degree of correlation exists between credit expansion and inflation in Belarus. Interestingly, a number of people in Belarus argue that this expansion of credit was required to compensate enterprises for inflation, and that new credits were needed to restore the working capital of enterprises so that they could continue working. In fact, the draft *Program of Social and Economic Development of Belarus in 1996-2000* ("Development Plan") that was approved by the President in September 1996 calls explicitly for more liberal monetary and credit policies to stimulate economic growth. Experience around the world makes it clear, however, that credit expansion is the cause, not the result, of inflation.

Extending more credit simply makes inflation worse. The increase in credit or net domestic assets is virtually the only source of increased money supply in the banking system, given that net foreign assets have been declining as a result of the rising trade and balance of payments deficits. As shown in Figure 1.3, the increase in consumer prices does not have a perfect month-by-month correlation with the expansion of credit and thus the money supply, but on a multi-month basis, the correlation is very high. Figure 1.3 also makes it clear that once credit expansion slowed after the beginning of 1995, the monthly rate of inflation dropped dramatically. Belarus is no exception to this universal law of economics that relates overall credit expansion in excess of real production increases to increases in inflation.

As stressed elsewhere in this report, *it was the Government's discipline in controlling credit expansion—not the fixed exchange rate—that brought inflation down after the beginning of 1995.* Credit, money supply, inflation, and exchange rates are all closely related, but the chain of causality must not be reversed. Lower inflation and exchange rate stability are the results of monetary discipline.

Figure 1.2: Excess credit expansion leads to inflation

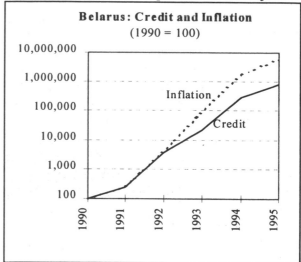

Source: Official data.

Credit expansion must be controlled to keep prices and the exchange rate stable. Efforts such as the recent decrees that reintroduce price controls, continue the artificial exchange rate corridor system, and control access to foreign exchange are implicitly trying to work this equation backwards. Such measures work on the symptoms of inflation, not on its causes. As such, they are doomed to fail. The draft Development Plan needs to be modified to make it very clear that these control-oriented, anti-market policies will be abandoned immediately and replaced by a firm commitment to sound monetary policies. To do otherwise would condemn Belarus to continued economic decline.

Figure 1.3: Inflation fell when monetary expansion slowed.

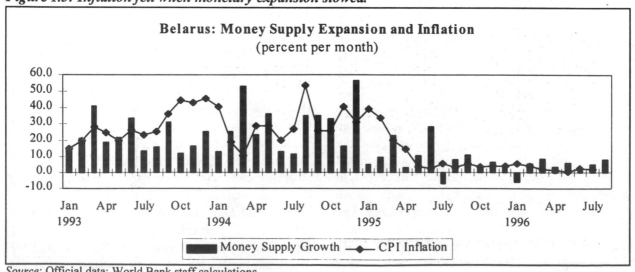

Source: Official data; World Bank staff calculations.

Sectoral Allocation of Credit

Of the credit that was extended to enterprises after independence, most went to those in the *agriculture* sector. In fact, while agriculture's share of credit rose from 7 percent to 28 percent of the total between 1992 and 1994 (Figure 1.4), its share in GDP fell from 22 percent to 13 percent. Gross credit to the agriculture sector nearly doubled between the last quarter of 1995 and the first quarter of 1996, an expansion made possible by the allocation of refinancing credits from the central bank to the commercial banks, largely the Agroprombank. Of the outstanding National Bank credit at the end of the first quarter of 1996, 75 percent was directed credit, and of this, 60 percent was directed to the agriculture sector (which accounts for only about 12 percent of GDP today). In sharp contrast, industry held less than four percent of the outstanding credit, even though it accounted for 30-35 percent of GDP on average over this period.

This disproportionate share of credit going to the loss-making agricultural sector —plus the fact that the interest rate to agriculture is about half the rate for credit that is auctioned —indicates the extent to which the Government has been misusing the central bank to bail out loss-making farms and agro-processing enterprises. The remaining directed credit was allocated primarily to the trade and housing sectors, both of which are also under financial stress, in part because of prices that are held to artificially low levels.

It should be stressed that the losses in the agricultural sector were not entirely the fault of farmers. These losses reflect in part the artificially low prices that farmers are allowed for their products, prices that were designed to subsidize urban consumers. The low returns on agricultural output, which result partly from price controls and partly from the lack of demand, have made it difficult for farmers to undertake the investments needed to improve production efficiency in general and energy efficiency in particular.

The credit squeeze that has resulted from wasting credit on loss-making enterprises is seen

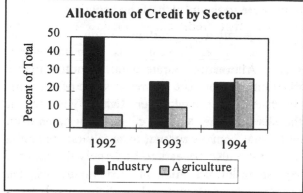

Figure 1.4: Agriculture got a rising share of credit.

Source: Official data; World Bank staff calculations.

even more dramatically when the stocks of credit are adjusted to take into account the inflation that was generated by misallocating the nation's scarce credit resources. Inflation has gradually eroded the real credit available to agriculture to a fraction of its previous levels. The situation in industry has been dramatically worse. Between 1993 and 1994, industry moved from a position of having over twice as much credit outstanding as agriculture (a reasonable situation given the relative size and nature of the two sectors), to a position of having less credit available than agriculture (Figure 1.5). The collapse in credit available to industry far exceeds the drop in production. In 1995, industry got less than 1 percent of the real credit that it got in 1990 for fixed capital investment, making it virtually impossible for the industrial sector to upgrade its capital stock to compete internationally in a post-Soviet world—or even to cover the depreciation of the existing capital stock.[5] It is therefore not surprising that enterprises are finding it extremely

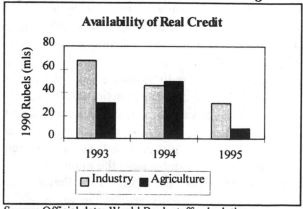

Figure 1.5: Real credit has been shrinking.

Source: Official data; World Bank staff calculations.

difficult to function in a normal manner or to contribute to the growth of the economy.

Another important drain on credit resources in recent years has been the energy sector. Although separate data are not available, this sector accounts for a major share of the credit traditionally reported under "Other." The jump in the share of the "Other" category between 1994 and 1995 from 32 percent to nearly 60 percent of total credit also appears to be largely the result of the increased allocation of credit to energy. The winter of 1995-96 was colder than normal, so oil consumption increased, requiring more financing. However, much of this increased demand for credit reflects (a) the lack of hard budget constraints on energy consumers, who therefore do not pay their bills on time, and (b) prices for household energy consumption that fail to recover the full cost of energy supplies. As a result, energy suppliers have to seek additional financing to insure continued energy supplies.

Despite the diversion of scarce credit resources from industry (and in 1995 from agriculture) to finance the purchase of energy supplies, this did not solve the energy supply problem. User payments plus loans were not enough to cover the cost of imports, resulting in the payments arrears to Russia mentioned above. In the end, increasing credit between mid-1994 and mid-1995 by five times in nominal terms while output fell by about ten percent did almost nothing to solve the fundamental structural problems of industry and agriculture—but did seriously aggravate inflation.

Where Did All the Credit Go? It is very important to note that the shortage of real credit faced by entrepreneurs in agriculture and industry cannot be cured simply by issuing more credit. Credit expansion to failing enterprises is inherently self-defeating. First, the inflation that is created by the credit expansion wipes out the real value of the credit expansion. As a result, despite massive emissions of credit over the past five or six years, the *real* credit available to enterprises has actually declined, as can be seen in Figure 1.5. Second, because the main impact of this type of credit expansion is inflation, the credit expansion actually erodes the value of the

working capital that the enterprises have on hand. It also erodes the value of the payments that the enterprises receive for goods that have already been sold. By undermining the financial strength of the enterprises, directed credit expansion has an effect that is exactly opposite of what was intended. While an individual enterprise might benefit in the short term from an injection of directed credit, the enterprise sector as a whole is seriously harmed by this process for the reasons just noted. When an entire sector is being propped up with directed credits, the entire sector suffers the negative impacts very quickly. Furthermore, when directed credit is used, efficient firms are denied the credit that they need to sustain their output—output that would help reduce inflationary pressures. Finally, by violating the principle of hard budget constraints, directed credit removes the incentives of financial discipline that would otherwise force the firms receiving directed credit to become more efficient and more competitive.

In terms of ultimate economic impact, this approach of extending inflationary directed credits through the banking system was just as bad as if the Government had borrowed the money itself from the central bank and given budgetary subsidies. In fact, the directed credit approach is probably worse because it hides the decisions from the normal process of budgetary review by the Cabinet and the Parliament, and it hides the results of these decisions in the balance sheets of the banks instead of making them appear transparently in the Government's budgetary accounts.

The self-defeating, damaging policy of directed credits should therefore be stopped immediately. In the future, new central bank emissions of credit should be held roughly in line with real GDP growth, based on credit emission rules worked out in cooperation with the IMF. This would minimize the risk of inflation caused by credit expansion. Any new central bank credit emissions should be auctioned, thus assuring that the credit is priced at a market-clearing interest rate, and helping to assure that the credits will go to those enterprises that will make the most efficient use of the money.[6]

Inflation and Families. The credit-induced inflation of the past five years has played a cruel trick on the households of Belarus. People temporarily felt good as the Government pushed up wages to keep up with inflation. But this very process created a wage-price spiral that ate up the value of household savings. The Government's policies were designed to ease the pain of transition, but in the end they only made it worse. Expanding the credit supply allowed people to spend more than they produced, but their actual consumption could exceed production only to the extent that the country: (a) borrowed from abroad, building up debts and payments arrears; (b) drew down the real value of their savings; (c) ate up the capital stock of the country by failing to invest enough to cover depreciation. In short, the attempts to soften the impact of the transition, while creating the illusion of a higher standard of living in Belarus compared to other FSU countries, actually ate away the foundations of the nation's economic structure, which is now collapsing.

In a very real sense, the policies of the past five years mortgaged the future of Belarus to pay for higher levels of consumption. Part of this mortgage is explicit—the burden of external debt and arrears that must be repaid in the future. But an even more important part is implicit—the loss of production capacity through erosion of the capital stock, and the loss of the real value of savings that could have been used to support investment and thus increased consumption in the future. To stop destroying the future prospects of the country and the lives of families in Belarus, the Government needs to stop printing money. It needs to stop directing credits from the central bank to the Government, to the banking system, and to the enterprises. And it needs to stop expanding credit at rates that exceed real output growth.

Credit Allocation and Bank Ownership. banking system credit is likely to continue to be directed to subsidize loss-making activities as long as the Government has a major voice in the allocation of credit because of its ownership and control of key parts of the banking system. The most clear-cut example of the problems created by government ownership and control is the national agricultural bank (Agroprombank). This bank, which had less than four percent of the share capital of the banking system at the end of 1995, absorbed 80 percent of total refinancing made available by the central bank, leading directly to the disproportionate share of total credit going to the agriculture sector.

To assure the efficient allocation of credit to activities that will increase national output instead of to those that will lead the nation into greater poverty, the Government should sell its controlling shares in all banks in the very near future. This would help assure that lending decisions are made on the basis of profitability and contribution to national output, not on the basis of social needs. A significant share of total banking system ownership should be sold to highly respected foreign banks who could introduce improved banking practices and who could provide access to the foreign capital that is needed so urgently by enterprises and investors in Belarus. Furthermore, the central bank should immediately stop all administrative allocation of refinancing credits (directed credit) and auction all such resources to a competitive commercial banking system. (For this to work, hard budget constraints and international-standard banking supervision and regulation must be in place so that failing banks eager to stay in business do not pay more than a reasonable competitive rate to attract funds).

Optimal credit allocation can only take place, however, if the necessary legal infrastructure is in place. More specifically, legal and judicial reforms are needed in Belarus to make assets such as land, buildings and equipment easier to use as collateral for loans, thus helping assure that those who have managed these assets well can use them to further expand economic activity and employment opportunities. In Belarus today, two basic obstacles arise.

- First, private ownership of real property, especially land, is still very limited and subject to laws that are not consistent with international practice. Recent moves to pass legislation correcting this problem were most welcome. Permission to own land privately is not enough. The state, which owns the vast majority of the land in Belarus today, needs to develop an active program for the sale of land to private individuals—a program which, incidentally, could make a significant contribution to relieving the financial constraints currently faced by the Government as it seeks to meet the costs of transition in an environment where the tax base is still declining.

- Second, major efforts are needed to develop the institutions and procedures that are required for real property to be used effectively as collateral for loans. For example, improvements should be implemented in areas such as cadastral surveys, land and real property registration systems, and systems for tracking third-party claims on real property. The latter is needed to make sure that a person does not use the same piece of land, for example, to secure five loans from five different banks without their knowledge that the property is already encumbered. Efforts will also be needed to make it easier for lenders, when borrowers default on loans, to take possession of the property that has been put up as collateral.

The Impact of Inflation on Growth. The levels of inflation that Belarus has experienced over the past half decade help explain why the economy continues to decline. Out of more than 130 countries for which comparative data are available for the period from 1980 to 1993, only 27 had average rates of inflation exceeding 25 percent per year. Of these, only three were able to maintain an average growth rate of per capita GDP exceeding one percent per year. Belarus should want to avoid the experience of these countries for several reasons. First, the odds are highly against Belarus being in this very small percentage of countries that manage to grow despite high rates of inflation. Second, those countries with positive rates of growth barely reached rates of over one percent per year. Such rates would restore the 1989 Belarusian standard of living only by some time in the second decade of the next millennium, a result that is highly inconsistent with the Government's declared and desirable objective of restoring living standards as quickly as possible. Belarus needs to look for a growth model that promises good prospects for a much faster rate of growth.

Finally, the countries that have managed to grow by more than one percent per year despite high inflation have generally managed to do so under very exceptional and very unstable circumstances. For example, Turkey has maintained its growth on the basis of high levels of borrowing from both domestic and foreign sources. The funds are on such short terms that Turkey needed to roll over roughly USD 1 billion of loans every week in the last quarter of 1996. Furthermore, its growth path has been highly erratic, swinging from rapid growth to virtually no growth from one year to the next. Belarus would not want to suffer the pain and uncertainty of such erratic economic performance. Nor would it want to emulate the situation in Guinea-Bissau, another of the small handful of countries that have attained modest growth despite high rates of inflation. This country, one of the smallest and poorest on earth, has managed to accomplish this through unprecedented dependence on external aid. Its dependence on massive foreign assistance has left it with a ratio of external debt to exports of 2,850 percent, the highest ratio in the world—and more than 10 times the level that marks entry into the World Bank's "severely indebted" category.

Further confirmation of the severely adverse impact on growth of high rates of inflation comes from a study by Bruno and Easterly of 127 countries from 1960-1992.[7] As seen in Figure 1.6, a very strong negative relationship exists between growth and rates of inflation exceeding 25 percent. This graph contains another very important message: that countries do not need to try to wring every bit of inflation out of the system. The emphasis in this report on controlling inflation should not be taken as a counsel of perfection. In fact, growth tends to turn negative when inflation is zero or negative. Price declines are usually associated with severe recessions or depressions. Furthermore, the graph demonstrates that, while reducing inflation towards zero improves growth rates on average, the variance in growth rates is small through the range of 0-25 percent per year. Some inflation may actually make it easier to adjust relative prices, thus providing more appropriate incentives that will lead to more efficient production. The key message from these two graphs is that the Government should make every effort at least to keep inflation below 25 percent per year if it wants to restore living standards for its people.

Social Protection. Although credit allocation from the banking system should not be used as a vehicle for subsidizing selected groups of producers and thus of consumers, social concerns are nevertheless very important. Rather than distorting the allocation of credit within the banking system, the Government should pursue its social objectives directly through policies and programs that improve the productivity and incomes of groups facing poverty. In the case of agriculture, for example, all price and margin controls should be removed at all levels of government so that farmers can charge their full cost of production to the consumers. If this results in certain households among the lower income classes falling below the poverty line, food stamps and other targeted methods of social assistance should be investigated as possible ways to address the Government's very legitimate social concerns. Given the low levels of output per worker on many of the farms in Belarus, measures also need to be implemented to improve the overall technical efficiency of the agricultural sector, and to facilitate the movement of excess and redundant labor from farms to alternative, more productive forms of employment.

Growth and Expenditure

GDP Decline After Independence. The previous section discussed the highly adverse impact that inflation has had on growth in countries around the world. Belarus is no exception. The very slow approach that Belarus pursued in implementing market-oriented reforms during the past five years did tend to moderate somewhat the decline in the economy. But this strategy, which was based on expanding credit and thereby postponing necessary adjustments, has already been costly in other ways, and it has delayed attaining the ultimate goal of restoring living standards. As a result, the slow-transition strategy will make the transition process more expensive than if a more rapid transition strategy had been pursued. Attempting to continue the current slow pace of economic reform in the face

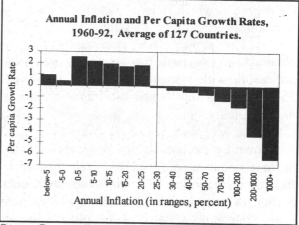

Figure 1.6: Growth falls as inflation rises.

Source: Bruno and Easterly, 1995b.

of a growing crisis in external payments and domestic enterprise profitability could even lead the country into a spiral of decline, leading ultimately to a low-level stagnation trap from which escape would be difficult.

Real GDP in Belarus at the end of 1995 was only 54 percent of the 1989 level, which is slightly lower than the 56 percent average for the rest of the FSU republics (excluding Armenia, Azerbaijan, Georgia and Tajikistan, which have experienced serious armed conflicts since the breakup of the FSU) (Figure 1.7).

If the people of Belarus today are somewhat worse off than the average person in the FSU in terms of GDP decline, what has been gained by the very cautious approach to implementing market-oriented reforms? Aside from the questionable political and social benefits of postponing the tough and sometimes unpleasant measures needed to adjust to the fundamental changes caused by the collapse of the former Soviet Union, the main benefit of the past policies is that they allowed the people of Belarus to live beyond their means for several years, thus allowing higher living standards than otherwise would have been possible given the real declines in output that could be sold. Although Belarus is at the same level today as the average non-combatant FSU republic in terms of percentage GDP decline, the people of Belarus have enjoyed several years of relatively greater prosperity. This is seen by the GDP trend lines in Figure 1.8. The gap between the line for Belarus and that for other countries in the region shows the degree to which Belarus was able in each year to retain its previous living standards.

The slower GDP decline that Belarus obtained in the past few years is even more noticeable with respect to the high performing FSU countries that began the transition process more quickly and more decisively (Estonia, Lithuania, Moldova, Latvia, Uzbekistan, Russia). As shown by the bottom line in Figure 1.8, GDP in these countries dropped more rapidly than for Belarus and for the FSU countries on average during 1991 and 1992. But after two difficult years, the rate of decline in these countries became slower than for the average FSU country—and much slower after 1993 than the rate of decline for Belarus, where, by this point the problems of non-reform were beginning to take their toll.

Recent Trends and Prospects. Figure 1.8 indicates that, by 1995, Belarus was continuing to decline while the average FSU economy had bottomed out, and the fast-reforming FSU economies were starting to grow again. But what lies ahead? The preliminary data for 1996, as shown in Figure 1.8, indicate a slight upturn in GDP. This may well have taken place, but serious concerns exist as to wheether or not this growth can be sustained, given the difficulty of continuing the policies that made this growth possible in 1996. These policies included: (a) allowing inventories of unsold goods to rise by 40 percent in 1996; (b) use of barter trade deals, which often appear not to have covered costs of production to reduce these inventories; (c) the "sale" of goods to agricultural enterprises on a "material credits" basis, which amounted to sale without payment in cash and only a future promise to repay in kind; (d) production for export despite an overvalued domestic currency that caused sharp reductions in the profitability of many goods; (e) substantial injections of credit to help loss-making enterprises pay wage arrears and to replace lost working capital; (f) policies that exempted loss-making enterprises from payment of certain taxes, or allowed them to pay taxes on generously extended terms; (g) further increases in enterprise arrears, and (h) increased arrears with Russia that financed gas imports. If

Figure 1.7: GDP decline in Belarus is about average for FSU.

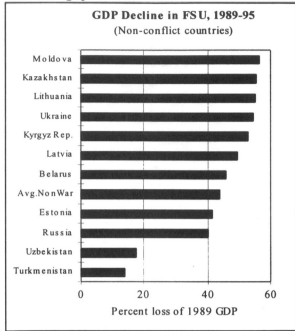

Source: Official data and World Bank staff calculations

Belarus continues these policies, will the economy turn around and start growing in 1997? Or will Belarus continue to decline? Knowing the answer is difficult, especially given the great uncertainties that face the country, but insights can be gained from the experience of Belarus in 1995, from the year-to-date results for the Belarusian economy in 1996, and from the experience of countries that have been in transition longer.

Figure 1.8: GDP declined more rapidly than the FSU average after 1993.

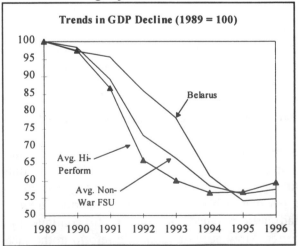

Source: World Bank data and staff calculations.

During 1995, Belarus had one of the sharpest rates of decline of all of the FSU republics, including those previously engaged in armed conflicts internally or externally (Figure 1.9). In fact, while Belarus and some other slow-reforming countries like Ukraine, Tajikistan and Azerbaijan continued to decline sharply, one third of the FSU republics were growing by rates ranging up to 5 percent per year or more.

Prospects for growth are guarded. Official figures on industrial output have been cited that indicate that the decline in the Belarusian economy has bottomed out, but interpreting the longer-term significance of the developments in 1996 is made difficult by factors in 1996 that would be difficult to sustain. The industrial data are also difficult to interpret because of methodological problems. For example, the conclusion that growth has been restored in 1996 is based on data from selected points in time, not on longer-term trends. Furthermore, the official constant price data on industrial output suffer from methodological flaws that distort the picture, giving the impression that each year output is rising. A recently developed series produces the pattern of industrial output shown in Figure 1.10.[8] This chart indicates a clear downward trend in industrial output that continued throughout the first half of 1996. During this period, this trend was interrupted only in March when industrial output expanded in response to administrative orders.

Another general indicator of the continuing economic crisis is the widespread deterioration of production facilities in Belarus that has resulted from levels of investment that, in many instances, have not even been sufficient to cover depreciation. In agriculture, for example, the stock of equipment is rapidly wearing out, and purchases of replacement equipment are a fraction of previous levels, (Table 1.1), which is adversely impacting the agricultural equipment manufacturing enterprises in Belarus. These trends also indicate that the productivity of the agricultural sector is declining significantly, that little is being done to improve the efficiency—especially the energy efficiency—of the sector, and that prospects for renewed growth—or even for maintaining past production

Figure 1.9: GDP decline was particularly sharp in 1995.

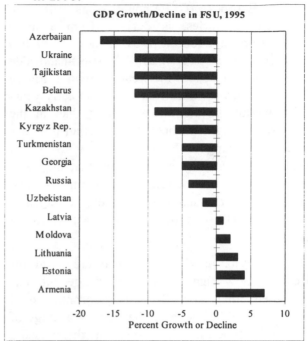

Source: World Bank data.

levels—are growing worse. Similar problems affect the industrial sector as well; with its declining profitability, it does not have the resources needed to maintain existing equipment adequately, much less to invest in the needed improvements. Thus prospects for renewed growth in this sector are also poor from the perspective of investment trends.

A final indicator of the limited prospects for a quick restoration of growth in Belarus under current economic policies lies in the experience of countries that have already gone through the transition process. Figure 1.11, which shows the

Figure 1.10: Industrial output declined in 1995.

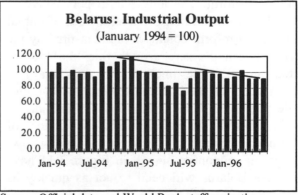

Source: Official data and World Bank staff projections.

trend in GDP growth rates for the fastest and the slowest transforming countries in the Central and Eastern European (CEE) countries as well as in the FSU countries, is derived from a more detailed presentation on p. 29 of the 1996 *World Development Report (WDR)*. The left-hand side of Figure 1.11 echoes the trends shown in Figure 1.8—GDP drops more sharply in the early years of transition in the fast-reforming than in the slow-reforming countries. But this chart provides what is missing in Figure 1.8—a view of the future, of what may happen now that the trend lines for the slow-reforming countries like Belarus have crossed and exceeded the indicator of total GDP decline for the fast-reforming economies.

What is the possible future trend for Belarus, now that its total GDP decline has exceeded that for the fast-reforming FSU countries and has equaled that for the average of all FSU economies, as shown by the crossing lines in Figure 1.11. The combined experience of the CEE and FSU countries shown in Figure 1.11 helps provide an answer. The "fast reform" countries, which are largely CEE countries, moved quickly to reform their economies. After the initial sharp decline in GDP, these economies turned around and pulled far ahead of the slow reforming economies starting in 1992. The shorter history of centrally planned economic systems in the CEE countries makes it impossible to claim a direct correlation between the experience there and what is likely to happen in Belarus and the other FSU republics. However, while differences in background may help explain the higher speed of reform that has been possible in the CEE countries, they do not affect the conclusion that slower reform is, in the long term, more costly than fast reform. The longer-term perspective of Figure 1.11 shows that the overall loss of output in the slow-reform countries (as measured by the area between the zero growth rate line and the actual growth rate line) far exceeds the loss experienced in the fast-transforming economies —despite the greater initial loss of output. To avoid repeating the experience of long periods of continued economic decline that the slow-reforming economies shown in Figure 1.11 have suffered, Belarus will need to act as quickly as

Table 1.1: Annual Purchase of Agricultural Equipment

Combine Harvesters	Units
1990	3,013
1995	42
Fodder Harvesters	
1990	1,040
1995	98
Tractors	
1990	9,085
1995	401

Source: Ministry of Agriculture.

Figure 1.11: Fast reformers drop faster—but also recover faster.

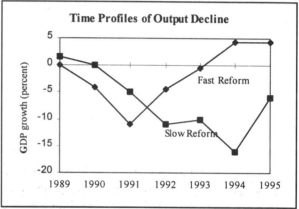

Source: World Bank, 1996.

possible to implement the necessary economic reforms.

Major institutional, organizational and physical changes will be needed in Belarus to provide a basis for renewed growth based on efficient, internationally competitive production. Given that such changes will take time to implement, we must therefore conclude that major efforts will be needed in the nearest future to avoid the continuing downward trend in output. Even if strong measures are implemented quickly, the industrial output decline shown for 1996 in Figure 1.10, plus other evidence such as declining investment, deteriorating capital stocks, foreign exchange shortages, the rising number of loss-making enterprises, and the experience of other slow-reforming countries, indicates that the Belarusian economy could easily decline by at least another five percent in 1996.[9]

Aggregate Demand. The rapid growth of consumption as a share of GDP—and the decline in the share of investment and in its productive efficiency—is one of the keys to understanding the current economic problems of Belarus. As shown in Figure 1.12, the share of consumption in GDP rose sharply between 1992 and 1994. Although investment fell during 1995, this decline was not enough to offset the surge in consumption. As a result, gross domestic expenditure exceeded 100 percent of GDP starting in 1993. This excess demand spilled over into the external sector and in 1993, the current account deficit approached 20 percent of GDP. With expenditures exceeding GDP by a significant margin, the country was living beyond its means.

This excessive expenditure level was driven largely by consumption expenditures, indicating that consumers, directly and indirectly, were being paid more than their output. Directly they received wages in excess of their productivity on average. This was only partly the result of relatively high wage rates. The common practice in state enterprises of keeping workers on the payroll who were redundant and had a low or zero marginal product has also played an important role in raising average remuneration above average productivity. Indirectly consumers have received income in kind from government expenditures on pensions, services, subsidies and the like. The relatively high level of government consumption in GDP has also been a major element in excessive aggregate demand. Government consumption, particularly in areas such as defense where the contribution to output is close to zero, has contributed significantly to the problem.

Investment. The declining and now inadequate level of real investment in fixed capital formation noted above is the inevitable result of allocating a rising share of declining GDP to consumption. Although the share of consumption in GDP has risen sharply and at the expense of investment since 1994, the rate of investment still appears to be relatively high, ranging from 25 to 30 percent of GDP. While lower than the East Asian rate of 30-35 percent of GDP, this rate is still above the world average.

Figure 1.12: Belarus lived beyond its means in 1993-1995.

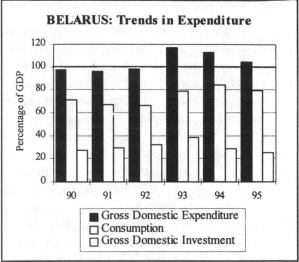

Source: Official data.

Despite this respectable rate of investment, Belarus is not getting the growth that such levels of investment should yield. With an incremental capital-output ratio (ICOR) of 5, for example, a 25 percent investment rate should yield a growth rate of 5 percent year, all other things being equal. Two factors help explain this low efficiency of reported investment in Belarus.

First, Belarus suffers from the same problem of low capital efficiency that Easterly and Fischer have identified as one of the key reasons for the decline and ultimate collapse of the command and control economic system of the former Soviet Union.[10] Their study found that while the Soviet investment rate rose from around 15 percent of GDP in 1950 to nearly 35 percent in the mid-1980s, the rate of return on capital in Soviet industry dropped from over 25 percent to virtually zero (Figure 1.13). With steadily falling Soviet GDP, of which a constantly rising share went to investment, the real resources available for consumption gradually disappeared, leading to the shortages of consumer goods and the monetary overhang that marked the final days of the command and control economic system of the former Soviet Union. The industrial sector that Belarus has inherited played a major role in the Soviet system, and like the rest of the FSU, it has very low average capital productivity. Unless Belarus improves the technical efficiency of its production structure—and more importantly—

unless it improves its business and policy environment, prospects for improving capital efficiency are poor.

A second reason that the economy of Belarus continues to decline despite high reported levels of investment is that part of the money counted as investment in the national accounts may be going to purposes other than fixed capital formation. For example, working capital is counted as investment. The accumulation of unsold stocks of goods thus counts as "investment" according to conventional national accounts procedures. Also, some of the transfers from the budget may be treated as equity investments in the enterprise sector. Under normal conditions, portfolio investments would be treated as "investment," but in Belarus, such resources have largely gone to pay workers, or to purchase goods from enterprises who in turn use the funds to pay workers. Thus government transfers should be treated as consumption, not investment.

Regardless of the exact explanation, it is empirically clear that the capital stock of Belarus is deteriorating at a worrisome rate, that plant and equipment are not being replaced and upgraded adequately, and that the overall productivity of both capital and investment is low. Correcting these problems will be a major challenge. Possible responses to this challenge are the central focus of this report.

Sources of Consumption Growth. One of the main causes of the unsustainable growth of consumption as a share of GDP has been the Government's credit policies. As noted above, credit was extended to failing enterprises in the industrial and agricultural sectors, allegedly to sustain production, but the underlying objective was to prevent unemployment and social unrest. Much of the net credit expansion from the banks passed through the enterprises to wages which, in real terms, have consistently exceeded the output generated by workers. As shown in Figure 1.14, the real wage index since early 1991 has, on average, exceeded the index of real GDP by a large margin. As can be seen by comparing Figure 1.12 and Figure 1.14, the impact of excessive real wages did not spill over into

Figure 1.13: Inefficient investment led to the collapse of the former Soviet Union.

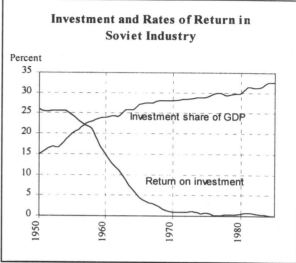

Source: Easterly and Fischer 1994.

aggregate consumption in 1991 as much as in 1993. This reflects the progress that Belarus made in moving towards a market system in the intervening years. In 1991, goods were still rationed, so excessive wages could not be spent. Consequently, the excess of wages over physical output built up as a "monetary overhang," the excess level of deposits in the banking system that developed towards the end of the Soviet era. By 1993, however, physical controls on consumer expenditure had been relaxed, and excessive

Figure 1.14: Real wage adjustments lagged the decline in GDP.

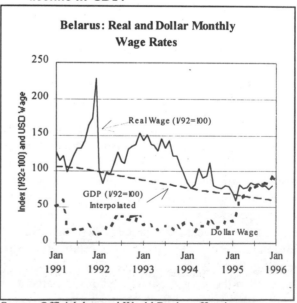

Source: Official data and World Bank staff estimates.

wages poured over into excessive consumer demand—including demand for imported goods.

Figure 1.14 also provides clear evidence of the improvement in government policies starting in 1993. As can be seen by the convergence of the real wage line with the GDP output line, wages have in fact been brought more in line with output. The surge in dollar wages in 1994—and even more in 1995—is a matter of great concern, however. High dollar-equivalent values for wages do almost nothing for the average consumer—except for energy prices—because most consumer purchases are of domestic goods. On the other hand, high dollar-equivalent wages—which reflect the overvalued exchange rate—make Belarusian goods noncompetitive with international products, thus ruining domestic enterprises and the jobs that they could offer if they were more competitive.

The sharp increase in energy and other externally determined prices certainly contributed to inflationary pressures. But the main factor explaining why inflation in Belarus has been so high and so persistent is the sharp expansion of the money supply. The money supply expanded more rapidly than output grew because of the Government's attempt to cushion the impact of transition by offering subsidies to the population. These subsidies were financed "off budget" by expanding banking system credit to cover the quasi-fiscal deficit that developed as public enterprises continued to pay wages which exceeded the value of worker productivity.

External Trade

One of the most visible dimensions of the current economic crisis in Belarus is the steep decline in the level of international reserves which, despite tight administrative controls on the purchase of foreign exchange, fell on a net basis from USD 260 million on July 1, 1995, to only USD 25 million on July 1, 1996. With imports running at USD 500-600 million per month, the reserves position is clearly completely inadequate. During this same period, Belarus has been accumulating USD 40-50 million per quarter of arrears in payments for gas imported from Russia. If payments had been made for even a month or two of these imports, Belarus would

have no net external reserves. The tenuous reserves position—and the extraordinary controls that the Government has imposed to preserve even the modest reserves that remain—are a clear indication of severe problems in the nation's external trade and payments policies. This section examines the origins of these problems, some of the factors, both internal and external, that have exacerbated the problems, and some of the measures that the Government needs to take immediately to restore more normal conditions for external trade and thus the basis for renewed economic growth.

The expansionary monetary, fiscal and wage policies that Belarus followed until early 1995 created demand pressures that spilled over into the external sector, leading to a current account deficit that peaked at over 15 percent of GDP in 1993. These expansionary pressures were gradually brought under control during 1994 as the Government sought to reach the inflation and deficit targets that had been agreed with the IMF. As a result, imports and exports were brought into balance by late 1994, and this balance was sustained though the first half of 1995, despite constantly rising imports (Figure 1.15). The current account deficit dropped from 12 percent of GDP in 1994 to about 2.5 percent of GDP in 1995.

During 1994, the undervalued Belarusian currency allowed domestic producers to compete successfully in international markets despite problems of product design, quality, and production efficiency. As shown in Figure 1.16, a trade surplus with the West counterbalanced the growing trade deficit with the East,[11] a deficit

Figure 1.15: The trade balance began to worsen by mid-1995.

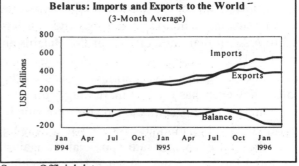

Source: Official data.

dominated by Belarusian imports of oil and gas from Russia.

The sharp deterioration in the trade balances with the West, starting in the second quarter of 1995, was initially offset by rising dollar prices of exports to Russia and other CIS countries as prices in these markets began to come into line with world prices.[12] However, as these prices began to match (or even exceed) world levels, and as the prices of oil and gas from Russia continued to rise, the trade deficit with Russia began to expand in late 1995. This aggravated the deteriorating trade position with the West (Figure 1.17). Thus, while improvements in the value (but not the volume) of trade with Russia initially masked the declining trade surplus with the West, the decline became highly visible during the first quarter of 1996 with the external trade deficit running at an annual rate of 15-20 percent of GDP, a clearly unsustainable level.

Exchange Rate

The rising external trade deficit was due in large measure to the increasing inability of the untransformed Belarusian enterprises to compete internationally. Belarusian products were intrinsically uncompetitive as noted earlier because of problems with design and production efficiency. Nevertheless, the products were able to compete in niche markets as long as the exchange rate made them price competitive. For example, Belarusian digital watches enjoyed considerable success in the low end of the Hong Kong market.

Because of the expansionary credit policies that the Government has continued to pursue in varying degrees over the past several years, domestic inflation continues to exceed world inflation. In the absence of appropriate adjustments in the nominal exchange rate, this has led to a sharp real appreciation of the Belarusian rubel. The continuing real exchange rate appreciation against hard currencies such as the dollar, however, has made it increasingly difficult for enterprises to compete in the potentially lucrative Western markets. As shown by Figure 1.18, the real exchange rate appreciation against the dollar has been going on since 1992.[13] Within

Figure 1.16: The trade surplus with the West has evaporated.

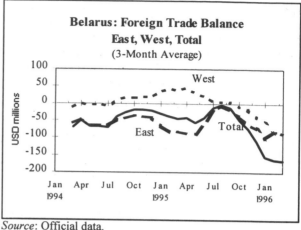

Source: Official data.

Figure 1.17: Real exchange rate appreciation undermined the trade balance

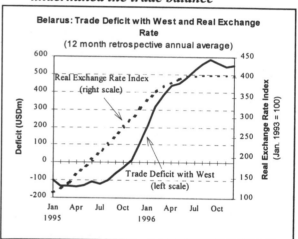

Source: Official data and World Bank staff calculations.

limits, this is a natural process seen in all transitional economies where the exchange rate of the new national currency was originally set at a highly depreciated rate. To the extent that a currency is still significantly undervalued with respect to its purchasing power parity rate, or to the extent that production efficiency increases as rapidly as the real exchange rate appreciates, enterprises can remain competitive. In the case of Belarus after late 1993, however, the real appreciation of the exchange rate moved more rapidly than productivity increases, resulting in a considerable erosion of price competitiveness—a common problem in countries which try to use nominal exchange rate anchors to control inflation (Box 1.1). If the Government had allowed the exchange rate to continue to move as

Box 1.1: *Fixed Exchange Rate Anchors*

Since late 1994 the Government of Belarus has used an "exchange rate anchor" in attempting to control inflation. Such anchors have been used widely in stabilization programs throughout the world—but often with very poor results. The international experience with exchange rate anchors was summarized in a 1995 seminar (IMF, 1995). The meeting concluded that exchange rate anchors were far more effective in halting inflationary expectations in hyperinflationary environments than in dealing with chronic inflation. Under conditions of chronic inflation, fixing the exchange rate had little immediate effect on inflation, and often led to "a real appreciation of the currency and to large trade and current account deficits, undermining the credibility of the strategy." This describes the situation in Belarus today.

The seminar also concluded that the success of an exchange rate anchor always requires appropriate supporting macroeconomic policies, *especially measures to control fiscal deficits and monetary expansion*. The highly successful program in Argentina in 1991, for example, did peg the exchange rate, but also "eliminated indexation and exchange controls, removed all legal tender provisions, provided for central bank independence and privatization of all public enterprises, and dealt with the quasi-fiscal deficit of the central bank. The absence of these measures in Belarus helps explain why its attempt to use an exchange rate anchor—first a pegged rate and more recently a fixed corridor or band—has not brought the desired results.

it had up to the end of 1994, the international competitive-ness of a major share of the enterprise sector in Belarus would not have been destroyed. However, as can be seen clearly in Figure 1.18, the Belarusian rubel began appreciating rapidly in real terms against the U.S. dollar starting in mid-1994, and this accelerated throughout 1995.

Convincing evidence exists today that the Belarusian rubel is overvalued and needs to be devalued significantly if Belarus is to avoid an even worse economic crisis and restore enterprise profitability and economic growth. Twelve indicators are commonly used to determine whether or not a currency is overvalued: the balance of payments position; export profitability; import competitiveness; compara-tive wage rates; purchasing power parity indicators; trends in real exchange rate valuation; the divergence between auction and cash rates; the degree of administrative interference in the local foreign exchange markets; movements in foreign exchange reserves in the central bank; evidence of capital flight; the sustainability of capital account inflows; and indicators of currency substitution, especially the use of foreign currencies for domestic transactions and for enterprise and household savings. The following discussion is designed only to present evidence of the need for devaluation based on the impact that the current overvaluation is having on the real economy of Belarus. Any future measures to realign the exchange rate should of course be designed and implemented in close cooperation with the IMF,

Figure 1.18: Real exchange rate appreciation followed years of relative stability.

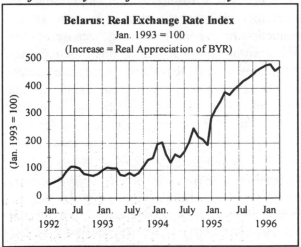

Source: Official data and World Bank staff calculations.

which would advise on issues such as the extent of realignment required, the mechanisms through which the interactions of market demand and supply for foreign exchange could be used to signal the appropriate exchange rate adjustments, the phasing of such adjustments over time, the anchors that could be used to minimize inflation during the adjustment process, and the complementary macro measures—especially those related to fiscal and monetary policies—that would have to be implemented at the same time to assure the sustainability of the new exchange rate and the stability of the economy. World Bank staff would work closely with the IMF and with Government authorities to help identify complementary structural adjustments that would also be required to sustain a new exchange rate regime.

Balance of Payments Position. The key role of the exchange rate is to create a sustainable balance between the price of traded goods and services (imports and exports) and non-traded goods and services. If traded goods become too cheap in domestic currency prices, exports will generate too little profit for domestic producers and imports will become highly attractive substitutes for domestically produced goods. Consequently, exports will decline, imports will increase, and an unsustainable balance of payments gap will emerge. As shown by the discussion above, this has already happened in Belarus. This is one of several indications that the domestic currency is indeed overvalued.

Export Profitability. Export profitability is another test of the exchange rate. If the production of exports is lagging because exports are becoming unprofitable, the domestic currency is probably overvalued. This is happening today in Belarus. As can be seen from Table 1.2, the profitability of many important Belarusian export products declined sharply between the end of 1994 and the end of 1995. In fact, many traditional products can now be exported only at heavy losses. This is clear evidence of exchange rate overvaluation given that: (a) world prices for these products were stable over this period; (b) key input prices did not move sharply higher (energy prices from Russia had already increased prior to December 1994 and have not increased by much since then); and (c) no major technological changes have occurred either inside or outside Belarus during this period which would explain the decline in profits. The only real explanation is the sharp appreciation of the real exchange rate. Between December 1994 and December 1995, producer prices increased by 2.4 times and consumer prices rose by 3.4 times—but the exchange rate was kept more or less fixed at roughly BYR 11,500 per U.S. dollar. As a result, producers faced a three-fold increase in rubel costs while revenues in rubels from export sales remained flat.

Under such circumstances it is surprising that any export oriented enterprise remained profitable. Some enterprises had previously been exceptionally profitable because of the residual undervaluation of the rubel, and thus were able to maintain some profitability when the Government pursued policies that were in part consciously designed to reduce the "excessive" profitability of enterprises. Unfortunately, the policies were not backed up by adequate analysis of their impact on enterprises in Belarus. As a result, these policies destroyed the financial viability of large parts of the agricultural and industrial sectors. Instead of allowing enterprises to make profits that could be invested in capital equipment to maintain and even improve the competitiveness of the heart and soul of the Belarusian economy, the Government's policies left enterprises with heavy debts and worn out equipment.

Recovering from this situation will be all the more difficult because of the loss of export markets. Knowing the importance of maintaining normal business relations with overseas customers, many enterprises continued to meet their export contract obligations, even when this meant operating at a loss. They tried to keep their clients, hoping that the Government would come to understand the seriously adverse impact that the fixed exchange rate policies were having on the enterprise sector. The deteriorating export levels during 1996 indicate that many enterprises have been forced to give up trying to export. As a result, clients are now being lost. The longer the current policies are continued, the more difficult the eventual turnaround will be, and the larger the devaluation will have to be to give Belarusian enterprises the competitive edge needed to regain lost markets.

Table 1.2: Decline in Export Profitability During 1995

	Profitability (%)	
	December 1994	*December 1995*
Motorcycles	38	-38
Combines	76	19
Watches	17	-4
Tractors	32	-11
Refrigerators	67	43
Footwear	38	23
Lingerie	41	-1
Chemical Fibers	19	-2

Source: Official data.

Import Competititivess. The ability of enterprises on average to remain profitable in the face of import competition is another key test of exchange rate valuation. As with export profitability, there is widespread evidence in Belarus that enterprises which once competed with imports are no longer able to do so—even though no major structural changes have taken place, either in domestic or foreign markets. For example, a clothing manufacturer who once bought Belarusian-made fabrics now imports equivalent materials from Poland because the exchange rate made the Polish fabrics cheaper. A farm cooperative that used to export beef to Poland now faces competition in Belarusian markets from Polish products. Pleas for tariff protection were once rare but now are common in Belarus, further evidence that the exchange rate has been allowed to appreciate in real terms to unsustainable levels.

Comparative Dollar Wage Rates. The dollar-equivalent wage rate for labor is a quick though very approximate indicator of the competitiveness of a country's exchange rate. If the dollar wage moves up sharply during a relatively short period without a comparable increase in either the level of exports or in the overall volume of industrial output, an exchange rate valuation problem probably exists—but this will need to be confirmed by the other indicators discussed in this section. A sharp upward movement in the dollar-equivalent wage rate relative to the dollar wage rate in competing countries is also a good indication in most cases that an exchange rate devaluation may be needed.

Both of these conditions exist in Belarus today. Figure 1.14 above highlighted the nearly three-fold increase in the dollar-equivalent wage rate during 1995, a period during which output declined steadily. Output per worker was clearly falling, not rising. Similarly, as can be seen in Figure 1.19, the dollar equivalent wages for Belarus have diverged sharply from those in Ukraine, Moldova, and Uzbekistan—all potential competitors of Belarus for export markets in Russia and the West.[14] These trends in dollar wages and output, combined with other evidence such as the falling profitability of enterprises and the rising trade deficit during the past year,

clearly indicate that the Belarusian rubel is overvalued.

Purchasing Power Parity Comparisons. Another indicator of the degree to which a currency may be overvalued or undervalued is the purchasing power parity (PPP) exchange rate. The PPP rate makes an average product cost the same in dollars in two different countries (Box 1.2). Up-to-date PPP calculations are not available for Belarus, but a quick survey comparing the prices of major consumption items in Belarus and the United States indicates a significant overvaluation of the Belarus rubel in PPP terms with respect to the dollar.

The exchange rate for a country in transition would normally be several times higher than the PPP rate, thus providing a margin of competitiveness that compensates domestic producers for their low productivity, for imperfections in the domestic market, and for the country's limited access to world markets. As an economy becomes more liberalized, and as a country's per capita income begins to rise towards the levels in industrialized countries, domestic prices can move closer to international price levels, and the PPP exchange rate will tend to converge with the market exchange rate. For a country at Belarus' current level of economic liberalization and per capita income, however, the

Figure 1.19: Belarusian wage increases outstrip those in comparator countries.

Source: Official data and World Bank staff calculations.

convergence of domestic prices and exchange rates with world market levels would normally not exceed 15-25 percent (see figures in Box 1.2).

With the current market exchange rate in Belarus, however, average domestic prices measured in PPP terms are now equal to about 50-60 percent of world levels. This has seriously eroded the competitive margin that Belarusian farms and factories need if they are to be able to compete with imports in the domestic market and with foreign countries in the world's export markets. Assuming that a major reduction of domestic prices is neither feasible nor desirable at this time for reasons discussed in more detail below, a substantial upward adjustment of the exchange rate (devaluation of the domestic currency) is the only feasible way to restore the urgently needed margin of competitiveness.

For reasons discussed in more detail in Annex E, this PPP calculation should not be interpreted as an indicator of the devaluation that will actually be required to make Belarusian enterprises competitive. However, the PPP calculations shown here do clearly confirm the conclusions of the other indicators presented in this section that the Belarusian rubel is overvalued at the current exchange rate and needs to be devalued. An exchange rate devaluation is the only feasible way to correct such a problem. The necessary amount of devaluation and its time phasing will have to be worked out with the IMF based on the various measures of exchange rate competitiveness presented here as well as other technical parameters used by the IMF, but some degree of devaluation is vital if Belarus is to restore the financial health of its enterprises and thus prospects for renewed economic growth and improved living standards.

Real Exchange Rate Index. The real exchange rate provides the final indicator that can be used to determine whether or not an exchange rate adjustment is needed. This calculation can also be used to help determine the approximate amount of adjustment that is required.

The rapid appreciation of the Belarusian rubel against the U.S. dollar, starting in early 1994, was seen clearly in Figure 1.18; its impact on the trade deficit with the West, starting in late 1994, was highlighted in Figure. The deterioration of the trade surplus with the West in the second half of 1995 was closely correlated with the rapid appreciation of the Belarusian rubel against the dollar and other western currencies. The real appreciation of the domestic currency had actually been going on for several years, but Belarusian products remained competitive for a while because of the strong initial undervaluation of the rubel. Starting in January 1995 and continuing through the first quarter of 1996, however, the Belarusian Government maintained the exchange rate at roughly BYR 11,500 per dollar. During this same period, the domestic price level increased by 3.6 times. This resulted in a further appreciation of the real exchange rate against world currencies by about 2.5 times, taking into account international inflation during the same period.[15]

The real appreciation during the latter half of 1995 was not offset by factors such as residual undervaluation, which had helped maintain trade competitiveness in the earlier periods. Consequently, the trade balance deteriorated in line with the increasing real appreciation of the exchange rate. Belarusian exports to the West stagnated after mid-1995, then gradually began to deteriorate. An even larger problem developed on the import side. As inflation continued to push up domestic prices, a wide range of imported products became competitive with those produced domestically, despite the fact that Belarusian wages were still less than five percent of those in major Western trading partner countries. Part of the increased flow of imports was in luxury goods such as hard drinks which were no longer significantly more expensive than Belarusian products. Even commodities such as butter and meat, where Belarus should have a comparative advantage, became more expensive than comparable imported goods.

In a normally functioning market economy, government authorities would have been forced by the erosion of external reserves to focus more quickly on the emerging overvaluation of the exchange rate, and this would have helped minimize the damage to the industrial sector. A quicker adjustment would also

Box 1.2: Purchasing Power Parity Indexes

What exchange rate would make a hamburger purchased in Japan cost the same in dollars as it does in the United States? Or taking a broader example, what exchange rate would give a dollar the same purchasing power in both countries, based on the average of all prices of goods in the average consumer basket? The exchange rate that makes the dollar prices equal is known as the "Purchasing Power Parity" or PPP exchange rate. The PPP, which can be calculated using dollars or any other reference currency, provides a useful—but by no means precise—measure of the degree to which a market exchange rate is overvalued or undervalued

Calculations of PPP rates are always subject to a significant margin of error because of the difficulty of finding exactly comparable products. Even goods that have similar characteristics may actually be different in ways that affect their prices. For example, the "Big Mac" hamburger sandwich that provides the basis for the "Big Mac Index" published yearly by *The Economist* is not a strictly homogenous product. In Europe, for example, the price includes a built-in VAT, while in the US a much smaller sales tax is added separately to the price. This alone could affect the advertised price by at least 15 percent. Also, conditions of service such as the quality of the facilities and the inclusion of extra dressings for the sandwich at no extra charge will vary from place to place. Other factors such as transport costs and tariff barriers can also distort PPP calculations. Furthermore, purchasing power parity calculations commonly include goods that are not traded internationally. Since the prices for such goods do not directly affect the balance of payments position, the market exchange rate (MER) can vary somewhat from the PPP exchange rates without causing a BOP problem.

The expected ratio of PPP exchange rates to the market exchange rate—the degree of convergence of national with world price levels—depends on the liberalization and income levels of a country. Economies that have a low liberalization rating as reported in the World Bank's *WDR* for 1996 do not yet have well-functioning markets, and this slows the process of equalizing domestic with international prices. Also, prices in relatively poor economies are held down by the low cost of labor. Thus the normal ratio of the PPP rate to the MER—the normal *convergence rate* with world prices—is usually far below 100 percent in such countries. Consequently, the MER has to be devalued more relative to the PPP rate in transitional and poor countries to provide adequate competitiveness for domestic producers. Whenever the PPP rate is significantly out of line with its expected value given the degree of transition of the economy and its income level, the market exchange rate is probably overvaluing the domestic currency.

Figures A and B indicate the price convergence ratios that are normally associated with different levels of liberalization and per capita income levels respectively. Belarus, with a liberalization index of about 50 percent, would have an expected price convergence ratio of about 17 percent—not the roughly 40 percent rate that is associated with the current overvalued market exchange rate.

Figure A: Prices converge as liberalization increases

Figure B: Prices converge with world levels as countries grow richer.

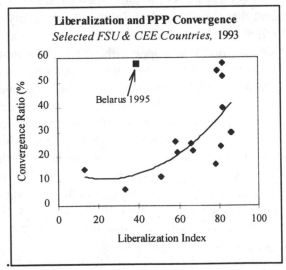

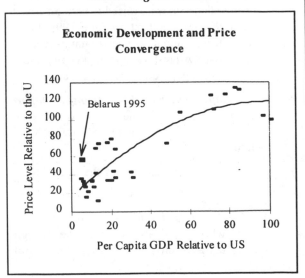

Source: See Appendix E.

have minimized the size of adjustment that would then be required. However, a series of factors operated in the part-command/part-market economy of Belarus during 1995 that prevented this early warning signal from emerging. Some of these factors were under the control of the Government and some were not. These factors made it possible for the Government to continue its pursuit of a fixed exchange rate without resorting to direct foreign exchange controls far longer than outside observers would have anticipated. Among the key factors behind this were the following (not all of which were in force at any given time).

- *Repatriation and surrender requirements* forced people to transfer foreign exchange earnings to the banks.

- *Sole legal tender rules* banned use of foreign exchange for transactions inside Belarus, thus stimulating flow of foreign exchange into the banking system by people who now needed local currency for transactions.

- *Barter deals* with foreign suppliers reduced the need for foreign exchange for imports.

- *Enterprise losses* forced managers to bring foreign exchange reserves back from overseas.

- *Bank capital requirements* were changed, forcing domestic banks to convert the foreign exchange component of their base capital into domestic currency, turning the foreign exchange over to the central bank.

- *Minimum reserve requirements* on foreign exchange deposits were raised from 5.5 percent in late 1994 to 8 percent by June 1995, to 10 percent in July, and have been maintained at 12 percent since August 1995, thus keeping more foreign exchange under central bank control.

- *Lower import duties and less stringent import controls* encouraged the flow of foreign exchange from Russia for imports through the Belarusian border.

- *Foreign exchange reserves* of the central bank were loaned to commercial banks "to put them to good use rather than keeping them idle," thereby injecting foreign exchange into the system while nominally keeping the foreign exchange assets on the books of the central bank.

- *Import taxes* had to be paid in foreign exchange, thus placing more foreign exchange under the control of the Government and of the central bank.

- *International arrears* accumulated, reducing demands for foreign exchange and allowing it to remain in the central bank.

- *Foreign exchange borrowing* of about USD 240 million during 1995 helped replenish and maintain foreign exchange reserves.

- *Interest rate arbitrage* between hard currencies and soft currencies brought foreign exchange into Belarus. With an implicit guarantee of convertibility at a fixed exchange rate, speculators borrowed deutschemarks and other hard currencies at 5-8 percent per year and invested them at 5-8 percent per month in Belarus.

- *A foreign exchange purchase tax* of 10 percent was imposed, allowing the Government to maintain the fiction of a fixed exchange rate while effectively devaluing it.

These measures enabled Belarus to maintain a fixed exchange rate without violating IMF agreements that required Belarus to avoid direct controls on the purchase of foreign exchange. But even these complex measures began to fail by the end of 1995.

On November 13, 1995, the Government suspended transactions on the Interbank Currency Market and began imposing administrative controls on the right to bid for foreign exchange in the central bank auctions, thereby seeking to assure that the allowed demand and the supply of foreign currency available would balance at a price within the supposedly free "corridor" (exchange rate band) that the Government had decreed. During 1996 the system became even more complex, with demand being strictly controlled through administrative review on Tuesdays and Thursdays, the "fixing days" when the official exchange rate was established. On the other days of the week, less strict controls on access to the market were imposed, allowing a dual exchange rate system to develop. At the same time, an even more depreciated street rate also began to emerge despite tight police controls. Most recently, the President of the central bank has allowed exchange dealers to charge "margins" for processing, thereby effectively widening the exchange rate band and allowing a more realistic rate to emerge legally on the street.

The net result of these measures was to disguise the serious shortage of foreign exchange that was developing during 1995 and to delay necessary adjustments in the exchange rate. This led to a serious deterioration both in the level of reserves and in the financial status of enterprises which could no longer make a profit at the highly appreciated real exchange rate. Reserves can be restored by borrowing from abroad, but the damage that these policies inflicted on the agricultural and manufacturing enterprises of Belarus will take considerably longer to repair.

Other Indicators of Exchange Rate Problems. In addition to the indicators discussed in some detail above, several other measures would normally be considered by the IMF in advising a government on exchange rate policies. A good indication of the need for a devaluation is *a substantial divergence between auction and cash rates for foreign exchange.* In Belarus this difference was minimized through mid-1996 by the measures mentioned above. In recent months, however, the market exchange rate has become so unrealistic that these measures no longer keep the rates unified. In November 1996, the official exchange rate ceiling of about BYR 15,500 per U.S. dollar was still being maintained in the central bank currency auctions (at least on the "fixing days"), but the street rate had risen to around BYR 20,000 per U.S. dollar, a difference of about 30 percent.

A high degree of *administrative interference in the local foreign exchange markets* is another good indication that the exchange rate is not realistic. In Belarus, as noted above, a committee in the central bank has been clearing applications for the purchase of foreign exchange for about a year in order to assure that the demand for foreign exchange at the officially decreed rate does not exceed the supply that is projected to be available. In addition to direct administrative controls on the demand for foreign exchange, the Government of Belarus has also taken the wide range of less direct actions noted above to influence both the demand and supply of foreign exchange.

The *movements in levels of foreign exchange reserves in the central bank* indicates the realism of the current exchange rate. The sharp decline in foreign exchange reserves in Belarus, which at points in the second half of 1996 were equivalent to only a few days of imports on a net basis, is clear evidence that the current exchange rate is overvalued. Similarly, the fact that up to 70 percent of demand for foreign exchange cannot be met in the foreign exchange markets on some days indicates the severe shortage of reserves.

The exact degree of overvaluation of the exchange rate cannot be determined directly from movements in reserves, however. Staff of the IMF also look at factors such as the *sources and sustainability of capital account.* For example, the IMF might conclude that a country's current exchange rate was appropriate despite a large current account deficit if (a) the deficit was caused by capital goods imports, and (b) the potential drain on the country's reserves position was being offset by large inflows of foreign direct investment. On the other hand, if the reserves position was being protected by heavy borrowing from abroad, the IMF might well conclude that the capital account position was not sustainable. An even less sustainable position would involve the accumulation of external payments arrears. Unfortunately, all of these indicators reveal serious problems in Belarus. Foreign investment inflows have been negligible. Foreign borrowing (including short-term flows to arbitrage interest rate differentials) has been substantial. And large external payments arrears have accumulated.

The presence of *capital flight* is another indicator of an inappropriate exchange rate. Unfortunately, because of the open border with Russia and weak systems for monitoring capital flight (which is difficult even in industrialized countries), we have no concrete data on this issue. Anecdotal reports indicate, however, that the problem has been significant—though counterbalanced in part by the flight of capital seeking higher interest rates in a country with an exchange rate that has effectively been fixed by Government decree.

Currency substitution is a final indicator worth examining for evidence that the exchange rate regime needs to be changed. Currency substitution or "dollarization" of domestic transactions was widespread prior to late 1994, at which time it was officially banned with the decree that made the rubel the "sole legal tender" in Belarus. Prior to mid-1995 when the Government began to bring inflation under control, currency substitution was also widespread by those seeking to protect the value of their savings—or even of their earnings from one week to the next. Although hard data are difficult to find, currency substitution in transactions and savings seems to have been less of a problem for the past year or so. It may return, however, as increased credit expansion raises concerns about price stability, and increased indications that the exchange rate should be devalued create uncertainty about the future value of the rubel.

Do Viable Alternatives to Devaluation Exist? Instead of making a substantial adjustment in the exchange rate, the Government of Belarus has been trying to restore the competitiveness of Belarusian enterprises in domestic and foreign markets by increasing tariffs on imports and by increasing the subsidies for exports. This approach can reduce imports and increase exports, but as proven by experience around the world over the past forty to fifty years, import tariffs and export subsidies are at best a poor substitute for an appropriate exchange rate regime. At worst, and this frequently happens, they create highly distorted patterns of production and high degrees of economic inefficiency. Even if tariffs and subsidies were equal and absolutely uniform across all activities, this would still be inferior to an appropriate exchange rate adjustment because of the administrative costs of collecting the taxes and allocating the subsidies. The really serious problem with the tax-and-subsidize approach, however, is that the rates of protection and subsidy provided to individual products and even individual producers tend to vary widely. This happens because producers and traders can make very substantial profits if a

product enjoys high rates of export subsidy or high rates of tariff protection. Consequently, producers are willing to pay government officials large sums of money for such protection. Those who have better political connections and those who are willing to pay larger bribes will get higher—and thus more distorting—levels of protection. The import tariff and export subsidy approach is thus highly inconsistent with the Government's announced desire to reduce corruption. An appropriate exchange rate adjustment can provide the same overall average competitiveness margin for domestic producers that is provided by import taxes and export subsidies, and a good exchange rate has the very substantial additional advantages of avoiding distortions, reducing inefficiencies, and accelerating economic growth.

Another option that has been attempted in some countries is to reduce the price of labor and other non-traded goods and services rather than increasing the prices of traded goods through a devaluation. However, this would require the authorities to force the economy into a depression, thereby driving domestic prices down—especially those for labor—to more competitive levels without changing the exchange rate. In the real world, however, this approach never seems to work. For example, authorities in the West African countries that were members of the French Franc Zone tried to do this for years. In the end this proved impossible, and they had to devalue the African currencies. Good monetary and fiscal policies can control the growth of domestic prices and wages, thereby avoiding the need for a devaluation, but they can rarely be used to avoid a devaluation once a currency has appreciated well beyond its equilibrium rate. Furthermore, worldwide experience has shown that downward adjustments of domestic prices only happen during recessions or depressions, and the last thing that Belarus wants at this point is a depression in the midst of its ongoing economic crisis. A devaluation is therefore the only feasible policy alternative.

Making Devaluation Work. All of the measures discussed here indicate that Belarus needs to devalue its exchange rate. Any sizable devaluation, however, involves inflation. The challenge is to handle the devaluation in a way that limits the inflation to the minimum required to accomplish the necessary adjustment of relative prices and to make certain that the devaluation does not generate an inflationary spiral as has happened in the past in Belarus and in so many other countries.

Inflation is an almost inevitable part of any devaluation for the following reasons. To attain the desired control of aggregate demand and to restore a sustainable balance of payments deficit, a significant devaluation needs to produce a short-term reduction in living standards. In theory, if a country were investing heavily in low-productivity activities, it could reduce aggregate demand by reducing investment activity, thus protecting consumption and living standards. In most countries facing severe economic problems, however, and certainly in Belarus today, the rate of investment is already well below desirable levels and needs to be raised, not lowered. Therefore, unless prospects for future improvements in living standards are to be sacrificed by reducing today's investment levels even further, the only way to restore a sustainable BOP position is to reduce consumption until growth resumes.

If done well, a devaluation will reduce aggregate demand by causing a one-time surge of inflation that erodes the purchasing power of people's wages.[16] Inflation is therefore not only unavoidable, it is an essential part of the adjustment process. Inflation, stimulated by the devaluation, drives up the prices of traded goods relative to those of non-traded goods and wages. This has two vitally important effects. First, it reduces the real purchasing power in the economy, thereby bringing real aggregate demand into line with real levels of output. Second, the increased prices of traded goods relative to those of non-traded goods makes imports more costly and exports more profitable, thus bringing the demand for imports into line with export earnings. The key to success is to make certain that the initial spurt of inflation is limited to the level induced by the devaluation and does not trigger an inflationary spiral of the kind Belarus suffered from 1992 to early 1995.[17]

If a devaluation is done poorly, it will rekindle long-term inflation, lead to an ongoing cycle of devaluations, and do nothing to solve the underlying macro imbalances. In fact, repeated cycles of inflation and devaluation are common in the world, and it is very important to understand why this happens and what can be done to prevent it from happening in Belarus.

Most devaluations fail because governments try to protect people from the reduction in aggregate demand, consumption, and thus in living standards—reductions that are the primary reason for having a devaluation in the first place. Governments do this either by failing to pass on the higher prices caused by the devaluation, or by giving people extra money to pay the higher prices. Either strategy is very dangerous and is likely to lead to further problems that, in the end, reduce rather than increase living standards.

The *failure to pass on the higher costs* and thus reduce consumption can come in indirect as well as direct ways, and the indirect ways are often the most serious. For example, if the price of an imported car or an imported bottle of vodka goes up because of a devaluation, governments are unlikely to do anything to cushion the price increase, and the consumption of these goods will decline, thus helping restore the balance of payments position.

Failure to pass on the *indirect* costs of a devaluation is much more likely and commonly causes devaluation efforts to fail. Energy provides one of the best examples. Aside from gasoline, which accounts for a small part of the imported energy products, few energy products are sold directly to consumers. Instead, the cost of imported energy is factored into the price of rent, utilities, and public transport. If the government does not raise the prices for rent, utilities, and public transport enough to fully cover the increased cost of the energy needed to provide these services, the devaluation will fail. It will fail because, unless the consumers are charged—and forced to actually pay—the full cost of these services, their consumption will not be reduced, and the external balances will not be restored.

The same is true for energy sources supplied to farms and factories. Unless these enterprises have to pay the full cost for the imported energy at the higher domestic prices resulting from a devaluation, they will not take the necessary steps to reduce consumption and to use energy more efficiently. Unless the full cost of directly and indirectly imported goods and services is passed on to the consumers—be they residential, commercial, or industrial—the devaluation will fail to achieve its goals. Devaluations around the world fail regularly for this reason. And this has been a central cause of the failures of past devaluations in Belarus. The domestic currency has been devalued by roughly 300,000 times since the final days of the Soviet Union, but it is still seriously overvalued today.

Attempts by governments to cushion the impact of a devaluation by giving people and enterprises more money to pay the higher costs is the second common reason that devaluations fail. Additional purchasing power to offset the higher post-devaluation prices is typically created either through expansionary credit policies or through lax fiscal policies. Over the past five years, the Government of Belarus has done both—with the expected results.

The Government has given enterprises and thus their employees more money to pay the higher prices following past devaluations by extending trillions of rubels of credit to these enterprises. This strategy had some short-term benefits, as seen in Figure 1.8. But in the end this approach has left the average Belarusian no better off than the average citizen of the other FSU republics—and has left Belarus still faced with making the fundamental structural adjustments required to move forward to prosperity after years of delay.

The only way to assure success of the next devaluation is to pass on to enterprises and individuals the full increased costs of the goods and services that are imported, directly and indirectly, to insist that enterprises and individuals pay for whatever they consume, and to resist pressures to provide additional credit, subsidies, or tax concessions that would increase purchasing power.

The poorest of the poor will always need help from the Government, especially after major devaluations. Government protection of those who would suffer from malnutrition and exposure if not assisted is necessary in any civilized country to protect human dignity and the fabric of society. Social assistance should be part of an efficient, fiscally sustainable social safety net as discussed in Chapter 4. But how can such subsidies be made consistent with the statement above that the Government should not increase purchasing power?

The secret is to finance the social safety net by *redistributing* purchasing power, not by increasing it. As a country, Belarus cannot afford to continue living beyond its means, but it can redistribute its means more equitably by taxing those with more comfortable incomes and using the revenues to help assure that the poor have the minimum income needed to preserve basic human dignity.

This approach is sharply different from the current approach in Belarus, which seeks to protect the poor (a) by distorting the prices for food and housing, holding them down to levels that do not recover the full cost of import and production; (b) by ordering inflation-fueling credit expansion from the banks to agricultural and industrial enterprises; and (c) by offering deficit-increasing subsidies and tax exemptions. The poor should be protected through *income redistribution*, not through *price distortions*.

The draft economic strategy issued by the Government in October 1996 calls for the creation of a "socially oriented market economy."[18] This is a highly desirable objective, one shared by most civilized nations of the world. The main difference between the countries that succeed and those that fail lies in the approach chosen to attain this objective. Countries that fail depend heavily on price distortions. To help selected groups of people, these countries create artificially low prices for goods and services such as food, energy, and transport. This causes losses to the producers of such goods and services. As a result, the Government is forced to support them through direct budgetary subsidies, cheap loans from the banking system, and concessional tax rates and other "tax expenditures." These measures leave the Government short of money, causing it to "borrow" from the central bank, which then prints money. Printing money increases prices, leading to cries for increased subsidies, thus triggering another spiral of distortions in prices, fiscal policies, and monetary policies. This distortion-based approach to creating a socially oriented economy has been attempted by well-meaning countries throughout the world. Sooner or later, such attempts always fail.[19]

If Belarus is to succeed in creating a socially oriented market economy, it needs to reject the current strategy of distorting prices and focus instead on redistributing purchasing power. It needs to stop destroying the production process with artificial prices and to focus instead on using the fiscal system to redistribute the fruits of an efficient production process that is based on market-determined prices.

Chapter 2 discusses ways in which market-determined prices that stimulate efficient production and consumption can be established. Chapter 3 focuses on the ways in which enterprises can be stimulated to maximize efficiency and economic growth, and Chapter 4 discusses the ways that the Government can use tax revenues from this growing economic base to finance programs that improve the incomes and living standards of the poor in a non-inflationary way that does not distort prices. If these measures are put into place, the next devaluation can be the last major devaluation, and Belarus will be on the road to economic recovery and higher living standards.

Enterprise Profitability

As noted above, the increasing inability of Belarusian enterprises to compete in domestic and export markets has been the result primarily of the low efficiency of Soviet-era enterprises, particularly in their use of energy inputs. These production efficiency problems were compounded by the low quality of their products, the loss of traditional markets in the FSU and CEE countries, and the rapidly appreciating domestic currency. As industrial output declined, the incomes of workers decreased, further reducing the domestic demand for these products.

The impact on enterprise profitability is seen in Figure 1.20.[20] The only export products which have sustained their competitiveness are those whose value depends on domestic natural resources such as potash fertilizer and timber, and products such as garments from factories which, because of their efficiency, have a low wage burden in total costs despite rapid increases in domestic prices and wages.

The profitability of enterprises has been seriously damaged by pressures from governments at the national and local levels to retain workers. Some factory managers indicate that they could easily shed half their workers without reducing output. Hidden unemployment has variously been estimated at 20-40 percent of total employment. Data on the cost structure of 55 major Belarusian exporters indicate, however, that wage and non-wage remuneration on average account for only 8-10 percent of total production costs. This, plus the long-term relationship between workers and managers, helps explain the reluctance of plant managers to fire redundant workers. However, since value added accounts for only 15-20 percent of the total cost of production on average for these enterprises, wage costs are in fact a significant burden on value added and thus on plant profitability. In cases where value added at world prices is negative (the cost of inputs exceeds the value of outputs), wages become an

Figure 1.20: The number of loss-making enterprises has grown sharply.

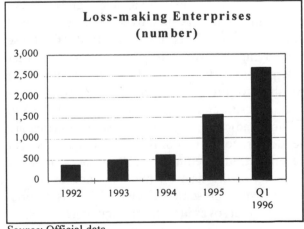

Source: Official data.

extremely large burden. Under such conditions, it may be cheaper to pay workers not to work by giving them a reasonably generous severance payment than to continue running the factory. In fact, the savings realized from halting the negative value added would generate a net gain to the economy even if the workers were to continue to be paid their working wage. The widespread collapse of enterprise profitability is having widespread negative effects on the rest of the economy—workers, other enterprises, energy suppliers, banks, and the Government.

Impact on Workers. According to the Bank's recently completed poverty assessment, about 95 percent of the increase in the poverty rate between 1992 and 1995 was the result of economic decline, not worse income distribution. Non-payment of wages and unemployment are the leading sources of poverty in Belarus today. Cases are regularly reported of delayed payments and non-payments to workers. In some instances, people work for weeks or months with no pay, partly out of dedication to their jobs, partly because alternative employment is hard to find in the current environment (which is not conducive to the establishment of new enterprises), and partly in the hope that their enterprises will get the necessary money from sales, the government, or the banks. In the meantime, the workers are able to take advantage of the housing and other services offered by enterprises.

Impact on Other Enterprises. Non-payments to other enterprises is a serious problem in Belarus, jeopardizing the financial health of enterprises that could otherwise be profitable. Total overdue non-payments grew from essentially zero in 1990 to over 40 percent of total inter-enterprise debts by early 1996. Of these non-payments, over 70 percent were to other enterprises, both inside and outside Belarus. The payables to foreign enterprises exceed receivables from these enterprises by nearly USD 500 million, indicating that Belarusian enterprises are net debtors to the rest of the world (since this debt began as trade credits in most instances, it is not included in the data on medium- and long-term external debt presented elsewhere in this report). Of the total overdues to foreign enterprises, a major share is for energy supplies from Russia.

Impact on Energy Suppliers. The large energy arrears underscore the need for hard budget constraints that would force enterprises either to remain current on their payments for energy or to shut down their operations. Russia has been reluctant to take measures such as shutting off gas and oil supplies that would press Belarus to meet its payments obligations, nor has the Government of Belarus effectively pressured the enterprises to meet their payment obligations. Arrears on payments for gas are a particularly severe problem; arrears to Russia grew to USD 400 million in late 1994 before a deal was struck, reducing this amount by half. By early 1996 gas arrears totaling over USD 900 million (including penalties) had again accumulated. In early 1996, the Presidents of Russia and Belarus signed a "zero option" agreement by which Russia would cancel these arrears in exchange for Belarus canceling its claims against Russia, including those for environmental damage, for nuclear weapons materials taken from Belarus to Russia, for the maintenance of Russian troops on Belarusian soil, and for deposits of the Belarus Vnesheconombank that are frozen in Moscow. Although implementation details were difficult to conclude—partly because of the negative impact on the financially strapped Russian budget—the deal was reportedly completed in September 1996.

The lack of payments discipline has had a very negative impact on the economic performance and prospects of Belarus. In the case of energy supplies from Russia, for example, the arrears have strained relations between the two governments. Further accumulations of arrears could lead Russia to shut off gas supplies to Belarus, as it has done for a number of the other FSU republics that have accumulated sizable arrears. Resolving such a situation could lead to demands that Belarus, in order to cancel its debts, give up partial or total ownership rights in important national assets such as refineries or the pipelines that transport Russian oil across Belarus to central and western Europe. Debt/equity swaps could therefore have seriously negative long-term impacts on the balance of payments and on the national income of Belarus. For example, the annual implicit value of gas and oil transportation by the pipelines across Belarus is probably in the range of USD 200-400 million. Even if this figure is significantly overstated, the loss of revenues that would result from a debt/equity swap that transferred ownership of such assets to Russia would obviously have a major impact on the net balance of payments position and long-term economic prospects of Belarus.

Impact on Exchange Rate. One of the most serious consequences of the lack of payments discipline and consequent payments arrears has been the distortions in the value of the Belarusian rubel and thus the erosion of the competitiveness and profitability of Belarusian enterprises. As a result of the failure of Belarusian enterprises to pay the Belarusian energy suppliers (Belgaz) for energy supplies, Belgaz has not had the Belarusian rubels needed to purchase foreign exchange in the domestic markets to pay these bills to Russia. Consequently, the demand for foreign exchange has been artificially low, contributing directly to the overvaluation of the domestic currency. The exchange rate overvaluation has been exacerbated by the fact that a significant share of the inflationary credit expansion during 1995 went to the gas company to help provide at least some of the resources that it needed to pay for imported gas. This plus other factors pushed total credit to expand more rapidly than GDP, leading to inflationary pressures that, in turn, contributed to even more overvaluation of the domestic currency, given the fixed exchange rate. This has resulted in a vicious cycle that can only be broken through a combination of appropriate policies including a flexible exchange rate, realistic domestic prices, and hard budget constraints.

The lack of payments discipline with respect to domestically supplied inputs, including labor, material inputs, bank loans, and government services, has also contributed to the overvaluation of the currency. Belarusian enterprises have continued to export—even at a loss—in order to obtain scarce foreign exchange. Enterprises have been able to do this because they can cover the losses by failing to pay their bills. As a result, loss-making exports have contributed to a much larger supply of foreign exchange in the domestic market than would have existed if

exporters had been forced—through the imposition of effective hard budget constraints—to pay all of their suppliers, workers, taxes, and bank loans.

Imposing hard budget constraints and financial discipline through mechanisms such as the effective threat of bankruptcy could greatly improve the competitiveness of Belarusian exports and thus the profitability of Belarusian enterprises. If such discipline were imposed, exports would initially decline as enterprises no longer exported at a loss. The drop in exports would increase the scarcity value of foreign exchange, creating pressures for an exchange rate devaluation. At the devalued rate, exports would become more profitable, allowing enterprises to return to exporting, but this time at a profit while fully covering their costs of production. In this way, financial relations within the economy could be put on a normal basis where enterprises paid their bills in full and on time, thus bringing an end to the spiraling cycle of non-payments.

Impact on the Banking System. The low profitability and non-payments of the enterprise sector have had a sharply negative impact on the banking sector. Between 1994 and 1995, arrears to commercial banks increased nearly three times as a share of credits outstanding (from 4 percent to 11 percent compared to an international norm of about 2 percent for a well-performing portfolio). These arrears are concentrated in the six largest commercial banks,[21] which account for about 70 percent of total arrears. Almost 50 percent of the banks' total capital funds in Belarus today needs to be set aside against bad loans. The loan losses and non-payment of interest have also hurt the profitability of the commercial banks. During the first quarter of 1996, about half of them were losing money. These developments, which threaten to undermine the already fragile condition of the banking system in Belarus clearly indicate the importance of imposing hard budget constraints. Without payments discipline, failing enterprises will bankrupt banks, which threatens the strength of otherwise healthy enterprises, which depend on a sound banking system. This in turn casts a dark shadow over prospects for renewed economic growth.

Impact on Government. Finally, enterprise non-payments are eroding the financial position of the Government. In addition to ordering the banking system to extend credits to failing enterprises, the Government has been making significant subsidies available directly from the budget—the equivalent of about 3.5 percent of GDP. Of the total subsidies in the 1996 state budget, over half are for the agricultural sector. Although the current subsidy number is still large—roughly equivalent to the entire budget deficit—it represents a major improvement compared to 1993, when budgetary subsidies were 15 percent of GDP.

Fiscal Policies and Performance

General government revenues have been declining relative to overall economic activity since 1993 when they reached 52 percent of GDP. In 1995 general government revenues were only 43 percent of GDP.[22] The Government hopes to raise them to 47 percent of GDP in 1996, but revenue collections are off sharply. By mid-year, only 33 percent of anticipated revenues for the year had been collected.

Many factors account for this shortfall in funds. First, economic activity in Belarus continues to decline. However, although this helps account for an absolute decline in tax revenues, it does not account for the decline relative to GDP. Second, the corporate profits tax accounts for about 20 percent of total tax revenues, and an increasing number of enterprises are now losing money, leaving them with no profits upon which to pay taxes. Third, to help keep failing enterprises afloat so that they will not have to lay off their workers, the Government has been granting some enterprises an extension for paying taxes and is completely exempting others from selected taxes; in addition to seriously eroding the tax base, these policies also result in an uneven playing field among enterprises and create conditions under which bribery and corruption are inevitable. Fourth, as the size of the informal economy grows relative to total GDP—a development reflecting in part the onerous government controls that make it difficult for an honest enterprise to run a profitable business—tax evasion has increased.

Despite the burden of subsidies and other expenditures, the Government has consistently done a good job of maintaining the nominal budget deficit at a modest 2-4 percent of GDP for the past several years. However, the picture is not as positive as it might seem for several reasons:

- Belarus has a sizable quasi-fiscal budget that is financed through the banking system.

- The Government has drawn down the reserves of the Social Protection Fund, both through direct transfers and by charging certain price adjustment compensation payments to consumers against the fund rather than against the budget, with the result that pensioners now receive their payments with substantial delays.

- In attempting to maintain the budget deficit and government borrowing targets agreed with the IMF, the Government is increasingly operating on a cash basis, paying its bills only as revenues are received. Consequently, wages and pensions are often paid with considerable delays, and the Government is in arrears to suppliers, thus worsening the financial crisis in the enterprise sectors. Expenditure arrears of the Government have grown from negligible levels to a substantial share of annual expenditures.

- With revenue collections falling well below projections, the Government is increasingly turning to sequestration of funds to prevent the deficit from exceeding the limits agreed with the IMF, and sequestration tends to be applied with little respect for the original budgetary priorities agreed with Parliament. For example, expenditures during the first half of 1996 were 33 percent of original plans for 1996, reflecting a similar shortfall in revenues. Within this total, however, expenditures on health were only 22 percent of the 1996 targets, but expenditures on defense were 41 percent of plans, the highest rate for any program area.

- The public investment program has been particularly hard hit; only 21 percent of the planned expenditures had been made by mid-1996. Capital expenditures of the central government have fallen from an average of 2.2 percent of GDP in 1992 and 1993 to only 0.7 percent of the sharply reduced GDP of the first quarter of 1996.

B. Restoring Economic Stability and Growth

Stability

Government policy reform efforts to date have focused primarily on controlling inflation and on softening the impact of the transition process on the people of Belarus. Unfortunately, the latter objective has frequently been given higher priority than controlling inflation. The Government's reluctance to impose hard budget constraints and to close loss-making enterprises where necessary, and its widespread use of directed credits and budget subsidies have created rather than controlled inflation. This approach may have reduced the amount of open unemployment, but has done little to improve the capacity of enterprises to grow and support an improved standard of living for the Belarusian people. A continuation of past policies will not do much good in the short run, and will make it even more costly in the long run to undertake the necessary structural reforms. Until enterprises, particularly those in the industrial and agricultural sectors, have been converted into efficient, profitable operations, the Government's objectives of stability and improved living standards will remain seriously at risk.

The priority actions in the area of stability are thus to free prices so that they may be determined by market forces, and to hold expansion of the money supply roughly in line with GDP growth to avoid inflation.

Growth and Structural Change

Policymakers in Belarus are very concerned about the efficiency and profitability of enterprises and have focused considerable effort on identifying how the necessary investment resources can be mobilized. An important paper was issued by the Government this summer on policies to stimulate investment in the economy, and the Government recently sponsored an international investment conference in Minsk to attract foreign investors. The need for massive investment in the economy cannot be questioned. The physical inefficiency of equipment and sub-standard designs of products cannot be fixed with simple stroke-of-the-pen policy changes.

However, the necessary level of investment will not take place until some other very important issues have been addressed.

A very rough estimate of the investment that will be required during the coming years can be calculated as follows. At the current market exchange rate, the GDP of Belarus in 1995 was equal to about USD 10 billion. If Belarus is to restore previous living standards and reverse the current trend towards increasing poverty in a timely manner, it would be desirable for the country to grow by at least 6 percent per year. Comparative data from around the world indicates that economies that grow in the range of 6-10 percent per year commonly have a ratio of investment to GDP of around 30 percent, compared to the rate of around 25 percent seen in Belarus today. This would imply annual investments starting at about USD 3 billion per year, and increasing thereafter in line with nominal GDP. A somewhat higher initial level of investment may be desirable to compensate for the very low status of much of the capital stock in 1990 in terms of energy efficiency and product design, and for the sharp deterioration in the capital stock since then. In 1995, for example, capital investment in the industrial and agricultural sectors was only about one third of the 1992 level in real terms.

According to official statistics, the actual gross fixed capital formation in 1995 was about USD 2.6 billion, which is close to the indicative USD 3 billion that is required. This underscores the point made earlier in this report that major improvements are needed in the efficiency of capital. Otherwise, increasing the GDP growth rate would require even higher levels of investment and corresponding reductions in the feasible levels of personal consumption. Given the compression of living standards that has already taken place, this is clearly not the desirable option. The remainder of this report therefore focuses on actions that the Government could take to improve the efficiency of investment in Belarus.

Although most enterprises today in Belarus are government-owned, most of the investment should come from private sources. The Government should be making relatively little investment in existing enterprises, and should focus instead on privatizing the enterprises so that they will be attractive to private investors. This recommendation is made from a purely practical, non-political perspective—the Government does not have the necessary financial resources, nor are there any prospects of its mobilizing more than a relatively small part of the required resources to make further investments in enterprises. Also, past experience in Belarus and elsewhere has shown that governments should focus on governing (including the establishment of a good investment climate), and should leave the business of business to the private sector.

Only three ways exist for Belarus to raise the rate of investment by the 5-10 percent of GDP that is needed to attain the level of investment required to grow at a desirable rate.

- Save and invest a higher share of GDP.

- Borrow from abroad.

- Attract foreign direct investment, including the repatriation of domestic capital that has sought safety and higher returns abroad.

Each of these strategies is viable and should be pursued. However, one conclusion is obvious in reading the list. Potential investors—be they Belarusian households and businesses, foreign lenders, or foreign investors—will require a much higher degree of safety and a much better real return on capital than exists in the Belarusian market today. This is axiomatic, for if the safety and returns in the Belarusian market were already sufficiently good, the investment would already be taking place. In short, attaining the required levels of investment will require major improvements in the business climate. The next section of this paper focuses on measures needed to establish a good business environment in Belarus.

C. CONCLUSIONS

This review of the sources of the current economic crisis in Belarus indicates that the main problems have included the following:

- The twin external shocks of higher energy prices and the loss of traditional markets triggered the current crisis.

- The poor quality and low production efficiency of Belarusian goods made it difficult for Belarus to redirect its exports to the international markets.

- These shocks, together with the breakup of the former Soviet Union, made unavoidable both a transition from the previous command economy to a market economy, and a fundamental restructuring and upgrading of domestic production capacity.

- Government policies implicitly sought to cushion the adjustment to these external shocks by expansionary credit and related policies that helped to maintain employment and living standards.

- The end result of these policies was excessive demand, rising consumption, falling investment, and high rates of inflation.

- These macroeconomic imbalances, together with cautious reforms in the areas of price decontrol and privatization, have created an unfavorable climate for investment in Belarus, and have significantly delayed the transition to a prosperous, market-based economy.

2

Establishing a Market-Friendly Environment

A. ATTRACTING INVESTMENT FOR GROWTH

The level of foreign investment that a country can attract is a good indication of the quality of its investment climate. Foreign investors have the freedom to invest almost anywhere in the world, so they will favor countries that have investment environments which provide maximum returns with minimum risks. Even resource rich countries like the oil producing states must be concerned about the quality of the business environment; investors stay away where they have to depend on case-by-case decisions of state and local authorities to get permission to invest, to purchase buildings and land, to set output prices, to define tax liabilities, and to enforce contracts for payments from customers. They prefer to go to countries where these issues are established by transparent laws that apply equally to all investors, and do not require case-specific appeals to the authorities, an environment that often fosters corruption.

The judgment of foreign investors in 1993 regarding the quality of the investment climate in Belarus compared to that in other FSU and CEE countries is quite clear from Figure 2.1. The picture would be even more dramatic if per capita investment in Belarus were measured against countries like Slovenia and Poland; compared to the USD 1.00 per person that Belarus attracts, they are attracting around USD 50. The Czech Republic and Estonia are attracting around USD 100 per person per year. These countries have few if any natural advantages over Belarus—which has an unsurpassed geographic location with close ties and good access to both Eastern and Western markets, a talented labor force, and an excellent basic physical infrastructure. Belarus obviously has great potential to expand the inward flow of foreign direct investment simply by improving its investment climate. Data on foreign direct investment (FDI) as a share of GDP for 1994 indicate no evidence of significant improvement for Belarus in the competition for foreign direct

investment (Figure 2.2), and anecdotal evidence for 1995 indicates that Belarus continued to face more difficulty than most other countries in attracting FDI.

Further evidence of the very low quality of the business climate in Belarus today comes

Figure 2.1: Belarus does not attract much FDI per person.

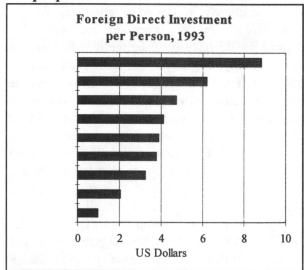

Source: World Bank staff calculations.

Figure 2.2: FDI as a percentage of GDP is low.

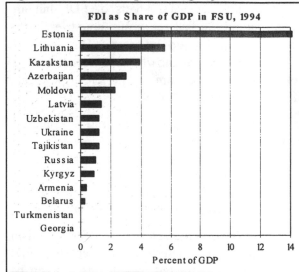

Source: World Bank staff calculations.

from the international business publications, which are highly influential in shaping the views of foreign investors. *Institutional Investor (1995),* rated the business climate in Belarus at 112 out of the 135 countries covered. *Euromoney (September 1996)* ranked Belarus at 142 out of 178 countries in terms of credit risk and at 136 out of 165 countries in terms of economic performance. The *1996 Index of Economic Freedom (Heritage Foundation 1996)* rates Belarus at 106 out of 140 countries in terms of its policies regarding areas such as trade, taxation, monetary policy, property rights, regulation and foreign investment.

Figures 2.1 and 2.2 indicate that Belarus has done poorly in terms of attracting foreign direct investment, but they do not prove that Belarus would have done better if it had moved more rapidly to establish a normal market economy. The link between FDI inflows and the speed of market-oriented reforms is seen more clearly in Figure 2.3. Here the 15 FSU and 10 CEE countries in transition are grouped in terms of their "Liberalization Index," a composite measure developed for the World Bank's *World Development Report* (*WDR*) showing the rate at which they have moved to establish a market economy of the kind found in OECD countries (IBRD, *WDR* 1996). As this figure shows, per capita FDI inflows are dramatically higher among the fast-reforming countries than among the slow-reforming countries. Countries undertaking a moderate pace of market-oriented liberalization are attracting increasing levels of FDI, but are falling behind the fast reforming countries in the race to attract foreign investors. The countries that are reforming slowly and very slowly, including Belarus, are experiencing severe difficulties in attracting FDI.

Are the fast-reforming countries fundamentally different from the slow-reforming countries? Are they attracting FDI for reasons other than their more rapid pace of reform? If countries like Belarus do accelerate their reforms, are they likely to attract the desired levels of FDI?

Figure 2.4 indicates reason for optimism on this score and underlines the fact that FDI waits for and is attracted by reforms. As can be

Figure 2.3: Fast reformers get more FDI.

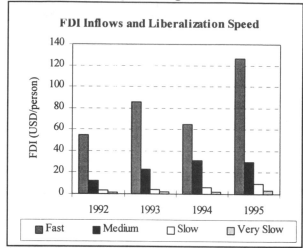

Source: World Bank (1996), World Bank staff calculations.

seen in this figure, the Liberalization Index (shown as a line) began moving up sharply after 1989, but FDI remained at extremely low levels. The pace of FDI inflow did not accelerate until these fast-reforming countries had gotten about 80 percent of the way towards establishing normal market-based economic structures. The lag is clear. But once a certain critical level of reforms was reached, the flows suddenly became substantial.

Belarus has a lot to learn from the experience of the fast-reforming countries. They are not a special case—nor is Belarus. The fast-reforming countries had to reach a certain stage in

Figure 2.4: FDI follows good liberalization performance.

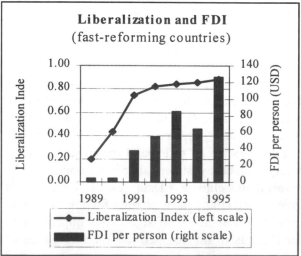

Source: World Bank (1996), World Bank staff calculations.

the transition process before large numbers of serious foreign investors were willing to come. Belarus faces exactly the same challenge today. Once it has implemented the reforms recommended in this report, it will also be able to attract significant flows of FDI.

In analyzing these graphs it is important to remember that the Liberalization Index does not measure levels of development. It only measures progress in establishing the pre-conditions for economic growth under a market-based economic system. A country does not have to become rich to attract FDI. In fact, Malaysia and Thailand, two of the star performers in Asia in terms of FDI, have per capita incomes similar to the level in Belarus. Even relatively poor countries like the Philippines and Indonesia, which have per capita incomes less than half the level in Belarus, are attracting large amounts of FDI (USD 760 million and USD 2.0 billion respectively in 1993). The secret is to create a normal, well-functioning market, and to do so as quickly as possible.

This chapter focuses on the measures that could be taken with relative ease to accomplish this goal—measures that could make a major contribution to obtaining the flow of investment that Belarus urgently needs to upgrade the productivity of its capital stock, its international competitiveness, and its standard of living. Action is needed in three major areas: (a) allowing prices to be set by competitive market forces; (b) developing a transparent and equitable legal framework that is consistent with international standards; and (c) maintaining a supportive environment.

The actions recommended here are just as important for attracting domestic as for attracting foreign investment, and the treatment given both domestic and foreign investors should be the same. Based on the experience in other countries, domestic investors are likely to account for 80-90 percent of the total investment that takes place in an economy in any given year. They are therefore extremely important to the overall growth strategy. This chapter is therefore not just about attracting foreign investors, but about improving the business environment of Belarus so that both domestic and foreign investors will want to invest in the nation's future.

B. ESTABLISHING MARKET-DETERMINED PRICES

One of the keys to success in making the transition from an administratively controlled system to a market economy is letting competitively-determined market prices provide the basis for allocating resources. Without competitively-determined prices, a market economy will fail. In market economies, prices are virtually the only guide to efficient resource allocation. Anything such as inflation, administrative controls on prices or profit margins, subsidies, monopolistic market structures, barriers to entry and exit, "socially-conscious" price setting by state-owned enterprises, ad hoc tax rates, and external trade barriers all distort prices, thereby reducing prospects for efficient resource use and rapid improvements in living standards. If an investor cannot depend on a government to allow market forces to set prices—if a serious risk exists that the government will intervene in determining prices—the risk that profits will turn into losses is great and the investor will look to other markets.

Belarus has made considerable progress since 1991 in moving from administratively determined to market-determined prices. Much remains to be done, however, to establish an environment where investors can be fully confident that their future profits will be determined by market forces, not by government interventions. This section reviews the progress made in various areas of price determination and the work that lies ahead to create a truly business-friendly pricing environment that will attract the levels of investment that Belarus wants and needs.

Price Decontrols

Under the administratively controlled system that Belarus inherited from the Soviet era, prices were more of an accounting convenience than a device to guide production and consumption decisions. Prices were fixed by decree, not by competitive forces of demand and supply. When an enterprise made "excessive" profits under the prevailing administered prices, the surplus was taken away through enterprise-specific tax rates, centrally determined dividend payments, or by imposing various social costs such as housing and district heating on the enterprise. When the administered prices for inputs and outputs led to losses, the government used subsidies, capital investments, and directed credits from the banking system to fill the gap.

As Belarus began the transition to a market economy, it started liberalizing prices so that they could be determined by market forces. In some areas the task is essentially completed. By 1995, virtually all manufactured products, for example, were free from all forms of price control. This was a major accomplishment. Most agro-industrial and agricultural products were also free of controls, but the process has taken longer. Profit margin controls still existed on dark bread, milk and meat in 1996. These limits on selling prices, combined with minimum procurement prices to farmers, have put a price squeeze on the trade sector, a situation further aggravated by the fact that the majority of enterprises in this sector are still government-owned and controlled. Local government officials pressure the managers of local wholesale and retail establishments to keep prices low "for social reasons." Because price controls had officially been abolished by the national Government, much of this control was not documented but took the form of "telephone control." The system of state orders, particularly for goods from the agricultural sector, also serves as a de facto system of price control and should be replaced by a procurement system based on competitive bidding. Nearly 60 percent of enterprises in this sector are now loss-makers, creating a severe crisis in the trade and catering sectors. Efforts to subsidize the poor by controlling prices of "socially sensitive" food items has been very costly. (Box 2.1). State orders

remain a serious barrier to the formation of competitive markets for the allocation of many agricultural goods and raw materials. Although the World Bank has been working with the national authorities through the Forestry Project to establish competitive markets for standing timber, most is still allocated administratively and transferred at a stumpage fee that is far below competitive market prices.

Unfortunately, the Government started moving in exactly the opposite direction in the latter part of 1996. In September, a decree was issued that reestablished price controls on a wide range of goods. Many of the goods explicitly listed in the decree were still under administrative control (for example,. goods and services produced by monopolistic enterprises). This part of the decree is of less concern, however, than the part that explicitly allows local governments to apply price controls on "socially important goods," a loophole that could easily be abused. The decree also froze prices through the end of 1996 on a number of important goods. The net effect of these measures is a significant reversal of previous policy progress, a reversal that will make it even harder than before to establish a market in Belarus where investors can depend on the price of their inputs and outputs being set by competitive market forces rather than by government decree.

The housing and utilities sector is also in deep crisis, with about 35 percent of the enterprises losing money, and price controls are the major problem here as well. Because of the monopolistic structure of these sectors, price controls are of course required. Major utilities like electricity are national level monopolies and will need price regulation for the foreseeable future. Housing, district heating, and water are provided by hundreds of different entities around the country, but are nevertheless effective monopolies in most cases as far as the individual householder or enterprise is concerned. The issue is therefore not the abolition of price controls, but rather to set prices that allow for full recovery of necessary costs.

Box 2.1: There is no free lunch.

Like many governments in third world countries, Belarus has sought to help the poor by imposing an artificially low price on bread. Bread is a particularly important source of nourishment for the poor, so this approach seems at first glance to make sense. However, it is seriously flawed and ends up costing everyone, even the poor.

If a loaf of bread costs, for example, 50 cents to make and is sold for 25 cents, the bakery has to be compensated for the loss or it will go out of business. In Belarus, part of this compensation comes in the form of artificially low prices for flour, which are based on the artificially low prices given to farmers for the grain procured through the state grain trading system. As of December 1995, for example, the state procurement price for grain was only $65 per ton, compared to a world price of $121 per ton.

This approach pushes the burden of subsidizing bread onto the farmers, who receive less than their cost of production. As a result of this and similar pricing practices for meat, milk, and other dairy products, the agriculture sector accounted for one of the largest concentrations of loss-making enterprises in Belarus as of the first quarter of 1996, followed by the trade and catering sector—where losses are also caused in part by controlled prices.

To help farmers survive the low grain prices, the Government has taken two different approaches. On the one hand, it has forced the banking system to lend heavily to the agricultural sector. As a result, agriculture's share of total credit has increased sharply while its share in total GDP has declined. The subsidization of agriculture with large volumes of cheap banking system credits has increased inflation and the interest rate cost of capital in Belarus. On the other hand, the Government also maintains an Agricultural Support Fund that provides direct budgetary subsidies to the agricultural sector for the purchase of inputs and capital equipment.

In the end, consumers pay more than the full cost of the cheap bread. They pay higher interest rates because of the drain of credit to loss-making enterprises in the agricultural sector. They receive lower wages due to the scarcity and high cost of investment funds that are needed to modernize the industrial sector and increase labor productivity, thus making it possible for enterprises to pay higher wages. And they pay higher taxes to finance subsidies to the farmers.

How much more efficient it would be simply to charge the full cost of the bread in the first place and give the poor a direct cash or food-stamp subsidy to help them pay the full cost of producing the bread. An income subsidy to the poor would cost a fraction of the current maze of subsidies required to compensate for the distorted price of bread, which ends up subsidizing everyone, not just the poor. Without the costs of compensating for all the losses caused by "cheap" bread, the Government could lower taxes and provide more adequate subsidies to those who are truly poor. If everyone paid the real cost of bread, everyone—including the poor—would eat better.

Under the Soviet system, housing and utilities were provided free or at token rates as part of the wage package for workers. Cost recovery for utilities became a major issue when the cost of energy increased from insignificant levels to levels close to world prices. Cost recovery for housing has also become an issue for several reasons: (a) current cost recovery rates are not enough even to cover maintenance costs, with the result that the housing stock is deteriorating; (b) with no capital cost recovery in most cases, resources are not available to replace obsolete housing units; (c) the implicit subsidization through under-recovery of costs from families in government-owned housing creates a serious bias against private home ownership because private owners will have to cover the full cost of home ownership and maintenance; and (d) the lack of resources to maintain existing and build new housing has caused a crisis in the building and construction materials industry.

The Government has made considerable progress since 1994 when the cost recovery rate for housing and utilities averaged barely 10 percent—cost recovery for rent and water was 2 percent or less, while that for heating was under 4 percent. Out of rent, heating, hot water, and electricity, the four significant[23] housing costs, only electricity had a recovery ratio exceeding 25 percent. Despite considerable social opposition, the Government made commendable progress during 1995 in increasing cost recovery rates to more realistic levels. By July 1995, the average cost recovery for all household costs was over 60 percent, and minor services such as radio, telephone and TV had reached 100 percent. Cost recovery on the major items was as follows: rent

(50%), heating (65%), hot water (54%), and electricity (84%). These efforts have stalled since then, however. Although average cost recovery as of mid-1996 was reportedly about 60 percent, this was possible only because, through negotiations with Russia, Belarus was able to get a concession on the cost of gas delivered to Belarus, bringing gas even further below world prices than before.

Demonopolization and Privatization

The previous section highlights one of the main problems that comes from not having prices determined by competitive market forces—that the government has to make decisions about appropriate prices. Unfortunately, few governments in the world do a good job of this for at least two reasons. First, being responsible for social welfare and sensitive to political pressures, governments usually find it easier to set prices with one eye on what is politically palatable rather than setting prices strictly on the basis of costs and finding other mechanisms, such as means-tested, targeted housing support funds, to meet social objectives. Second, setting prices requires a decision, which requires committees, meetings, and reports. All this takes time. Consequently, prices are very likely to be out of line with costs by the time the decision is finally reached and implemented—the well-known problem of *regulatory lag*. These problems are universal and almost unavoidable whenever governments try to set prices.

The best way around this problem is to create an environment where the market forces of demand and supply, rather than the government, set prices for goods and services—prices that will accurately reflect true scarcity values, thus assuring maximum efficiency and growth. To establish a market structure in Belarus that can accurately determine prices, the authorities need to break up monopoly structures and reduce government ownership.

Monopolistic Markets. The Government established a special Anti-Monopoly Ministry to deal with these problems; with the help of outside experts, it has done a good job of establishing the basic laws needed to eliminate monopolistic market structures and to control monopolistic practices.[24] The most serious monopolistic

structures in Belarus in terms of their impact on consumers are the retail and wholesale trading organizations. Some progress has been made in this area.[25] However, local political pressures have made it difficult for the national Government to break these up as quickly and completely as would be desired. For example, a national plan for demonopolizing the trading organizations—a condition for the past year for a World Bank loan to support private enterprise development—has been prepared, but its implementation has been delayed.

Government Ownership and Privatization. Despite an initial spate of activity right after independence, progress in reducing the presence of the state in retail trade has slowed markedly since 1992 (Figure 2.5). Action in this area needs to be accelerated sharply. Breaking up trading companies into smaller, independent units helps, for this introduces some degree of competition among them. In Gomel, for example, newly-separated units of the former retail trading organization are competing with each other in terms of service, product line, and accessibility. This does not really solve the problem, however. As long as the demonopolized enterprises are still owned by the state, they will be subject to the same pressures noted above to price goods and services on the basis of "social" rather than purely economic considerations. Also, state ownership of wholesale organizations can make it difficult for privatized shops to get supplies. Even without explicit instructions, the old-line managers of

Figure 2.5: State dominance in retail sales is falling.

Market Share of State in Retail Sales (%)

Source: Official data.

state-owned organizations often feel a strong allegiance to other state-owned enterprises, and distrust the motives and social conscience of the private shops, which leads them to supply and price goods to other state-owned enterprises on a non-market basis. This helps explain why trading organizations are among the least profitable and most highly indebted enterprises in Belarus. The existence of large state organizations, with their well-established infrastructure of warehouses and cold stores, can therefore make it difficult for new private enterprises even to get established, much less compete. The fact that private trading enterprises are nevertheless a rather dynamic sector in Belarus indicates the contribution that they could make to economic development and growth if freed of the many shackles and constraints under which they currently must work.

Although the existence of large and often monopolistic state-owned trading enterprises creates problems for private enterprise, it would be a mistake to simply privatize these large state enterprises. They first need to be demonopolized. A private monopoly is more likely to distort prices and to harm the public interest than a well-run public monopoly. Thus, neither demonopolization nor privatization is sufficient. Both are required, and both should be implemented as quickly as possible. In addition to allowing a more competitive pricing environment, this would improve the business climate and attract investors who would create new jobs that would cushion the impact of reforming the over-staffed large-scale enterprises. Small-scale enterprises like retail shops are one of the best possible sources of employment because of the small amount of investment required per job place created. But Belarus will not be able to take advantage of this opportunity, and thus will find it difficult to avoid poverty and social unrest, unless it sharply accelerates efforts to privatize and demonopolize the wholesale and retail trade sectors, not only for food and household goods, but also for trade in agricultural inputs and raw materials (Annex B).

Demonopolization and privatization should also be accelerated in the *housing industry*. A significant share of the total housing stock is already in private hands (38 percent), and

this represents a significant improvement over the situation in 1992 when only 7 percent had been privatized. The process slowed down significantly in 1995, however. As with retail trade, accelerating the privatization of housing could open up major opportunities for new jobs and new economic activity. Housing is very labor intensive, requires little in the way of imported materials, could build on the capacities of the substantial building materials industry that already operates in Belarus, and could help improve the quality of life for thousands of families in Belarus.[26]

Developing a comprehensive strategy for the demonopolization and privatization of the housing sector so that it can attract both household and commercial investments is beyond the scope of this paper. However, a strategy should include the establishment of (a) a condominium law to protect the rights of individuals in multi-family dwellings and to help assure adequate maintenance of buildings; (b) a full private land ownership system including adequate mechanisms for recording both titles and third-party claims against titles; and (c) the laws and institutions needed so that existing commercial banks can undertake long-term, mortgage-backed lending.

External Trade Policy

The external trade policies of Belarus are important not only from the macroeconomic and balance of payments perspective, as noted in Chapter 1, but also from the perspective of creating an attractive business environment based on market-determined prices. In this context, an open foreign trade policy with minimal barriers to the free flow of goods and capital offers two very important advantages.

Control of Monopolies. Open borders provide the best possible way for Belarus to control the monopolistic tendencies of its very large industrial enterprises. For large enterprises such as the tractor factory and the truck plants, demonopolizing in terms of final products makes no sense. For example, breaking up the tractor factory so that Belarus had multiple domestic brands among which farmers could chose would be a very costly policy. To be internationally competitive, factories producing such products require very large-scale production, and such factories need to be internationally competitive because they are too large to survive based on the limited demand of the domestic market in Belarus. Some of the ancillary activities of these factories, such as the production of parts like hydraulic cylinders that are common to other vehicles and equipment, should almost certainly be spun off to specialized producers who could, with multiple clients, produce at larger and therefore more efficient scales. However, breaking up production of the core products such as tractors would make no sense from an economic perspective.

The monopolistic power of such enterprises should instead be controlled by forcing them to compete with little or no tariff or non-tariff protection against producers from around the world. Besides assuring domestic consumers that they can buy tractors at world prices, this strategy would also assure that Belarusian products are competitive internationally, and thus much more attractive to investors who could help improve the quality and competitiveness of Belarusian exports.

Customs Union with Russia. Most decisionmakers in Belarus seem to be convinced that an outward-oriented strategy is appropriate for a country like Belarus that depends so heavily on international trade. The viability of this strategy is being jeopardized, however, by the customs union with Russia. Russia, being a much larger country, could pursue a protectionist, inward-oriented policy more easily than Belarus, and could more easily bear the probable economic costs of such a strategy because of its rich endowment of natural resources. Nevertheless, such an inward-oriented strategy would be costly for Russia—and very costly for Belarus. Recent moves by Russia to increase protection against third-country imports, such as increasing tariffs on automobiles, are thus of great concern.

Tariff-free trade between Russia and Belarus is an excellent idea from the Belarusian perspective because (a) it should give Belarus access to imported inputs at prices prevailing in the Russian market; and (b) it makes a much larger market available for Belarusian products, thereby allowing Belarusian factories to attract more investment and to produce on a more economic scale. Whether or not Belarus will benefit depends, however, on the degree of tariff protection against third countries.

The main risk of preferential trading agreements—whether customs unions or free trade areas—is that, instead of *creating* more economical trade by breaking down tariff barriers between two or more countries, trading partners will *divert* their purchase of imports from low cost external sources to high cost sources within the trading area because of high external tariffs. Belarusian consumers and producers are already suffering from this problem under the customs union agreement with Russia. Some manufacturers now find that duties on imported materials can be 100 percent higher than before. In fact, a recent survey of leading export-oriented manufacturing enterprises in Belarus indicates that the most serious problem preventing them from developing a higher volume of exports was the *high taxes and tariffs for imported parts and materials*, second only to the appreciation of the real exchange rate noted in Chapter 1. Similarly, consumers face prospects of sharply higher duties for imported Western cars, which could force them to buy inferior Russian cars at unreasonably high prices.

One of the initial attractions of joining the customs union with Russia was the prospect of being able to purchase energy inputs at prices well below those prevailing in world markets. This is turning out to be a false hope for two reasons. First, the real appreciation of the Russian ruble plus domestic taxes has already put some Russian energy products above world prices. Second, Russian prices increased by 36 times from January 1993 to December 1995. As of September 1995, motor vehicle gasoline cost USD 327 per ton in Russia versus USD 183 on the world market, and diesel fuel was USD 236 per ton versus USD 160. The only "bargains" of importance to Belarus in the Russian market today are natural gas and crude oil. These were selling at 70-75 percent of world prices in September 1995. However, Russia has agreed with the IMF to raise domestic energy prices to world-equivalent prices, which means that Belarus will also have to pay world prices for energy from Russia.

To attain the advantages of a preferential trade area without the costs of being forced to accept and bear the costs of whatever protectionist measures Russia may decide to impose, Belarus should consider letting the current arrangement evolve from a *de facto* free trade area into a *de jure* free trade area. Free trade areas are now being used both in parts of Europe and throughout North America. Such arrangements are particularly advantageous for countries of markedly different size that have different levels of economic development and economic resource endowments. Such a move would of course require modification of the existing legislation and international agreements that established the customs union with Russia.

The main difference between a customs union and a free trade area is that, under the former, only one set of duties prevails with respect to the rest of the world, at least in theory, while under the latter each country sets its own policies with respect to the rest of the world. Given that significant differences already exist in the external trade policies of Belarus and Russia, the main change required to move to a free trade area would be to establish a customs border between the two countries. This is necessary for the following reason. Under a free trade system, it would be possible, for example, for Russia to have 100 percent duties on television sets and for Belarus to have zero duties. Without a border, Russians would import TVs from Japan into Belarus at zero duties, then take them on into Russia where they could be sold for half the price of those imported from the same source through St. Petersburg.

For obvious reasons, this would not be acceptable to the Russian authorities, or to the Russian TV manufacturers. Under a free trade arrangement, a customs border is therefore established to prevent such abuses. However, as part of a free trade area agreement, Belarus should still be able to send its own television sets into Russia free of duty. To make it possible for the customs officers to determine which TVs

come from Japan and which come from Belarus, each shipment between partners in a free trade area agreement is accompanied by a *"certificate of origin"* indicating where the product was made. Free trade areas have been in operation elsewhere in the world for decades; consequently, procedures such as rules of origin are well established and should not be difficult for Belarus and Russia to implement. Moving in the direction of a free trade area with Russia would help assure that Belarus was free to set policies that would assure potential investors that they could purchase inputs and sell their outputs at world market prices.

Trade with Non-CIS Markets. Although strengthening ties with Russia and other traditional CIS trading partners has many attractions such as familiarity and lower average quality standards than found in Western markets, Belarus needs to avoid trading arrangements with the CIS that will, at the same time, discourage the development of improved trading relations with non-CIS markets. Trade with Western markets will offer Belarus access to the technology needed to upgrade design and production efficiency, something that is needed not only to compete profitably in the rich but demanding Western markets, but increasingly to compete in the more profitable, high-end segments of the traditional CIS markets. As income levels increase, consumers in countries like Russia and Kazakstan will increasingly demand goods of international quality. Learning to compete in non-CIS markets will thus provide Belarus the experience and expertise needed to remain competitive in its traditional markets to the East.

Trade Policy and International Agreements. Another good way for Belarus to guarantee investors that they will enjoy continued access to imports at close to world prices would be for Belarus to join the World Trade Organization (WTO). As part of the accession process to the WTO, Belarus would have to "bind" its tariffs at a maximum rate, promising that actual rates will always be equal to or lower than the bound rates. Belarus is making good progress in this direction. It was granted observer status to the General Agreement on Tariffs and Trade (GATT) in 1992 and to WTO as successor to GATT in 1995. In December 1995 the Belarusian memorandum on trade and economic policies was forwarded to WTO, and Belarus is now in the process of responding to the questions that WTO member countries raised regarding the memorandum as part of the process.

Financial Discipline, Price Formation, and Bankruptcy

Prices are irrelevant if enterprises and consumers are not forced to pay for what they consume. Efforts to decontrol prices, to establish competitive markets, to control monopolistic pricing, and to implement sensible foreign trade policies will be wasted if financial discipline is not strictly enforced. Producers and consumers must learn to observe "hard budget constraints" and to live within their means.

Without financial discipline, markets cannot set realistic prices that stimulate efficiency in both production and consumption. If enterprises and consumers have no intention of paying for the goods and services that they consume, they will offer to pay prices that are grossly inflated in hopes of being given access to scarce commodities. The resulting prices will be both unrealistic and inflationary.

In well-functioning market economies, financial discipline becomes a self-enforcing virtue. If an enterprise knows that it must pay for *all* of the inputs that it uses, it will insist that its customers pay for the goods and services that they receive from the enterprise. This puts financial pressure on the consumers, who will in turn insist on being paid for what they produce. Enterprises will enforce payment on consumers, and workers will insist on being paid so that they can pay their own bills.

The banking system has two very important roles to play in enforcing financial discipline. First, banks should only lend in cases where the borrower can provide solid evidence of being able to repay. This would be a major change from the current practice in many of the banks in Belarus today, especially those owned by the state. These banks are regularly used, as under the Soviet system, as a conduit for subsidized credit to loss-making enterprises in the agricultural and industrial sectors. Such lending should stop immediately, because it creates entirely the wrong kind of environment and priorities within commercial banks, and causes banks to become agents working to loosen rather than tighten financial discipline, which is their second major role. If subsidies must be given, they should be channeled directly from the budget to those being subsidized. Banks should be left to operate on a commercial basis. Once they are in a position to make all loans on the basis of normal commercial criteria, they will also be in a position to enforce repayment on the same basis. When a bank is forced or allowed to make loans for political reasons, it is in no position to insist that the loans be repaid. However, if the loans are made on a commercial basis, the banks have every right—and strong incentives—to make certain that the loans are repaid. When necessary, banks should use the threat of bankruptcy to force repayment of loans.

Bankruptcy plays an important but widely misunderstood role in the process of developing financial discipline and respect for hard budget constraints in an economy. The *threat* of bankruptcy is far more important that bankruptcy itself. If the owner of an enterprise knows that his enterprise could be taken away from him if he fails to pay his bills, he will do whatever is necessary to assure that he can pay, thereby avoiding bankruptcy. The *threat* of bankruptcy will, for example, encourage him to improve production efficiency, sell unused assets, and reduce labor redundancy. The percentage of enterprises that are actually taken into bankruptcy in a market environment is actually very small. In 1988, for example, only 0.4 percent of businesses in the United States filed for bankruptcy. Furthermore, only 0.2 percent of all bankruptcy filings were involuntary.[27] The vast majority of bankruptcies are initiated by the enterprises themselves to secure protection from creditors while reorganizing in ways that will allow creditors to be repaid as fully as possible out of the future earnings of the reorganized firm.

Prices, Subsidies, and Social Protection

Governments around the world fall into the trap of distorting prices in a vain attempt to "protect the people." They control the prices of bread, milk, rent, and energy in the name of "social justice." Unfortunately, the Government of Belarus is no exception, and this is creating serious distortions in the pricing of such goods and services. These distortions lead to inefficient, wasteful use of these resources; they fail to achieve their objectives in the most cost effective manner; and they end up costing the consumers more than if the consumers had paid the full cost of production in the first place.

The inefficiencies caused by underpricing are a perfectly natural and rational response to bad pricing policies. For example, the high level of energy inefficiency in the factories and homes of Belarus was a perfectly rationale response to the cheap energy prices that prevailed in the former Soviet Union. Why spend extra money on insulation and energy-efficient equipment when energy costs almost nothing? Energy pricing is now being corrected, and this is leading to investments in its more efficient use, but more needs to be done to pass these costs fully on to the consumers, both industrial and residential, to assure fully efficient use of energy.

Some types of bread are currently underpriced in Belarus, as noted in Box 2.1, and this is also leading to serious waste. For example, it is reported that farmers in the Soligorsk region have been feeding bread to their cattle and pigs because the bread is priced below the cost of the grain in the bread. From the farmers point of view, feeding bread to the animals is simply a sound economic decision based on the current relative prices of bread and grain. But Belarus cannot hope to restore and maximize growth if it allows such waste to continue.

The poor do need help, especially during the transition period, but distorting the price of valuable goods like bread and energy is not an efficient approach. First, as noted with energy and grain, artificially low prices lead to waste in consumption. Second, they discourage production, thus leading to scarcities that may actually increase the real cost, further widening the gap between cost and price. Third, most subsidies based on artificially low prices are poorly targeted, going to the rich as well as the poor. Because the rich often consume more than the poor, the total subsidy to the rich is often far greater than the subsidy to the poor. As a result, the subsidy increases the disparity of incomes rather than reducing it. For example, artificially low prices for household electricity are paid by rich and poor households alike. However, with their air conditioning, electric heating, refrigerators, and electric stoves, rich households will benefit far more in absolute terms than poor households with only a few light bulbs. (This phenomenon also helps explain why subsidies for goods and services like electricity are so hard to eliminate—the rich who benefit the most from such subsidies are also those who have the most political power.)

A key point to remember in setting prices and in designing social protection systems is that *it is impossible to reduce the price of any good or service below its cost of production for the society as a whole. Sooner or later, the people will have to pay the full cost of everything that is consumed* —assuming, of course, that Belarus does not default on international payments obligations. This was highlighted in Box 2.1 above and is further demonstrated here in Box 2.2.

Monetary and Credit Policies

Another very important price in any economy is the price of capital. In Belarus this price is widely distorted, leading to wasteful uses of this scarce commodity. The most serious problem is the highly subsidized interest rate charged to farmers. In the first quarter of 1996, for example, the NBB was lending directed credit funds to the Agroprombank at an annual rate of 37 percent, far below the auction rate of 68 percent. Housing loans, at an annual rate of 3.4 percent, were even more seriously out of line with the cost of capital in Belarus.

Partly as a result of the artificially low interest rates in Belarus, Russian entrepreneurs have been borrowing from Belarusian banks to finance projects outside of Belarus, thereby draining capital that is urgently needed to finance working and fixed capital investments inside Belarus. The IMF has therefore recommended that the central bank authorities increase the discount rate to parity with that in Russia, and that all new credit from the central bank be auctioned. These steps would make a major contribution to "getting the prices right" for capital resources.

Box 2.2: *There is no free ride.*

A city bus ticket in Minsk only cost the equivalent of 10 U.S. cents in early 1996, and this modest price was collected from only a fraction of those who ride the public transport system. Similarly low fares are charged for the subway in Minsk and for inter-city rail transport. As a result of these highly subsidized prices, the average consumer spends only four percent of his income for public transport services according to the consumption basket maintained by the Ministry of Statistics for calculating the Consumer Price Index. But in the end, the consumer will pay the full cost and more.

Other forms of publicly owned transportation including inter-city trucking, rail, and air are also heavily subsidized. Although these prices have increased significantly from the Soviet era in nominal terms, they have failed to keep up with the sharply higher real cost of energy. Nor have nominal price increases overcome the failure of the previous centrally planned system to recover capital costs. As a result, tariffs recover only a fraction of the full cost of supply. But there is no free ride for the Belarusian consumer.

Although ticket prices for passenger traffic and tariffs for freight fail to recover the cost of these services from the users, the average Belarusian citizen pays their full cost in the end. Assuming that Belarus does not risk being shut off from international assistance and from world markets by defaulting on its foreign loans, the citizens of Belarus will eventually have to pay the difference between the cost of supply and the revenues collected. The payments to fill this gap will come in many different and often indirect ways. The inefficiencies and transaction costs of indirectly recovering the full cost of production mean that Belarusian consumers will end up paying more for transport services than if the costs had been collected directly from the users. The people of Belarus will pay in many different ways.

- *Higher taxes* are the most obvious additional cost. The Government must charge higher taxes to cover the cost of the subsidies that must be paid to the transportation authorities so that they can continue to keep the transportation systems in operation. The cost of collecting taxes and disbursing them to the transport authorities further increases the cost to the consumer.

- *Capital stock deterioration* is another major cost imposed by failing to recover full costs from the users of transport services. In the long term, the people of Belarus will have to pay to replace the capital stock that is wearing out. In the short run, capital depreciation brings another more severe cost in the form of increased operating costs.

- *Higher operating costs* due to the inability of the transport authorities to invest in more energy efficient equipment is a serious problem now that energy prices are about ten times higher in real terms than they were when the equipment in use today was originally purchased.

- *Poor service* hurts consumers every day as they wait in long lines for buses that do not show up on time because so many of them are out of service due to the lack money to buy replacement parts. The aggravation of waiting in the cold for a bus or tram, increased commuting times, late arrivals at work, and lost production are additional costs of failing to recover an adequate share of costs directly from the users.

In short, cheap transportation is costing the people of Belarus dearly. Measures to increase cost recovery should be implemented as quickly as possible, accompanied by means-tested assistance to the poor to help them pay the higher transit fares. Externalities such as reduced congestion from automobile traffic may argue for modest public subsidies for urban transport systems, but the majority of the transport services in Belarus should be placed on a full cost recovery basis as quickly as possible, thereby reducing the cost to the average citizen.

C. TRANSPARENT, EQUITABLE LEGAL FRAMEWORK

Risks and Investment

Next to the potential for profit, an investor's most important concern is risk. One of the most frequent concerns expressed by enterprises about investing in Belarus is the high level of risk created by the lack of a transparent, equitable legal framework. Investors need a predictable environment where they can anticipate with a reasonable degree of certainty the rules of the game that they will face during the life of the proposed investment.

Physical and commercial risks are probably no higher in Belarus than in any other country, and the risk from criminal activity may well be less than in many of the other former Soviet states. However, investors see excessive risks in the current policy framework for business in Belarus for the following reasons:

- laws—the rules of the game—are constantly changing, which means that rules could be imposed in the future that would turn profits into losses;[28]

- when the Government changes laws, it sometimes imposes them with retroactive effect, which is harmful to businesses;[29]

- laws are often ambiguous, leading to the risk of adverse interpretations by those enforcing the laws;[30]

- since laws are open to interpretation and administrative discretion, a change in government personnel could result in a reversal of interpretations upon which major investment decisions had been made;

- competitors may be given a more favorable interpretation, placing the investor in a non-competitive position;

- some actions which in normal industrial countries would not require any governmental approval must, in Belarus, be taken all the way to the national Parliament, a costly and time-consuming process with very uncertain results;[31]

- whenever laws are subject to administrative interpretation, corruption is inevitable, especially in the area of tax law.

To provide potential investors with the assurance of a level playing field where "rules of the game" for the conduct of business are easily understood and evenly enforced for all investors, the Government should minimize the actions for which government approval is needed, and should make certain that the rules by which any application will be judged are transparent. Applications that conform to the rules should be approved automatically, and the rules should be sufficiently clear and limited so that there will be no question as to whether or not the application conforms to the rules.

To provide potential investors with the assurance of a level playing field where rules of the game are easily understood and evenly enforced, the Government needs to: (a) minimize the barriers to entry and exit; (b) enforce hard budget constraints, including the real threat of bankruptcy; (c) clarify, simplify and clean up the rules and administration of foreign trade and payments; and (d) establish a transparent, equitable tax code and system of tax administration which assures that all businesses pay taxes that are modest, even, and equitably enforced. To this end, the Government is now preparing a formal tax code, the first part of which has already been presented to Parliament.

Barriers to Entry and Exit

In 1993, about 100 different activities required prior discretionary licensing by the Government for establishment, a process that was so time consuming and costly that few if any new enterprises were set up in these fields. The situation has improved considerably since then; only a limited number of activities now require an establishment license. However, virtually all licensing requirements should be removed as soon as possible; this would improve the attractiveness of Belarus to investors and, by eliminating another area of discretionary bureaucratic intervention, help the Government achieve its announced objectives of reducing opportunities for corruption.[32] Entry licensing should be limited to narrowly defined areas such as weapons, explosives, and nuclear materials where the purchase of the necessary equipment by criminal elements could pose an immediate danger to public safety.

In most other areas such as food, medicines, transport services and building materials, regulation is a better approach than entry licensing because it addresses the critical issue—which should not be to control or prevent the production of the materials, but to assure that the products are safe to use.

One of the most serious barriers to entry in Belarus today is the difficulty that legal entities face in purchasing land suitable for commercial use. Ownership of real property provides valuable insurance against the risk of losing control and use of property once investments have been made. Furthermore, property provides collateral that can be used to obtain bank financing for productive investments. The laws of Belarus should be amended immediately to provide unrestricted ownership for both physical and legal persons, foreign and national, of land plots up to, say, 25 hectares for commercial purposes. This would considerably improve the attractiveness of Belarus as a venue for investment. Concerns about appropriate use of land in terms of public interest and environmental safety should be handled through zoning regulations, not through controls on ownership. Unless Belarus establishes the right to private ownership of land along lines similar to those prevailing in Western Europe and other competing investment locations in Eastern Europe, prospects for attracting foreign investment will be very limited, thus casting doubt on the ability of Belarus to stop its economic decline and restore previous standards of living. Where this is politically difficult, the Government should quickly implement policies that would allow long-term transferable leases that would allow security of tenure and right to mortgage.

Unreasonable *labor laws* and practices provide another potential barrier to investors. In Belarus the labor code itself appears to be sensible, allowing employers to dismiss workers for due cause with reasonable severance payments. The main problem appears to be instead the informal pressure that government officials place on public enterprises to retain labor. (There is so little private investment in Belarus at present, and most private enterprises are so new and small, that it is difficult to know if they are also subject to such pressures.) After making certain that the labor code is consistent with normal practice in other countries competing with Belarus for investments, the Government should announce that it will not take any actions that would make it difficult for investors to adjust their labor force as necessary. As noted above, the old Soviet-era "propiska" system should also be abolished.

Contracts, Hard Budget Constraints and Bankruptcy

Potential investors are willing to face normal business risks, but they want assurances that they will be given the same treatment by the Government that every other investor gets in terms of laws and their enforcement.

Modern business requires scales of operation that make it impossible for managers to know personally the character and reliability of every customer. Yet modern businesses rely on customers to pay their bills. Business in the industrialized world therefore depends on contracts and their enforcement. The explosion of enterprise debts noted in Chapter 1 indicates that investors cannot depend on other enterprises in Belarus to respect contracts—nor can they depend on the Government to enforce these contracts, making Belarus a highly risky place to invest.

This problem can be solved without great difficulty—and with tremendous benefits. In the absence of any effective penalty for non-payment, debtors can always find other uses for their money. But if faced with the effective threat of penalties like bankruptcy, they will find a way to control and pay their bills.

The Government of Belarus has not taken the necessary actions to this end. In particular, it needs to rescind the current policy which says that some accounts payable are more important than others, and it needs to begin immediately to take into bankruptcy a number of companies with high levels of accounts payable that have little prospect of repaying these amounts out of their own earnings.

For at least the past year, the Government has followed a policy of setting priority among various categories of enterprise arrears. For example, energy bills and taxes are given higher priority than payments to suppliers. This sends the wrong signal to enterprise managers, giving them the impression that some bills do not really have to be paid on time, that some payments obligations are less valid and binding than others. This encourages enterprise managers to delay payments to the creditors who are given lower priority by the Government, undermining financial discipline in the use of resources. Enterprises should learn that no resource should be used unless the enterprise is going to be able to pay for it in a timely manner, that unpaid bills are likely to lead to bankruptcy, regardless of the creditor. Financial discipline will encourage enterprises to restructure, selling off unneeded assets in order to focus on viable core business activities, and will encourage enterprises to be more careful regarding the retention of excess labor, which, as noted in Chapter 1, reduces the competitiveness of Belarusian products and creates inflationary pressures.

The lack of an effective bankruptcy system in Belarus is underscored by the fact that, despite the widespread presence of enterprises that are deeply in debt and have no prospects for repaying their debts, no enterprise has ever been closed on the basis of bankruptcy proceedings. The country has a 1992 bankruptcy law, but neither the law nor the supporting judicial structure are effective. By mid-1995, only 13 bankruptcy cases had been brought forward, and none of these had been resolved. A new bankruptcy law of international standards is now before Parliament and should be approved as soon as possible. At the same time, the judicial institutions needed to enforce bankruptcy—and related actions such as creditor-led reorganization along the lines of the "Chapter 11" bankruptcy process in the United States—should be created.

The Government should also undertake a campaign to educate the public about the nature of bankruptcy, which in Belarus is often regarded as a socially and economically harmful process that destroys jobs and capital. The purpose of bankruptcy is just the opposite. Jobs are lost and capital is destroyed when enterprises are badly managed and lose money. Therefore, bankruptcy and related processes such as court-ordered restructuring are designed to transfer the ownership of assets to new managers who will use the capital more efficiently, thereby preserving and creating jobs. With public understanding of the true nature and purpose of bankruptcy, the Government should find it relatively easy to move forward with bankruptcy proceedings in a few highly visible cases, thereby sending the message that non-payment and the lack of financial discipline and responsibility will no longer be tolerated. This would immediately create a better investment climate in Belarus.

Foreign Trade and Payments

Foreign Trade Administration. An earlier section of this chapter discussed the important contributions that good foreign trade policies could make to market-determined prices, efficiency, and economic growth. Good trade policies are also important to investors, and the current policies of Belarus need considerable improvement. A recent survey of Belarusian enterprises, for example, indicated that the Customs Administration was, by a wide margin, the government agency that creates the most serious problems for export activities. Customs was cited as the source of the most serious problems by 35 of the leading firms, compared to only 20 who cited the Tax Inspectorate. The main problem is the lack of transparency and equity in the way that the current foreign trade regulations are written and administered. The present laws provide wide scope for administrative discretion regarding the allowability, classification, and thus taxation of various products. A plethora of special ministerial, cabinet, and presidential decrees, issued on an ad hoc basis to resolve specific problems, have contributed to the atmosphere of obscurity, and have increased opportunities for corruption.

Experience in other countries indicates that cleaning up the inefficiency and corruption that is common in customs administrations in many developing countries can be very difficult. The best way to start is to *convert all import duties to a single ad valorem rate*. With only one rate applicable to all imports with no exemptions, the classification of goods under different categories becomes relatively unimportant and is therefore no longer an issue that delays processing or that creates opportunities for corruption.

In addition to removing a major problem for investors, such a tariff policy would also have major benefits in terms of removing price distortions, particularly if the new ad valorem rate is kept relatively low (for example, 10 to 15 percent). Highly differentiated tariffs distort relative prices, making it difficult for investors to produce efficiently and for products made in Belarus to compete internationally. Thus, even if it is not possible to move to the theoretical ideal of free trade, a low uniform tariff rate would greatly improve the situation.[33]

Another trade-related problem that reduces the ability of Belarusian enterprises to compete internationally relates to the duties that must be paid on imported inputs. The Government appears to be working towards the implementation of some form of duty drawback system that would allow exporters who depend on imported inputs to avoid having to cover the cost of these duties in the price of the exported goods. A variety of different ways exist in which this can be done—bonded processing areas where import duties are never paid, rebates of taxes upon export, crediting of taxes paid towards new imports, and so on, and not all of them are mutually exclusive. Regardless of the method(s) chosen, some form of drawback should be put into place as soon as possible.

Additional measures may also be suggested to improve the administration of customs. First, to reduce the problems of over- and under-invoicing, arrangements can be set up to obtain indicative information from international sources on prices for a wide range of products moving in world trade. Specific duties (for example, U.S. dollar per cubic meter) are sometimes used to avoid the valuation problems,

but specific duties involve so many other problems that it is better to move to ad valorem duties and reinforce the system with indicative information on product values. Furthermore, this invoicing problem will become much less severe if Belarus moves to a low, uniform import tax rate and if, in addition, it makes foreign exchange freely convertible as discussed below. When measures like these do not solve the customs administration problem, countries such as Indonesia have hired international inspection services like the Société Générale de Surveillance (SGS) to administer the customs services. The increased revenues and reduced corruption are often more than enough to pay for these expert services, and the reduced corruption makes it much easier for serious investors to conduct business in a normal manner. This may soon become a moot point, however. Recent reports indicate that Russia has become so concerned with the manner in which Belarusian customs are being operated—especially the diversion of potential customs—that it is planning to replace the Belarusian customs service with Russian officers.

Foreign Exchange Management. The current foreign exchange management system has seriously hurt the investment climate in Belarus in two major ways. First, the domestic currency is overvalued, which makes it difficult to compete with artificially cheap imports, and makes exporting unprofitable for many products that previously were quite profitable. Second, the administrative controls on foreign exchange make it difficult to conduct trade in a normal manner.

As noted in Chapter 1, the real exchange rate appreciated by about 2.4 times between January 1995 and March 1996. As policymakers began to realize the extremely adverse effect that this real exchange rate appreciation was having on the viability of the enterprise sector and on the nation's balance of payments position, an "exchange corridor" was announced, and the rate was allowed to rise to a somewhat more realistic level. However, the central bank is still intervening heavily in the market (primarily by rejecting applications for foreign exchange purchase), foreign exchange reserves have been reduced to perilously low levels, and the interbank market has been virtually shut down, making it almost impossible for the commercial banks to respond in a normal manner to customers' daily requests for foreign exchange. All of these factors, plus the dramatic decline in the profitability of exporting many of the leading export products of Belarus (discussed in the next chapter), are clear evidence that the 35 percent exchange rate adjustment that has been allowed under the current administratively determined exchange rate corridor between January and October 1996 has not offset enough of the 250 percent real appreciation in the proceeding period to restore the competitiveness of Belarusian products either in domestic or in foreign markets. Until an appropriate adjustment has been implemented in consultation with the IMF, prospects for renewed economic growth will remain bleak.

The administrative barriers to foreign exchange transactions are also a serious problem for enterprises in Belarus. Under current policies, the only imports that qualify for the preferential official rate are those determined by a small group of officials to be "priority" imports. Considerable administrative discretion is involved because there is no clear list indicating what will be of sufficiently high "priority" at any point in time. This creates an environment which, in most countries, would lead to administrative delays if not corruption.

The investment climate in Belarus could be improved by establishing the free convertibility of the Belarusian rubel at a uniform rate determined by unrestricted forces of market supply and demand. The exchange rate will of course change over time to compensate for changes in domestic price levels, but until inflation is brought more firmly under control, a fixed nominal rate does not appear to be feasible. Most businessmen will find it easier to anticipate market driven exchange rate movements than to guess the rate that the government might decide to set at any point in time. Furthermore, with a normally functioning foreign exchange market, investors will be able to hedge their import and export contracts by buying and selling foreign exchange futures, thereby locking in the rates used in their profit and loss calculations.

Taxation

The single most common complaint by businesses about the investment climate in Belarus is that "taxes are too high." For example, in a recent survey of 55 major Belarusian enterprises, nearly 90 percent indicated that the most important restraint to increasing exports was the excessive tax burden. The problem, however, is much more complex than simply the level of taxes. Tax reforms will have to address a number of distinct problems: level and incidence, transparency, equity, administrative burden, compliance, consistency with international norms, stability of the current tax system, and the avoidance of earmarking and extrabudgetary funds.

Level and Incidence of Taxes. Complaints about the level of taxes on business in Belarus miss a fundamental point—that businesses are only legal fictions. Enterprises physically pay taxes, but never actually bear the burden of taxes. The burden is ultimately borne by workers (directly or through deductions from wages), by customers (through higher prices for goods and services produced by the enterprises), and by the individuals who own the businesses (through reduced after-tax profits). The taxation of businesses is simply an administratively easy way for the government to take resources from these far-flung groups of people—who also pay taxes on income, sales, and services.

The share of total taxes that should be collected indirectly through enterprises rather than directly from these three groups is of legitimate concern, but this is more an issue of administrative efficiency and financial incentives rather than economic burden. The real issue is the *total level of taxes* collected by the government from the economy. Here the answer with respect to Belarus is unambiguous. The level of taxes is about twice the level that would be expected in a country at Belarus' current level of per capita income. As can be seen by the trend line in Figure 2.6, the average ratio of general government revenues to GDP in countries (at the current Belarusian income level) is about 25 percent—compared to about 40 percent in Belarus. Incidentally, the burden of government on the economy is not a recent problem; in 1992, Belarus had the highest ratio of government revenue to GDP in the twelve FSU republics for which data are available.

Taxes in Belarus should be reduced to provide an environment that is similar to that found in other countries at a similar level of income. This would improve the efficiency of resource allocation and will provide investors with a tax environment comparable to what they would find in other countries competing for their investment resources. Reducing the tax burden would almost inevitably lead to a highly desirable reduction in the role of government in the economy, thereby creating a more market-oriented environment.

Transparency of Taxes. One of the most serious problems with the current tax system in Belarus is its lack of transparency and certainty. As discussed above, various ambiguities and inconsistencies in the various tax laws, regulations and decrees currently in force make it difficult for a business to determine what taxes it owes. This issue is ultimately resolved through negotiations with the tax authorities, a process vulnerable to corruption, thereby creating an environment that is unfavorable to serious investment. The existing tax system should be reviewed carefully and revised to make the applicable tax rates absolutely clear. Attaining this objective will also require major improvements in accounting and auditing practices within Belarus. The Soviet accounting system does not provide financial information in the manner needed to determine unambiguously the real costs and profits of an enterprise. Investors will be hesitant to invest in any business that presents its accounts in a manner which the investor finds difficult to interpret. The old system should therefore be replaced with the International Accounting Standards (IAS) conventions.

Equity of Taxes. The best ways to increase the transparency of the tax system are to reduce the number of different taxes (22 at present), to limit the number of differential rates for each tax, and to eliminate virtually all tax exemptions. The recently introduced waivers and

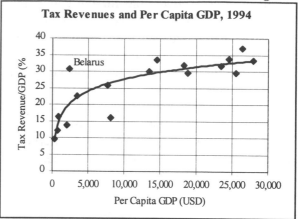

Figure 2.6: The tax burden in Belarus is high.

Tax Revenues and Per Capita GDP, 1994

Source: World Bank data and staff calculations.

deferrals of the payment of VAT for selected enterprises is one of the worst problems in this context. Not only does the possibility of obtaining special tax treatment create an environment that destroys transparency and fosters corruption; it also creates an environment where the tax burden is shared unequally among investors, making the business climate less attractive. Unequal tax rates and exemptions also create distortions in relative prices that reduce competitiveness, efficiency, and economic growth. Reducing special exemptions broadens the tax base, making it possible to lower overall taxation rates. This makes the investment climate more attractive, and makes tax administration easier by reducing incentives to evade taxes. The social protection concerns that motivated well-targeted tax exemptions should be addressed instead with social safety net measures.

Administrative Burden. Businessmen in Belarus often complain as much about the administrative burden of the tax system as about the amount of taxes paid. Simplifying the structure of taxes as recommended in the previous paragraph would greatly reduce the administrative burden. The burden should also be reduced by eliminating a wide range of extra-budgetary funds, many of which are financed by special earmarked taxes. Subsidies for agriculture and other activities that are deemed necessary as a transitional measure should be financed out of general revenues, not with special ear-marked taxes. Nuisance taxes should be eliminated. For example, there is no reason to maintain a separate

Fire Brigade Tax, which requires businesses to fill in a multiple page form and, in the end, generates a trivial share of total revenue. Similarly, the Emergency (Chernobyl) Tax could well be consolidated with the other payroll taxes, thus reducing the administrative burden. Better yet, the tax could be eliminated as a separate item and the Chernobyl amelioration programs could be funded out of general revenues.[34] The only extra-budgetary funds for which clear justification exists are a few user-specific ones like the Road Fund and the Pension and Health Funds. To reduce administrative costs and the burden on tax payers, all national-level taxes should be collected by a single agency to the extent possible.

Tax Compliance. Serious investors seek an environment with a "level playing field"—where all investors face and pay the same taxes for the same level of activity or profit. In addition to implementing a system of uniform tax rates without exemptions, the highest possible level of compliance is required so that all tax payers are treated equally. No firm data are available on tax evasion in Belarus, but anecdotal information indicates that the problem is widespread. This creates an uneven playing field, making it hard for the honest businesses to compete. It also means that, to raise a given amount of revenue, the tax rates have to be excessively high on those who do pay, further discouraging serious investors.

Tax compliance should be enforced as it is in industrialized countries, not as it is in Belarus today. Under the current Belarusian system, the powers of the Tax Inspectorate are far too broad and are not subject to the necessary checks and balances. Tax authorities should audit business accounts and impose fines, but they should not have the authority to confiscate property. This power should be left to the courts, and businesses should have the right to appeal rulings of the tax authorities to these courts. The process of improving tax compliance in a manner consistent with practices in industrialized countries would be greatly enhanced by reducing the number of different tax rates, eliminating ad hoc concessions like tax exemptions, and moving towards international accounting standards.

Consistency with International Norms. Regardless of the exact level of taxes, investors will feel much more comfortable if the tax system is broadly consistent with international standards. Belarus has made excellent progress in this area, with a standard array of income, profits, payroll, excise and VAT taxes. The main task now is fine tuning. A complete review of the tax system in terms of compatibility with international standards is beyond the scope of this report, but a few comments on some special problems related to the value added tax might be in order here.

Like most CIS countries, Belarus practices a dual VAT system, applying the "destination principle," common in most world trade, to trade with the West, and the "origin principle" to trade with the CIS. This creates a competitive disadvantage for enterprises that are investing in Belarus in order to produce for markets in Russia and other CIS countries. Because of the destination principle, enterprises must pay VAT on goods imported from the West and, because of the origin principle, must pay VAT again on goods that are being exported to Russia and other CIS countries.

For goods moving in the opposite direction, the mix of origin and destination principles adversely affects government revenues. The Government of Belarus does not receive VAT payments on goods imported from Russia because the Russian Government collects these taxes. If the same goods are subsequently exported to the West, either directly or as inputs to Belarusian products, the Government of Belarus again loses out because VAT will be paid on such goods only in the destination country. This problem can be even more severe in the case of goods based on CIS inputs that go through intermediate transactions and processing in Belarus before being exported to the West. If such goods are zero rated for export purposes, a standard practice in international trade, the Government of Belarus has to rebate the VAT that was paid to the Government of Russia. Thus, the Government and the business community would both benefit if Belarus, Russia and the other CIS states were to agree on moving to the world standard destination principle with respect to VAT taxation. This is but one example of the need for greater consistency between Belarusian and world standards of taxation. Several more (such as moving from the subtraction to the invoice/credit method) could be mentioned for the VAT, and tax policies in other areas need adjustment as well. Many of these changes would be facilitated by the widespread adoption of International Accounting Standards in Belarus. The task of making the tax and accounting system consistent with international standards is considerable, but one that Belarus needs to take seriously if it is to attract sizable flows of foreign investment.[35]

Stability. Most businesses can learn to live with almost any set of laws, including bad tax laws, provided the laws remain stable so that business decisions can be made accordingly. Retroactive changes in tax laws are particularly damaging. The highly unstable and rapidly changing legal environment for business in Belarus in the past five years has created serious problems, but the current paper suggests more changes. How can these conflicting objectives be reconciled? This can be done by announcing and implementing, according to a predefined schedule, a multi-year legal reform program designed to create a legal environment that is as consistent as possible with European standards. Although the details would have to be worked out as the process proceeded, businesses could make their investment plans knowing the general direction and pace of the reforms.

The Government has already begun to do this by preparing the *Plan to Attract Investment* into Belarus, and the *Plan for the Year 2000*. These documents could be augmented with more specific details and commitments regarding plans for legal reforms, including reforms of the tax system, then could be approved by Parliament and published by the President as a binding commitment to the business community. This would give investors the confidence that the current problems listed above in the tax and legal environment of Belarus will be fixed but, at the same time, would provide a reasonable degree of stability of expectations.

Extra-Budgetary Funds and Earmarked Taxes. These two budgeting problems tend to go hand in hand, and they are usually inflicted on fiscal systems with the very best of intentions. For example, if the environment has been damaged—and this certainly was the case in Belarus with the Chernobyl disaster—policy makers want to assure that adequate funds are available to resolve the problem. To make certain that resources are not diverted to other "less worthy" purposes, an extra-budgetary fund is commonly established, and to make certain that the fund has adequate resources, a special tax is commonly introduced and "earmarked" to finance the fund. Belarus now has an exceptionally large number of such earmarked taxes and extra-budgetary funds. It has the standard extra-budgetary funds for pensions, employment and health insurance, and some arguments can be made for continuing these on the basis that they are insurance programs where those contributing can expect to receive corresponding benefits at some point in their lives.

Far more questionable, however, are special funds such as those for the environment, roads, housing, agriculture, price regulation, foreign exchange, exporters,[36] and fire brigades (Statistical Annex Table 5.6 provides further information on these funds). The big problem with such funds and their associated earmarked taxes is that both tend to be perpetuated long after the original problem has been partially or fully resolved. Because such funds are not reviewed by all concerned parties (including Parliament) as part of the annual budgetary review process, the necessary efforts are not made to assure that the resources are still needed more urgently to solve the original problems than to meet new needs that have arisen in the meantime. For example, many of the emergency expenses required to ameliorate the effects of the Chernobyl disaster have now been completed, but the earmarked tax continues to be collected and, at least in theory, allocated to solving the Chernobyl problem.[37]

Another problem with extrabudgetary funds is that fragmenting the budget into a number of different pockets makes it difficult to get a complete picture of how funds are being spent and what the total financing requirements are. To avoid the distortions created by earmarked taxes and extra-budgetary funds, the Government should seek to eliminate all but a few of the funds associated with social insurance programs in the next budget cycle. In addition to providing a better mechanism for reviewing and prioritizing the use of funds, this would make it possible to reduce the number of different taxes, thus making compliance—and the enforcement of compliance —a much easier task. The Government could continue to fund existing programs at current levels; until the World Bank has been able to carry out a Public Expenditure Review in Belarus, it would be difficult to suggest which programs might be cut and which might be expanded. However, moving to an integrated budgetary framework with minimal reliance on earmarked taxes and extrabudgetary funds would greatly facilitate the process of assuring that scarce budgetary resources are used only for the highest priority programs.

Expenditure Reduction - The Other Side of the Coin. Unfortunately, reducing taxes is more complex than simply cutting tax rates. Without adjustments in expenditures, the Government would face: (d) highly inflationary budget deficits, destroying prospects for renewed economic growth; (e) growing arrears in payments, aggravating the already serious problem of non-payments in the economy; or (f) random, ad hoc expenditure cuts that are not consistent with the Government's longer-term social and economic priorities. Any effort to reduce the overall level of taxes therefore needs to begin with the definition of a strategy for reducing government expenditures. This strategy should begin by identifying, on the one hand, the highest priority areas that only the Government is in position to handle, and on the other, the areas that should be left to the private sector.

This report was not designed to examine government expenditures; if the Government agrees, the very important issues of expenditure prioritization and management would be addressed in a proposed Public Expenditure Review. A cursory review of the current situation indicates, however, that expenditures could be reduced in the following areas without hurting national welfare. In fact, by reducing the role of Government in the following areas, prospects for economic development and restored living standards could probably be improved:

- eliminate production subsidies, replacing them as needed in agriculture, for example, by income support programs for poor households;

- eliminate consumer subsidies, again with the proviso that a well-targeted social safety net would be put in place as required;

- eliminate most extra-budgetary funds other than those such as pensions and social insurance where those who contribute the money will ultimately be the beneficiaries;

- sharply reduce government involvement in production activities, and assure that any remaining activities are essentially self-financing from user charges;

- reduce expenditures on defense now that Belarus has peaceful relations with neighbors both to the East and to the West; and

- reduce excess staffing wherever it may exist, especially in the branches of the bureaucracy that are no longer needed because of the natural reduction of the role of Government as the economy moves from central planning and control to a market-based economy.

D. SUPPORTIVE ENVIRONMENT

The most important contribution that the Government can make to developing an attractive investment climate in Belarus is to create a supportive policy environment. However, government expenditures are also important. In market economies, investors expect governments to focus on law and social order, and on basic public goods and services.

Law and Social Order

Law and order is a precondition for efficient, equitable economic development. Investors need to be reasonably certain that they can conduct their business without significant risk of theft, destruction of property, personal harm, or extortion. Belarus has been quite successful in this area since independence. Efforts will be needed to assure the continuation of this success in a manner consistent with protecting basic human rights and the right of enterprises to operate without excessive and ad hoc government interference. This will require improvements in the court system and the guaranteed right of appeal to the courts.

A far bigger challenge is that of creating the administrative and judicial system needed to implement the Government's economic policies. Problems in customs administration were noted above. Major investments in staffing, training, equipment, facilities and procedures will be needed to resolve them. Similar efforts will be needed to improve general tax administration as well as the management and control of expenditures. Another major task will be to build the capacity within the economic courts system to handle the complex issues of various forms of bankruptcy, restructuring and administration. Finally, since most of the task of privatization and restructuring of public enterprises still lies ahead, the Government needs to make substantial investments in capacity building here as well.

Vital Public Goods and Services

The second major area on which the Government of Belarus should focus is the provision of basic social services. Serious investors want to make long-term commitments, but will hesitate to do so if the country does not have the systems of education, health, housing, sanitation, and related services needed to assure a continuing supply of healthy, well-educated workers who can focus on their work rather than being distracted by problems of daily survival. Because of social externalities—benefits to the country at large that are hard to recover from specific recipients at any point in time—most education and public health services should continue to be provided by the Government. In other areas such as housing and, eventually, certain public utilities such as electricity and telecommunications, the Government should focus on creating an environment where the private sector can take primary responsibility. This will allow public officials to focus scarce government resources on tasks which the private sector cannot handle, and to reduce the overall burden of taxes and other government claims on national resources from the current level of 42 percent to about 30 percent (a more normal level for a country with Belarus' per capita income), thereby stimulating economic activity and growth. Improved cost recovery from users to the extent possible is vitally important for reducing the fiscal burden, for making the provision of such goods and services more attractive to private sector investors, and for encouraging efficient use by consumers, especially of energy-based services such as heating and electricity.

Potential investors also look for good production-supporting physical infrastructure facilities, especially serviced sites with reliable access to good quality supplies of power, water, and telecommunications. In Belarus, these services will almost certainly have to be provided by the Government for the foreseeable future. Given the relatively good physical plant inherited from the Soviet era, the Government should focus its increasingly limited resources on maintaining these services, not on restructuring the state-owned factories—a task best left to the private sector.[38] The net revenue burden of providing such services should be close to zero. The owners and users of the land who benefit from the improved infrastructure should repay the cost of providing these services through user fees, improvement "district" assessments, valorization charges and the like. On the other hand, government investments in long-distance transport facilities such as highways, and in improved border crossing infrastructure, would help reduce the transportation bottlenecks that currently add an estimated 3-4 percent to transport costs in Belarus, according to a World Bank study. The availability of good transport and transit facilities is of key importance to the type of investors that Belarus most wants to attract—those who will generate export earnings.

E. CONCLUSIONS

Market-Determined Prices

To be able to assure potential investors, both domestic and foreign, that prices will be determined by competitive market forces rather than by ad hoc administrative decisions, Belarus needs to:

- introduce an exchange rate regime that allows the value of the Belarusian rubel to be determined by the free interaction of demand and supply;

- finish eliminating all forms of implicit and explicit price controls on competitively marketed products;

- eliminate monopolistic market structures wherever possible by fostering domestic and foreign competition;

- reduce the risk of government interference in setting prices by privatizing virtually all trade, manufacturing and agricultural activities, a process that will also improve overall production efficiency; and

- minimize barriers to international trade.

Transparent, Equitable Legal Framework

To provide potential investors with the assurance of a level playing field where the rules of the game are easily understood and evenly enforced, the Government needs to:

- minimize the barriers to entry so that efficient firms can start up and grow;

- minimize the barriers to exit so that the physical assets of poorly managed enterprises can be released for more productive uses;

- enforce hard budget constraints, including a real threat of bankruptcy;

- establish a judicial system that enforces contracts, including those for payment and delivery; and

- establish a tax code and system of tax administration which assures that all businesses pay taxes that are modest, even, and equitably enforced.

Supportive Environment

To provide an attractive and supportive environment for business development in Belarus, the Government should:

- assure the maintenance of law and social order in a manner consistent with basic human rights;

- provide support for education, health, and other vital social services which the private sector, under current conditions, would not be able to supply equitably, efficiently or adequately;

- develop and maintain an adequate system of physical infrastructure, especially transport and public utilities.

3

Establishing Profit-Oriented Producers

The previous chapter summarized the measures that the Government needs to take to establish a normal market-based economy in Belarus, one that will attract both foreign and domestic investors. Without the suggested framework of laws, policies and supportive services, most businessmen would find it difficult to operate profitably and would choose to invest elsewhere.

Background

The problems in Belarus go beyond shortcomings in the macro and sectoral environment. They go right into the core of most enterprises operating in Belarus today, be they in the agricultural, the industrial, or the service sector. These enterprise-level problems are the direct result of over 75 years of operating within the confines and distortions of a centrally planned economy. The most pervasive problem is that, unlike the situation in many of the FSU and CEE countries, most people in Belarus still work in enterprises that are owned by the state, and many of these enterprises still operate more like extensions of government than as profit-oriented, efficiency-maximizing centers of production. In theory—and occasionally in practice—state enterprises can be run with the same high standards of corporate governance that is found in the best-run private enterprises. But for reasons discussed in this chapter, this is rare. Consequently, privatization is commonly needed to create the incentives required to assure profit-oriented behavior among enterprise managers.

At the same time, a number of the largest state-owned enterprises are likely to remain in the public sector for some time. Thus means that, where privatization is not immediately feasible, measures will need to be taken to create an environment within public sector corporations that encourages their managers to operate with the same focus on corporate profitability that is found in private enterprises. Finally, while the efficient operation and ultimate privatization of existing state enterprises is important, experience in other countries indicates that the development of new private enterprises is one of the most important sources of growth and employment in transitional economies—and this is an area given great importance today by the senior policymakers in Belarus.

The key problems of Belarusian enterprises are like those in many other FSU economies. The industrial sector comprised over 40 percent of GDP in 1991, concentrated in industries such as automobiles, electrical and mechanical engineering, and chemicals. At the breakup of the U.S.S.R., Belarus was left with 1,313 republican[39] enterprises and 291 all-union enterprises that had previously been subordinated to the Government of the U.S.S.R.. These enterprises, totaling about 1,600, were highly vertically integrated, many of which served the all-union markets as well as markets in Eastern Europe. Exports to the West were minimal for most enterprises, although products such as tractors, motorcycles, watches, synthetic fibers and potassium fertilizers did find a major share of their market in non-CIS countries. A few large enterprises, accounting for only 15 percent of all units, controlled 60 percent of production. Products were heavily biased towards capital and energy intensive heavy industry, and many focused on electronics, optics, and transport equipment for the military. Management skills in finance, sales and marketing were limited —financial management and marketing decisions were commonly handled from Moscow. Apart from the republican level enterprises, there are about 10,000 communal enterprises operating in distribution, transport, construction, and catering, and employing about 30 percent of the industrial workforce. This proportion is relatively small, reflecting the concentration of industry, and the comparatively low value-added in distribution as opposed to production.

The structural problems faced by the larger state-owned enterprises (SOEs) producing tradable goods were exacerbated by the collapse of the inter-republic payments system and market demand in the area. The slowness of the Government to address these problems, including an exceptionally slow privatization process, has made the situation worse. Recent government regulations have further exacerbated the situation by creating constraints on private enterprise development and banking. In the enterprise sector (which is still predominantly state-owned and in particularly bad shape), more and more enterprises are operating at losses.

This chapter reviews the situation in the state enterprises, the slow progress of the privatization program, the constraints on private enterprise development, and the need to relieve enterprise managers from responsibility for the provision of housing and other fringe benefits based on "social assets" owned by the enterprises.

A. STATE ENTERPRISES: THE CURRENT SITUATION

The state-owned enterprise sector is in crisis. Although only 3 percent of the labor force is officially unemployed, up to 25 percent have either been laid off, are working shortened hours, or are working without pay. The enterprise sector as a whole has suffered badly since independence from the decline in capital investment. Between 1990 and 1995, for example, the following declines were recorded: fuel industry (-60 percent); machine building and metal working (-77 percent); and building materials (-81 percent). Some sectors have benefited from expanded investment during the same period: oil (+13 percent); and forestry and wood processing (+2 percent). Overall, however, new investment fell far below the required levels during this period—and fell by another 8 percent overall in real terms in 1996. Output has fallen by over 50 percent in many plants, and overall industrial output is at half of its 1991 level (Table 3.1). As a share of GDP, industry has fallen from 40 percent to 26 percent over this period. Employment has fallen more slowly, with the 1995 level about 14 percent below that of 1991. This reflects the SOEs' efforts to protect jobs, which has provided an informal social safety net, but has resulted in over-manning and a significant fall in output per capita. The rate of gross investment in manufacturing and processing has fallen particularly steeply—to 5.6 percent of GDP in 1995—and is negative in net terms.

During 1995, production continued to fall drastically, not only in the traditional engineering and high-tech goods, but also in consumer goods such as shoes and clothing. Furthermore, unsold stocks of finished goods have proliferated, rising faster than GDP. The problem of unsold inventories is particularly acute at some of the leading industrial enterprises (Table 3.2).

The number of loss-making SOEs[40] has increased exponentially (Figure 3.1 and Table 3.3). In the first quarter of 1996, there were 2,677 enterprises making losses (29 percent of the total recorded by the Ministry of Statistics). Total recorded losses for the sector rose to BYR 2,508 billion by 1995, or 2.1 percent of GDP.

Table 3.1: Production, Employment, and Investment in Industry

	1990	1991	1992	1993	1994	1995
Output (1/90=100)	100	99	89.7	80.7	66.9	59.1
Employment (000)	5,148	5,020	4,887	4,824	4,696	4,405
Investment (index)	100	106.0	74.8	66.3	74.5	47.7

Source: Belarus Ministry of Statistics and IMF.

Figure 3.1: The share of loss-making enterprises is increasing.

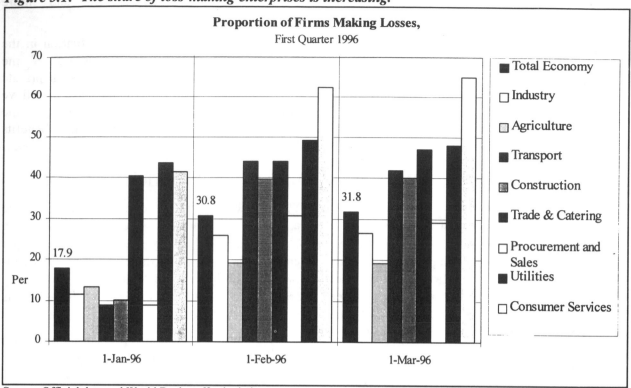

Proportion of Firms Making Losses,
First Quarter 1996

Source: Official data and World Bank staff calculations.

Causes of Loss-making

Loss-making by SOEs is caused by problems that are not unique to Belarus—namely, excess capacity in relation to the local market, inappropriate product mix, energy intensity, and over-manning. In addition, over the past 18 months a further factor—exchange rate appreciation—has reduced the profitability of traded goods for producers in both state and private sectors. In addition, the manufacturing sector has had particular difficulties in obtaining credit, and plant rehabilitation has virtually come to a halt. The age structure of industrial plants has increased. In 1994, one third of equipment surveyed was over 20 years old, and only about one fifth less than 10 years old.[41] The tax system has acted to the detriment of enterprises, especially in high inflation, because of the use of historic costs combined with price controls.

One of the biggest causes of losses in enterprises in Belarus today is the sharp appreciation of the real exchange rate that was discussed in the previous chapter. The benefits of a modest increase in price stability for production

Table 3.2: Unsold Stocks, April 1996

Product	Percent of Annual Production Unsold as of April 1996
Trucks	34
TV Sets	36
Refrigerators	48
Bicycles	51
Tractors	76

Source: Belarus Ministry of Economy.

Table 3.3: Loss-Making Enterprises by Subsector

	1992	1993	1994	1995	1996 Q1
Industry	10	42	46	192	441
Construction	24	24	33	114	432
Agriculture	65	128	179	380	550
Trade, catering	42	50	121	529	645
Other	238	258	239	356	613
Total	379	602	618	1,571	2,681

Source: Belarus Ministry of Economy.

in Belarus have been overwhelmed by the negative impact that this exchange rate appreciation has had on the profitability of enterprises which, compared to their current costs, now receive only about one third of what they did a year ago for their exported products. They must also compete with imported goods that, because of the failure to adjust the exchange rate in a way that avoided excessive real appreciation, now cost the domestic consumer about one third of what they did a year ago in real (inflation-adjusted) terms. No enterprise can hope to remain profitable under such conditions. Many products, such as motorcycles and refrigerators, moved from profit to loss positions over 1995-96 as a direct result of the change in currency values.

Price and distribution control (including state orders) have also depressed enterprise profitability. Indicative prices and margin limits still apply to products such as meat, grain, sugar, oil, timber and leather. Milk, for example, has been sold to processors at less than 50 percent of the open market price. Such controls were officially abolished for a few months, but as discussed in Chapter 2, informal controls continued at the local level and have recently been reintroduced on an explicit, legal basis, thus reversing the policy gains that had been made earlier.

State Enterprise Response and Adjustment

Survival Tactics. In order to survive, many enterprises have restructured or liquidated assets such as inventories, or have simply stopped payments to suppliers and have run up tax and wage arrears. Some have taken steps to reduce taxes by revaluing assets for inflation, thereby establishing a more realistic basis for calculating depreciation charges. Some have entered barter agreements to avoid foreign exchange surrender requirements. Along with the increase in domestic inter-enterprise arrears, cash advances from customers and contract manufacturing for foreign firms have also been important elements in survival since the end of 1992. Barter has also increased, especially in inter-republican transactions. Despite these survival tactics, the overall financial strength of enterprises has fallen sharply since 1991 (Figure 3.2).[42]

Financial Restructuring and Arrears. The survey of state enterprises showed that restructuring had not taken place except through the ad hoc build-up of debt to the tax authorities,

labor, and other enterprises, with a relative decline in real long-term and short-term bank borrowings. In the firms surveyed there tended to be a decline in bank borrowing and a rise in other current liabilities, including accounts and taxes payable. The build-up of arrears has constituted an involuntary expansion of credit in the economy that has fueled inflation. Receivables and payables of enterprises have continued to rise, with overdue arrears increasing steadily (Table 3.4). In the first quarter of 1996, they increased by a further 23 percent. Total accounts payable stood at about 40 percent of GDP in April 1996, of which 41 percent was overdue. Industry accounts for half of the total. Tax collections decreased from 37 percent of GDP in 1993 to 27 percent as of May 1996 as tax arrears accumulated. Budgetary loans in default to agriculture and agro-processing have reached serious proportions, despite the heavy budgetary and banking system subsidies to agriculture noted in the previous chapter. Similarly in the industrial sector, the Government has provided millions of

Figure 3.2: Enterprise assets have fallen sharply. *(Constant BYR billions)*

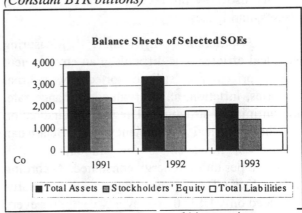

Source: Pilot Enterprise Survey of 14 enterprises.

Table 3.4: Enterprise Arrears
(USD millions)

Payable to:	1994	1995	6/30/96
Enterprises	746	1,461	2,143
Government	4	77	107
Labor	2	47	42
Banks	2	41	55
Other	125	530	512
Total	879	2,158	2,860

Source: Belarus Ministry of Statistics.

dollars in assistance to major companies such as Horizont, MAZ and MTZ, but this has not fostered the recovery of these plants. Wage arrears became a serious issue in the first part of 1996 because so many enterprises were no longer profitable. The Government "fixed" this problem by ordering the banks to extend credit to the enterprises so that they could pay the arrears, but this monetary expansion contributed to continued inflation, which was running at an annual rate of 35-40 percent by mid-1996, well in excess of levels normally associated with positive economic growth.

Product Diversification. Some progress has been made in converting military industries to civilian goods. In 50 major producers of military products, the share of such products was reported to have declined from 45 percent of output in 1988 to 20 percent in 1992. State-owned firms have, for example, converted production from rocket guidance systems to precision instruments for civilian use (including medical applications), and from micro-circuits to consumer durables such as television sets. Similarly, a large enterprise that once made optical equipment for military use now produces medical instruments, glasses, and lenses.

Production Efficiency. Measuring technical efficiency is difficult in an environment where prices are still distorted by internal rigidities, inflation, an overvalued exchange rate, and unfinished structural changes. One indication of the physical inefficiency of Belarusian enterprises, however, is the amount of GDP produced per unit of energy consumed. According to the *World Development Report 1995*, Belarus produced only USD 0.70 (seventy cents) for every kilogram of oil equivalent (koe) in 1994. In the same year, countries in the group of "middle income economies" to which Belarus belongs produced an average of USD 1.70 of GDP per koe—nearly 2.5 times as much. The cold Belarusian climate explains part of the difference, but similarly cold Nordic countries like Norway and Denmark produced an average of USD 5-7 of GDP per koe. The low energy efficiency of Belarusian production is not surprising given the artificially low energy prices that Belarus enjoyed during the Soviet era. Such prices are gone now,

however, and are never likely to return. Belarus therefore needs to give high priority to investing in the new technologies that provide not only higher product quality, but also higher energy efficiency. Such investments will not be made, however, until enterprises are forced, by threat of bankruptcy when necessary, to pay their energy bills. Market prices for energy mean nothing if the bills are not paid. Again, a respect for financial discipline and the imposition of hard budget constraints are vital if the Government of Belarus is to have any hope of restoring the living standards of its people.

Divestiture of Social Assets. In addition to product diversification, enterprises have started to shed ancillary activities which can be efficiently performed by others. The divestiture of "social assets" such as housing and district heating from enterprises to municipalities has been one of the more prominent examples of such restructuring. Other social responsibilities such as day-care facilities, clinics, and recreation facilities are also being transferred from enterprises to municipalities and, in some cases, to non-profit organizations or even to for-profit enterprises in the private sector. Such restructuring should be encouraged, for it allows enterprise managers to focus more clearly on the core business activities of their firms. The process is not as critical to enterprise viability as might be thought, however. Based on the widely accepted view that non-production responsibilities such as these are a considerable problem for enterprises, the mission undertook a special study of the issue, which is summarized in Annex A. This study determined that the financial burden created for the average Belarusian firm by such responsibilities is now quite modest. In fact, as enterprises sought to survive by controlling their costs, their expenditures on fringe benefits of this type decreased from 35 percent to 12 percent of total employee remuneration expenses—which in turn were only 5-10 percent of the total costs of the average enterprise. Further moves to divest social assets is a logical way for firms to restructure, but given the relatively small size of this problem compared to other problems (such as the exchange rate at which enterprises export their products), it is not a top policy priority.

Furthermore, the process needs to be handled with care for several reasons: (a) many services such as housing have a high social value and help provide a form of social safety net at relatively modest out-of-pocket costs; (b) many of the municipalities are not financially able to accept full responsibility immediately, which could jeopardize the delivery of these important services; and (c) some time is needed to attain the levels of cost recovery that will make the transition to municipal or private sector provision relatively easy.

Divestiture of Other Peripheral Activities. In addition to the employee-related activities such as housing and sports facilities, many enterprises were also heavily involved in other non-core activities such as construction, and farming to supply food to workers. Such responsibilities are more appropriately carried out by enterprises, preferably in the private sector, for whom such activities are the core business. Enterprises also need to consider shedding specialized manufacturing activities where the factory's own demand is not enough to support efficient scales of production.

Declining Dominance of State Enterprises in Distribution. The share of state and quasi-state agencies (for example Belcoopsoyuz) in distribution has fallen steadily as private agencies have started to increase, reaching an overall market share of 33 percent in 1996. The traditional state distribution companies such as Agrosnab and Agrochemia have been dismantled, or have started diversifying into other areas of business. As private enterprise gains control, administered pricing and distribution will disappear. In many cases procurement is now being done through direct dealings between processors, traders, and producers. Also, the President has issued a recent decree that all agro-processing enterprises should be corporatized by the end of 1996, which would facilitate autonomous decision making, even though it falls short of privatization. Restrictions remain a burden particularly on state-owned enterprises, and measures are needed to loosen the hold of the regional administrations and their agricultural departments. The most effective way to achieve this is through the transfer of ownership and demonopolization of the distribution authorities. The Ministries of Agriculture and of Trade, their branches, and the regional Executive Councils need to shed most of their business administration functions and retain only their public administration functions.

Restructuring Strategy for the Future

Even under the most optimistic assumptions about privatization, many enterprises will remain under state ownership for some time. For reasons discussed in the previous chapter regarding the importance of profit-maximizing enterprises for making a market system work, the Government should seek to privatize virtually all of the small and most of the medium-sized enterprises within the next 12 to 18 months. Some of the larger enterprises will, however, take considerably longer to privatize (beyond the portion sold for vouchers under the mass privatization program) because there are fewer investors able to buy them or bring the new capital, technology, market access, and management skills needed to restructure them. In the meantime, the Government needs to take actions to prevent the irreversible depletion of potentially valuable assets (of both fixed and human capital).

Corporatization is a first step towards restructuring, by creating a buffer between the Government and enterprises. This has effectively removed enterprises from micro-management by the branch Ministries and from automatic access to budgetary resources, and can provide the necessary framework for attracting buyers, including cash investors as well as voucher and buyout sales. However, corporatization needs to be accompanied by systematic measures to enforce privatization or closure.

Experience in other countries suggests that major investments by the state in restructuring are generally not cost-effective. Government restructuring efforts should instead focus on repair and maintenance, reorganization, downsizing (including labor reduction) and, to a limited extent, product mix.

Two approaches are key to this process.

- First, as discussed in the previous chapter, *hard budget constraints* must be imposed on state enterprises to provide the incentives needed for them to seek efficiency improvements and to search for new investments and investors. The hard budget constraint must apply to all forms of credit and grants, including budgetary funding, bank credit, and arrears to supplier enterprises and labor.

- Second, to prevent further depletion of human and fixed capital assets in state-owned enterprises (including those corporatized), and to transfer these assets to the private sector where they could be more efficiently utilized in combination with injections of new capital, technology and management expertise, a program should be introduced whereby a group of selected enterprises would be prepared for privatization or liquidation. The enterprises should be put under the control of an agency fully autonomous of government, empowered to make independent privatization or liquidation decisions on appropriate economic and financial

viability criteria alone. The program would focus on packaging each enterprise as one or more marketable entities by downsizing, spinning off or closing areas (such as social assets), reducing costs, improving management systems, and restructuring product mixes towards target markets. Entry to the program for each enterprise would require agreement between the Government (as owner), creditors, management and workers. Such an agreement could be framed under a memorandum of understanding which would: (a) set appropriate deadlines for decisions based on a business plan to be produced by the enterprise, and; (b) define access to financing facilities (strictly limited to essential operational requirements) during a program period of about one year maximum. The agency would market each enterprise in whole or in part, and those assets that cannot be sold as part of a going concern within the deadline period would be sold independently, or scrapped. This process, combining privatization and liquidation, would provide a demonstration impact which, if successful, could be replicated in the case of other enterprises.

B. THE PRIVATIZATION PROCESS

A law on privatization was adopted in 1993, and was followed by a law on vouchers that introduced the mass privatization program. Various privatization programs were passed by Parliament, and the original plan was to privatize 30 percent of state assets at the republican level by 1995. Consensus on privatization was not achieved, however, and the program has flagged (Figures 3.3 and 3.4). Privatization did not exceed 10 percent of republican and communal assets combined by mid-1996. The trade and transport sectors have come nearest to meeting privatization targets, exceeding 50 percent of the target, including the Ministry of Trade retail outlets which have largely been spun off as corporate entities or privatized. As a result of powerful state and municipal lobbies preventing ownership transfer of food enterprises, privatization has been particularly slow in agro-processing, where only 20 units have been corporatized, and few if any have actually been privatized. At the republican level, a total of 428 enterprises had been privatized or corporatized by June 30, 1996, with zero progress in the first half

of 1996. By the end of 1996, about 130 additional enterprises had been privatized, corporatized or otherwise restructured (Table 3.5)

Of the total number of transactions at the republican level, corporatizations amounted to 278, and buyouts amounted to 128. Only 22 enterprises were sold by auction or tender. The

Figure 3.3: State sector employment still dominates.

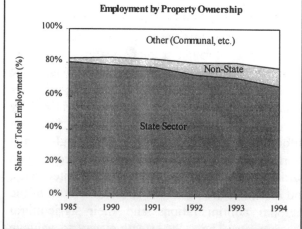

Source: Belarus Ministry of State Property and World Bank staff calculations.

total, excluding corporatizations still in the state sector, amounted to about 6 percent of republican assets. At the communal level, the trend in privatizations has been similar to those of the republican level, with about 10 percent of units privatized, largely through auctions and buyouts.[43] The year 1994 saw the peak of the privatization effort, when the program was not too far below target. Since then, however, activity has all but halted as the result of strong resistance to more rapid advance by the top levels of the Government administration.

The mass privatization program has played a part—so far quite small—in some of the privatizations. As of June 30, 1996 (the second deadline for closing the distribution process), about 40 percent of the people of Belarus had received privatization certificates, about one third of which had been actually traded. Of these, most went to investment funds rather than being exchanged for directly-held shares in companies. Since the total number of certificates issued was fixed in terms of the book value of 50 percent of all assets (republican and communal), then less than 5 percent of assets has been traded through the voucher program (40 percent of the population holding vouchers times 50 percent of assets, times 33 percent of vouchers traded, minus the proportion of vouchers traded to investment funds). A few percent more have been sold through periodic auctions of shares to corporate entities, including investment funds and banks.

No trade sales have taken place, despite efforts by Treuhand and by Coopers and Lybrand teams, and no public offers have been made. A handful of joint venture agreements with existing SOEs took place in 1991-93. Inadequate capacity

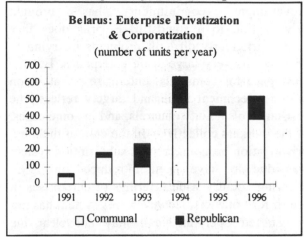

Figure 3.4: Enterprise reform is slowing.

Source: Belarus Ministry of State Property and World Bank staff calculations.

exists within the Government to conduct sale negotiations.

At the most, if we take units transformed as representative of assets transformed, including voucher sales, 13 percent of all assets have been privatized, and at the most 11 percent of republican assets as of mid-1996, three years after the passing of the privatization laws. This clearly puts Belarus into the small group of formerly planned economies that have made very little progress with privatization.

Privatization Policy Perspectives

The 1996 privatization program adopted some procedural changes designed to accelerate the process. These changes increased the power of the Privatization Ministry to initiate corporatizations, allowed increases in share capital to accommodate outside investors, decentralized corporatization to the enterprise level, and allowed more price flexibility in initial

Table 3.5: Enterprises Transformed through Privatization and Corporatization (by year)

	1991	1992	1993	1994	1995	1996	Total
Republican							
Total units	19	32	140	184	53	134	564
Industry units	12	23	68	58	15	36	212
Total employment (ths)	18	30	125	115	31	47	366
Industry employment (ths)	16	28	106	76	25	14	265
Communal							
Total units	42	157	99	457	413	390	1,558

Note: 1996 is for 2 quarters.
Source: Belarus Ministry of Economy.

share pricing. Despite this, the lack of Government commitment has brought privatization to a standstill. Belarus does face some particularly difficult problems in trying to privatize its very large scale enterprises. But the slow pace for communal enterprise privatization is not a technical issue and largely reflects the resistance of the city councils, and in some cases, of the workers collectives. In the case of the mass privatization program, a mass subscription system was due to have been introduced in 1995, allowing country-wide offerings of enterprises in return for vouchers. However, this system has not yet started operating, and may not clear the market under current rigid share pricing rules. The Government allowed a few voucher auctions to parallel the subscription process, but these have been jeopardized by intensive regulation and auditing of the investment funds that were supposed to intermediate sales. The Government closed all of these investment funds for a period in 1995, and three of the firms were still closed in October 1996.

The sale of shares for vouchers has also been slowed by the sporadic and inadequate supply of enterprise shares. This has been the result of the very slow pace of "corporatization" or setting up departmental enterprises as joint stock corporations with their own boards of directors. Progress during 1995 was sporadic, despite government commitments to do 2,000 enterprises by the end of the year. Virtually no corporatizations had occurred in the first three quarters of 1996, and only a small number is expected to be complete before year-end—a major shortfall compared to the program for 1996 announced by the President in January. The slow pace of corporatization has been partly the result of indecision and continuing efforts to find the ideal legal and administrative procedures. For example, during the past year the Government has had to work on establishing a more transparent valuation method, and has introduced a mechanism by which the reservation price for enterprise shares can be reduced if they do not sell in the first offering.

The delays in the privatization process also reflect the fact that the Government has given workers collectives in the enterprises the effective right to block corporatization of the enterprise where they work, at a time when broader government policies have made it very difficult even for well-established privatized enterprises to make successful use of their increased flexibility in decision-making. Although technically only a change in legal structure, corporatization in Belarus is actually very significant. As part of the process, the shares are allocated, which generates serious discussions about the rights of various groups to corporate control. Furthermore, the process of corporatization creates a desirable distance between the corporation and the Government, thus reducing the likelihood that the Government will subsidize the unit. This potential or actual loss of access to subsidies, plus widespread knowledge that many public enterprises, especially the larger ones, are significantly over-staffed and thus likely to be downsized when the enterprise can no longer depend on budgetary support, leads many workers collectives to obstruct the corporatization and thus the sale of vouchers and privatization.

The Government needs to exercise strong leadership to convince workers that corporatization and privatization are not only necessary, but also good for them in the long term since this will increase efficiency, the development of new small enterprises, and thus employment opportunities and income. The Government needs to convey with unswerving clarity the message that restoring growth and expanding economic opportunities is going to benefit everyone—even the poor who must depend on governmental income support programs paid for out of taxes on a growing economy—far more than spending months trying to assure that every decision regarding the allocation and use of assets inherited from the old regime is "fair." Unfortunately, the most recent government decrees tend to be moving in the opposite direction. Although the recovery plan through the year 2000 generally gives strong support to privatization and "de-statization," it also proposes that workers' collectives be given the right to block any corporate restructuring initiative. Unless changed, this is likely to become a serious barrier to the economic transition in Belarus because, especially in large enterprises, most workers, many of whom are redundant, have a strong vested interest in the status quo.

Incentives to Privatization

The pace of privatization is slow largely because the Government has not been prepared to make the efforts needed to implement effective privatization laws. The process has been paralyzed by both inadequate drive from the center and objections of local authorities and enterprise managers who have successfully blocked transactions, usually on the belief that rescue is around the corner, either through re-establishment of traditional (Soviet) markets, or through government credit and financing, or both. The imposition of *hard budget constraints* on enterprises, as discussed above, is therefore a key factor in encouraging and facilitating needed structural change, including privatization.

C. PRIVATE ENTERPRISE DEVELOPMENT

Employment in single-owner companies grew at 40 percent per annum over 1990-95. By 1995, recorded employment in such companies reached 345 thousand, or about 8 percent of the labor force (up from 1.3 percent in 1991). While cooperative enterprises have gone into decline, the number of registered small enterprises (according to the tax authorities) rose by 80 percent per year between 1992 and early 1996, probably reflecting the transformation of cooperatives into private enterprises. The tax registry records 200,000 "tax bearers" in the private sector in January 1996, up from 6,000 in 1992. Ministry of Statistics data on the other hand show less aggressive growth, recording rapid increases up to 1994 but slowing thereafter, which may reflect the restrictions imposed on business by the current Government and the tendency of enterprises to move into the informal (non-reporting) sector in response to excessive government regulation and intervention. Table 3.6 shows some key statistics. The inconsistencies in the table in data from alternative sources also highlights the severe difficulties faced in finding reliable information on this sector which is playing an increasingly important role in the economy despite the many handicaps that it faces in the current policy environment. Its importance is underscored, for example, by the fact that, if the private sector did not exist in Belarus, the current official unemployment rate would increase by a factor of two to three times.

Three categories of private sector enterprise can be identified—the privatized enterprises, the spin-offs, and the new starts. Generally the spin-offs grow fastest because they have the advantages of both ready access to equipment and materials, and entrepreneurial owners. Given the apparent dynamism of the private sector, it may be wondered what exactly are the constraints. First, it must be remembered that the starting point was low, and the share of private sector activity remains low. Second, there are indications of a falloff after 1994 which could probably be attributed to the imposition of controls following the arrival of the new regime, and to a decree in early 1996 requiring the re-registration of companies.

Table 3.6: Private Business Growth

Enterprise Types	(Thousands - end of period)						
	1990	1991	1992	1993	1994	1995	1996 (Q1)
Taxation Department data							
Registered small units	-	-	7.9	14.45	33.3	44.1	54.5
Cooperative units	-	-	5.6	4.3	3.4	2.9	2.6
Employment in single owner units	65.6	116.3	169.8	225.6	293.1	344.9	-
Ministry of Statistics data							
Small Scale Enterprises (SSEs)	-	-	3.3	5.7	10.0	13.1	14.0
Employment in SSEs	-	-	82.9	120.0	128.1	100.4	123.4

Source: Official data and World Bank staff calculations.

The problems faced by private enterprises, particularly new starts, have been: (a) the effects of the exchange rate regime; (b) the continuation of state monopolies, especially in trading and distribution, although this is reducing; (c) the continuation of (informal) price controls at the local level; (d) a relatively onerous and complicated tax system; (e) the lack of a supportive legal framework, especially with respect to private property; (f) government regulations such as the re-registration decree; and (g) the financial crisis and the consequent increased difficulty of securing financing, particularly for fixed investment. A recent survey also identified the following problems.

- At present, there is great uncertainty because no new permits to operate businesses are being issued.[44]

- The large number of licenses, permits, registrations, and approvals from various levels of government required for each location or line of business—and the delays and uncertainty in receiving them—severely discourage private businesses.

- Rents for space in the premises of state enterprises are excessive, and in some cases have become so high as to preclude doing business.

- Application of regulations sometimes discriminates against private companies; for example, local officials or tax authorities in some jurisdictions reportedly harass private firms that successfully compete with a state firm.[45]

- Tax inspectors harass private companies, for example by attempting to levy draconian fines for relatively minor infractions.

- State enterprises discriminate against private firms, for example by insisting on pre-payment for supplies sold to private firms, but tolerating large arrears from other state enterprises.

D. FRINGE BENEFITS AND SOCIAL ASSET DIVESTITURE

Firms in Belarus spend money on many functions classified in their enterprise accounting systems as "social"—housing for employees, summer camps for the children of employees, spas for employees, health and dental clinics on site and specialized medical and dental facilities off-site, subsidized food, crèches and kindergartens, and vocational schools. In some areas, firms also provide local infrastructure services such as district heating, electricity, and water and sewer systems. Extensive provision of such local infrastructure is also common among state and collective farms.

The divestiture of such "social" functions is commonly regarded as an important way to improve the competitiveness of enterprises in transition economies. Such obligations reduce the profitability of enterprises by diverting money that could better be used to finance investments in increased productivity, and they divert management attention from core business activities. This section examines (a) the need to divest "social assets;" and (b) measures that can be taken to reduce the costs of providing such fringe benefits. (A more complete discussion of this topic is presented in Annex A.)

Need for Divestiture

Conceptual Issues. Before discussing the need for divestiture, the terminology should be clarified. Although the services just described are commonly referred to as "social assets," they should really be called non-wage or "fringe" benefits because most are private rather than social in nature and, under current conditions, many are liabilities rather than assets from the perspective of the enterprises.[46] The term "social assets" is thus quite misleading and will generally not be used in this discussion. "Fringe benefits" will be used instead.

Fringe benefits are by no means unique to enterprises in the former Soviet Union. Most enterprises, including the World Bank, offer various fringe benefits such as pensions, life insurance plans, clinics for treatment of minor medical problems, food service facilities, and day care for children of employees. Such fringe benefits are often not entirely free, however; some contribution to full cost recovery is often required from the employee. Other fringe benefits such as housing, public utilities, and foodstuffs, however, are generally provided in industrialized countries only by enterprises operating in remote areas where the private sector cannot be depended on to provide these goods and services. The real issue is therefore not the existence of fringe benefits, but the scope, cost, and the administrative burden on the enterprise of physically providing such benefits.

A rough idea of the scope and cost of fringe benefits in Belarus is seen in Table 3.7. This table highlights the facts that: (a) many of the fringe benefits such as housing and utilities are not as important today as commonly believed in the total cost of fringe benefits; and (b) as a percentage of labor costs, fringe benefits on average were a fairly minor burden, accounting for only 12 percent of the total in 1995. As a share of total costs, fringe benefits averaged only one percent. These numbers, however, fail to show the significant progress that enterprises in Belarus have already made to control such costs. In 1994, for example, fringe benefits accounted for 35 percent of total labor costs. As economic pressures on enterprises increased between 1994 and 1995, enterprises chose to reduce such employee fringe benefits, and while data are not available, anecdotal evidence indicates that the burden on enterprises of providing fringe benefits was even higher in the years prior to 1994. Enterprise spending on the construction of houses and infrastructure was particularly hard hit in 1995 when almost no spending took place. Earlier research viewed continued enterprise social provision as cushioning the effects of sharp falls in real money wages in the process of transition,[47] but managers interviewed in Belarus regarded many fringe benefits as poorly targeted and low priority—obvious candidates for reduction or elimination in cost-cutting drives.

Although the burden of fringe benefits on enterprises has obviously become much less of a problem than previously, reforms are still needed for at least four reasons. First, even though fringe benefits may now represent a small share of total costs, they can still be a significant share of value added, particularly at world prices. Second, considerable inequities exist in the access that workers have to such benefits when they are provided by enterprises rather than by

Table 3.7: Expenditures on Non-Wage Benefits, 1995

| Item | Percentage Share of | | |
	Fringe Benefits	Labor Costs	Total Costs
Total Costs			**100**
Non-Labor Costs			89
Labor Costs		**100**	11
Wages		88	10
Fringe Benefits	**100**	12	1
Capital Costs			
Housing & Infrastructure	17		
Current Costs			
Housing	14		
Heating, electricity, etc.	12		
Clinics, day care, etc.	27		
Subsidies in kind	25		
Other	49		

Note: Cells are left blank to focus attention on the key relationships between fringe benefits and various cost concepts in corporate accounts.
Source: Official data and World Bank staff calculations.

government agencies. Third, the provision of certain fringe benefits diverts management attention from more important matters. Fourth, fringe benefits commonly represent a tax loophole that should be closed.

Burden on Value Added. As indicated in Table 3.7, fringe benefits still constitute over 10 percent of wage costs. Data limitations prevent calculating the share of fringe benefits in total value added, but the widespread enterprise losses and arrears to suppliers indicate that many enterprises probably have small or negative value added, that is, the cost of material inputs exceeds the value of the finished product. If the value of inputs and outputs is measured at world prices rather than at domestic prices—which are distorted by artificially low prices for energy inputs and import duties on competing imported outputs—even more products would probably show negative value added. When value added margins are very slim, increasing labor costs by 10-15 percent can make the difference between profit and loss. Therefore, enterprises should continue to reduce the costs of fringe benefits where these contribute significantly to the lack of competitiveness of their products.

Inequity in Access. Enterprises in the top quartile in terms of firm size spent the equivalent of 15 percent of total employee compensation on fringe benefits in 1995. During the same period, firms in the bottom quartile spent only two percent. Employees in small firms clearly have less access to fringe benefits than those in large firms. The Government of Belarus could improve the equity of access to services such as kindergartens and health care by making these services available directly rather than through enterprises. Similarly, services such as housing and utilities, which are not "social" or "public" goods, should be made available through the private sector or by non-profit organizations, thus assuring equal access to all workers regardless of the size of the enterprise in which they work. Such changes would of course require changes in the distribution of the gross earnings of enterprises. Workers would have to be paid more so that they could afford to pay for services that were previously provided as a condition of employment, and governments would have to receive more in taxes (or reduce expenditures in lower-priority areas). The financing of "social asset divestiture" is discussed in more detail below.

Diversion of Management Attention. In order to provide fringe benefits, firms in Belarus frequently engage *directly* in activities that are extraneous to their core business activities. For example, producers of television sets and heavy construction equipment are also involved in running truck farms to produce vegetables and other foodstuffs for their employees. This diverts management's attention from core business activities, thereby reducing efficiency and prospects for economic recovery. To correct this problem, firms should try wherever possible to replace in-kind fringe benefits, such as food, with additional cash payments which workers can use to purchase products from normal market sources. When in-kind fringe benefits such as cafeteria services or daycare must be provided within the enterprise, enterprises in market economies often find that this can be done most efficiently by hiring specialist enterprises to provide these services, thus freeing enterprise management to focus on core business activities. "Out-sourcing"

or "contracting-out" services like this will be difficult until the market mechanisms in Belarus have developed more fully, but this option should be considered when possible.

Fringe Benefits and Tax Loopholes. One of the key attractions to both enterprises and workers of non-cash fringe benefits compared to regular pay is that both parties gain from tax loopholes with non-cash compensation under current tax legislation. Expenditures by enterprises on fringe benefits such as daycare centers and resort facilities are commonly allowed as deductible business expenses that reduce profits and thus the taxes owed by an enterprise. However, if the cost of providing the fringe benefits were instead given to the employees in cash so that they could purchase the same services from other sources, the additional cash given to the employees would increase the enterprises' wage bill, thereby increasing its payroll tax liability. The current tax system creates a similar bias in favor of fringe benefits in the minds of employees. Fringe benefits received in kind are generally not subject to taxation, but cash received in lieu of fringe benefits would immediately be subject to income taxes.

To remove this bias, thereby facilitating the transfer of "social assets" to private operators, municipalities and other more appropriate providers, the Government and Parliament should change the national tax legislation, as has been done in Russia and many OECD countries, to make all fringe benefits, regardless of whether they are paid in cash or in kind, subject to the same rate of income taxation. This would make employees indifferent from a tax perspective, and since cash can be used for whatever purpose is most important to the worker, most would then prefer to receive compensating adjustments in cash wages, thereby making it easy for the enterprise to shed the social assets. Wages would remain a deductible business expense, allowing the enterprise to continue to reduce its profit tax burden. To remove the payroll tax bias in favor of non-cash compensation, the payroll tax rate could be lowered by an amount that compensates on average for the increased cash payments to workers, thereby leaving the Government with the same amount of tax revenue and removing the bias of enterprise managers against offering cash compensation to workers. In fact, such a reform could be used as an opportunity for a broader reform of the payroll tax system that would reduce the current bias against employing workers and in favor of using more capital equipment.

Approaches to Divestiture

With the possible exceptions of kindergartens and some forms of medical care, most of the fringe benefits provided directly to individual employees do not warrant continued public subsidy, either through government-owned enterprises or directly by state and local government bodies. But many of the services like housing and utilities that formerly were provided by enterprises will clearly need to be supplied to prevent adverse impacts on individuals and communities. The following key problems must therefore be addressed when reducing the burden of fringe benefits on enterprises—especially benefits that are provided in-kind: (a) how can enterprises be encouraged to reduce their expenditures on fringe benefits; (b) who should provide goods and services no longer provided by enterprises; and (c) how should the goods and services be paid for once the enterprise no longer provides them as part of the wage package?

Reducing Fringe Benefit Expenditures. The solution to this problem is relatively easy. The Government should make certain that all enterprises are subject to hard budget constraints—that they are forced to pay all of their debts or be subject to bankruptcy proceedings. Under such conditions, enterprise managers will do whatever is required to remain competitive. The reduction of fringe benefits in the total cost structure of enterprises from 35 percent to 12 percent of labor costs between 1994 and 1995 as described above is clear evidence that this process is already working in Belarus. The main task now, as highlighted by the excessively high levels of overdue accounts payable in the enterprise sector, is to enforce the hard budget constraints much more effectively than has been done in the past. This will provide the incentives needed to assure that enterprises maximize the efficiency of their provision of

fringe benefits, providing them only when it is necessary to attract and retain needed employees. Likewise, workers will have the incentive to seek out new, more productive jobs with employers who can afford to offer attractive fringe benefit packages. Other than imposing effective hard budget constraints on enterprises, there is little else that the Government needs to do to stimulate the necessary action on the part of enterprises.

Provision of Goods and Services. The Government will, however, need to implement substantial changes in the allocation of staff and resources to assure that critical services continue to be available once the enterprises no longer provide them as fringe benefits. In this context, two basic groups of goods and services should be distinguished—those which are "public" in nature, and require provision by the Government, and those which are "private," and can be supplied by the private sector.

Very few of the fringe benefits traditionally provided by the enterprises are really "public" as defined above. For example, enterprises rarely provided public health services (as opposed to clinics) or general education (as opposed to day care services). Most of the fringe benefits were goods and services like resorts, housing, utilities, and food, which in a market economy should be provided by the private sector and paid for by users. Fringe benefit reduction by enterprises therefore need not necessarily create an additional burden for the Government.

Nevertheless, because of the very weak condition of the private sector in Belarus today, the Government may have to play a transitional role in providing certain goods and services. This is particularly true for housing, which is critical to labor mobility and hence to economic growth.[48] Belarus has already made very good progress in privatizing its housing stock; by the end of 1995, 62 percent of housing was in private hands (including cooperatives). Most housing should be privatized as rapidly as possible, but until the necessary conditions are fully in place, such as condominium-type laws, property registration systems, and mechanisms for mortgage financing, local governments will almost certainly have to pick up some of the responsibility for housing units no longer being maintained by enterprises —and this in fact is already happening. In the longer term, most public utilities could and probably should be privatized (subject to appropriate regulatory controls), but in the meantime, quasi-governmental bodies such as district heating and electric power companies will have to bear the responsibility. Kindergartens are increasingly being used to provide daycare for infants because economic difficulties are causing women to cut short maternity leave, and provisions would also need to be made to assure the continued availability of such services.

In some cases, especially where the enterprises are large compared to the communities where they are located, the most sensible approach during the transition period may be to have the enterprise continue to supply the services, especially when: (a) the cost is a small percentage of enterprise value added; (b) a program for moving to more or less full cost recovery is implemented; and (c) the services are managed by a semi-autonomous part of the enterprise, thus leaving plant management free to focus on production, efficiency and marketing. Special arrangements will need to be made when enterprises are closed to assure continuity of critical public services, but the fact that enterprises provide such services should not be used as an excuse to maintain activities that are not profitable.

The *responsibility* for functions should be distinguished from their *physical provision*. Even when services become the responsibility of local government bodies, they do not necessarily have to be provided by government staff. Actual delivery of these functions can be accomplished by a number of alternative organizations, including private contractors, non-governmental organizations and even other levels of government under contract.

Financing the Provision of Goods and Services. Regardless of whether goods and services previously provided as fringe benefits will be provided in the future by the national government, by local governments, by quasi-governmental bodies, by non-profit organizations, or by the private sector, the costs must be financed. Three basic classes of goods and services can be identified: (a) those to be financed by the workers themselves; (b) those to be financed by the government; and (c) those that must be temporarily discontinued.

For goods and services such as housing and utilities that are of high priority, people will find the money out of their own pockets to pay the costs. Part of this additional burden will be covered by additional wages paid by enterprises in compensation for the fringe benefits no longer provided. Part will be met through household budget reallocation from less critical household expenditure categories. Finally households will reduce their use of services such as heat and electricity—something that happens naturally as prices are raised to reflect the true cost of supply. In the case of the very poor households, the Government will need to continue providing an appropriate social safety net, as discussed in the next section.

To finance services such as housing that the public sector may temporarily have to continue to supply, the Government can take two measures. First, it can increase cost recovery from the users. Second, it can reallocate tax revenues (which should increase as enterprises become more profitable), transferring them to local governments—which will probably have to bear most of the burden of supplying services previously supplied by enterprises—so that they will have adequate resources.

As an unfortunate but unavoidable result of the collapse of the previous economic system, which provided a stable and, by comparison with some parts of the Soviet Union, good standard of living to virtually all people in Belarus while it lasted, some services from the previous period may have to be suspended until economic conditions improve. Spas, resorts, and other recreational facilities, for example, are non-essential luxuries under current conditions.

E. SUMMARY

Priority needs to be given to the following policy measures if Belarus is to establish a business environment that stimulates the reform and growth of enterprises in Belarus:

- **Hard Budget Constraints.** Eliminate as rapidly as possible all forms of subsidized credit and involuntary grants. This would force enterprises to find solutions that cut costs, increase revenues, and attract new capital.

- **Privatization.** Remove barriers to privatization and accelerate the process by (a) facilitating management/ labor buyouts of small and medium enterprises; (b) starting to force the "corporatization" of all enterprises not sold by April 1997, thereby improving the supply of enterprises available for voucher privatization; (c) modifying the state-determined reservation prices for enterprises so that they have a reasonable chance of being sold at a competitive, market-clearing price; (d) establishing the capacity to negotiate trade sales with international investors for large enterprises; (e) setting up a fully autonomous agency to implement plans for the privatization or liquidation of selected enterprises according to a schedule agreed between the Government, creditors and management.

- **Price Controls.** Phase out price and all related controls so that enterprises can base their production decisions on prices determined by the free interaction of demand and supply in the markets.

- **Private Sector Development.** Remove barriers to new private sector development.

- **Macroeconomic Policies.** Implement the policies needed to improve the investment climate that were outlined in the previous chapter.

- **Social Asset Divestiture.** Free enterprise managers from the responsibility for providing in-kind fringe benefits such as housing, pre-schools, and food by transferring the associated "social assets" from the enterprises to individuals, private enterprises, non-profit organizations, or local governments.

4

Protecting the People

If implemented in a timely manner, the policy measures outlined in this report will make a major contribution to reducing poverty in Belarus by gradually reversing the 40 percent economic decline of the past five years. This decline has been the source of almost all incremental poverty, which has increased from 5 percent in 1992 to 22 percent on a yearly basis in 1995.[49] Enterprise reforms are urgently needed to increase productivity, increase jobs, raise incomes, and reduce poverty.

If not managed well, however, such reforms will result in factory closures, mass layoffs, open and hidden unemployment, growing regional inequalities, disruptions in local community life, and growing poverty. These costs can be minimized with good economic and social policies that maximize the recovery of economic efficiency and output in a way that favors employment. Such policies need to be carefully designed, however, to be fiscally viable and to avoid creating welfare dependence by reducing incentives to work. The remainder of this chapter is arranged as follows. Section A discusses strategies for maximizing employment to minimize poverty during the transition period, and Section B looks at policies that the Government can implement to help those who do fall into poverty. Despite the immense importance of the topic, this chapter is relatively brief because the World Bank has recently completed a separate report specifically on the issues of poverty and social protection in Belarus during the transition. This *Poverty Assessment Report* provides a more complete discussion of the social protection policy issues.

A. MAXIMIZING EMPLOYMENT TO MINIMIZE POVERTY

In addition to increasing output by accelerating the rate of foreign and domestic investment as rapidly as possible by taking the measures recommended earlier in this report, the following actions are recommended to increase employment opportunities. First, the Government should give special attention to measures that will stimulate the development of small businesses. Second, enterprises should be allowed to adjust wages and employment levels without interference from the Government, thus assuring labor market flexibility.

Small Enterprise Development

Experience from countries around the world, including countries already more advanced than Belarus in the transition to a market economy, indicates that the best way to create new job opportunities is to encourage the development of small-scale enterprises. As indicated in the previous chapter, this experience is already confirmed in Belarus by the rapid development of new jobs in the services sector—despite the many handicaps that private entrepreneurs currently face. Small firms require relatively little capital per job created, and can respond quickly to emerging market conditions. In addition to the policies noted above for general business development, the Government could take the following actions to stimulate the development of small-scale enterprises:

- accelerate the privatization of shops and other small enterprises owned by government bodies at all levels, and sell the land with the buildings;

- allow legal as well as natural persons to own land for business purposes;

- launch a special program that would encourage large enterprises to "spin off" small production units, allowing workers to set up their own businesses with assets bought from the large enterprises when appropriate;

- create an office or publication where any potential investor can find out about public enterprise assets that managers, once they begin to face hard budget constraints, become ready to sell.

- set up "business incubator centers" where small enterprises can get easy access, on a month-by-month rental basis if necessary, to building space and shared support facilities like accounting, shipping and advertising; and[50]

- establish business promotion centers such as those now being initiated with help from TACIS.

Such measures would greatly facilitate the transition of workers from unproductive jobs in failing plants to new, more productive jobs, thus reducing the risk of long-term unemployment and poverty. The savings in direct income support to unemployed workers can easily compensate for the budgetary costs of these modest programs. In implementing such measures, care should be taken not to introduce special incentives based on enterprise size, such as special tax concessions for small-scale enterprise development. Such incentives create distortions that can hurt employment generation by encouraging firms to stay small in order to take advantage of size-linked incentives. Such incentives also lead to corruption; with such policies, entrepreneurs commonly break up enterprises into fictionally separate entities so that they can take advantage of the tax giveaways.

B. An Effective, Fiscally Sustainable Social Safety Net is Needed

Since independence, the standard of living for the Belarusian population has eroded, with per capita GDP falling from USD 3,440 in 1990 to USD 2,160 in 1994, and with the incidence of poverty rising from 1 percent in 1990 to 22 percent in 1995. Movements in and out of poverty have been highly volatile—the share of people living in poverty was 36 percent in the first quarter of 1995, but this dropped to about 25 percent during the more temperate months when more in-kind income from garden plots becomes available (without in-kind income, poverty incidence would have risen to 51 percent in 1995).[51] Over two-thirds of all households were poor at some point during the year, with one in six experiencing poverty for five months or more. Poverty has been periodic and brief for most households to date, but there is evidence that the poor are experiencing longer periods of poverty as the severe economic decline continues.

The increase in poverty is primarily due to the drop in overall levels of production and income. On average, wage income permits the poor to satisfy only 40 to 60 percent of the minimum consumption basket.[52] Some 90 percent of poor households have one or more workers, but they earn wages that cannot support a family. The degree to which the overall decline in income (rather than the increasing inequality in the distribution of income) has been the primary source of poverty can be demonstrated as follows. Assume that total household income had remained at 1992 levels but was distributed among families in a way that reflected the less equal distribution of income that developed between 1992 and 1995. If this had happened, fewer than 10 percent of families would have fallen below the poverty line instead of the 36 percent that were in poverty during the first quarter of 1995. The other 26 percent of families in poverty during the first quarter of 1996 were therefore in poverty because of the overall decline in incomes.[53] If we look not just at the families in poverty for a single quarter but rather than those who were on average in poverty throughout the year, we find that the percentage of families defined as poor drops from 36 percent to 22 percent. Rising income inequality, which is an expected feature of the transition as the dispersion of incomes increases to reflect the relative market demand and scarcities of different skills, added less than five percentage points to the increase in the poverty rate. The remaining 25 percentage points of increased poverty for the first quarter of 1995 was caused by falling national product and thus falling aggregate household income.

Poverty tends to be higher for larger families and for children to age 6. Single parents with children face a risk of poverty exceeding 50 percent. Poverty is lower in rural than in urban areas, largely because of the greater access to income in kind in the rural areas; and there is an equal incidence of poverty among women and men in percentage terms (though numerically, more women are poor due to the demographic balance). The elderly face a relatively low risk of poverty, as they have been able to accumulate retirement, labor, and garden plot income.

The Government has introduced an extensive array of social insurance and social assistance benefits that consume a high level of resources (36 percent of total public spending), but which have done little to reduce poverty because of their weak targeting. Overall, the non-poor receive 1.5 times more benefits than the poor, while 37 percent of poor families are not paid family benefits even though they qualify. Under the current system, introducing a 50 percent increase in family benefits would only reduce poverty by an estimated 1 percent, while correspondingly increasing the tax burden. The financing of some benefits through high payroll taxes (50 percent for pension, Chernobyl, and nursery school programs) both drives down employment levels and depresses wages, exacerbating the household income problem noted above.

Developing a New Social Protection Strategy

Since most of the poverty in Belarus today results from economic decline rather than from distribution problems, *the best long-term solution to poverty would be to restore economic growth*. Fairly modest increases in average incomes would significantly reduce the poverty rate, even with no change in the pattern of income distribution. At the same time, achieving the transition will involve shifts in relative prices, imposing costs on some households that will require development of an effective national social assistance policy. Demographic and fiscal trends will also challenge the sustainability of social insurance programs, which include old age and unemployment benefits. The Government therefore should develop and implement a three pronged social sector reform strategy that would:

- improve Belarusian welfare by redeploying labor to the more productive sectors of the economy, and by supporting policies that sustain real wage growth;

- ensure that a well-targeted social safety net is in place to support the transition; and

- establish a fiscally sustainable and equitable social insurance system.

Improving Labor Market Flexibility

As was shown in Chapter 1, average wages since 1991 have stayed well above output. This disconnect between output and labor income has created internal inflationary pressures, and external payments deficits. While wages are often a small percentage of enterprise costs, they are a large share of total value added given the heavy weight of energy and material input costs. In fact, wages for many enterprises have become so large compared to the margin between selling price and input costs that the enterprises cannot pay workers—or if they pay the workers, cannot pay for their materials, energy, bank loans and taxes.

Wage Flexibility. If wage rates continue to exceed labor productivity, enterprises will be forced to fire workers once badly-needed hard budget constraints are in place. Unemployment can be reduced, however, by allowing more flexibility in wages. If real wages in each enterprise fall in line with its real, inflation-adjusted output, the burden of wage payments will remain constant relative to sales revenues, and enterprises will be able to continue paying their workers in a timely manner, thereby avoiding the severe poverty that comes to workers who must continue working without pay, or who are fired. Downward flexibility in real wages was quite successful in Estonia, for example, where average real wages fell by about 40 percent during early stages of the transition process, reflecting the decline in real output. This wage flexibility, together with policies that created an excellent environment for the development of small enterprises, allowed Estonia to pass through the worst part of the transition process with unemployment levels that stayed below those common today in the countries of Western Europe. The economy is now recovering, and wages are rising in line with increased labor productivity.

Wage flexibility spreads the cost of the transition process across all workers, allowing almost everyone to remain employed as the transition progresses, an approach that seems highly consistent with the Government's objectives of social justice. This approach also allows workers to improve their situations as the transition progresses. As investors begin to improve conditions in the best enterprises, these will become more profitable and will increase wages—both to hold onto their skilled workers and to attract good workers from other enterprises that are not as efficient and thus less able to pay competitive wages. Workers will be able to move to these higher paying jobs as the economic situation improves in response to a good investment climate.

Other Labor Market Policies. Wage flexibility needs to be complemented, however, with other policies to improve labor market flexibility. In particular, the Government needs to (a) eliminate any barriers to the dismissal of workers other than the requirement of reasonable notice and reasonable severance pay; (b) eliminate *propiska* (residency and work permit) requirements so that workers can move freely to the best jobs; (c) improve housing market flexibility so that workers can find rental housing at competitive costs where good jobs are developing;[54] (d) assure that employment benefits are structured so that they do not reduce incentives to seek work; and (e) develop training programs in cooperation with the private sector to help workers prepare for and identify better jobs. The employment and retention of workers could also be encouraged by sharply reducing the various payroll taxes.

Establishing a Well Targeted Social Safety Net

The current social assistance system, which consists of an array of child and birth allowances, payments to single parents, compensation programs, and other benefits, has failed to meet the underlying objectives of poverty reduction and support to families in need. In response, the Government should introduce a new and well-integrated system that is cost-effective in relation to its objectives, and which minimizes disincentives to work. Implementation of a reform strategy will have to address the country's lack of experience with developing, monitoring and evaluating social policy, the lack of exposure to best practice in social assistance, and weak administrative capacity.

With the establishment of a new household survey, the Government is well positioned to identify vulnerable segments of the population, and to monitor changes in household income, consumption, and behavior. This information will help the Government to target its scarce resources away from the well-off and towards assisting the most needy. For example, the Government might consider replacing the universal program of family benefits (which takes more from families in taxes than it redistributes in benefits, with no relative gain to the poor) with a means-tested benefit of last resort. This type of benefit should be designed to minimize labor disincentives—for example, each rubel of income should not result in the loss of a full rubel of benefit. Whatever the cash benefit mix, the Government will need to evaluate program effectiveness through use of survey and administrative data, and periodically adjust its spending in line with its available resources and the needs of the population.

Community social services provide support to vulnerable groups that can reduce reliance on cash benefits, keep populations at risk (such as the elderly and disabled, children) out of less effective and more expensive institutional care (which was extensively relied on by the Soviet system), and improve the quality of life. Community services are particularly effective at introducing a client focus that is missing in most cash benefit and institutional programs. The range and quality of services provided in Belarus could be improved through a review of expenditure assignments for social care and consideration of new community programs, with a view towards delivering high quality services and reducing the currently high levels of institutionalization.

Reforming Social Insurance

The Belarusian social insurance system (covering old age, disability, and survivors pensions, unemployment benefits, maternity benefits, and sick pay) is facing a severe medium-term crisis. The ratio of those on pensions to those working and paying pension contributions was 49 percent in 1991, and is expected to rise to 60-70 percent by the end of the decade (which will require correspondingly higher taxes or lower pensions, or both, if not addressed). Consolidated extra-budgetary social fund expenditures are expected to rise from 8.9 percent of GDP in 1992 to a projected 12.9 percent in 1996 (pension expenditures are 16 percent higher as a percentage of GDP than the OECD average). Social fund revenues are frequently used to finance non-fund expenditures, and the benefits delivered under this system bear no relationship to lifetime contributions. Eligibility criteria are highly generous—women and men can retire at ages 55 and 60, respectively, with many eligible for earlier retirement. Disability pensions are often granted to individuals whose earning capacities have not been significantly affected by the disability.

The Government of Belarus therefore urgently needs to develop a social insurance system that will ensure (a) fiscal sustainability; (b) system transparency, so that revenues and expenditures can be tracked in accordance with International Accounting Standards; (c) an actuarially-sound relationship between social insurance benefits and the contributions of each individual so that people can shift some of their income from their active years to old age, with different individuals receiving identical benefits for identical contributions; (d) improved service to system clients (employers, employees, and beneficiaries); and (e) the establishment of a legal, regulatory, and institutional environment that will foster the development of private pension alternatives over the longer term. All state social insurance benefits should be viewed as a package and harmonized (for example, sickness and disability benefits).

To meet these objectives, the Government should review the fiscal and social impact of a range of reform options, including movement over the long term from the current single-tier old-age pension system to an appropriate multi-pillar system with both public and private tiers.[55] In the short term, ensuring fiscal sustainability and lowering tax rates will require aggressive measures such as raising the retirement age, curtailing early retirement, tightening disability criteria, introducing waiting periods and revalidation requirements for unemployment benefits, developing improved eligibility certifi-

cation procedures, reducing the replacement rate (the ratio of the pension to working life income) from the current rate of over 40 percent to a level that is consistent with the prevailing support ratio, and introducing income taxation of social insurance to improve equity and incentives to work (by treating labor and benefit income equally). The Government should broaden the tax base, especially by moving the Chernobyl benefit off of the payroll tax and onto the budget. There is a further need to develop the institutional capacity of the Government to develop a social insurance policy, and to implement that policy effectively and transparently, while delivering a high rate of accurate processing, rapid claim turnover, and efficient service.

The Government needs in particular to make a radical change in its approach to providing a social safety net for the poor. In the past, the Government has sought to help the poor—and many other groups in society—by distorting prices. Food, housing, energy, and transport were all made available at artificially low prices that did not cover the cost of production. The Government has made it very difficult for enterprises to get rid of excess labor, thus distorting the normal functioning of the labor market. To compensate farming, manufacturing, and public transport enterprises for the losses forced on them by the artificially low prices that they were able to charge consumers and the excess workers that they were forced to retain, the Government has distorted the prices and allocation of credit, energy, raw material inputs, and foreign exchange. These distortions in prices to the enterprise sector led to further economic problems such as the high levels of payments arrears to Russia for gas because the gas distribution companies did not receive enough money from the enterprises to buy the foreign exchange needed to pay Russia. This restricted the demand for foreign exchange, contributing to the overvaluation of the domestic currency, and thereby inflicting further losses on exporters in the industrial and agricultural sectors. In short, in the name of protecting the people, the Government's policies have nearly destroyed the economy. The damage can be repaired. But doing so will require a fundamental shift in the way the Government goes about protecting the poor.

The Government's draft economic plan, *The Major Trends of Social and Economic Development of the Republic of Belarus for 1996-2000,* stresses that Belarus wants to create a socially oriented market economy. This is the objective of virtually every civilized nation in the world. People are very important. But the way in which governments help people is also very important. Belarus should be supported in its desire to create a market-based economy that provides a good living environment for people, but for this strategy to succeed, Belarus needs to use the approach normally followed by successful industrialized countries. *The Government needs to move from a social assistance strategy based largely on price distortions to one based on income redistribution.*

Adjusting prices to attain social objectives may have been an adequate approach in a centrally planned system where production was driven more by administrative decree than by prices and profits. In market systems where prices and profits are the main factors guiding production decisions, efficiency and thus the living standards of the nation depend on prices that are not distorted. Price distortions can kill a market system.

Income redistribution provides a much more solid basis for social protection in a market-based system, because it does not distort the prices upon which production decisions are based. A social protection system based on income redistribution takes very small amounts of production-based income from enterprises and individuals throughout the country through the taxation system, then provides meaningful levels of support to those who are truly poor. Since the resources going to the poor are obtained by taxing income downstream from the production process rather than by distorting the prices of inputs and outputs associated with the production process, correct price signals for producers are maintained. As a result, production efficiency is maximized, thereby increasing total income levels. By generating a higher standard of living for all, this approach reduces the number of poor needing

government support and increases the resources available to provide this support. By moving from a social protection system based on price distortions to one based on income redistribution, the Government can stop the current vicious circle of distortions that lead to losses that lead to more distortions. Moving to a system based on taxation and income redistribution will replace this vicious circle with a virtuous one where undistorted prices lead to efficiency and higher incomes, reducing both the number of poor and the burden on the non-poor to support them.

A system of social protection based on taxation and income redistribution has another advantage—it makes the costs of the system more visible than they are with a system based on price distortions. Furthermore, the actual costs of income redistribution are far lower than those of price-distorting systems like the present one in Belarus. With the present system, the price-distorting costs are very real but hard to measure. For example, it is difficult to measure the costs of a farm failing to invest in cost-saving, efficiency-enhancing equipment because its earnings were reduced by artificially low prices for the food it produced. Nor is it easy to see the production losses caused by the fact that farm managers were forced to use their meager revenues to pay wages to redundant workers—workers who sooner or later could have produced more and earned more in alternative employment if they had been forced to go look for a new job.

A fundamental principle is that hiding the costs of helping poor by distorting prices does not reduce the costs. In fact, hiding the costs through price distortions increases the costs, thereby reducing the ability of the economy to restore living standards.

One of the strong virtues of a tax-based income redistribution system is that the costs are visible. This tends to focus more attention on the costs and efficiencies of the programs, helping to assure their more efficient operation.

The system for protecting the poor needs to be redesigned so that it depends more heavily on means-tested social assistance programs. Given the administrative cost of means-testing, short-cut approaches will be required. For example, programs should be made "self-selective," placing the burden on those who want assistance to come forward and prove their eligibility. Claims from high risk groups such as families headed by a single parent and families with a large number of children could generally be accepted at face value with only limited random audits. Actual means testing, aside from reviewing the papers submitted to support such claims, could be limited to groups falling outside the high-risk categories, thus minimizing the administrative burden of introducing a means-tested income transfer program. Improvements are also needed to increase the efficiency of the insurance programs for unemployment, health insurance, and old age.

C. CONCLUSIONS

Maximizing Employment to Minimize Poverty

- Facilitate the development of small scale enterprises.

    - Encourage rapid small scale privatization.

    - Facilitate access to land and buildings.

    - Develop business incubator programs.

    - Create a transparent, equitable legal framework.

- Labor market flexibility.

    - Allow wage flexibility.

    - Abolish propiska requirements.

    - Remove constraints other than reasonable severance payment and notice on dismissal of labor.

    - Encourage the development of rental housing in growing job market areas.

    - Refuse to grant subsidies to prop up failing enterprises.

Fringe Benefit Restructuring

- Although fringe benefits ("social asset expenditures") are not a significant share of enterprise costs on average, they can be a heavy burden on enterprises with low value added.

- Provision by enterprises of in-kind benefits such as housing and food diverts management attention from core business activities.

- Many social services should therefore be taken over by municipalities, non-profit organizations, or the private sector.

- Improved cost recovery is needed to help finance the divestiture process and to improve the efficiency with which such services are used.

Programs to Reduce Poverty During the Transition

- Increase opportunities for remunerative employment to reduce poverty.

- Social assistance programs to supplement the income of the poor should:

    - require a waiting period, given the short-term nature of most poverty in Belarus, to avoid disincentives to seeking new jobs; and

    - be means-tested and targeted wherever possible.

Social Insurance Programs

- The financial sustainability of the pension system is at risk unless measures are taken to:

    - reduce expenditures on underage and questionable disability pensions;

    - move to a system of individual accounts;

    - link pensions above a certain subsistence level to lifetime earnings and pension contributions; and

    - increase reliance on individual contributions while lowering the payroll tax burden.

5

Reform Agenda and Macro Prospects

Although Belarus has made considerable progress since independence in liberalizing and stabilizing prices, the success of these reforms can be sustained only if Belarus accelerates the structural reforms required to create an investment climate that will attract the necessary investment. Without fundamental structural reforms, pressures on the budget and on the central bank to subsidize failing enterprises could easily rekindle inflation. This, plus the failure of reforms to break up and privatize state-owned monopoly structures, would prevent the establishment of the business climate needed to attract investment from both foreign and domestic sources. Without the investment needed to improve enterprise efficiency and international competitiveness, prospects for improved living standards will remain poor.

A. REFORM AGENDA

With rapid implementation of the reforms suggested in this paper, prospects for sustained economic growth are excellent. Belarus has tremendous advantages over many if not most developing countries in the world—a highly educated work force, a good basic infrastructure, a long tradition of high tech industrial production, a history of unusual openness to international trade, and excellent proximity to both the large Russian and rich European markets. With these favorable initial conditions, Belarus should be able to improve the quality and efficiency of its production so that it competes well in international markets, thus providing the foundation for good economic growth and improved living standards.

Upgrading production facilities will require substantial investments, however, and Belarus will be able to finance them only by attracting foreign and domestic private investment resources. The Government should therefore create a business environment similar to that in other countries which are competing with Belarus for investment resources. Without such an environment, foreign investors will continue to avoid the Belarusian market, potential domestic investors will continue to take their money abroad, and any investment that does take place would probably not be competitively efficient. As will be demonstrated in the remainder of this chapter, efficient investment and production will be vital to the future economic health of Belarus, and these can only be accomplished with strong participation from private sector investors, both Belarusian and foreign, within the context of a supporting, market-oriented investment climate.

B. MACROECONOMIC PROSPECTS

This section presents three scenarios of the future prospects of the Belarusian economy—the Policy Reform scenario, and two low case scenarios—GDP Decline and High Debt. The latter show what is likely to happen if Belarus does not implement the policy reforms suggested in this report.

These scenarios are designed to define the outer limits of what is likely to happen over the next few years, but none of these scenarios should be regarded as "most likely." While the "most likely" or "base case" scenario will almost certainly lie within the range delimited by the cases presented here, the current political situation in Belarus makes it impossible to define a most likely scenario. At time of writing, an emergency economic plan had just been released that stresses increased state control on prices, administrative determination of the allowable range of exchange rate movement, protection from imports for domestic producers, and an expansionary monetary policy to stimulate growth.

79

If these policies are implemented in their present form, the most likely case will probably be some combination of the GDP Decline and High Debt scenarios presented here. If the President does decide to move forward with rapid reforms on all fronts as other transitional economies have, along lines recommended by international organizations, Belarus could move towards the results of the Policy Reform case.

All three scenarios are based on implementation during 1996 of the "zero option" agreement that was signed by the Presidents of Belarus and Russia in February 1996. The scenarios also assume convergence of prices of energy imported from Russia with world levels by 1998.

Policy Reform Scenario

This scenario assumes a rapid and consistent implementation of the market-oriented reforms described in this report. GDP would bottom out with zero growth in 1997 and grow by six percent per annum thereafter. The projected GDP growth rate is ambitious but feasible given the scope for increased productivity once appropriate policies are in place.

The relatively high rate of GDP growth would be ensured by increased investment in the traded goods sector, financed with foreign direct investment and external borrowing. As this scenario includes the maximum amount of public and publicly guaranteed borrowing deemed feasible, the rest of the financing would have to come through foreign direct and portfolio investments into the private sector. But such flows will materialize only if Belarus implements the policy measures needed to create a favorable investment climate.

Given the sharp declines in the economy since 1990, export recovery will be starting from an exceptionally low base. Export volumes are projected to pick up sharply following significant real devaluations between now and the end of 1997, and by 1998, these exchange rate adjustments would have restored the price competitiveness of Belarusian exports. With improved capacity utilization in existing enterprises, export growth would accelerate, then stabilize towards the end of the projection period at around 7 percent per year, just above the real GDP growth rate. Once the credibility of reforms had been established and an environment

Table 5.1: Policy Reform Scenario

Key Indicators	1995	1996	1997	1998	2002
Growth Rates (%)					
GDP	-10.1	2.6	0.0	6.0	6.0
Exports	-6.0	—	3.4	12.2	7.1
Imports	11.0	—	-4.0	5.2	5.7
Prices (CPI Inflation)	709.0	52.0	58.8	31.0	10.6
Percent of GDP					
Exports	45.6	38.0	51.7	68.3	61.3
Imports	53.8	51.0	56.8	73.3	64.4
Current Account Balance	-2.5	-9.0	-5.1	-5.3	-4.9
Investment	25.2	24.6	30.0	30.0	30.0
Government Expenditures	32.8	32.8	30.1	23.8	22.0
Government Budget Deficit	-1.9	-5.8	-3.6	-1.2	-0.4
External Debt Indicators					
Gross Annual Borrowing (USDm)	432.0	187.8	784.4	936.2	1,185.1
Debt Service/Exports (%)	3.6	2.7	3.1	5.9	13.8
Debt/GDP (%)	24.0	7.6	17.1	27.0	29.8
Foreign Direct Investment (USDm)	7.0	19.0	92.3	166.1	527.9
As percentage of GDP	0.1	0.2	0.9	1.5	4.8
Real GDP (1990=100)	62.7	63.6	63.6	62.4	78.8

Source: Official data and World Bank staff calculations.

conducive to investment was created, new private businesses would enter the market with new export product lines, providing a further impetus to export growth. The accelerated pace of enterprise restructuring and private sector development would be focused on export production, with emphasis given to manufactured goods.

An export-driven growth strategy would require enhanced efforts to integrate Belarus with the European Union and other non-CIS markets, and to reduce barriers to trade. Such integration would provide Belarus with greater access to inputs and technology from the industrialized world, and put pressure on the domestic producers to become more efficient, thus increasing the potential for producing competitive exports. It would also expand Belarusian focus on the European market, which is likely to be much more profitable during the foreseeable future than the Russian market. The share of exports to non-CIS markets is therefore projected to rise from 35 percent in 1995 to 50 percent in 2006.

Import volumes in real terms would be initially constrained by the availability of financing (assuming no further recourse to payment arrears). Import growth would accelerate during the next few years as the investment climate improved and capital goods imports increased, much of which would be financed by counterbalancing foreign direct investment resource flows. Import growth would thereafter drop back to rates in line with GDP growth.

The current account deficit is projected to fall in dollar terms in 1997 as a result of the external financing constraint and a cessation of further external payments arrears accumulation, and then grow over the period 1998-2002, reflecting import-intensive investment financed with debt. Total external debt would exceed $5.5 billion by year 2006. However, the rapid growth of exports would secure the sustainability of the external debt and current account positions of the economy. The ratio of debt service to total exports is projected to peak at about 13 percent in 2002, thus keeping Belarus comfortably below the 18 percent benchmark for moderately indebted economies. The debt service ratio and

the current account deficit would both decline thereafter. Although the ratio of total debt to GDP would initially exceed the 30 percent benchmark for moderately indebted economies, peaking at 33 percent in 2000, this reflects the low valuation of GDP in dollar terms that will result from the real devaluations needed to restore export competitiveness. In the outer years, as productivity improvements allow a real appreciation of the domestic currency, the ratio of debt to GDP would decline to 27 percent by 2006, the last year of projections.

High Debt Scenario

This scenario demonstrates the futility of trying to restore living standards through higher levels of borrowing without taking the actions needed to improve the investment climate in Belarus. It demonstrates that, if the Government does not implement the reforms suggested in this report—reforms designed to make Belarusian products more competitive in both the international and the domestic markets—the external debt that would be required to attain the same rate of GDP growth projected in the Policy Reform scenario would quickly become unsupportable.

The High Debt scenario assumes that the authorities would persist with their current exchange rate policy, and that the nominal devaluation rate would fall short of the inflation rate, thus producing further real appreciation. The overvalued domestic currency would exacerbate pressures on loss-making exporters. At the same time, imports that were increasingly inexpensive in relative terms would be substituted for domestically produced goods, leading to an import-driven consumption boom. Private consumption would increase by 24 percentage points over the projection period, and private savings would decline by 13 percentage points.

To attain the same rate of GDP growth that is projected in the Policy Reform scenario without exchange rate and other appropriate policy adjustments, the Government would have to sustain the same investment rates, and would have to support the growing trade deficit by borrowing heavily abroad. Even with subsidies to domestic exporters, however, the export growth

Table 5.2: High Debt Scenario

Key Indicators	1995	1996	1997	1998	2002
Growth Rates (%)					
GDP	-10.1	2.6	0.0	6.0	6.0
Exports	-6.0	—	-0.2	7.9	4.3
Imports	11.0	—	3.7	7.4	6.9
Prices (CPI Inflation)	709.0	52.0	51.1	26.7	9.3
Percent of GDP					
Exports	45.6	38.0	32.4	31.7	28.8
Imports	53.8	51.0	40.0	40.1	40.6
Current Account Balance	-2.5	-9.0	-7.5	-9.0	-15.2
Investment	25.2	24.6	30.0	30.0	30.0
Government Expenditures	32.8	32.8	31.3	27.1	26.9
Government Budget Deficit	-1.9	-5.8	-5.0	-3.7	-4.3
External Debt Indicators					
Gross Annual Borrowing (USDm)	432.0	187.8	1,697.7	2,462.4	7,907.5
Debt Service/Exports (%)	3.6	2.7	3.2	10.8	57.2
Debt/GDP (%)	24.0	7.6	16.8	25.7	68.7
Foreign Direct Investment (USDm)	7.0	19.0	60.2	74.3	0.0
As percentage of GDP	0.1	0.2	0.6	0.7	0.0
Real GDP (1990=100)	62.7	63.6	63.6	67.4	78.8

Source: Official data and World Bank staff calculations.

rate is projected to fall by two percentage points relative to the Policy Reform scenario, and imports are projected to accelerate and grow at an average annual rate of 7 percent. The resulting current account deficit would grow rapidly, and the ratio of current account deficit to GDP would reach 15 percent in 2002. The debt service ratio is projected to exceed the benchmark for moderately indebted economies as early as 1999 and to grow at an accelerating rate thereafter, reaching the totally insupportable level of 118 percent in 2006.

The mounting export and investment subsidies would not allow the Government to bring down its budget deficit significantly in the initial years of the projection period, with the deficit actually starting to grow after 2000. Financing the budget deficit with domestic credit from the monetary sector would create inflationary pressures and undo the disinflation effect generated by the fixed exchange rate regime. Consequently, the average rate of inflation would decline by only 2 percentage points over the entire projection period from the levels projected in the Policy Reform scenario. Such a negligible improvement in inflation performance clearly refutes the authorities' claim that a fixed exchange rate policy helps keep inflation low and that real devaluation would re-ignite inflation. The price paid for such pseudo-stability would be a skyrocketing external debt burden and plummeting trade balance, factors which generate an external position that is unsustainable even in the very short run.

Low Growth Scenario

The external reserves of Belarus have fallen to such low levels that a foreign exchange or import crisis could easily develop. For example, with only about a week of net reserves, it could be very difficult to buy the oil and gas needed to provide heating this coming winter. When told that the exchange rate should be devalued because external reserves were falling to unacceptably low levels, some Government officials replied that the country should simply restrain imports to a level consistent with foreign exchange availability—which is exactly what the Government proceeded to do by imposing a prioritization scheme under which potential importers were allowed to buy foreign exchange only if the goods that they proposed to import were deemed to be of sufficiently high priority. The Low Growth scenario presented in this section demonstrates that the strategy that the Government has been pursuing over recent months—the maintenance of an exchange rate that has been kept at unrealistic levels, and the restriction of imports to the level of available export earnings to prevent erosion of net foreign exchange reserves—is clearly unsustainable in the medium term and completely inconsistent with the Government's objective of eliminating poverty and raising living standards.

In countries that are essentially self-sufficient, either because they are very large or because they are very poor, restricting imports to levels consistent with available export earnings can be a viable (though not desirable) strategy. In a country like Belarus, however, such a strategy would create extreme economic difficulties. Trade turnover (exports plus imports) have traditionally been more or less equal to GDP in Belarus. This reflects the deep dependence of the productive sectors on imported raw and intermediate materials, and on export markets for sales. Reducing imports in a country like Belarus will immediately and directly reduce economic growth and exports because farms and factories will not have access to the inputs that they need to continue production. With falling production and limited imports, severe scarcities will also develop in consumer goods markets, leading to a sharp increase in inflationary pressures. These pressures will be exacerbated by the subsidies that the Government and the banking system will find necessary to prevent the collapse and closure of loss-making enterprises that cannot function for lack of imported inputs and export earnings. Inflation will quickly erode living standards, bringing real consumption into line with falling real output. The possible results of this strategy are simulated in Table 5.3.

As the Government continues with its policy of overvalued domestic currency, exports are projected to drop by about ten percent in 1997, with export volume decline continuing throughout the projection period. To prevent the total erosion of net foreign exchange reserves, the authorities would have to cut imports drastically. Total volumes of imports are projected to decline by over 20 percent in 1997, with the brunt of the cuts being borne by consumer and manufactured goods imports from non-CIS countries.

Falling export earnings would reduce the economy's effective demand (as opposed to need) for energy, capital, and intermediate goods. At the same time, the supply of working capital needed

Table 5.3: Low Growth Scenario

Key Indicators	1995	1996	1997	1998	2002
Growth Rates (%)					
GDP	-10.1	2.6	-7.0	-6.0	-3.0
Exports	-6.0	—	-9.5	-7.6	-5.8
Imports	11.0	—	-21.3	-15.4	-9.3
Prices (CPI Inflation)	709.0	52.0	110.3	109.4	305.2
Percent of GDP					
Exports	45.6	38.0	29.3	24.1	7.5
Imports	53.8	51.0	30.9	25.1	7.6
Current Account Balance	-2.5	-9.0	-1.6	-1.2	-0.3
Investment	25.2	24.6	25.2	25.2	25.2
Government Expenditures	32.8	32.8	34.2	35.1	30.4
Government Budget Deficit	-1.9	-5.8	-4.6	-5.1	-6.5
External Debt Indicators					
Gross Annual Borrowing (USDm)	432.0	187.8	580.6	339.3	527.2
Debt Service/Exports (%)	3.6	2.7	3.5	7.0	15.5
Debt/GDP (%)	24.0	7.6	9.8	9.0	4.5
Foreign Direct Investment (USDm)	7.0	19.0	53.2	61.9	0.0
As percentage of GDP	0.1	0.2	0.6	0.6	0.0
Real GDP (1990=100)	62.7	63.6	59.2	55.6	44.2

Source: Official data and World Bank staff calculations.

same time, the supply of working capital needed to sustain production would be severely circumscribed by the external financing constraint. As a result, output is projected to continue to decline at an average rate of three to four percent throughout the projection period. The GDP and exports decline rates are projected to be most acute in 1997, and then to slow down in the outer years of projections as the economy slips into self-sufficiency. The continuing GDP decline over the 1996-2002 period is projected to bring GDP down to only 40 percent of the level at the time of independence, a result that would parallel the experience of Zaire and Zambia between 1980 and 1987.

To keep the external debt position manageable, the authorities would have to keep the current account deficit close to zero throughout the period. The debt service ratio is projected to reach about 17 percent towards the end of the projection period, then decline thereafter as the Government continued to artificially constrain imports, thereby destroying the basis for renewed economic growth.

The Government would seek to keep failing enterprises afloat with budgetary subsidies and directed credit. Consequently, the budget deficit is projected to increase over the period and to reach an unsustainable level of 10 percent of GDP in 2006. Financing the budget deficit and the rapidly growing portfolio of non-performing loans of commercial banks with central bank credit, coupled with increasing scarcities of consumer goods would rekindle high inflation. (CPI increases are projected to reach 300 percent on a year-on-year basis in 2006.) Real private consumption is projected to fall by over 30 percent relative to its 1995 level, bringing about a dramatic deterioration of living standards. Private consumption per capita in constant 1995 prices would drop from USD 513 in 1995 to USD 347 in 2006, thereby increasing the share of families below the poverty line to over 60 percent.

Financing Requirements

The financing requirements for the high debt and low growth scenarios do not need to be discussed in detail here because neither scenario is sustainable. They are presented only to demonstrate the serious problems that would result from a continuation of current government policies. The Policy Reform scenario, however, indicates the financing that will be required if Belarus implements the necessary policy measures and maximizes its economic growth, subject to the constraints of the nation's initial conditions in terms of the physical and financial resources available to it today. This scenario also represents the feasible upper limit of borrowing for the following reasons. First, it assumes optimal economic policy performance, and if policy performance falls below the levels assumed here, Belarus will not be able to attract either the debt or the equity (FDI) financing that has been assumed. If policy performance does fall below the levels assumed here, higher levels of borrowing might be desired in order to sustain consumption and living standards in the absence of good economic performance, but higher levels of borrowing would be neither available nor sustainable. Second, unless Belarus were to attain considerably better export performance than the generous levels assumed in the Policy Reform scenario above, and this is unlikely for a variety of physical reasons, higher levels of borrowing cannot be sustained even in the Policy Reform case. Thus any financing scenario other than that shown for the Policy Reform scenario in Table 5.1 is likely to involve lower levels of borrowing—but if these take place without good economic performance, the debt service indicators will nevertheless be less satisfactory than in the Policy Reform case. The corresponding balance of payments picture is presented in Table 5.4.

Table 5.4: Balance of Payments, 1995-2000
(millions of USD)
Base-case (most likely) projection

	1995	Estimate 1996	Projection 1997	1998	1999	2000	2005
Total exports of GNFS[a]	5235.0	5925.0	5363.7	6264.4	6920.0	7610.9	11691.8
Merchandise (FOB)	4621.0	5264.0	4583.8	5252.2	5789.0	6357.7	9653.2
Nonfactor services	614.0	661.0	779.9	1012.3	1131.0	1253.2	2038.5
Total Imports of GNFS	5501.0	7161.0	5897.0	6716.5	7368.6	8095.6	12091.8
Merchandise (FOB)	5149.0	6919.0	5530.5	6331.2	6950.0	7640.3	11407.9
Nonfactor services	352.0	242.0	366.5	385.3	418.6	455.3	683.9
Resource balance	-266.0	-1236.0	-533.4	-452.1	-448.6	-484.6	-400.1
Net factor income	-65.1	-66.0	-53.9	-98.0	-148.3	-201.5	-537.3
Factor receipts	1.9	0.0	13.1	37.8	61.6	87.8	170.1
Factor payments	67.0	66.0	67.1	135.8	209.9	289.3	707.4
Interest (scheduled)	67.0	66.0	66.2	127.5	187.1	241.6	405.8
Total interest paid [b]	67.0	66.0	66.2	127.5	187.1	241.6	405.8
Net adjustments to scheduled interest	0.0	0.0	0.0	0.0	0.0	0.0	0.0
Other factor payments	0.0	0.0	0.9	8.2	22.9	47.7	301.6
Net private current transfers	-24.7	52.0	59.6	61.1	62.7	64.3	72.2
Current receipts, of which	-53.3	32.0	29.8	30.5	31.3	32.1	36.0
Workers' remittances	28.5	28.0	29.8	30.5	31.3	32.1	36.0
Current payments	-28.6	-20.0	-29.9	-30.6	-31.4	-32.2	-36.1
Net official current transfers	101.8	0.0	0.0	0.0	0.0	0.0	0.0
Current account balance	-254.0	-1250.0	-527.7	-488.9	-534.3	-621.9	-865.2
Official capital grants	7.3	0.0	0.0	0.0	0.0	0.0	0.0
Private investment (net)	7.0	19.0	92.3	182.7	311.1	436.9	840.2
Direct foreign investment	7.0	19.0	92.3	166.1	259.3	349.6	672.1
Portfolio investments	0.0	0.0	0.0	16.6	51.9	87.4	168.0
Net LT[c] borrowing	78.0	-484.0	596.9	529.7	523.0	590.3	433.1
Disbursements[b]	240.0	58.0	684.4	736.2	864.4	1079.4	1200.9
Repayments (scheduled)	113.0	542.0	87.4	206.4	342.4	489.2	767.8
Total principal repaid[b]	113.0	542.0	87.4	206.4	342.4	489.2	767.8
Net adjustments to scheduled repayments	0.0	0.0	0.0	0.0	0.0	0.0	0.0
Net other LT inflows	-49.0	0.0	0.0	0.0	1.0	0.0	0.0
Other capital flows	-50.3	1437.0	150.0	0.0	0.0	0.0	0.0
Net short-term capital	10.0	0.0	0.0	0.0	0.0	0.0	0.0
Net capital flows n.e.i.[d]	-101.0	451.0	150.0	0.0	0.0	0.0	0.0
Errors and omissions	40.7	986.0	0.0	0.0	0.0	0.0	0.0
Change in net international reserves	212.0	278.0	-311.6	-223.5	-299.8	-405.4	-408.1
(- indicates increase in assets)							
Memorandum items							
Total gross reserves, of which	377.0	469.0	745.5	1142.1	1578.9	2096.2	3199.8
Total reserves minus gold	377.0	469.0	745.5	1142.0	1578.9	2096.2	3199.8
Gold (at year-end London price)	0.0	0.0	0.0	0.0	0.0	0.0	0.0
Total gross reserves (in months' imports G&S[e])	0.8	0.9	1.5	2.0	2.5	3.0	3.0
Exchange rates							
Annual average (LCU/US$)[f]	11525.0	15458.0	27660.0	41490.0	46549.8	46317.0	61667.7
At end year (LCU/US$)	11500.0	15500.0	34575.0	44019.9	46433.4	46201.2	64021.0
Index real average exchange rate (1995 =1)	1.00	0.72	0.98	1.21	1.21	1.12	..
Current Account Balance as % GDP	-2.5	-9.0	-5.1	-5.3	-5.4	-5.3	-4.6

a. Goods and nonfactor services.
b. Historical data from Debt Reporting System (DRS); other data projected by country operations division staff.
c. "LT" denotes "long-term."
d. "n.e.i." denotes "not elsewhere included."
e. "G & S" denotes "goods and services."
f. "LCU" denotes "local currency units."
g. The index of the real exchange rate reflects US$/LCU, so an increase is an appreciation at the real exchange rate.
Sources: Actual data for 1995 and estimates for 1996 are IMF staff calculations. Others are Bank staff projections.

C. KEY THEMES AND CONCLUSIONS

The analysis presented in this report has led to the following important conclusions, which were developed in the preceding chapters.

- First, a return to the past is not feasible. The previous system, to which many people in Belarus would still like to return because of the many benefits they enjoyed, collapsed because the system was intrinsically inefficient. It tried to allocate resources based on decisions made by a relatively small group of Government administrators based on a variety of economic, social and political considerations. This system, despite its high ideals, cannot compete in the real world with economic systems where resources are allocated to maximize profits and consumer welfare is based on the individual decisions of those most directly affected.

- Second, the inefficiency by world standards of Belarusian enterprises today, particularly those in industry and agriculture, is the main source of the country's economic decline and poverty.

- Third, this inefficiency can only be overcome by creating the competitive, efficient product and factor markets and the profit-maximizing production systems in Belarus that exist in Europe and elsewhere in the industrialized world.

- Fourth, substantial investments will be required to physically transform the production sector in Belarus, and this level of investment can only be attained if Belarus creates (a) an investment climate that attracts private investment from both domestic and foreign sources, and (b) a market-driven incentives framework that ensures efficient production and sales decisions.

- Fifth, these goals cannot be reached in a system where the majority of production activities are still controlled by the state. Attempting this would simply perpetuate the problems of the past. Consequently, privatization, which has moved very slowly to date, must be accelerated dramatically to assure appropriate incentives for and focus on profit-maximizing behavior of managers within a market-oriented environment such as exists in all successful industrialized countries.

- Sixth, hard budget constraints—rules that force enterprises to spend no more than they earn or can responsibly borrow—must be imposed to control inflation and to provide the incentives that will lead to spontaneous, efficiency-oriented privatization and production decisions.

- Seventh, the transition process will involve hardships for those who must leave their present jobs and look for new ones. The social safety net needs to be focused on protecting these workers and their families while, at the same time, maintaining their incentive to find new, more productive jobs.

Notes

1. Easterly, William and Stanley D. Fischer, 1994. "The Soviet Economic Decline," The World Bank Economic Review 9(3): 341-71.

2. This report is based primarily on data and information collected largely in mid-1996. Where possible, key indicators have been updated through the end of 1996. Although some data were somewhat out of date at time of publication, the situation had not changed materially in terms of the nature of the economic problems facing Belarus, and almost all of the recommendations were still fully relevant at the time of final revision of the published version in mid-April 1997.

3. The emphasis here is on manufacturing enterprises. The Belarusian authorities already accept that most sales and service enterprises should be in the private sector, and even in relatively industrialized countries, public utilities and mass transit services are often provided by public enterprises because of the problems of economies of scale and the risk of non-competitive market structures.

4. Trade data from the period do not adequately reflect the benefits derived by Belarus under the Soviet system. For example, the trade data for 1990 indicate a commodity trade surplus of close to RUR 2.4 billion, indicating that Belarus was effectively a capital exporter. However, if the trade is revalued at world prices, adjusting in particular for the artificially low price of energy supplies, Belarus had a trade deficit of RUR 1.2 billion. In other words, through the artificial pricing of this period, Belarus enjoyed a net gain in commodity trading of RUR 3.6 billion, the equivalent of 9 percent of GDP. (Zlotnikov, 1996).

5. The data on credit available to industry in 1990 make its position look more favored than it actually was. Much of the "credit" available to industry at this time could not be spent. It was just part of the "monetary overhang" that built up in the banking system towards the end of the Soviet era because administrative controls had prevented prices from rising to equilibrate the supply of money with the supply of investment and other goods in the Soviet economy.

6. This system will work only if hard budget constraints and financial discipline are applied to all enterprises equally. Otherwise, enterprises that are desperate for money will be willing to pay exorbitant rates of interest knowing that, in the end, they will probably not be forced to repay the loan. The same caveat applies if interest rates charged by commercial banks are decontrolled.

7. Bruno, Michael, and William Easterly. 1995. "Inflation Crises and Long-run Growth." Washington, DC: The World Bank (processed).

8. The problem centers on the procedure for converting current price output data to constant prices. The methodology currently in use produces a constant or comparable price series for industrial production that, in each year since the early 1990s, has shown a rising trend throughout each year, with a particularly large surge in the last two or three months of the year, followed by a major contraction between December and January. This pattern of year-end surges became increasingly exaggerated in 1992-94 with higher rates of inflation, which tends to confirm that the flaw in the methodology relates to the treatment of prices. For an alternative approach to calculating the real growth of industrial output in Belarus, see *Belarus Economic Trends*, August 1996, Table 6.1.

9. Many Belarusians believe that the economic crisis has already been so severe that the economy could not possibly decline further. Unfortunately, evidence from other countries demonstrates that the economy of Belarus will probably continue to decline absolutely, or at least relatively to other countries, unless serious structural reforms are initiated. Argentina is an excellent case in point. In the early part of this century, Argentina was a prosperous nation of well-educated people having a per capita income similar to that in the United States. However, a combination of extensive state ownership of production, control-oriented government policies, non-transparent rules of business conduct and taxation, populist wage and expenditure policies, and an increasingly inward-oriented trade policy led to inflation and economic decline. By the early 1990s, Argentina's per capita income was only about one tenth that of Canada. The parallels to the current situation in Belarus are extremely

clear. Since 1990, Argentina has begun implementing measures consistent with those recommended in the present report. Hopefully, Belarus will do the same without first going through years of economic stagnation and falling living standards.

10. Easterly and Fischer, 1994.

11. "East" and "West" are used as short-hand terms for the CIS and non-CIS markets respectively. Russia dominates trade with the East, accounting for 80-90 percent of such trade. Trade with the West is more diversified, but Germany is the leading partner, accounting for about one fourth of Belarusian imports and about one seventh of its exports to the rest of the world.

12. The dollar equivalent prices of goods traded with Russia and other CIS countries were artificially low in the early days of independence. Since then, unit prices in dollars for a wide range of important products have increased considerably faster than world dollar prices on average. This welcome convergence with world market prices, however, has important implications for the valuation and assessment of trends in the real volume of Belarusian exports to these markets. Because aggregate import and export price index data do not exist for Belarus, dollar equivalent values for trade are commonly used as a proxy for volumetric data. However, if the dollar prices for trade with Russia are deflated to take account of the sharp increase in the dollar prices of goods moving in this market over the past few years, it becomes apparent that Belarusian exports have fallen more seriously than previously reported. For example, between 1993 and 1995 the nominal dollar value of exports increased by 140 percent, but the constant dollar value of these exports, indicating actual physical volumes, decreased by over 50 percent (Zlotnikov 1996, Tables 1 and 10).

13. Real exchange rate appreciation occurs when domestic inflation, which reduces the purchasing power of a unit of domestic currency, is not offset by an exchange rate adjustment. For example, if domestic prices increased by 10 percent, and there was no inflation in world prices, the exchange rate would have to be devalued by 10 percent to maintain competitiveness unless other factors, such as increasing productivity or the ability to accept lower profits on exports, compensated for the domestic inflation. The real exchange rate, in its most straightforward form, is calculated by dividing the nominal exchange rate

by the ratio of domestic to world inflation. The result is usually then expressed in index number form, setting the index to 100 at some point in time (January 1993, for example). Unfortunately, the economics profession has not agreed on whether world prices or domestic prices should go into the numerator when calculating the real exchange rate. Depending on the choice made, a rising line can show either real exchange rate appreciation or real exchange rate devaluation. The convention adopted here is that real appreciation or *rising real purchasing power* of the domestic currency in international trade is shown with a *rising line*.

14. Wage rates in Russia now exceed those in Belarus, but this reflects special conditions. The higher dollar wages in Russia are linked to rising levels of production and to a strong balance of payments position that is supported by energy exports for dollars in western markets. The higher purchasing power of wages in dollars is thus matched by export earnings in dollars.

15. The Belarusian rubel has also appreciated against the RUR, but to a much lesser extent than against the USD, the DEM and other hard currencies. Consequently, the real appreciation of the trade-weighted exchange rate, in which trade with Russia has a weight of about 50 percent, is significantly lower than the real appreciation against the USD as shown in the charts presented here. The lower appreciation of the BYR versus the RUR as compared to the USD reflects the fact that the RUR has also been appreciating in real terms. This has been less of a problem for Russian than for Belarus, however, because with its strong natural resource base, including exportable quantities of oil and gas, the Russian balance of payments situation is more sustainable than is the case in Belarus. Belarus needs to establish and keep an exchange rate that is competitive in all of its markets, not just with respect to the West. Adjustments of the exchange rate against the dollar are much easier to monitor and interpret than adjustments against the RUR because of the greater stability of absolute and relative prices on international as opposed to FSU markets, and adjustments in BYR/USD exchange rates will automatically produce parallel changes in the BYR/RUR exchange rates because of the opportunities for arbitrage.

16. If Belarus chooses to devalue its currency, this means that it has rejected the even more painful and probably harmful option of creating a

depression that will drive domestic prices and wages down until they are consistent with the current exchange rate. Given the size of adjustment in relative prices that is needed, together with the fact that Belarus is already in a severe depression, the price reduction approach must be rejected, leaving devaluation as the only feasible alternative.

17. The reader may think that there is a fundamental inconsistency in this paragraph. On the one hand it speaks of restoring balances by reducing domestic prices. On the other hand it says that the necessary balance can be restored by raising prices in the domestic market. The apparent inconsistency is easily resolved and centers on the presence or absence of a devaluation. The underlying problem is to reduce purchasing power and thus aggregate demand. This can be done directly by reducing nominal wages, in which case there is no inflation; in fact, prices would be reduced under this approach. Aggregate demand can also be reduced by reducing the purchasing power of the nominal wages through inflation. However, unlike the situation with a deflationary solution to the problem, the inflationary solution requires a substantial devaluation at the same time, thereby establishing a sustainable balance between domestic and foreign (or better non-traded and traded) prices. Devaluation is the only way, in the inflation-based approach, to assure appropriate prices for imported goods relative to those for domestic goods, thereby assuring that the purchasing power of workers is reduced for imported as well as for domestic goods. (A key problem during 1995 in Belarus was that the fixed exchange rate plus rising wages actually expanded aggregate demand rather than contracting it.)

18. Government of Belarus. 1996. *The Major Trends of Social and Economic Development of the Republic of Belarus for 1996-2000.*

19. Minor distortions can of course be absorbed by any healthy economy without creating serious problems. However, minor distortions are usually not sufficient to attain the degree of support for the poor that is needed. As a result, the distortions sooner or later are increased to the point that they causes the system to break down.

20. These figures seriously understate the true level of losses. The Soviet accounting system still used by most enterprises does not take inflation and the cost of replacing inputs into account, and a number of business costs such as marketing expenses are not counted until after profits have been calculated.

21. Sberbank/Belarusbank, Promstroibank, Agroprombank, Belbusinesbank, Priorbank, and Vnesheconombank.

22. In these years, revenues of the State Budget (excluding social funds and extrabudgetary funds) were 35 percent and 30 percent respectively.

23. Under full cost recovery, the share of each of these items in the total during the winter would be as follows: heating (36%), electricity (15%), rent (13%), and hot water (13%). Source: Ministry of Housing and Communal Services, as reported in IMF, *Recent Economic Developments 1995*, Table 74.

24. The Anti-Monopoly Ministry was abolished in the summer of 1996, but the new Ministry of Entrepreneurship will continue the anti-monopoly work of the former ministry in addition to working on the development of private entrepreneurship.

25. For example, based on the assets of 128 marketing conglomerates and trusts, about 1,200 independent economic entities had been set up by the end of 1996. As a result of work during 1996, 25 trade and public catering companies out of 54 that were under control as monopolistic entities lost their dominating position and were stricken off the State Register of dominating companies.

26. As a result of anti-monopoly efforts, a reasonably competitive environment has been established in housing construction in all regions except Minsk, where the Minsk Leased Company of Industrialized House Building remains a monopolist. To help remedy this problem, the Program of Demonopolizing the Belarusian Economy for 1996-97 envisages (a) improving a system of compulsory open bidding in the construction sector, and tenders for all construction works; (b) facilitating the development of a market infrastructure for contractors; (c) creating leasing, consulting and other firms; and (d) providing services to the construction sector.

27. U.S. Dept. of Commerce, 1992. *Statistical Abstract of the United States, 1992.* Tables 826 and 849.

28. For example, the survey of exporters noted above found that, other than excessive taxation, the most important problem restraining the

development of exports was the "unstable legislative and regulatory environment" in Belarus.

29. Examples of this are the recent Chernobyl tax modification, which was applied retroactively, and the taxes on turnover for the Road, Agricultural Protection, and Housing extra-budgetary funds, which were also applied with retroactive effect.

30. For example, enterprises may be exempted from the payment of VAT and other taxes for a variety of reasons at the discretion of the Government; imports may be subject to differential rates—or even exempted entirely from duties as in the TorgExpo case—depending on the discretion of various government officials; certain expenditures may or may not be allowed as capital investments, which can have a major impact on future tax liabilities; certain expenses, such as those for marketing, may not even be allowed as costs but must be paid for out of profits, depending on the judgment of the tax inspector.

31. For example, a major international soft drink company wants to purchase land near Minsk to set up a bottling plant, but permission to purchase land can only be obtained by special application to the Supreme Soviet. At time of writing, the decision is still being debated in the parliamentary body.

32. The international literature on reducing corruption in government indicates that most corruption arises because governments create "rent-seeking" opportunities—situations where government officials are given the right to approve or reject private applications for special privileges. The risk of corruption is especially great when the decision-making is not based on a transparent, competitive process, such as auctions.

33. One argument for retaining import duties is that they provide a low cost, reliable basis for revenue generation, particularly in economies where tax administration systems are weak and officials are not accustomed to dealing with a growing number of enterprises not directly owned and controlled by the government.

34. The "levy for fire service upkeep" is based on "0.005% of the value of production and non-production assets, stock of goods and valuables of the objects of mentioned purposes, located in the Republic, taking into account adjusted ratios."

The 1997 State Budget of the Republic of Belarus envisages both the abolition of payments to the fund for maintenance of fire brigades and a reduction in the rate of the Emergency Chernobyl tax.

35. The Government recognizes the desirability of moving to the world-standard destination form of VAT but rightly notes that agreement must first be reached with Russia, which so far is only applying the destination principle in its trade with Ukraine. WTO has requested that Russia switch to the destination principle. The Government also sees the lack of a customs border with Russia as a problem for good management of the VAT in cross-border trade; although this problem is handled among the highly-developed countries in the European Union, this would be a further argument for moving to a free trade area relationship with Russia at this time.

36. The State Fund to Support Exporters has now been eliminated.

37. The 1997 State Budget proposes to eliminate most extrabudgetary funds other than the State Employment Fund and the Social Protection Fund which, according to international practice, will continue to be kept separate because they are essentially insurance rather than current expenditure programs. It appears that the Government plans to keep the extra-budgetary fund to support agricultural producers, but this fund may at least be integrated with the budget during the course of the year.

38. A full definition and defense of the role of government proposed here is beyond the scope of this report, but will form a central focus of the dialogue which is anticipated in connection with the proposed Public Expenditure Review for Belarus.

39. This report follows the Belarusian convention of distinguishing between "republican" enterprises, which were under the control of ministries at the level of the Republic of Belarus, and "communal" enterprises, which were owned by governments at the oblast and municipal levels. Republican enterprises are usually medium- and large-scale manufacturing and infrastructure operations, while communal enterprises are generally small-scale operations such as shops and small processing plants.

40. Any data on the profits of enterprises in Belarus should be treated with great caution, since profitability is consistently overstated under the

Soviet style accounting system that is still used by most enterprises in Belarus. First, the system does not allow for taking into account the impact of inflation on the cost of purchasing replacements for material inputs used in production, a serious problem given the triple-digit rates of inflation that have prevailed until recently in Belarus. On the other hand, certain expenses, generally related to marketing, cannot be subtracted as working expenses but must be paid out of profits, thus reducing the measure of profits.

41. World Bank survey of 14 state enterprises, 1994.

42. The positive net worth shown in Figure 3.2 is probably overstated because of asset over-valuation.

43. The universe of enterprises varies according to data source. MinStat reported 4,812 republican and 8,906 communal enterprises as of January 1996. However, the Tax Department reported 8,687 republican and 10,050 municipal enterprises.

44. Registration of new and existing enterprises has now resumed. It is not going smoothly, however, for several reasons: (a) the local offices responsible are not adequately staffed, so long queues form, wasting hours of valuable time for the entrepreneurs and investors; (b) the national and local authorities have not adequately defined the requirements for registration (e.g. copies of leases on premises required); and (c) they do not have adequate programs of public information so that entrepreneurs can know the requirements in advance, collect all required information, and handle the entire process in one trip. In addition to wasting time that should be spent on increasing output and helping Belarus grow, the combination of long lines and non-transparent regulations creates a breeding ground for corruption. These problems could all be solved rather easily by reducing, clarifying, and announcing the detailed requirements for (re)registration in advance.

45. Such actions are strictly illegal, however, and the Anti-Monopoly authorities make every effort to detect, punish and prevent such activity. In 1996, for example, 289 cases were inspected for compliance with anti-monopoly regulations. Some cases were initiated on the basis of complaints received, and others were initiated by the Anti-Monopoly Ministry. As a result of this work, 56 violations were exposed, and 45 orders were issued by the Anti-Monopoly Ministry to assure restoration of fair practices. These cases included an injunction against the Polotsk Executive Council, which had issued a resolution making it mandatory for companies selling alcoholic beverages to limit sales of vodka only to vodka produced by the Polotsk wine-making factory, and an injunction against the Ministry of Health, which had given the state enterprises Belbiopharm, BelPRO "Pharmacia," and OPO "Pharmacia" the right to control the issue of permits to others to import medicines and pharmaceutical substances.

46. From an economics perspective, a "social" service or good is commonly regarded as one (like public health, sanitation, or public safety) that has significant externalities that benefit society at large, and which the private sector would not supply in optimal amounts without government support given the difficulty of charging individual beneficiaries. The most costly "social assets" in transition economies —housing and public utilities—are in fact goods and services which individuals pay for in normal market economies and which are usually provided largely if not entirely by private enterprises.

47. See Simon Commander and Richard Jackman, "Providing Social Benefits in Russia: Redefining the Roles of Firms and Government." Policy Research Working Paper WPS 1184, Economic Development Institute, The World Bank, 1993.

48. It has been estimated, for example, that a quarter of all unemployment in 1992 in Poland was due to limitations on labor mobility caused by lack of housing. See Fabrizio Coricelli, Krysztof Hagemejer and Krysztof Rybinski, "Poland," in Simon Commander and Fabrizio Coricelli (eds), Unemployment, Restructuring, and the Labor Market in Eastern Europe and Russia, EDI Development Studies, Washington, DC, The World Bank, 1995, p. 74.

49. All references to "poverty" and "poverty rates" in this paper refer to the percentage of households with less than the minimum level of income in cash and in kind that, given the household's composition (number, age and gender), is needed to provide the minimum acceptable level of nutrients and other necessities of life.

50. A network of business promotion centers is now being established in Belarus, and a pilot business incubator is being established in Gomel.

51. These figures are based on a poverty assessment done in 1996 by the World Bank in collaboration with the Government of Belarus. Official data from the Ministry of Statistics are based on a slightly different methodology and, as a result, the poverty impact figures vary by a few percentage points from those shown here, but the two sets of numbers are very close and show a completely consistent story.

52. Unlike the poverty line used by the Government, the World Bank's poverty line is differentiated according to family size and structure, making it more accurate in its measurement of the incidence of poverty. However, for the average family, the poverty line used by the World Bank is very close to that defined by the Government, which it takes as 60 percent of the minimum consumer budget.

53. If we look not just at the families who were in poverty for a single quarter, but rather at those who were on average in poverty throughout the year, we find that the percentage of families defined as poor drops from 36 percent to 22 percent.

54. Housing market flexibility can be improved by a variety of measures such as eliminating legal barriers to sub-leasing apartments, to renting out rooms, and to the entry of private real estate developers who can rehabilitate existing housing and build new housing. Governments can also facilitate housing market development by improving privatization programs, creating the conditions needed to establish an active housing mortgage market, facilitating the access of real estate developers to land served by basic utilities such as water and electricity, and establishing a transparent process for obtaining building permits.

55. Choosing an appropriate strategy and reform plan will require careful analysis of a wide range of options, and development of appropriate transition strategies. A public pillar, in theory, could have the objective of limiting old age poverty and redistributing income to the poor, while a mandatory, fully funded and privately managed pillar could encourage lifetime savings and smooth the level of individual income over one's lifetime, while also supporting financial market development. Appropriately regulated private savings plans would complement these pillars. There are a variety of models—the public pillar could link contributions to benefits by channeling taxes to individualized personal accounts, which would serve as the basis for setting an actuarially fair pension at retirement, or could consist of a social assistance benefit along with a mandatory, privately managed second pillar. Given the current state of the Belarusian legal and regulatory environment, as well as complex transitional issues, it will be important not to rush into any one model, but to (a) determine the appropriate longer-term objective for reforming the social insurance system; and (b) develop a strategy for getting there. For a good overview of the underlying issues, see World Bank, Averting the Old Age Crisis—Policies to Protect the Old and Promote Growth. (Oxford: Oxford University Press, 1994.)

References

Bruno, Michael 1996a. "Why crises can be good for growth." *DEC Notes - Research Findings*. Washington, D.C.: The World Bank.

_____. 1996b. "Deep Crises and Reform: What Have We Learned?" *Directions in Development*. Washington, D.C.: The World Bank.

Bruno, Michael, and William Easterly. 1995a. "Could Inflation Stabilization be Expansionary?" *Transition* 6:7-8, pp 1-3.

_____. 1996. "Inflation's Children: Tales of Crises That Beget Reforms." *American Economic Review* 86(2):213-17.

de Melo, Martha, Cevdet Denizer and Alan Gelb. "From Plan to Market: Patterns of Transition." Washington, D.C.: The World Bank.

Easterly, William. 1996. "When is Stabilization Expansionary?" *Economic Policy*, April 1996.

Easterly, William and Stanley D. Fischer. 1994. "The Soviet Economic Decline," *The World Bank Economic Review* 9(3): 341-71.

EBRD (European Bank for Reconstruction and Development). 1994. *Transition Report* 1994. London.

_____. 1995. *Transition Report 1995: Investment and Enterprise Development*. London.

EuroMoney. 1996. "Country Risk: Asia's Economies Start To Slip," September, pp. 200-205.

Government of Belarus Statistics. 1996. *Expenditures and income of the population in the Republic of Belarus (household sample survey) 1995*. Minsk.

Gwartney, James, Robert Lawson and Walter Block. 1996. *Economic Freedom of the World: 1975-1995*. Washington, D.C.: Caito Institute and others.

IMF. 1995. "Using Exchange Rate anchors in Adjustment Programs: When and How?" *IMF Survey*. November 20, 1995.

Institutional Investor, December 12, 1995.

Johnson, Bryan T. and Thomas P. Sheehy. 1996. *1996 Index of Economic Freedom*. Heritage Foundation, Washington, DC.

Kaufmann, Daniel. 1994. "Diminishing Returns to Administrative Controls and the Emergence of the Unofficial Economy." Kiev: The World Bank.

Kiguel, Miguel A. and Nita Ghei. 1993. *Devaluation in Low-Inflation Economies,* (Policy Research Working Paper 1224). Washington, D.C.: The World Bank.

Lipton, David and Jeffrey Sachs. 1990. "Creating a Market Economy in Eastern Europe: The Case of Poland," *Brookings Papers on Economic Activity* 1:1990.

Mansur, Ahsan Habab. 1984. "Determining the Appropriate Exchange Rate in LDCs," *Finance & Development*. December 1984, pp. 18-21.

McAuley, Alastair. 1991. "The Economic Consequences of Soviet Disintegration," *Soviet Economy* 1991:7:3, pp. 189-214.

Wells, Louis T. Jr. and Alvin G. Wint. 1991. *Facilitating Foreign Investment: Government Institutions to Screen, Monitor, and Service Investment from Abroad.* Washington, D.C.: Foreign Investment Advisory Service (FIAS), Occasional Paper 2.

World Bank. 1996. *From Plan to Market.* World Development Report 1996. New York: Oxford University Press.

Statistical Appendix

STATISTICAL APPENDIX

Table 1.1 - Labor Market Indicators
(In thousands of persons)

	1992	1993	1994	1995	1996 Q1
Employment	4,887	4,824	4,696	4,405	4,005 [1]
Job leavers	829	705	721	779	172
Jobs taken up	678	628	551	585	142
Activity of the Employment Bureau					
Applications from job seekers	196	185	205	231	82
Placements	86	97	106	119	24
Unemployed					
Officially recognized	24	66	101	131	166
Of which:					
Benefit recipients	20	35	52	69	88
Memorandum items:					
Vacancies	18	13	18	11	12
Unemployed [2]					
Officially recognized (%) [3]	0.5	1.4	2.1	2.7	3.5
Of which:					
Benefit recipients	0.4	0.7	1.1	1.5	1.9

[1] Quarterly for large and medium sized enterprises.

[2] The definition of unemployment was widened effective January 1993.

[3] The unemployment rate is calculated as registered unemployed as a percentage of employed plus registered unemployed.

Sources: Data provided by the Belarussian authorities; and IMF staff calculations.

Table 1.2 - Average Employment by Sector

	1991	1992	1993	1994	1995	1996 Q1	1992	1993	1994	1995	1996 Q1
	(In thousands)						(Percentage change on year earlier)				
Annual survey 1/	**5,020**	**4,887**	**4,824**	**4,696**	**4,405**	**4,005**	**-2.6**	**-1.3**	**-2.7**	**-6.2**	**-9.1**
Monthly survey 2/	**4,646**	**4,469**	**4,318**	**4,124**	**3,812**	**3,625**	**-3.8**	**-3.4**	**-4.5**	**-7.6**	**-4.9**
Industry	1,495	1,433	1,366	1,294	1,160	1,093	-4.1	-4.7	-5.3	-10.4	-5.8
Agriculture 3/	1,035	990	940	882	803	710	-4.3	-5.1	-6.2	-9.0	-11.6
Construction	408	385	374	336	278	242	-5.6	-2.9	-10.2	-17.3	-12.9
Transport and communication	343	332	308	297	279	275	-3.2	-7.2	-3.6	-6.1	-1.4
Trade and related services 4/	310	287	270	253	223	212	-7.4	-5.9	-6.3	-11.9	-4.9
Communal services 4/	105	106	101	104	110	122	1.0	-4.7	3.0	5.8	10.9
Health and social services	244	247	255	261	260	262	1.2	3.2	2.4	-0.4	0.8
Education, culture, science	487	475	463	466	461	467	-2.5	-2.5	0.6	-1.1	1.3
Banks and insurance	29	31	33	39	44	46	6.9	6.5	18.2	12.8	4.5
Administration 4/	57	60	66	70	73	74	5.3	10.0	6.1	4.3	1.4
Other 4/	133	123	142	122	121	122	-7.5	15.4	-14.1	-0.8	0.8

	1991	1992	1993	1994	1995	1996 Q1
	(Share in total) 2/					
Monthly survey	100.0	100.0	100.0	100.0	100.0	100.0
Industry	32.2	32.1	31.6	31.4	30.4	30.2
Agriculture	22.3	22.2	21.8	21.4	21.1	19.6
Construction	8.8	8.6	8.7	8.1	7.3	6.7
Transport and communication	7.4	7.4	7.1	7.2	7.3	7.6
Trade and related services 4/	6.7	6.4	6.3	6.1	5.8	5.8
Communal services 4/	2.3	2.4	2.3	2.5	2.9	3.4
Health and social services	5.3	5.5	5.9	6.3	6.8	7.2
Education, culture, science	10.5	10.6	10.7	11.3	12.1	12.9
Banks and insurance	0.6	0.7	0.8	0.9	1.2	1.3
Administration 4/	1.2	1.3	1.5	1.7	1.9	2.0
Other 4/	2.9	2.8	3.3	3.0	3.2	3.4

	1991	1992	1993	1994	1995
	(In percent)				
Memorandum items:					
Labor force participation rate 5/	52	50.3	49.8	48.6	45.9
Labor force as share of working age population	93.6	90.7	89.9	87.5	82.4
Share of woman in the labor force	54.4	53.6	53.5	53.9	54.5

1/ Based on comprehensive annual survey data that include small enterprises.
2/ Based on monthly survey data, which accounted for approximately 91 percent of the employment covered by the annual survey in 1993.
3/ Approximately two thirds from collective farms.
4/ Data for 1993 through 1995 reflect reclassification from January 1993 on.
5/ Labor force participation rate defined as employed and registered unemployed in percent of total population.
6/ Excluding kolkhozes.

Source: Ministry of Statistics and Analysis.

Table 2.1 - Gross Domestic Product by Sectors and Expenditures at Current Prices
(millions of BRub)

	1990	1991	1992	1993	1994	1995
By Sector						
Agriculture and forestry	**9,883**	**17,438**	**207,460**	**1,690,248**	**2,417,790**	**14,268,542**
Agriculture	9824	17285	204635	1642660	2,324,443	13,422,496
Forestry	59	153	2825	47588	93,347	846,046
Industry and construction	**19,598**	**41,027**	**398,417**	**3,697,738**	**5,904,773**	**36,978,369**
Industry	16,251	34,523	334,683	2,931,627	4,851,800	30,396,015
Construction	3,347	6,504	63,734	766,111	1,052,973	6,582,354
Other	**12,121**	**23,943**	**263,719**	**3,777,108**	**7,664,715**	**55,643,991**
Transport	2,348	3,735	66,362	937,909	1,750,842	12,565,229
Road maintenance	..	..	..	..	..	..
Communication	427	733	6,879	109,010	202,474	2,072,506
Wholesale trade	..	..	..	..	..	..
Retail trade and catering	1,490	4,006	44,842	864,614	1,798,071	10,972,272
Material supply	376	836	10,508	169,504	743,801	3,587,518
Procurement	149	462	5,220	74,879	87,064	381,505
Information and computing services	103	155	769	13,370	17,545	168,681
Other sectors of material production	296	535	3,435	44,241	81,986	811,028
Housing	654	1,028	9,856	141,751	296,370	4,321,108
Public utilities and personal services	903	1,633	26,950	285,807	582,347	6,297,455
Health care, social security, and sports	925	2,260	26,473	321,923	525,268	4,077,162
Education	877	2,367	29,888	399,834	598,144	5,278,923
Culture and art	217	402	6,440	70,599	76,041	550,204
Science and research	1,297	2,110	6,971	75,975	140,552	1,187,373
Credit	139	1,226	14,252	870,227	1,324,543	5,012,694
Insurance	37	62	686	12,175	15,433	157,870
General administration and defense	1,797	3,485	18,858	229,727	616,441	3,968,008
Private nonprofit institutions	86	244	1,126	10,605	14,467	118,531
Financial intermediaries, imp. chrg.	..	-1,336	-15,796	-855,042	-1,206,674	-5,884,076
Total gross value added 1/	**41,602**	**82,408**	**869,596**	**9,165,094**	**15,987,278**	**106,890,902**
Net Taxes on production and imports	2,582	4,243	74,136	962,925	2,146,716	16,418,538
Taxes on production and imports	9,745	11,491	176,953	1,985,513	3,253,013	19,941,707
Subsidies on production and imports	7,163	7,248	102,817	1,022,588	1,106,297	3,523,169
Total GDP at factor cost	**40,151**	**81,663**	**839,826**	**8,812,903**	**15,514,600**	**102,103,082**
Net Indirect taxes	2,582	4,243	74,136	962,925	2,146,716	16,418,538
Total GDP at market prices	**42,733**	**85,906**	**913,962**	**9,775,828**	**17,661,316**	**118,521,620**
By Expenditure Category						
Gross Domestic Expenditure	**42,733**	**85,906**	**913,962**	**9,775,828**	**17,661,316**	**118,521,620**
Consumption	**30,265**	**57,657**	**605,449**	**7,680,865**	**14,897,526**	**94,313,718**
Private consumption	18,657	35,917	419,958	5,299,241	9,987,894	59,905,270
Government consumption	10,160	18,174	146,200	1,920,726	3,766,773	25,961,638
Non-Profits	1,448	3,566	39,291	460,898	1,142,859	8,446,810
Gross domestic investment	**11,508**	**25,269**	**295,134**	**3,752,603**	**5,107,838**	**29,818,540**
Gross fixed investment	9,533	19,267	234,626	3,049,591	5,165,515	29,789,525
Change in stocks	1,975	6,002	60,508	703,012	-57,677	29,015
Resource balance (net export GNFS)	**960**	**2,980**	**13,379**	**-1,657,640**	**-2,344,048**	**-5,610,638**
Exports of goods and NFS	19,889	32,070	548,035	6,514,670	12,644,222	50,646,122
Imports of goods and NFS	18,929	29,090	534,656	8,172,310	14,988,270	56,256,760

..: Data not available.

Note: The table uses consistent currency from 1990 to 1995.
1/ In 1990-93, this line includes "Other taxes on production".

Table 2.2 - Gross Domestic Product by Sectors and Expenditures at Comparable Prices
(millions of 1990 BRub)

	1990	1991	1992	1993	1994	1995
Sector of Origin						
Agriculture and forestry	**9,883**	**9,567**	**8,186**	**7,334**	**6,213**	**5,744**
Agriculture	9,824	9,504	8,126	7,267	6,155	5,688
Forestry	59	61	57	58	58	56
Industry and construction	**19,598**	**19,762**	**18,676**	**16,485**	**13,206**	**11,459**
Industry	16,251	16,419	15,571	13,930	11,297	10,100
Construction	3,347	3,343	3,105	2,556	1,909	1,359
Services	**12,121**	**11,636**	**10,042**	**9,198**	**9,198**	**8,600**
Transport	2,348	2,335	1,875	1,524	1,173	1,044
Communication	427	310	225	178	172	149
Retail trade and catering	1,490	1,425	1,183	1,028	939	704
Material supply	376	402	343	309	547	484
Procurement	149	129	109	97	79	60
Housing	654	670	699	708	712	708
Public utilities and personal services	903	893	809	802	773	710
Health care, social security, etc.	925	931	940	959	973	994
Education	877	883	868	841	841	862
Culture 1/	1,514	1,500	1,150	930	814	737
Credit and Insurance 2/	37	39	41	46	58	68
General administration and defense	1,797	1,560	1,107	1,038	968	956
Financial intermediaries, imp.. chrg.2/	624	560	693	739	1,149	1,125
Total gross value added 3/	**41,602**	**40,969**	**36,831**	**32,853**	**28,516**	**25,322**
Total GDP at factor cost	**40,151**	**40,969**	**37,132**	**33,549**	**29,469**	**26,532**
Net Indirect taxes	2,582	1,251	1,035	572	353	278
Total GDP at market prices	**42,733**	**42,220**	**38,167**	**34,121**	**29,822**	**26,810**
Expenditure Category						
Consumption	28,817	26,915	24,143	23,250	20,739	17,317
Private consumption	18,657	17,407	16,025	15,778	13,490	10,266
Government consumption	10,160	9,373	7,935	7,102	6,889	6,765
Gross domestic investment	11,508	13,267	11,190	9,894	6,580	4,862
Gross fixed investment	9,533	9,956	8,155	6,896	5,710	4,168
Change in stocks	1,975	3,311	3,035	2,998	..	..

..: Data not available.

1/ Culture, art, science and research;

2/ Preliminary estimates;

3/ In 1990-93, this line includes "Other taxes on production".

Table 2.3 - Structure of Gross Domestic Product at Current Prices
(Percentage Distribution)

	1990	1991	1992	1993	1994	1995
Sector of Origin						
Agriculture and forestry	**23.1**	**20.3**	**22.7**	**17.3**	**13.7**	**12.0**
Agriculture	23.0	20.1	22.4	16.8	13.2	11.3
Forestry	0.1	0.2	0.3	0.5	0.5	0.7
Industry and construction	**45.9**	**47.8**	**43.6**	**37.8**	**33.4**	**31.2**
Industry	38.0	40.2	36.6	30.0	27.5	25.6
Construction	7.8	7.6	7.0	7.8	6.0	5.6
Services	**28.4**	**27.9**	**28.9**	**38.6**	**43.4**	**46.9**
Transport	5.5	4.3	7.3	9.6	9.9	10.6
Road maintenance	..	..	..	..	..	..
Communication	1.0	0.9	0.8	1.1	1.1	1.7
Wholesale trade	..	..	..	..	..	..
Retail trade and catering	3.5	4.7	4.9	8.8	10.2	9.3
Material supply	0.9	1.0	1.1	1.7	4.2	3.0
Procurement	0.3	0.5	0.6	0.8	0.5	0.3
Information and computing services	0.2	0.2	0.1	0.1	0.1	0.1
Other sectors of material production	0.7	0.6	0.4	0.5	0.5	0.7
Housing	1.5	1.2	1.1	1.5	1.7	3.6
Public utilities and personal services	2.1	1.9	2.9	2.9	3.3	5.3
Health care, social security, etc.	2.2	2.6	2.9	3.3	3.0	3.4
Education	2.1	2.8	3.3	4.1	3.4	4.5
Culture and art	0.5	0.5	0.7	0.7	0.4	0.5
Science and research	3.0	2.5	0.8	0.8	0.8	1.0
Credit	0.3	1.4	1.6	8.9	7.5	4.2
Insurance	0.1	0.1	0.1	0.1	0.1	0.1
General administration and defense	4.2	4.1	2.1	2.3	3.5	3.3
Private nonprofit institutions	0.2	0.3	0.1	0.1	0.1	0.1
Financial intermediaries, imp.. chrg.	..	-1.6	-1.7	-8.7	-6.8	-5.0
Total gross value added 1/	**97.4**	**95.9**	**95.1**	**93.8**	**90.5**	**90.2**
Net Taxes on production and imports	6.0	4.9	8.1	9.9	12.2	13.9
Taxes on production and imports	22.8	13.4	19.4	20.3	18.4	16.8
Subsidies on production and imports	16.8	8.4	11.2	10.5	6.3	3.0
Total GDP at factor cost	**94.0**	**95.1**	**91.9**	**90.1**	**87.8**	**86.1**
Net Indirect taxes	6.0	4.9	8.1	9.9	12.2	13.9
Total GDP at market prices	**100.0**	**100.0**	**100.0**	**100.0**	**100.0**	**100.0**
Expenditure Category						
Gross Domestic Expenditure	**100.0**	**100.0**	**100.0**	**100.0**	**100.0**	**100.0**
Consumption	70.8	67.1	66.2	78.6	84.4	79.6
Private consumption	43.7	41.8	45.9	54.2	56.6	50.5
Government consumption	23.8	21.2	16.0	19.6	21.3	21.9
Non-Profits	3.4	4.2	4.3	4.7	6.5	7.1
Gross domestic investment	26.9	29.4	32.3	38.4	28.9	25.2
Gross fixed investment	22.3	22.4	25.7	31.2	29.2	25.1
Change in stocks	4.6	7.0	6.6	7.2	-0.3	0.0
Resource balance (net exports of GNFS) 2/	2.2	3.5	1.5	-17.0	-13.3	-4.7
Exports of goods and NFS	46.5	37.3	60.0	66.6	71.6	42.7
Imports of goods and NFS	44.3	33.9	58.5	83.6	84.9	47.5

1/ In 1990-93, this line includes "Other taxes on production".
2/ Due to average exchange rate estimates, there are discrepancies between this table
and table 5.1, table 5.2, and table 5.3 in the text.

Table 2.4 - Gross Domestic Product at Comparable Prices
(annual growth rates)

	1991	1992	1993	1994	1995 1/
Sector of Origin					
Agriculture and forestry	**-3.2%**	**-14.4%**	**-10.4%**	**-15.3%**	**-7.6%**
Agriculture	-3.3%	-14.5%	-10.6%	-15.3%	-7.6%
Forestry	3.4%	-5.9%	0.3%	0.5%	-2.9%
Industry and construction	**0.8%**	**-5.5%**	**-11.7%**	**-19.9%**	**-13.2%**
Industry	1.0%	-5.2%	-10.5%	-18.9%	-10.6%
Construction	-0.1%	-7.1%	-17.7%	-25.3%	-28.8%
Services	**-4.0%**	**-13.7%**	**-8.4%**	**0.0%**	**-6.5%**
Transport	-0.6%	-19.7%	-18.7%	-23.0%	-11.0%
Communication	-27.4%	-27.4%	-20.8%	-3.5%	-13.1%
Retail trade and catering	-4.4%	-17.0%	-13.1%	-8.6%	-25.1%
Material supply	6.9%	-14.7%	-9.9%	77.0%	-11.5%
Procurement	-13.4%	-15.5%	-11.0%	-18.6%	-24.1%
Housing	2.4%	4.3%	1.4%	0.5%	-0.6%
Public utilities and personal services	-1.1%	-9.4%	-0.9%	-3.6%	-8.1%
Health care, social security, etc.	0.6%	1.0%	2.0%	1.5%	2.1%
Education	0.7%	-1.7%	-3.1%	0.0%	2.5%
Culture 2/	-0.9%	-23.3%	-19.2%	-12.4%	-9.5%
Credit and insurance	4.5%	5.4%	13.5%	24.4%	18.1%
General administration and defense	-13.2%	-29.0%	-6.3%	-6.7%	-1.3%
FISIM 3/	-10.3%	23.9%	6.6%	55.4%	-2.1%
Total gross value added 4/	**-1.5%**	**-10.1%**	**-10.8%**	**-13.2%**	**-11.2%**
Total GDP at factor cost	**2.0%**	**-9.4%**	**-9.6%**	**-12.2%**	**-10.0%**
Net Indirect taxes	-51.5%	-17.3%	-44.7%	-38.3%	-21.2%
Total GDP at market prices	**-1.2%**	**-9.6%**	**-10.6%**	**-12.6%**	**-10.1%**
Expenditure Category					
Consumption	-6.6%	-10.3%	-3.7%	-10.8%	-16.5%
Private consumption	-6.7%	-7.9%	-1.5%	-14.5%	-23.9%
Government consumption	-7.7%	-15.3%	-10.5%	-3.0%	-1.8%
Non-Profits	1.7%	-8.7%	-2.5%	-0.6%	0.1%
Gross domestic investment	15.3%	-15.7%	-11.6%	-33.5%	-26.1%
Gross fixed investment 5/	4.4%	-18.1%	-15.4%	-17.2%	-27.0%
Change in stocks	67.6%	-8.3%	-1.2%	..	..

1/ Provisional estimates currently under revision.
2/ Culture, art, science and research.
3/ Undistributed imputed payments to financial intermediaries.
4/ In 1990-93, this line includes "Other taxes on production".
5/ Includes residential investment and business fixed investment.

Table 2.5 - Capital Investment by Sectors at Constant Prices

	1991	1992	1993	1994	1995
(1990=100)					
Total	104.1	74.2	63.4	56.5	39.2
Industry	106	74.8	66.3	74.5	47.7
Agriculture	95	46.8	32.5	17.4	11.6
Transport and communication	127.4	88.5	97.2	75.9	85.2
Construction	127.4	58.6	51.5	41.2	21.6
Residential construction	110.4	97.8	79.1	70.9	40
Other	94.6	89.3	81.5	75.5	56.4
(Share of total)					
Total	100.0	100.0	100.0	100.0	100.0
Industry	24.8	24.6	25.5	32.1	29.7
Agriculture	26.4	18.2	14.8	8.9	8.5
Transport and communication	9.0	8.8	11.3	9.9	16.0
Construction	3.9	2.5	2.6	2.3	1.7
Residential construction	20.8	25.9	24.5	24.6	20.0
Other	15.1	20.0	21.3	22.2	24.1
Memorandum items					
Index (1990=100)					
Real gross investment 1/	115.3	97.1	85.0	56.5	41.8
Fixed capital	104.4	85.5	72.3	59.9	43.7
Stock building	167.6	153.7	151.9	72.5*	...
As share of GDP (%)					
Gross investment 1/	29.4	32.3	38.4	28.9	25.2

*/ Estimation.

Note: The data differ from the national accounts tables due to different sources.
1/ According to national accounts.

Source: Ministry of Statistics and Analysis.

Table 3.1 - Balance of Payments, 1993 - 96
(millions US$)

	1993	1994	1995	1996 Estimate
Current Account	-1,113	-641	-254	-1,250
Merchandise Trade	-1,051	-710	-529	-1,655
Exports	2,812	2,641	4,621	5,264
Imports (fob)	-3,863	-3,351	-5,149	-6,919
Services	-131	19	196	353
Non-factor services, net	-119	52	262	419
Interest, net	-12	-33	-66	-66
Transfers, net	69	50	79	52
Capital and Financial Account	550	790	83	-14
Medium and Long term capital	320	193	78	-484
Disbursements	322	283	191	58
Amortization	-2	-90	-113	-542
Foreign direct investment, net	18	10	7	19
Other	212	587	-2	451
Errors and omissions 1/	381	-410	-41	986
Overall Balance	-182	-261	-212	-278
Financing	182	261	212	278
Claims of banking system	-206	-138	8	52
Central Bank, net (- increase)	-152	-55	-90	41
Commercial banks, net (- increase)	3	-83	98	11
Exceptional financing	388	399	204	226
of which gas arrears accumulated	0	399	196	203
(in percent, except where otherwise indicated)				
Memorandum items				
Current account /GDP 2/	-31	-13	-2	-9
Exports/GDP 2/	77	55	45	38
Imports/GDP 2/	106	69	50	51
Export Volumes (change on year earlier	..	-17	-6	..
Import Volumes (change on year earlier	..	-39	10	..
Gross reserves (millions US$) 2/	91	101	377	469
in months of imports	0.3	0.3	0.7	0.9
External debt (e.o.p., millions US$)	1,014	1,251	1,513	947
External Debt/GDP 2/ 4/	28	26	15	7
Debt service/exports of goods and nonfactor services	0	4	3	2

1/ Excluding arrears of Beltrangaz to RAO Gazprom (shown separately as exceptional financing).

2/ The sharp real appreciation of the rubel against the dollar in 1995-96 implies a rapid increase in dollar GDP, complicating the interpretation of ratios to GDP.

3/ Gross official reserves excluding CIS currencies.

4/ Excludes arrears for imports of natural gas. Reflects cancellation in February 1996 of debt to Russia amounting to US$ 417 million.

Sources: Data provided by the National Bank of Belarus, the Ministry of Statistics and Analysis, and the Ministry of Finance; and the Fund staff estimates.

Table 3.2 - Balance of Merchandise Trade, 1992 - 95

	1992	1993	1994	1995
(billions of BRB)				
Total foreign trade (turnover)	1,071	14,246	25,940	117,789
export	540	6,225	11,676	54,036
import	531	8,021	14,264	63,753
balance	9	-1,796	-2,588	-9,717
CIS countries (turnover)	762	8,218	16,608	75,665
export	359	3,731	6,878	33,559
import	403	4,487	9,730	42,106
balance	-44	-756	-2,852	-8,547
o/w Russia (turnover)	495	6,093	14,102	57,763
export	216	2,498	5,385	23,855
import	279	3,596	8,717	33,908
balance	-63	-1,098	-3,332	-10,053
ROW (turnover)	309	6,028	9,332	42,124
export	181	2,494	4,798	20,477
import	128	3,534	4,534	21,647
balance	53	-1,040	264	-1,170
(millions of USD)				
Total foreign trade (turnover)	7,052	4,509	5,578	10,268
export	3,558	1,970	2,511	4,706
import	3,494	2,539	3,067	5,562
balance	64	-569	-556	-856
CIS countries (turnover)	5,015	2,601	3,571	6,606
export	2,364	1,181	1,479	2,930
import	2,651	1,420	2,092	3,676
balance	-287	-239	-613	-746
o/w Russia (turnover)	3,257	1,928	3,030	5,054
export	1,420	790	1,157	2,089
import	1,837	1,138	1,873	2,965
balance	-417	-348	-716	-876
ROW (turnover)	2,037	1,908	2,007	3,662
export	1,194	789	1,032	1,776
import	843	1,119	975	1,886
balance	351	-330	57	-110

Source: Ministry of Statistics and Analysis.

Table 3.3.a - Exports by Commodity Group at Domestic Prices to CIS
(millions of current rubles)

Commodity group	1987	1988	1989	1990	1991	1992	1993	1994	1995
Industry	16,825	17,796	17,813	16,782	28,225	348,639	3,650,176	6,850,099	33,294,329
Energy									
Electric power	25	26	33	42	153	21	56	894	5,571
Oil and gas	1,134	1,157	1,311	1,204	1,226	5,894	852,022	1,470,178	4,729,321
Coal	..	0	..	..	..	..	150	..	197
Other fuel	..	..	..	..	..	..	111	..	9,534
Ferrous metallurgy	171	198	172	189	383	9,308	104,975	249,500	256,739
Nonferrous metallurgy	67	69	73	78	78	359	32,457	78,261	23,602
Chemical and petroleum	2,122	2,249	2,227	2,128	4,122	65,950	626,806	571,574	5,596,224
Sawmill and lumber industry	445	455	455	442	993	7,979	102,688	311,995	2,143,005
Machinery and metal works	7,170	7,686	7,893	7,856	12,628	192,063	1,451,508	2,822,061	14,238,609
Building materials	219	231	236	290	228	3,127	51,124	220,164	1,071,603
Light industry	3,606	3,718	3,568	3,270	5,130	36,695	240,266	717,170	1,858,525
Food and beverage production	1,583	1,693	1,568	984	2,740	19,767	135,097	306,270	2,882,651
Other industries	283	313	277	299	544	7,476	52,918	102,018	208,750
Agriculture	370	389	263	228	908	10,761	47,528	19,269	243,934
Other material production	34	37	234	214	37	...	33,786	8,647	20,618
Total exports	**17,229**	**18,222**	**18,310**	**17,225**	**29,170**	**359,400**	**3,731,490**	**6,878,015**	**33,558,881**

Table 3.3.b - Exports by Commodity Group at Domestic Prices to CIS
(millions of USD)

Commodity group	1987	1988	1989	1990	1991	1992	1993	1994	1995
Industry	25,884	27,378	27,404	2,811	1,023	2,294	1,155	1,473	2,907
Energy									
Electric power	39	..	..	7	6	0	..	..	..
Oil and gas	1,745	1,780	2,017	202	44	39	270	316	413
Coal	..	1	..	..	..	..	0	0	..
Other fuel	..	..	..	..	..	..	0	0	1
Ferrous metallurgy	262	304	265	32	14	61	33	54	46
Nonferrous metallurgy	103	106	112	13	3	2	10	17	2
Chemical and petroleum	3,264	3,461	3,427	356	149	434	198	123	489
Machinery and metal works	..	..	..	..	..	1,264	460	607	1,243
Sawmill and lumber industry	685	699	700	74	36	52	32	67	187
Building materials	337	355	363	49	8	21	16	47	94
Light industry	5,547	5,720	5,488	548	186	241	76	154	162
Food and beverage production	2,435	2,605	2,412	165	99	130	43	66	252
Other industries	435	482	427	50	20	49	17	22	18
Agriculture	568	599	405	38	33	70	15	4	21
Other material production	52	56	360	36	1	..	11	2	2
Total exports	26,505	28,033	28,170	2,885	1,057	2,364	1,181	1,479	2,930

Note: The data for this table were calculated by using data in BRB and average yearly exchange rate BRB/USD.

M:\JH\BEL\CEM\GRAY\DATA\[AN03.XLS]MGeorg.%.y

Table 3.4.a - Exports by Country at Domestic Prices
(millions of current belarus rubels)

	1987	1988	1989	1990	1991	1992	1993	1994	1995
Total export	18,864	19,917	20,301	18,995	31,330	541,000	6,225,000	11,676,000	54,036,000
Total export to CIS	17,228	18,222	18,310	17,225	29,170	359,368	3,731,500	6,878,000	33,558,879
Armenia	276	295	287	252	291	1,071	5,300	6,000	30,851
Azerbaijan	285	300	293	258	299	5,685	19,200	18,800	71,937
Belarus	..	..	..	..	..	..	..	..	..
Estonia	202	214	216	204	294	..	..	..	..
Georgia	271	289	283	252	307	1,696	3,800	8,000	41,115
Kazakhstan	779	823	801	751	1,292	19,340	149,300	116,500	880,940
Kyrgyz Republic	143	154	153	143	236	1,629	5,100	10,700	68,122
Latvia	431	449	459	430	527	..	..	..	..
Lithuania	567	596	613	577	693	..	..	..	..
Moldova	388	413	410	396	642	9,073	160,900	130,400	816,761
Russia	10,279	10,882	10,947	10,276	17,733	215,833	2,497,700	5,385,100	23,854,814
Tajikistan	150	159	150	136	143	1,597	16,000	5,300	60,985
Turkmenistan	101	104	102	92	183	4,188	13,000	5,700	37,287
Ukraine	2,835	2,997	3,062	2,966	5,324	86,476	808,200	1,142,300	7,004,823
Uzbekistan	521	547	534	492	1,206	12,780	53,000	49,200	691,244
Total export to ROW	..	..	..	..	..	181,000	2,494,000	4,798,000	20,477,000
EC	..	..	..	..	..	62,000	833,000	1,722,000	6,638,000
Others	..	..	..	..	..	119,000	1,661,000	3,076,000	13,839,000

*Table 3.4.b - **Exports by Country at Domestic Prices***
(percentage distribution)

	1992	1993	1994	1995
Total export	100.0	100.0	100.0	100.0
Total export to CIS	66.4	59.9	58.8	62.1
Kazakhstan	3.6	2.4	1.0	1.6
Moldova	1.7	2.6	1.1	1.5
Russia	40.0	40.1	46.1	44.1
Ukraine	15.8	13.0	9.8	13.0
Uzbekistan	2.4	0.9	0.4	1.3
Others	2.9	0.9	0.4	0.6
Total export to ROW	33.6	40.1	41.2	37.9
EC	11.4	13.4	14.7	12.3
Austria	3.1	1.4	0.7	0.4
Germany	1.8	5.2	6.5	5.7
Italy	0.6	1.4	1.3	1.3
Netherlands	1.2	1.4	1.0	1.6
Poland	4.5	4.5	4.4	5.8
Latvia	1.5	0.9	1.0	4.2
Lithuania	1.6	1.1	1.4	3.1
China	0.8	1.5	1.7	0.3
Others	13.8	18.7	18.0	12.2

Table 3.5 - Exports to Non-CIS Countries
(in millions USD)

	1993	1994	1995
Europe	512	707	1374
Austria	27	17	18
Germany	98	155	268
Italy	26	32	61
Poland	86	104	271
Switzerland	27	40	8
Turkey	31	29	34
Other	217	330	714
United States	39	55	58
Other	238	270	402
Total	789	1032	1776
Memorandum items			
Barter transactions 1/	271	236	145

1/ Included in Totals.

Source: Ministry of Statistics and Analysis.

Table 3.6.a - Imports by Commodity Group at Domestic Prices from CIS
(millions of Belarus rubles)

Commodity group	1987	1988	1989	1990	1991	1992	1993	1994	1995
Industry	13,576	13,717	14,349	14,067	24,464	382,146	4,349,144	5,533,550	41,375,546
Energy	1,964	1,997	2,050	1,892	4,196	41,127	1,961,357	5,709,778	21,691,851
Electric power	118	136	147	154	633	...	124,191	191,688	1,104,062
Coal	53	59	56	40	60	3,085	35,675	61,707	701,500
Oil and gas	1,792	1,801	1,846	1,697	3,502	38,042	1,801,184	5,456,283	19,836,736
Other fuel	1	1	1	1	1	...	301	...	49,553
Ferrous metallurgy	1,273	1,329	1,310	1,333	2,553	48,001	397,968	725,703	4,005,495
Nonferrous metallurgy	365	406	411	411	856	14,155	118,408	214,831	445,672
Machinery and metal works	1,841	1,974	1,987	1,980	3,188	52,574	559,983	945,687	5,469,079
Sawmill and lumber industry	4,775	4,729	4,972	5,045	6,857	118,033	770,512	1,061,016	5,108,742
Building materials	371	383	397	408	929	15,367	51,308	118,601	577,076
Light industry	240	239	258	178	359	6,066	63,677	120,918	365,163
Food and beverage production	1,478	1,367	1,547	1,552	2,678	40,157	132,558	231,863	613,228
Chemical and petroleum	1,029	1,035	1,143	909	2,089	34,375	104,699	173,568	2,732,214
Other industries	240	258	274	359	759	12,290	188,680	231,693	367,026
Agriculture	389	337	283	468	1,085	17,518	132,900	179,841	701,615
Other material production	118	117	202	306	123	18,417	5,826	16,920	28,622
Total imports	**14,083**	**14,171**	**14,834**	**14,841**	**25,672**	**418,081**	**4,487,870**	**5,730,311**	**42,105,783**

Table 3.6.b - Imports by Commodity Group at Domestic Prices from CIS
(millions of USD)

Commodity group	1987	1988	1989	1990	1991	1992	1993	1994	1995
					Industry total				
Industry	20,886	21,103	22,075	2,356	886	2,514	1,376	2,049	3,613
Energy	3,021	3,072	3,154	317	152	270	620	1,227	1,899
Electric power	182	209	226	26	23	..	39	41	96
Coal	81	91	86	7	2	..	..	..	..
Oil and gas	2,757	2,771	2,840	284	127	250	570	1,173	1,732
Other fuel	2	2	2	0	0	20	11	13	6
Ferrous metallurgy	1,958	2,044	2,015	223	93	316	126	156	350
Nonferrous metallurgy	561	625	633	69	31	93	37	46	39
Chemical and petroleum	2,832	3,037	3,057	332	116	346	177	203	478
Machinery and metal works	7,346	7,275	7,649	845	248	777	244	228	440
Sawmill and lumber industry	571	589	610	68	34	101	16	25	50
Building materials	368	368	396	30	13	40	20	26	32
Light industry	2,273	2,103	2,381	260	97	264	42	50	54
Food and beverage production	1,583	1,592	1,758	152	76	226	33	37	239
Other industries	369	397	421	60	28	81	60	51	32
Agriculture	598	519	436	78	39	115	42	39	61
Other material production	182	180	311	51	4	22	2	4	2
Total imports	**21,666**	**21,802**	**22,822**	**2,486**	**930**	**2,651**	**1,420**	**2,092**	**3,677**

Note: The data for this table were calculated by using data in BRB and average yearly exchange rate BRB/USD.

Table 3.7.a - Imports by Country at Domestic Prices
(millions of current belarus rubel)

	1987	1988	1989	1990	1991	1992	1993	1994	1995
Total import	17,707	17,844	19,348	19,766	29,650	531,000	8,021,000	14,264,300	63,752,635
Total import from CIS	14,083	14,171	14,834	14,841	25,672	403,000	4,487,000	9,730,300	42,105,783
Armenia	139	138	147	146	81	1,380	1,700	4,300	11,993
Azerbaijan	240	236	252	249	632	2,774	13,300	15,600	49,462
Estonia 1/	135	132	143	140	199	925	4,500	..	..
Georgia	226	223	241	233	203	1,193	4,100	7,700	34,586
Kazakhstan	302	288	304	322	842	15,165	262,500	152,000	645,564
Kyrgyz Republic	117	115	121	127	206	1,230	11,500	15,800	33,709
Latvia 1/	333	333	354	340	728	5,164	28,300	..	..
Lithuania 1/	468	475	502	522	995	7,955	66,600	42,200	403,397
Moldova	276	269	288	277	721	6,356	34,500	8,716,700	33,908,255
Russia	8,844	8,941	9,350	9,349	14,081	279,248	3,595,500	13,300	34,249
Tajikistan	55	51	55	56	216	991	4,600	1,800	9,355
Turkmenistan	49	45	50	50	169	2,194	8,000	694,200	6,552,982
Ukraine	2,720	2,749	2,841	2,842	5,804	85,013	511,700	66,700	422,231
Uzbekistan	179	176	186	188	795	7,492	40,500		
Total import from ROW	3,624	3,673	4,514	4,925	3,978	128,000	3,534,000	4,534,000	21,646,852
EC	..	..	..	..	..	49,000	1,866,000	2,707,000	10,635,681
Others	..	..	..	..	..	79,000	1,668,000	1,827,000	11,011,171

1/ Since 1992 Baltic states are classified as ROW countries.

Table 3.7.b - *Imports by Country at Domestic Prices*
(percentage distribution)

	1992	1993	1994	1995
Total import	100.0	100.0	100.0	100.0
Total import from CIS	77.9	65.2	70.2	66.0
Kazakhstan	2.9	3.8	1.1	1.0
Moldova	1.2	0.5	0.3	0.6
Russia	54.0	52.2	62.9	53.2
Ukraine	16.4	7.4	5.0	10.3
Uzbekistan	1.4	0.6	0.5	0.7
Others	2.0	0.7	0.4	0.2
Total import from ROW	22.1	34.8	29.8	34.0
EC	7.9	24.0	17.1	16.5
Austria	1.6	1.6	1.2	0.8
Germany	3.2	14.9	10.6	7.6
Italy	0.4	0.7	0.6	1.5
Netherlands	0.7	0.9	0.8	1.6
Hungary	0.5	1.4	2.1	1.6
Latvia	0.0	0.4	0.5	1.0
Lithuania	0.0	0.9	0.4	2.1
Poland	2.8	3.8	4.2	3.5
Others	10.9	4.3	5.5	9.3

Table 3.8 - Imports from Non-CIS Countries
(in millions USD)

	1993	1994	1995
Europe	893	744	1,365
Austria	39	36	28
Germany	369	299	412
Italy	18	19	82
Poland	94	112	196
Switzerland	53	23	40
Turkey	23	10	7
Other	297	245	600
United States	87	51	82
Other	139	180	92
Total	1,119	975	1,539
Memorandum items			
Barter transactions 1/	291	179	130

1/ Included in Totals.

Source: Ministry of Statistics and Analysis.

Table 3.9 - Trade by State Foreign Trade Organizations (FTOs) in 1993-95
(in millions of US dollars)

	1993	1994	1995
Total exports	1,741.1	2,608.2	4,362.9
By state foreign trade organizations	156.0	70.4	30.9
Petroleum products	42.6	15.9	..
Timber and furniture	6.2	3.4	0.4
Fertilizer	55.4	18.5	..
Cars	..	..	..
Nonferrous metal	4.0	6.8	..
Trucks	0.4	..	..
Horses	0.4	0.4	..
Dairy products	4.7	2.2	12.7
Salt	2.7	1.4	1.7
Other	39.6	21.8	16.1
Total imports	2,119.5	2,723.9	4,795.2
By state foreign trade organizations	340.4	93.6	45.9
Equipment for food industry	18.5	8.6	1.4
Construction equipment	0.2	..	..
Grain	40.6	11.2	7.2
Medicine	33.3	22.9	13.2
Sugar	56.1	9.0	4.7
Edidle oil	18.8	0.7	0.7
Grape wine	0.3	0.1	0.1
Herbicides	24.6	3.2	0.5
Natural rubber	4.6	..	..
Leather footware	0.7	0.1	..
Cars, vans, and mini-buses	1.3	0.0	0.0
Other	141.4	37.8	18.1
Memorandum items			
Trade by FTOs in percent of overall trade			
Exports	9.0	2.7	0.7
Imports	16.1	3.4	1.0

Source: Ministry of Statistics and Analysis.

Table 4.1 - External Debt Outstanding, 1992 - 96(Q1)
(In millions of U.S. dollars; end of period)

	1992	1993	1994	1995	1996 Q1
Total debt outstanding 1/	**570**	**969**	**1,272**	**1,649**	**1,555**
Medium-/long-term	**570**	**866**	**1,100**	**1,256**	**775**
Public and publicly guaranteed	570	865	1,100	1,256	775
Official Creditors	570	865	1,100	1,256	775
Multilateral (excluding IMF)	118	112	173	188	189
World Bank	--	0	100	112	116
EBRD	--	4	10	39	35
Other (EC)	118	108	63	37	38
Bilateral	452	753	927	1,068	586
FSU	--	573	543	575	150
Russia 2/	--	573	543	575	150
Non-FSU	--	180	384	493	436
Japan	--	0	57	54	47
Germany	--	152	254	326	310
USA	--	28	56	76	76
Other	--	--	17	38	3
Private creditors	--	--	--	--	--
Private non-guaranteed	--	1	0	0	0
Short-term & n.i.e.	--	**7**	**70**	**110**	**504**
IMF	--	**96**	**102**	**283**	**276**

Note: Stocks are valued at end-of period exchange rates.
1/ Due to data different sources, there are discrepancies from those in table 5.3.
2/ Reflects cancellation of US $471 million in technical credit, effective January 1, 1996.

Sources: Ministry of Finance and the Bank staff estimates.

Table 4.2 - *Distribution of External Interenterprise Debts by Country, 1994 - 95*
(End-of-period stocks; in billions of rubels)

	1994		1995			
	September	December	March	June	September	December
Payables	2,848.0	6,113.5	7,300.9	8,729.1	10,030.2	11,613.2
Azerbaijan	2.2	8.5	10.4	7.3	7.1	2.3
Armenia	0.5	0.5	0.6	0.8	3.1	2.6
Kazakhstan	6.1	82.1	22.1	18.9	33.3	23.2
Kyrgyz republic	3.0	9.0	3.6	2.6	4	3
Moldova	5.9	8.2	10.6	14.5	14.6	20.1
Russia	2,716.4	5,422.6	6,310.2	6,944.7	8363.2	9532.1
Tajikistan	0.9	0.7	0.6	7.4	7.9	2
Turkmenistan	--	0.9	1.9	10.9	11.4	2.8
Uzbekistan	4.3	12.6	17.3	95.7	106.3	135.5
Ukraine	67.5	124.6	190.5	225.5	263.1	335
Georgia	0.1	0.3	0.8	1.1	2	12.1
Lithuania	9.3	104.2	129.5	157.2	127.1	303.4
Latvia	13.1	15.3	29.9	50.3	43.9	75.1
Estonia	1.0	1.8	2.9	8.3	3.6	5.6
Other	17.7	322.2	570.0	1,183.9	1039.6	1158.4
Receivables	828.7	2,653.0	3,371.1	4,530.6	5,614.0	5,877.5
Azerbaijan	0.8	2.3	2.5	1.7	2.6	2.6
Armenia	0.2	0.4	1.9	2.1	2.3	2.7
Kazakhstan	12.0	44.8	34.3	27.0	62.9	77.3
Kyrgyz republic	0.6	0.5	0.4	0.3	1.2	1.6
Moldova	5.3	6.0	17.4	20.2	26.4	30.5
Russia	630.6	1,564.9	1,776.7	2,668.9	3,144.4	3,702.2
Tajikistan	0.4	1.7	1.0	1.1	1.7	1.9
Turkmenistan	0.2	1.4	0.9	0.7	1	3.3
Uzbekistan	3.2	12.9	8.0	40.4	95.1	99
Ukraine	103.9	210.3	324.6	354.1	492.1	423.1
Georgia	0.8	0.2	1.4	1.6	2.6	2.5
Lithuania	7.0	17.7	94.9	137.9	166	92.8
Latvia	13.8	34.6	36.8	104.0	82.8	92
Estonia	2.3	3.0	3.4	8.8	9.1	8.1
Other	47.6	752.3	1,066.9	1,161.8	1,523.8	1,337.9
Net debt	-2,019.3	-3,460.5	-3,929.8	-4,198.5	-4,416.2	-5,735.7
Azerbaijan	-1.4	-6.2	-7.9	-5.6	-4.5	0.3
Armenia	-0.3	-0.1	1.3	1.3	-0.8	0.1
Kazakhstan	5.9	-37.3	12.2	8.1	29.6	54.1
Kyrgyz republic	-2.4	-8.5	-3.2	-2.3	-2.8	-1.4
Moldova	-0.6	-2.2	6.8	5.7	11.8	10.4
Russia	-2,085.8	-3,857.7	-4,533.5	-4,275.8	-5,218.8	-5,829.9
Tajikistan	-0.5	1.0	0.4	-6.3	-6.2	-0.1
Turkmenistan	-0.2	0.5	-1.0	-10.2	-10.4	0.5
Uzbekistan	-1.1	0.3	-9.3	-55.3	-11.2	-36.3
Ukraine	36.3	85.7	134.1	128.6	229.0	88.1
Georgia	0.7	-0.1	0.6	0.5	0.6	-9.6
Lithuania	-2.3	-86.5	-34.6	-19.3	38.9	-210.6
Latvia	0.8	19.3	6.9	53.7	38.9	17.1
Estonia	1.3	1.2	0.5	0.5	5.5	2.5
Other	29.9	430.1	496.9	-22.1	484.2	179.5

Source: Ministry of Statistics and Analysis.

Table 4.3 - Sectoral Distribution of Interenterprise Receivables and Payables
(End of period stocks in billions of rubels)

	Dec-94			Mar-95			Dec-95		
	Receivables	Payables	Net Owed	Receivables	Payables	Net Owed	Receivables	Payables	Net Owed
Total	**18,154**	**23,578**	**5,424**	**27,021**	**38,543**	**11,522**	**49,820**	**66,007**	**16,187**
Industry	8,484	10,707	2,223	12,751	18,351	5,600	23,402	30,583	7,181
Agriculture	418	676	258	818	1,692	874	1,427	3,781	2,354
Transportation, incl. pipelines	3,169	4,802	1,633	4,786	5,803	1,017	8,669	8,446	-223
Communications	44	73	29	192	184	-8	329	348	19
Construction	867	1,042	175	1,641	2,150	509	3,545	4,691	1,146
Trade and public catering	884	1,692	808	1018	2,263	1,245	2,529	5,576	3,047
Distribution	435	544	109	928	1,026	98	1,820	1,981	161
Housing and communal services	3,671	3,623	-48	4,214	5,658	1,444	7,465	9,597	2,132
Other	182	419	237	673	1,416	743	634	1,004	370
Domestic debts	**15,501**	**17,465**	**1,964**	**23,650**	**31,242**	**7,592**	**43,942**	**54,394**	**10,452**
Industry	6,501	9,301	2,800	9,922	15,951	6,029	18,752	27,040	8,288
Agriculture	406	671	265	799	1,682	883	1,378	3,759	2,381
Transportation, incl. pipelines	2,753	376	-2,377	4,440	1,149	-3,291	7,987	1,229	-6,758
Communications	42	72	30	186	184	-2	308	344	36
Construction	818	1,016	198	1,587	2,127	540	3,445	4,653	1,208
Trade and public catering	717	1,475	758	944	2,129	1,185	2,240	4,992	2,752
Distribution	426	530	104	913	997	84	1,784	1,900	116
Housing and communal services	3,670	3,623	-47	4,209	5,653	1,444	7,464	9,597	2,133
Other	168	401	233	650	1,370	720	584	880	296
Foreign debts	**2,653**	**6,113**	**3,460**	**3,371**	**7,301**	**3,930**	**5,878**	**11,613**	**5,735**
Industry	1,983	1,406	-577	2,829	2,400	-429	4,650	3,543	-1,107
Agriculture	12	5	-7	19	10	-9	49	22	-27
Transportation, incl. pipelines	416	4,426	4,010	346	4,654	4,308	682	7,217	6,535
Communications	2	1	-1	6	0	-6	21	4	-17
Construction	49	26	-23	54	23	-31	100	38	-62
Trade and public catering	167	217	50	74	134	60	289	584	295
Distribution	9	14	5	15	29	14	36	81	45
Housing and communal services	1	0	-1	5	5	0	1	0	-1
Other	14	18	4	23	46	23	50	124	74

Sources: Ministry of Statistics and Analysis; and IMF staff calculations.

Table 4.4 - Sectoral Distribution of Energy Debts of Enterprises, 1995-96 (March).
(In billions of rubels)

Item	1-Jan-95					1-Jan-96					1-Mar-96				
	Total	Gas	Oil	Electricity	Other	Total	Gas	Oil	Electricty	Other	Total	Gas	Oil	Electricty	Other
Domestic debts	**5,280**	**3,937**	**317**	**836**	**200**	**13,754**	**10,102**	**221**	**2,932**	**521**	**17,311**	**11,543**	**314**	**4,842**	**612**
Industry	3,293	2,171	209	745	168	7841	5380	29	2315	117	10240	5995	58	4020	167
Agriculture	66	22	5	30	9	506	112	28	301	65	724	171	33	449	71
Transportation, incl. pipelines	17	—	8	8	1	88	3	4	80	1	73	7	13	52	1
Communications	2	—	—	2	—	—	—	—	—	—	—	—	—	—	—
Construction	16	4	1	9	2	51	11	1	34	5	61	13	2	40	6
Trade and public catering	3	—	—	3	—	7	1	1	5	0	6.1	0.8	—	5	0.2
Distribution	103	4	92	—	7	429	9	154	12	255	473	19	195	13	246
Housing and communal services	1,776	1,736	2	25	13	4820	4584	4	175	57	5719	5336	13	251	119
Other	4	—	—	14	0	12	2	0	10	21	14.9	1.2	0	11.9	1.8
Foreign debts	**4,700**	**4,313**	**29**	**331**	**26**	**6,838**	**6,487**	**118**	**234**	**0**	**7,469**	**7,152**	**72**	**245**	**0**
Industry	366	4	26	331	5	352	1	118	234	0	317	—	72	245	0
Agriculture	—	—	—	—	—	—	—	—	—	—	—	—	—	—	—
Transportation, incl. pipelines	4,309	4,309	—	—	—	6486	6486	—	—	—	7152	7152	—	—	0
Communications	—	—	—	—	—	—	—	—	—	—	—	—	—	—	—
Construction	—	—	—	—	—	—	—	—	—	—	—	—	—	—	—
Trade and public catering	24	—	3	—	21	—	—	—	—	—	—	—	—	—	—
Distribution	—	—	—	—	—	—	—	—	—	—	—	—	—	—	—
Housing and communal services	—	—	—	—	—	—	—	—	—	—	—	—	—	—	—
Other	1	—	—	—	—	—	—	—	—	—	—	—	—	—	—

Source: Ministry of Statistics and Analysis.

Table 5.1 - *Summary of General Government Operations*
(In billions of rubels)

	1992	1993	1994	1995	1996B	96 Q1-Q2E
State budget						
Revenue	30	362	6,493	35,468	55,429	19,276
Expenditure	31	417	7,111	38,817	61,157	20,859
Balance (commitment basis)	-2	-55	-618	-3,349	-5,728	-1,583
Social funds						
Revenue	9	822	1,708	13,023	23,204	8,856
Expenditure	8	789	1,555	13,131	23,163	9,188
Balance	1	33	153	-108	41	-332
Extrabudgetary funds 1/						
Revenue	3	107	571	3,926	7,199	...
Expenditure	2	89	447	3,609	7,199	...
Balance	1	18	124	317	0	...
General government 2/						
Revenue	43	535	8,463	51,203	84,147	30,108
Taxes on income and profits	10	133	2,465	11,634	16,211	5,122
Social security and payroll taxes	12	126	1,737	14,219	24,974	9,653
Taxes on goods and services	15	178	3,209	15,504	26,251	9,035
Other revenue	6	97	1,052	9,845	16,711	6,298
Expenditure	42	571	8,915	53,440	89,836	31,496
Interest payments	1	8	77	961	2,041	361
Subsidies	8	156	1,131	4,078	6,684	1,873
Social protection	9	117	1,998	15,434	27,802	10,529
Health and education	8	104	1,973	12,415	22,748	8,271
Defense	2	26	302	1,734	2,583	1,209
Net lending	0	12	416	1,928	-1,800	566
Other expenditure 3/	14	148	3,018	16,890	29,778	8,687
Balance (cash basis)	0	-18	-452	-2,237	-5,687	-1,387
Financing	...	18	452	2,237	5,687	1,387
Foreign financing, net 4/	...	9	-154	-589	929	-149
Domestic financing 4/	...	8	554	2,518	3,510	1,238
Banking system	...	8	554	2,518	3,510	1,238
Other domestic	...	...	...	...	...	...
Privatization receipts	...	1	53	307	1,248	...
Memorandum items						
Wage bill of budgetary organizations 4/	...	52	852	9,365	17,117	...
Expenditure arrears (end-period)	...	...	...	2,510	...	3,329
Interest on domestic debt	...	3	53	407	...	...
Interest of foreign debt	...	5	199	781	...	...
Nominal GDP	91	1,038	17,518	118,522	179,600	70,495

1/ State Foreign Exchange Fund (until 1994), Road Fund, Agricultural Support Fund,
   Fund for the Support of Exporters, and net expenditures of other extrabudgetary funds identified
   from IMF account data.

2/ Total of State Budget, Social Funds, and Extrabudgetary Funds, excluding interbudgetary transfers.

3/ Adjustments include changes in expenditure arrears, cash adjustment for changes in deposits of
   budgetary organizations and extrabudgetary funds, and the financing discrepancy between
   above-the-line and below-the-line items.

4/ Budget support loans extended by the Europen Union are included under domestic financing.

Sources: Data provided by authorities; and staff estimates (IMF).

Table 5.2 - *Summary of General Government Operations*
(In percent of GDP)

	1992	1993	1994	1995	1996 B	1996 Q1-Q2E
State budget						
Revenue	32.4	37.1	36.8	29.9	30.9	27.3
Expenditure	34.4	42.6	40.3	32.8	34.1	29.6
Balance (commitment basis)	-2.0	-5.5	-3.5	-2.9	-3.2	-2.2
Social funds						
Revenue	10.4	8.4	9.7	11.0	12.9	13.0
Expenditure	8.9	8.1	8.8	11.1	12.9	-0.5
Balance	1.5	0.3	0.9	-0.1	...	0.0
Extrabudgetary funds 1/						
Revenue	3.5	11.0	3.2	3.3	4.0	...
Expenditure	2.7	9.1	2.5	3.0	4.0	...
Balance	0.8	1.8	0.7	0.3	...	...
General government 2/						
Revenue	46.1	51.6	48.3	43.2	46.9	42.7
Taxes on income and profits	10.8	12.9	14.1	9.8	9.0	7.3
Social security and payroll taxes	12.9	12.1	9.9	12.0	13.9	13.7
Taxes on goods and services	16.0	17.2	18.3	13.1	14.6	12.8
Other revenue	6.4	9.4	6.0	8.3	9.3	8.9
Expenditure	46.1	53.4	50.9	45.1	50.0	44.7
Interest payments	0.7	0.8	0.4	0.8	1.1	0.5
Subsidies	9.2	15.0	6.5	3.4	3.7	2.7
Social protection	10.3	11.3	11.4	13.0	15.5	14.9
Health and education	8.9	10.0	11.3	10.5	12.7	11.7
Defense	1.6	2.5	1.7	1.5	1.4	1.7
Net lending	0.2	1.2	2.4	1.6	-1.0	0.8
Other expenditure	15.3	12.6	17.2	14.3	16.6	12.3
Balance (cash basis)	0.1	-1.8	-2.6	-1.9	-3.2	-2.0
Financing	...	1.8	2.6	1.9	3.2	2.0
Foreign financing, net 4/	...	0.9	-0.9	-0.5	0.5	-0.2
Domestic financing, net 4/	...	0.8	3.2	2.1	2.0	1.8
Banking system	...	0.8	3.2	2.1	2.0	1.8
Other domestic	...	...	...	...	...	...
Privatization receipts	...	0.1	0.3	0.3	0.7	...
Memorandum items						
Wage bill	...	5.0	...	7.9	9.0	...
Expenditure arrears (end-period)	...	...	...	2.1	...	4.7
Interest on domestic debt	...	0.3	...	0.3	0.3	...
Interest of foreign debt	...	0.5	...	1.1	0.7	...

1/ State Foreign Exchange Fund (until 1994), Road Fund, Agricultural Support Fund,
Fund for the Support of Exporters, and net expenditures of other extrabudgetary funds identified from IMF account data.

2/ Total of State Budget, Social Funds, and Extrabudgetary Funds, excluding interbudgetary transfers.

3/ Adjustments include changes in expenditure arrears, cash adjustment for changes in deposits of budgetary organizations and extrabudgetary funds, and the financing discrepancy between above-the-line and below-the-line items.

4/ Budget support loans extended by the Europen Union are included under domestic financing.

Sources: Data provided by authorities; and staff estimates.

Table 5.3 - Government Debt, 1992 - 96(Q1)
(In billions of rubels, end of period unless otherwise indicated)

	1992	1993	1994	1995	1996 Q1
Total debt	**290**	**6,864**	**16,653**	**18,576**	**18,639**
Domestic debt 1/	**-1**	**-26**	**-220**	**1,223**	**1,286**
Republican government	3	-2	242	2,598	3,507
Local governments	-1	-7	-146	-535	-492
Extrabudgetary funds 2/	-3	-17	-129	-136	-189
Budgetary organizations 3/	--	--	-187	-704	-1,540
Foreign debt	**291**	**6,890**	**16,872**	**17,354**	**17,354**
Memorandum items					
Foreign debt (millions of USD) 4/ 5/	570	987	1,592	1,509	1,555
Domestic debt (in percent of GDP)	-0.9	-2.6	-1.2	1.0	...
Exchange rate (BRbl/U.S. dollar)	511	6,980	10,600	11,500	11,500
Nominal GDP (billions of rubels)	91	978	17,661	118,522	...

1/ The data are derived from NBB balance sheets; a break in the series occurs in December 1995.

2/ Including social funds.

3/ Cash balances end-period in budgetary organizations.

4/ As recorded in the balance of payments; includes IMF. Enterprise debt is usually government-guaranteed.

5/ Due to different sources, there are discrepancies from those in table 4.1.

Sources: Belarussian authorities and IMF staff estimates.

Table 5.4 - Tax Arrears, 1993 - 96(Q1)
(In billions of rubels; end of period)

	1993	1994	1995	1996 Q1
Total tax arrears (State budget)	7	119	1364	1861
Taxes on income and profits	3	62	339	374
Personal income tax	...	...	2	10
Profit tax	3	62	329	360
Enterprise income tax	...	...	7	4
Social security contributions	...	...	...	...
Chernobyl payroll tax	1	6	226	347
Taxes on property	...	2	126	148
Real estate tax	...	2	92	123
Land tax	...	...	34	26
Domestic taxes on goods and services	3	49	673	991
VAT	3	39	531	773
Excises 1/	1	7	73	83
Fuel tax	...	3	10	14
Natural resource tax	...	...	15	48
Forestry	...	...	44	74
Taxes on international trade	...	...	...	...
Social Protection Fund		61	960	1413
Fund for Support of Agricultural Producers	...	...	185	239
Memorandum item				
Total tax arrears	7	180	2510	3514
as percent of GDP	0.7	1.0	2.1	...
Deferred taxes 3/	...	...	1	155
GDP (billions of rubels, previos year)	977.6	17661.3	118522.0	...

1/ Data are not available for arrears on Customs duties, and excises on imports.

2/ This fund was introduced in 1995.

3/ Tax deferments may be granted by the Ministry of Finance (Republican taxes) or by oblasts and
   Minsk city (local taxes). Tax deferments carry a penalty of 50 percent of the refinancing rate
   of the National Bank of Belarus (instead of the usual penalty of 150 percent of the NBB refinancing rate).

Source: Ministry of Finance.

Table 5.5.a - State Budget, 1992 - 96(Q1)

(in billions of rubels)

	1992	1993	1994	1995	1996B 1/	1996 Q1E
Revenue	30	362	6,493	35,468	55,429	8,603
Taxes on income and profits	10	133	2,465	11,634	16,211	2,454
Individual income tax	2	26	473	3,300	4,631	1,081
Profit taxes	8	108	1,992	8,334	11,579	1,373
Chernobyl surcharge	3	28	319	2,753	3,815	843
Taxes on property	--	5	104	1,202	2,803	230
Domestic taxes on goods and services	14	153	2,613	13,337	21,406	3,473
VAT	11	100	1,780	9,934	15,245	2,571
Excises	2	44	688	2,806	5,991	734
Fuel levy	1	9	145	597	170	168
Taxes on international trade	1	25	596	2,013	4,845	418
Other taxes	--	1	18	267	618	116
Nontax revenue 2/	2	16	378	3,812	5,731	1,069
Expenditure	31	417	7,111	38,817	61,155	8,777
Interest payments	1	8	77	961	2,041	88
Subsidies	6	83	1,131	4,078	6,684	833
Price differentials	--	33	367	1,219	740	222
State subsidies	--	24	486	1,476	1,209	254
Agricultural subsidies	--	14	222	1,264	3,457	257
Other subsidies	--	12	55	119	1,277	100
Transfers to other budgets	--	5	224	1,075	1,321	263
Transfers to households	4	54	436	2,490	4,638	643
Education	5	58	1,039	6,644	11,852	1,931
Health	3	46	935	5,770	10,896	1,555
Expenditure related to Chernobyl	4	40	492	3,002	4,639	783
Expenditure state reserves	--	5	134	835	1,180	127
Capital expenditure 3/	2	24	310	1,558	2,660	237
Lending minus repayments	--	12	416	1,928	-1,800	171
Other expenditure 4/	6	59	2,050	10,476	17,044	2,145
Balance (commitment basis)	-1	-55	-618	-3,349	-5,728	-175
Financing	2	34	752	2,938	5,728	175
Foreign financing, net	--	9	-154	-589	929	173
Domestic financing	2	24	853	3,220	3,551	2
Banking system	2	24	853	3,220	3,551	2
Monetary authorities	--	--	226	3,234	2,700	55
o.w. EU disbursements 5/	--	--	--	2	440	--
Banks	--	--	627	-14	851	-53
o.w. securities 6/	--	--	--	632	850	185
Other domestic financing 6/	--	--	--	--	--	--
Privatization receipts	--	1	53	307	1,248	--

1/ As approved by the President on July 12, 1995.
2/ Excludes debt reimbursements and some privatizatioin receipts that are included in the State budget.
3/ Includes only capital expenditure financed by national economy budget.
4/ Adjustments include expenditure arrears and the financing discrepancy between above-the-line and below items.
5/ European Union loans are to the NBB and become domestic credits to the budget.
6/ The negligible amount of nonbank holdings of government securities are included under bank financing.

Sources: Data provided by authorities; and staff estimates.

Table 5.5.b - State Budget, 1992 - 96(Q1)
(percentage distribution)

	1992	1993	1994	1995	1996B 1/	1996 Q1E
Revenue	100	100	100	100	100	100
Taxes on income and profits	33	37	38	33	29	29
Individual income tax	7	7	7	9	8	13
Profit taxes	27	30	31	24	21	16
Chernobyl surcharge	10	8	5	8	7	10
Taxes on property		1	2	3	5	3
Domestic taxes on goods and services	47	42	40	38	39	40
VAT	37	28	27	28	28	30
Excises	10	12	11	8	11	9
Fuel levy	3	2	2	2	0	2
Taxes on international trade	...	7	9	6	9	5
Other taxes	...	0	0	1	1	1
Nontax revenue 2/	7	4	6	11	10	12
Expenditure	100	100	100	100	100	100
Interest payments	3	2	1	3	3	1
Subsidies	19	21	16	11	11	9
Price differentials	...	8	5	3	1	3
State subsidies	...	6	7	4	2	3
Agricultural subsidies	...	4	3	3	6	3
Other subsidies	...	3	1	0	2	...
Transfers to other budgets	...	1	3	3	2	3
Transfers to households	...	14	6	7	8	7
Education	16	15	14	18	19	22
Health	10	12	13	15	18	18
Expenditure related to Chernobyl	13	10	7	8	8	9
Expenditure state reserves	...	1	2	2	2	1
Capital expenditure 3/	...	6	4	4	4	3
Lending minus repayments	...	3	6	5	-3	2
Other expenditure 4/	...	15	28	25	28	24
Balance (commitment basis)	-7	-9	-12	-8	-9	-2
Financing	100	100	100	100	100	100
Foreign financing, net	...	26	-20	-20	16	99
Domestic financing	100	71	113	110	62	1
Banking system	100	71	113	110	62	1
Monetary authorities	...	...	30	...	47	31
o.w. EU disbursements 5/	...	...	...	...	8	...
Banks	...	...	83	...	15	-30
o.w. securities 6/	...	...	...	...	15	106
Other domestic financing 6/	...	...	...	...	...	...
Privatization receipts	...	3	7	10	22	...

1/ As approved by the President on July 12, 1995.
2/ Excludes debt reimbursements and some privatizatioin receipts that are included in the State budget.
3/ Includes only capital expenditure financed by national economy budget.
4/ Adjustments include expenditure arrears and the financing discrepancy between above-the-line and below items.
5/ European Union loans are to the NBB and become domestic credits to the budget.
6/ The negligible amount of nonbank holdings of government securities are included under bank financing.

Sources: Data provided by authorities; and staff estimates.

Table 5.6.a - Extrabudgetary Funds, 1992 - 96
(in billions of rubels)

	1992	1993	1994	1995	1996 B	1996 Q1E	1996 3/
State Foreign Exchange Fund							
Revenue	1.3	46.5	34.8	--	--	--	--
Expenditure	0.8	43.6	25.2	--	--	--	--
Balance	0.5	2.9	9.6	--	--	--	--
Price Regulation Fund							
Revenue	--	37.4	17.4	--	--	--	--
Expenditure	--	32.8	19.0	--	--	--	--
Balance	--	4.6	-1.6	--	--	--	--
Road Fund 1/							
Revenue	1.9	23.3	518.7	2459.0	4500.0	618.0	3680.4
Expenditure	1.7	25.1	377.6	2479.0	4500.0	618.0	3700.0
Balance	0.2	-1.8	141.1	-21.0	0.0	0.0	-19.5
Agricultural Support Fund							
Revenue	--	--	--	1467.0	2599.0	622.0	2601.7
Expenditure	--	--	--	1390.0	2599.0	508.0	2618.1
Balance	--	--	--	77.0	0.0	114.0	-16.3
Fund for Support of Exporters 2/ 3/							
Revenue	--	--	--	--	100.0	64.0	201.3
Expenditure	--	--	--	--	100.0	0.0	200.8
Balance	--	--	--	--	0.0	64.0	0.5
Other extrabudgetary funds 4/							
Net expenditure	--	-12.2	25.2	-260.0	--	--	--
Balance	--	12.2	-25.2	260.0	--	--	--
Consolidated extrabudgetary funds							
Revenue	3.2	107.2	570.9	3926.0	7199.0	1304.0	6483.4
Net expenditure	2.5	89.3	447.0	3609.0	7199.0	1126.0	6518.8
Balance	0.7	17.9	123.9	317.0	0.0	178.0	-35.4

1/ Preliminary data for 1996.

2/ Fund operative in 1996, financed by 10 percent fee on purchases of foreign exchange for certain imports.

3/ Fund is liquidated, balance is closed, remaining sums transferred to budget.

4/ Estimates based on banking account data.

Sources: Belarussian authorities; and staff estimates.

Table 5.6.b - Extrabudgetary Funds, 1992 - 96(Q1)
(in percent of GDP)

	1992	1993	1994	1995	1996 B	1996
State Foreign Exchange Fund						
Revenue	1.4	4.8	0.2	--	--	--
Expenditure	0.9	4.5	0.1	--	--	--
Balance	0.5	0.3	0.1	--	--	--
Price Regulation Fund						
Revenue	--	3.8	0.1	--	--	--
Expenditure	--	3.4	0.1	--	--	--
Balance	--	0.5	0.0	--	--	--
Road Fund 1/						
Revenue	2.1	2.4	2.9	2.1	2.5	2.0
Expenditure	1.9	2.6	2.1	2.1	2.5	2.1
Balance	0.2	-0.2	0.8	0.0	0	0.0
Agricultural Support Fund						
Revenue	--	--	--	1.2	1.4	1.4
Expenditure	--	--	--	1.2	1.4	1.5
Balance	--	--	--	0.1	0	0.0
Fund for Support of Exporters 2/ 3/						
Revenue	--	--	--	--	0.1	0.1
Expenditure	--	--	--	--	0.1	0.1
Balance	--	--	--	--	0	0.0
Other extrabudgetary funds 4/						
Net expenditure	--	-1.2	0.1	-0.2	--	--
Balance	--	1.2	-0.1	0.2	--	--
Consolidated extrabudgetary funds						
Revenue	3.5	11.0	3.2	3.3	4.0	3.6
Net expenditure	2.7	9.1	2.5	3.0	4.0	3.6
Balance	0.8	1.8	0.7	0.3	0	0.0

1/ Preliminary data for 1996.

2/ Fund operative in 1996, financed by 10 percent fee on purchases of foreign exchange for certain imports.

3/ Fund is liquidated, balance is closed, remaining sums transferred to budget.

4/ Estimates based on banking account data.

Sources: Belarussian authorities; and staff estimates.

Table 5.7.a - Social Funds
(in billions of rubels)

	1992	1993	1994	1995	1996 Budget	1996 Q1 Estimate
Social Protection Fund 1/						
Revenue	9	798	1,658	12,622	22,491	3,981
Pension fund contributions	9	776	1,382	10,829	20,723	3,447
Transfers from state budget	--	--	224	1334	1,683	334
Other revenue	--	22	52	459	85	200
Expenditure	8	785	1,512	12,763	22,492	4,399
Pensions	5	573	905	9,023	16,285	3,487
Child allowances	2	77	100	528	1,363	363
Other expenditure	1	135	507	3,212	4,845	549
Balance	1	13	146	-141	--	-418
Employment Fund						
Revenue	--	24	50	401	712	180
Employment fund contributions	--	24	35	278	436	86
Transfers from state budget	--	--	--	--	--	--
Other revenue	--	--	15	123	276	95
Expenditure	--	4	43	368	671	74
Unemployment benefits	--	3	6	49	314	31
Other expenditure	--	1	37	319	357	43
Balance	--	20	7	33	41	106
Consolidated Social Funds						
Revenue	9	822	1,708	13,023	23,204	4,161
Expenditure	8	789	1,555	13,131	23,163	4,473
Balance	1	33	153	-108	41	-311
Financing	-1	1	-146	-79	-41	311
Domestic	-1	-3	-82	-79	-41	311
Foreign						
Memorandum items:						
Average pension (rubles per month)	...	2,303	32,308	327,200	448,731	--
Average wage (rubles per month)	...	5,893	93,356	804,702	1,083,100	--
Pension replacement rate 2/	...	0.39	0.35	0.41	0.4	--

1/ Data for 1992 and 1993 include Social Insurance Fund.

2/ Defined as ratio between average pension and average wage.

Sources: Data provided by authorities; and staff estimates.

Table 5.7.b - Social Funds
(in percent of GDP)

	1992	1993	1994	1995	1996 B	1996 Q1E
Social Protection Fund 1/						
Revenue	10.1	8.1	9.4	10.6	12.5	11.8
Pension fund contributions	10.0	7.9	7.8	9.1	11.5	10.2
Transfers from state budget	--	--	1.3	1.1	0.9	1.0
Other revenue	0.1	0.2	0.3	0.5	--	0.6
Expenditure	8.7	8.0	8.6	10.7	12.5	13.0
Pensions	5.4	5.8	5.1	7.6	9.1	10.3
Child allowances	2.1	0.8	0.6	0.4	0.8	1.1
Other expenditure	1.2	1.4	2.9	2.7	2.7	1.6
Balance	1.4	0.1	0.8	-0.1	--	-1.2
Employment Fund						
Revenue	0.3	0.2	0.3	0.3	0.4	0.5
Employment fund contributions	0.2	0.2	0.2	0.2	0.2	0.3
Transfers from state budget	--	--	--	--	--	--
Other revenue	0.1	0.1	0.1	0.1	0.2	0.3
Expenditure	0.2	0.0	0.2	0.3	0.4	0.2
Unemployment benefits	--	0.0	0.0	0.0	0.2	0.1
Other expenditure	0.2	0.0	0.2	0.3	0.2	0.1
Balance	0.1	0.2	0.0	0.0	0.0	0.3
Consolidated Social Funds						
Revenue	10.4	8.4	9.7	11.0	12.9	12.3
Expenditure	8.9	8.1	8.8	11.1	12.9	13.2
Balance	1.5	0.3	0.9	-0.1	--	-0.9

1/ Data for 1992 and 1993 include Social Insurance Fund.

Sources: Data provided by authorities; and staff estimates.

Table 6.1 - Monetary Survey
(End of period balances in billions of rubels)

	1994	1995				1996		
	Dec	Mar	Jun	Sep	Dec	Mar	Apr	Jun
BANKING SYSTEM:								
Broad money, M3 1/	**6,940**	**9,798**	**14,278**	**15,853**	**17,935**	**19,269**	**19,956**	**21,448**
Currency, M0	736	1,242	2,633	3,179	3,779	3,989	4,190	5,515
Ruble deposits	2,437	4,149	6,689	7,636	8,652	10,204	10,313	10,590
Population	487	618	2,358	2,422	2,404	4,324	4,549	4,603
Enterprises	1,951	3,530	4,331	5,214	6,248	5,880	5,764	5,987
Liquid forex deposits	3,767	4,407	4,956	5,038	5,504	5,076	5,453	5,343
Net Foreign Assets	**2,732**	**2,968**	**4,286**	**3,655**	**3,198**	**2,441**	**2,366**	**2,798**
Net foreign assets (convertible) 2/	2,613	2,903	4,110	3,453	3,055	2,508	1,978	2,426
Gross foreign reserves	4,294	6,373	7,578	7,895	7,378	7,144	7,403	7,636
Gross foreign liabilities	-1,681	-3,470	-3,468	-4,442	-4,323	-4,636	-5,425	-5,210
Net foreign assets (non-convertible)	119	65	176	201	143	-67	388	372
Foreign assets	623	238	458	596	579	499	775	867
Foreign liabilities	-504	-173	-281	-395	-436	-565	-387	-495
Net Domestic Assets	**4,208**	**6,830**	**9,992**	**12,199**	**14,736**	**16,829**	**17,589**	**18,651**
Credit to non-government	6,012	9,295	10,963	13,196	14,057	16,234	16,905	17,778
In rubles	3,336	4,892	5,907	8,086	8,978	10,813	11,031	11,727
In foreign currency	2,677	4,403	5,057	5,110	5,079	5,421	5,874	6,051
Claims on non-financial public enterp.	2,878	4,626	4,664	6,332	6,659	6,733	7,339	7,452
Claims in rubel	2,125	3,019	3,461	4,974	5,351	5,827	5,987	6,106
Claims in foreign currency	753	1,607	1,203	1,358	1,308	906	1,352	1,346
Claims on private sector	3,134	4,669	6,299	6,864	7,398	9,501	9,566	10,326
Claims in rubel	1,211	1,873	2,446	3,112	3,627	4,986	5,044	5,621
Claims in foreign currency	1,924	2,796	3,854	3,752	3,771	4,515	4,522	4,705
Claims on general government (net)	979	812	1,758	2,886	4,136	4,172	4,294	5,435
Net claims on general government	979	812	1,758	2,886	4,136	4,172	4,294	5,435
In rubel	28	-234	228	527	1,757	1,778	1,953	3,316
In foreign currency	951	1,046	1,531	2,359	2,379	2,394	2,341	2,119
Gross claims on local government	...	...	...	...	...	...	...	...
Other items (net)	**-2,783**	**-3,277**	**-2,729**	**-3,883**	**-3,457**	**-3,578**	**-3,610**	**-4,562**
Restricted deposits	-42	-67	-107	-250	-407	...	...	...
Capital account	-1,407	-2,704	-3,107	-3,678	-5,257	-5,093	-5,097	-5,442
Inter-bank (net) (float)	194	23	-15	-9	122	-510	-146	-344
Revaluation account (net)	-1,068	-1,040	-1,299	-1,068	-980	-752	-1,056	-1,268
Other items (net) (other)	-459	512	1,799	1,121	3,065	2,777	2,689	2,492
								(Continued)
MONETARY AUTHORITIES								
Reserve (Base) money	**1,773**	**2,780**	**5,111**	**6,662**	**6,836**	**7,097**	**7,186**	**8,693**
Required reserves	128	632	1,002	1,563	1,376	1,581	1,695	1,887
Excess (free) reserves	800	695	801	631	526	931	1,058	700
Correspondent accounts	706	555	648	341	301	405	618	337
In rubel	364	446	585	284	184	343	469	201
In foreign currency	342	109	63	56	113	62	149	136
Vault cash (031)	94	140	153	290	225	526	440	363
Other sector deposits	88	159	538	177	135	116	143	149
rubel deposits	75	141	525	164	116	-	-	-
forex deposits	13	18	13	13	19	-	-	-
Currency outside banks, M0	757	1,294	2,727	3,179	3,779	3,989	4,190	5,515
Banks' deposits and holdings of NBB securities	-	-	43	1,112	1,020	480	100	442
Net Foreign Assets	**-37**	**853**	**2,078**	**1,966**	**1,207**	**1,213**	**544**	**681**
In convertible currencies 2/	-108	898	2,051	1,763	1,020	1,190	508	652
Gross foreign reserves	1,071	3,415	4,584	5,091	4,336	4,889	4,864	4,823
Gross foreign liabilities	-1,179	-2,517	-2,533	-3,328	-3,316	-3,699	-4,356	-4,171
In non-convertible currencies	71	-45	27	203	187	23	36	29
Foreign assets	156	40	109	279	259	96	110	103
Foreign liabilities	-85	-85	-82	-76	-72	-73	-74	-74
Net Domestic Assets	**1,810**	**1,927**	**3,032**	**4,697**	**5,630**	**5,884**	**6,641**	**8,012**
Net Domestic Credit	**2,754**	**3,025**	**4,481**	**6,052**	**6,986**	**7,295**	**8,398**	**9,961**
Credit to non-financial public enterprises	12	81	66	84	88	65	52	39
In rubels	11	39	51	65	67	61	47	34
In foreign exchange	1	42	16	19	21	5	5	5
Claims on private sector	7	9	48	57	38	3	15	20
In rubels	4	9	12	12	24	3	15	20
In foreign exchange	3		36	45	15	...	...	...
Net claims on general government	1,299	1,442	2,473	3,765	4,530	4,585	5,054	6,251
Net claims in rubel	208	302	737	1,057	1,758	1,782	2,115	3,052
Net claims in foreign currency	1,091	1,140	1,736	2,708	2,772	2,803	2,939	3,199
Net claims on local government	...	...	...	...	...	...	...	...
Claims on banks	1,435	1,493	1,894	2,146	2,329	2,642	3,277	3,651
In rubels	652	627	703	1,295	1,486	1,827	2,271	2,615
In foreign currency	783	866	1,191	851	843	814	1,006	1,036
Other claims	19	90	114	142	126	68	67	59
Claims in rubel	15	48	63	77	91	64	62	54
Claims in foreign currency	4	42	51	64	35	5	5	5
Other Items (net)	**-944**	**-1,098**	**-1,449**	**-1,355**	**-1,355**	**-1,411**	**-1,757**	**-1,949**
Capital account	-301	-595	-525	-467	-637	-1,037	-955	-1,074
Revaluation counterpart	-654	-598	-972	-903	-875	-764	-1,012	-1,272
Fixed assets	15	115	119	127	316	362	362	401
Interbank settlements	-4	-7	-24	-30	-18	41	47	46
Other items (net, Other)	-1	-13	-47	-83	-141	-13	-199	-50

1/ Includes local government deposits.
2/ Excludes Russian rubels.
Source: National Bank of Belarus (NBB).

Table 6.2 - Real Movements in Monetary Aggregates
(End of period balances in billions of rubels)

		1995						1996				
	Dec	**Jan**	**Feb**	**Mar**	**Jun**	**Sep**	**Dec**	**Jan**	**Feb**	**Mar**	**Apr**	**Jun**
Indicators in Real (12/90) Prices												
Banking System:												
Broad money	0.391	0.295	0.242	0.247	0.297	0.289	0.294	0.262	0.265	0.280	0.276	0.269
NFA	0.154	0.118	0.082	0.075	0.089	0.067	0.052	0.045	0.046	0.035	0.029	0.033
NDA	0.237	0.177	0.160	0.173	0.208	0.223	0.242	0.217	0.219	0.239	0.246	0.236
Non-government	0.339	0.272	0.245	0.235	0.228	0.241	0.230	0.000	0.000	0.231	0.233	0.223
Government	0.055	-0.030	-0.029	0.021	0.037	0.053	0.068	0.051	0.054	0.059	0.063	0.070
Monetary Authorities:												
Base money	0.100	0.065	0.059	0.070	0.106	0.122	0.112	0.092	0.093	0.101	0.097	0.104
NFA	-0.002	0.018	0.023	0.022	0.043	0.036	0.020	0.013	0.015	0.017	0.007	0.009
NDA	0.102	0.047	0.035	0.049	0.063	0.086	0.092	0.080	0.079	0.084	0.089	0.095
Government	0.073	-0.003	0.004	0.036	0.051	0.069	0.074	0.064	0.066	0.065	0.070	0.078
Banks	0.081	0.052	0.037	0.038	0.039	0.039	0.038	0.034	0.032	0.038	0.043	0.040
Real Monthly Growth												
Banking System:												
Broad money		19.3	-18.0	2.4				-11.0	1.4	5.7	-1.8	
NFA		-24.6	-30.9	-8.4				-14.7	2.6	-24.3	-15.3	
NDA		-25.6	-9.4	7.8				-10.2	1.2	9.0	2.8	
Non-government		-19.9	-9.9	-4.1				-100.0			1.1	
Government		-155.0	-5.2	-171.3				-25.2	5.7	10.6	5.4	
Monetary Authorities:												
Base money		-34.6	-10.5	19.9				-17.8	1.4	8.1	-4.2	
NFA		-956.3	27.9	-6.5				-36.5	18.2	16.3	-57.7	
NDA		-53.6	-25.1	37.1				-13.8	-1.3	6.5	6.8	
Government		-103.6	-242.2	878.0				-13.5	2.7	-1.2	7.3	
Banks		-35.4	-28.3	0.8				-12.1	-3.6	16.2	13.6	
Index (base=100)												
Banking System:												
Broad money	49.7	37.4	30.7	-113.0					-113.1	295.8	-130.8	
NFA	-90.7	-69.7	-48.2	-72.9					-117.4	-1046.9	-37.1	
NDA	24.8	18.4	16.7	-183.3					-111.9	644.2	-68.6	
Non-government	34.3	27.5	24.8	-58.4				-100.0				
Government	49.1	-27.0	-25.6	3193.3					-122.6	87.2	-48.9	
Monetary Authorities:												
Base money	32.5	21.3	19.1	22.9	34.6	39.6	36.5	30.0	30.4	32.9	31.5	
NFA	1.0	-8.5	-10.9	-10.2	-20.5	-17.0	-9.4	-5.9	-7.0	-8.2	-3.5	
NDA	19.7	9.1	6.8	9.4	12.2	16.5	17.8	15.4	15.2	16.1	17.2	
Government	74.6	-2.7	3.8	37.1	52.4	70.0	75.6	65.4	67.1	66.4	71.2	
Banks	17.3	11.2	8.0	8.1	8.4	8.4	8.2	7.2	6.9	8.0	9.1	
Memo												
Consumer Price Index (12/90 = 100)	1,773,321	2,468,285	3,299,357	3,958,898	4,804,471	5,476,064	6,099,581	6,438,717	6,696,266	7,031,079	7,242,012	7,963,317

Note: CPI for June 1996 are estimated.

Table 6.3.a - Bank Lending by Type of Credit and Sector at Current Prices
(billions of rubels, end of period balances)

	1990	1991	1992	1993	1994	1995
Type of credit - Total	1.1	2.6	40.2	230.3	3,176.8	8,771.8
Working capital	0.8	2.1	37.8	209.2	2,791.4	7,611.3
Industry	0.3	0.7	19.3	54.0	636.4	1,777.8
Agriculture	0.1	0.2	2.6	24.9	844.2	477.2
Construction	0.1	0.2	0.4	3.9	93.3	222.7
Trade and catering	0.1	0.2	3.3	20.5	355.1	1,113.0
Other	0.2	0.8	12.2	105.9	862.4	4,020.6
Investment credit	0.2	0.3	1.7	8.0	244.8	787.7
Industry	0.1	0.1	0.6	4.5	181.1	83.3
Agriculture	0.1	0.2	0.3	2.0	37.9	92.1
Other	0.0	0.0	0.8	1.5	25.8	612.3
Housing	0.1	0.1	0.3	11.7	133.0	321.7
Consumer credit	0.0	0.1	0.4	1.4	7.6	51.1
Total Credit	1.1	2.6	40.2	230.3	3,176.8	8,771.8
Industry	0.4	0.8	19.9	58.5	817.5	1,861.1
Agriculture	0.2	0.4	2.9	26.9	882.1	569.3
Construction	0.1	0.2	0.4	3.9	93.3	222.7
Trade and catering	0.1	0.2	3.3	20.5	355.1	1,113.0
Other	0.3	1.0	13.7	120.5	1,028.8	5,005.7
Type of borrower - Total	1.1	2.6	40.2	230.3	3,176.8	8,771.8
State enterprises	0.8	1.9	28.0	128.9	1,970.0	4,853.1
Working capital	0.7	1.7	27.3	122.9	1,725.2	4,417.4
Investment	0.2	0.2	0.7	6.0	244.8	435.7
Cooperatives	0.2	0.3	4.3	56.1	450.6	2,333.9
Working capital	0.1	0.2	4.1	54.5	447.7	2,257.0
Investment	0.1	0.1	0.2	1.6	2.9	76.9
Private enterprises	0.0	0.1	1.3	11.1	523.5	219.8
Working capital	0.0	0.1	1.3	11.0	523.5	38.4
Investment	0.0	--	--	0.1	--	181.4
Households	0.0	0.1	0.7	12.9	137.7	276.9
Housing	0.0	0.1	0.3	11.4	130.1	225.8
Other	0.0	0.1	0.4	1.5	7.6	51.1
Other	0.0	0.2	5.9	21.3	95.0	1,088.1

Source: National Bank of Belarus.

Table 6.3.b - Bank Lending by Type of Credit and Sector at Current Prices
(percentage shares based on end of period balances)

	1990	1991	1992	1993	1994	1995
Type of credit - Total	100.0	100.0	100.0	100.0	100.0	100.0
Working capital	69.6	80.7	94.0	90.8	87.9	86.8
Industry	26.3	26.9	48.0	23.4	20.0	20.3
Agriculture	6.2	7.7	6.5	10.8	26.6	5.4
Construction	12.5	7.7	1.0	1.7	2.9	2.5
Trade and catering	8.1	7.7	8.2	8.9	11.2	12.7
Other	16.6	30.7	30.3	46.0	27.1	45.8
Investment credit	22.1	11.6	4.2	3.5	7.7	9.0
Industry	11.2	5.1	1.5	2.0	5.7	0.9
Agriculture	10.2	5.9	0.7	0.9	1.2	1.0
Other	0.6	0.7	2.0	0.7	0.8	7.0
Housing	4.8	3.8	0.7	5.1	4.2	3.7
Consumer credit	3.5	3.8	1.0	0.6	0.2	0.6
Total Credit	100.0	100.0	100.0	100.0	100.0	100.0
Industry	37.5	32.0	49.5	25.4	25.7	21.2
Agriculture	16.4	13.5	7.2	11.7	27.8	6.5
Construction	12.5	7.7	1.0	1.7	2.9	2.5
Trade and catering	8.1	7.7	8.2	8.9	11.2	12.7
Other	25.5	39.1	34.1	52.3	32.4	57.1
Type of borrower - Total	100.0	100.0	100.0	100.0	100.0	100.0
State enterprises	77.3	73.0	69.7	56.0	62.0	55.3
Working capital	61.6	65.3	67.9	53.4	54.3	50.4
Investment	15.8	7.7	1.7	2.6	7.7	5.0
Cooperatives	19.1	11.5	10.7	24.4	14.2	26.6
Working capital	7.9	7.7	10.2	23.7	14.1	25.7
Investment	11.2	3.8	0.5	0.7	0.1	0.9
Private enterprises	2.4	3.8	3.2	4.8	16.5	2.5
Working capital	0.0	3.8	3.2	4.8	16.5	0.4
Investment	2.3	...	...	0.0	...	2.1
Households	3.5	3.8	1.7	5.6	4.3	3.2
Housing	2.8	1.9	0.7	5.0	4.1	2.6
Other	0.7	1.9	1.0	0.7	0.2	0.6
Other	-2.3	7.8	14.7	9.2	3.0	12.4

Source: National Bank of Belarus.

Table 6.4 - Bank Lending by Type of Credit and Sector at Comparable Prices
(millions of 1990 rubels, end of period balances)

	1990	1991	1992	1993	1994	1995
Type of credit - Total	1,088	1,051	979	267	179	144
Working capital	757	848	921	243	157	125
Industry	286	283	470	63	36	29
Agriculture	67	81	63	29	48	8
Construction	136	81	10	5	5	4
Trade and catering	88	81	80	24	20	18
Other	180	323	297	123	49	66
Investment credit	241	122	41	9	14	13
Industry	122	54	15	5	10	1
Agriculture	111	62	7	2	2	2
Other	7	7	19	2	1	10
Housing	53	40	7	14	8	5
Consumer credit	38	40	10	2	0	1
Total Credit	1,088	1,051	979	267	179	144
Industry	408	337	485	68	46	31
Agriculture	179	142	71	31	50	9
Other	278	411	334	140	58	82
Type of borrower - Total	1,088	1,051	979	267	179	144
State enterprises	842	768	682	150	111	80
Working capital	670	687	665	143	97	72
Investment	172	81	17	7	14	7
Cooperatives	208	121	105	65	25	38
Working capital	86	81	100	63	25	37
Investment	122	40	5	2	0	1
Private enterprises	26	40	32	13	30	4
Working capital	1	40	32	13	30	1
Investment	25	...	...	0	...	3
Households	38	40	17	15	8	5
Housing	30	20	7	13	7	4
Other	8	20	10	2	0	1
Other	-25	82	144	25	5	18
Memo						
Consumer Price Index	100	248	4,106	86,096	1,773,321	6,099,581

Source: National Bank of Belarus.

Table 6.5 - *National Bank Credit by Sector, 1993(Q4) - 1996 (Q1)*
(gross credit in billions of rubels, end of period balances)

| | 1993 | 1994 | | | | 1995 | | | | 1996 |
	Q4	Q1	Q2	Q3	Q4	Q1	Q2	Q3	Q4	Q1
Directed credit										
Agriculture	31.9	96.3	107.1	443.6	501.4	402.4	319.9	520.5	457.8	851.7
Trade	4.6	0.2	0.4	24.7	24.6	88.7	113.9	200.5	125.6	126.9
Industry	18.4	15.6	18.1	24.7	27.9	25.9	32.1	53	48.3	48.3
Housing	...	...	10	9.9	49.2	49.2	48.7	47.7	45.6	140.6
State Emergency Reserv	1	2	3.1	5	10.8	35	61.8	100.3	145.1	182.3
Auctioned credit	20	1.2	...	3	38	26.6	126.8	373	663.5	436.2
Total credit	76	115.3	138.8	511	652.3	627.3	703.3	1295	1486.1	1786

Source: National Bank of Belarus.

Table 6.6 - Average Interest Rates of NBB, 1993(Q4) - 1996 (Q1)

	1993 Q4	1994 Q1	1994 Q2	1994 Q3	1994 Q4	1995 Q1	1995 Q2	1995 Q3	1995 Q4	1996 Q1
Directed credit										
Agriculture	98.4	29.9	47	91.7	120.6	188.7	95.5	65.4	65.3	37.3
Trade	60.9	73	100	100	300	300	96	66	69.4	50.3
Industry	24.5	17.3	35.9	53.8	78.1	72.5	61.7	60.6	60.9	73.3
Housing	...	...	6.5	6.5	6.5	6.5	6.5	6.5	6.5	3.4
State Emergency Reserves	...	...	...	...	...	...	...	...	...	...
Auctioned credit	175	170	...	223.1	336.9	400	100	66.6	64.6	68.3
Average interst rates on all credit	102.2	62.6	53.6	95.9	147.2	187.7	80.6	58.4	56.7	48.5

1/ Excluding credit extended for state emergency reserves.

Source: National Bank of Belarus.

Table 6.7 - Purchases of Foreign Exchange by the NBB and Commercial Banks
(thousands of US dollars)

	1995											
	Jan	Feb	Mar	Apr	May	June	July	Aug.	Sept.	Oct.	Nov.	Dec.
NBB	35,848	30,060	24,550	53,362	13,805	73,401	84,126	(22,536)	(46,264)	(40,162)	(27,018)	38,669
Non-cash	24,606	13,441	19,573	48,377	13,190	66,922	80,808	(22,706)	(42,051)	(41,067)	(28,032)	34,323
At the ICE 1/	24,871	14,414	12,658	41,293	22,917	58,671	88,911	1,246	(61,561)	(69,374)	(44,979)	(14,943)
Outside the ICE	(4,088)	(4,450)	2,585	4,273	(17,484)	(2,914)	(20,548)	(40,727)	258	6,307	(647)	15,410
Taxes	3,823	3,477	4,329	2,811	7,757	11,165	12,445	16,775	19,252	21,999	17,594	33,856
Cash	11,242	16,618	4,978	4,985	614	6,479	3,318	170	(4,212)	906	1,014	4,346
From households	10,743	16,331	4,950	4,984	621	6,479	3,318	170	(4,212)	904	1,014	4,346
From legal entities	499	288	28	1	(7)	0	0	0	0	1	0	0
Commercial banks	26,105	9,993	(55)	(35,209)	951	(61,363)	(36,874)	7,214	40,080	37,488	2,511	(38,346)
Non-cash	(24,831)	(15,091)	(12,718)	(40,802)	(1,332)	(66,364)	(48,556)	9,014	47,874	50,057	11,248	(32,388)
At the ICE	(24,871)	(14,412)	(12,658)	(41,293)	(1,333)	(58,602)	(88,911)	(1,246)	61,561	69,374	44,979	14,943
Outside the ICE	39	(679)	(60)	491	0	(7,762)	40,354	10,260	(13,687)	(19,317)	(33,731)	(47,331)
Cash	50,936	25,084	12,663	5,593	2,284	5,001	11,683	(1,800)	(7,794)	(12,569)	(8,737)	(5,958)
From households	50,936	25,084	12,663	5,593	2,284	5,001	11,683	(1,800)	(7,794)	(12,569)	(8,737)	(5,958)
From legal entities	0	0	0	0	0	0	0	0	0	0	0	0
Total	61,953	40,053	24,495	18,152	14,756	12,038	47,252	(15,322)	(6,184)	(2,673)	2,511	323
Non-cash	(226)	(1,650)	6,854	7,575	11,858	558	32,252	(13,692)	5,823	8,990	(16,784)	1,935
At the ICE	0	2	0	0	21,584	69	0	0	0	0	0	0
Outside the ICE	(4,049)	(5,129)	2,525	4,764	(17,484)	(10,676)	19,806	(30,467)	(13,429)	(13,009)	(34,378)	(31,921)
Taxes	3823	3477	4329	2811	7757	11164.9	12445	16775.4	19252.5	21999.4	17594	33856
Cash	62,178	41,702	17,641	10,577	2,898	11,480	15,001	(1,630)	(12,007)	(11,663)	(7,723)	(1,612)
From households	61,679	41,415	17,613	10,576	2,905	11,480	15,001	(1,630)	(12,007)	(11,664)	(7,723)	(1,612)
From legal entities	499	288	28	1	(7)	0	0	0	0	1	0	0

Note: Includes transactions in Russian rubles.
1/ ICE stands for Interbank Currency Exchange.

Source: National Bank of Belarus.

Table 7.1 - Agricultural Production

	1990	1991	1992	1993	1994	1995
(In thousands of tons, unless indicated otherwise)						
Grain	7,035	6,296	7,230	7,508	6,095	5502
Potatoes	8,590	8,958	8,984	11,644	8,241	9504
Flax	52	76	61	57	49	60
Sugar beets	1,479	1,147	1,120	1,569	1,078	1172
Meat	1,758	1,590	1,442	1,242	1,138	995
Milk	7,457	6,812	5,885	5,584	5,510	5070
Eggs	3,657	3,718	3,502	3,514	3,400	3373
Live animals (1,000 heads) 1/						
Cattle	6,975	6,577	6,221	5,851	5,403	5054
Pigs	5,051	4,703	4,308	4,181	4,005	3895
Sheep	403	380	336	271	230	204
Horses	217	212	215	215	220	229
(Percentage changes from previous year)						
Grain	-4.7	-10.5	14.8	3.8	-18.8	-9.7
Potatoes	-22.6	4.3	0.3	29.6	-29.2	15.3
Flax	-40.2	46.2	-19.7	-6.6	-14	22.4
Sugar beets	-18.3	-22.4	-2.4	40.1	-31.3	8.7
Meat	-1.6	-9.6	-9.3	-13.9	-8.4	-12.6
Milk	0.5	-8.6	-13.6	-5.1	-1.3	-8
Eggs	0.2	1.7	-5.8	0.3	-3.2	0.8
Live animals 1/						
Cattle	-2.7	-5.7	-5.4	-5.9	-7.7	-6.5
Pigs	-2.9	-6.9	-8.4	-2.9	-4.2	-2.7
Sheep	-15.3	-5.7	-11.6	-19.3	-15.1	-11.3
Horses	-0.9	-23	1.4	--	2.3	4.1

1/ End of period stocks.
Source: Belarus Ministry of Statistics and Analysis.

Table 7.2 - Agricultural Production Sold Through State Procurement Organizations
(In percent of total production)

	1990	1993	1994	1995
Grain	17.6	24.7	30.1	31.4
Potatoes	16.1	6.1	3.0	1.8
Sugar beets	89.0	89.3	87.7	60.5
Vegetables	50.1	15.5	12.1	7.6
Meat 1/	93.1	81.2	71.7	56.1
Milk 1/	82.8	66.0	58.6	48.9
Eggs 1/	49.6	50.8	48.0	46.2

1/ Excluding amounts used for breeding and catering or sold at farmers' markets.
Source: Statistical Bulletin, Ministry of Statistics and Analysis.

Table 7.3 - Private Sector in Agriculture

	1991	1992	1993	1994	1995
Gross agricultural output 1/	27.0	33.6	38.6	39.6	44.0
Crops	33.6	40.9	47.8	49.0	53.0
Livestock	22.3	27.7	29.6	32.2	35.9
In physical volumes:					
Potatoes	65.0	72.4	74.6	85.4	86.9
Vegetables	54.6	70.3	75.0	76.1	77.3
Fruits and berries	96.1	92.5	92.6	94.6	94.8
Grain	2.1	3.9	5.5	6.5	6.5
Sugarbeets	--	0.2	0.4	0.6	0.4
Meat	13.7	15.3	18.0	20.2	23.7
Milk	26.3	31.7	34.7	35.8	39.6
Eggs	38.4	40.8	40.7	42.6	41.6
Live animals					
Cattle	12.2	13.0	13.9	15.1	16.2
Pigs	31.5	34.1	36.4	38.6	40.1
Sheep	54.4	59.5	69.7	74.8	82.5
Horses	9.2	13.5	20.3	24.7	29.9

1/ At comparable 1983 prices.
Source: Ministry of Statistics and Analysis.

Table 8.1 - Industrial Production at Comparable Prices, 1994-1996(Q1)
(percentage change)

	1993 Weight	1991	1992	1993	1994	1995	1996 Q1
Total	100.0	-1.0	-9.4	-10.0	-17.1	-11.7	-2.9
Power generation	14.6	0.9	-3.1	-10.9	-11.3	-15.8	3.2
Refineries	8.0	-5.4	-42.9	-36.9	-45.2	11.2	3.9
Chemicals and petrochemical	12.4	-6.7	-14.7	-12.3	-16.8	8.9	11.5
Ferrous metallurgy	1.9	13.1	-13.7	-13.9	-12.5	-1.4	32.6
Machine building	22.1	5.1	-7.4	2.8	-14.1	-20.5	-5.6
Wood and paper	4.5	6.9	-7.2	-3.4	-12.7	-9.6	-2.8
Construction materials	5.7	5.0	-10.6	-13.9	-28.8	-21.2	-18.4
Light industry	11.3	1.0	0.7	1.7	-23.0	-34.1	-20.2
Food processing industries	13.1	-9.4	-17.6	0.1	-5.5	-12.7	-8.8
Index: 1990 = 100	1990	1991	1992	1993	1994	1995	
Total	100.0	99.0	89.7	80.7	66.9	59.1	
Power generation	100.0	100.9	97.8	87.1	77.3	65.1	
Refineries	100.0	94.6	54.0	34.1	18.7	20.8	
Chemicals and petrochemical	100.0	93.3	79.6	69.8	58.1	63.2	
Ferrous metallurgy	100.0	113.1	97.6	84.0	73.5	72.5	
Machine building	100.0	105.1	97.3	100.0	85.9	68.3	
Wood and paper	100.0	106.9	99.2	95.8	83.7	75.6	
Construction materials	100.0	105.0	93.9	80.8	57.5	45.3	
Light industry	100.0	101.0	101.7	103.4	79.6	52.5	
Food processing industries	100.0	90.6	74.7	74.7	70.6	61.7	

Sources: Ministry of Statistics and Analysis; and IMF staff calculations.

Table 8.2 - Production of Selected Industrial Products, 1990-96(Q1)
(units as indicated)

	1990	1991	1992	1993	1994	1995	1996(Q1)
Timber (million m3)	6.9	6.7	6.5	6.2	5.6	5.5	1.6
Plywood (1,000 m3)	192	164	157	127	104	94	30
Cardboard (1,000 t)	219	207	149	117	109	106	23
Paper (1,000 t)	198	166	118	59	22	27	7
Lime (1,000 t)	1,089	1,080	1,057	939	589	453	57
Mineral fertilizers (million t)	6	5.2	4.1	2.5	3	3.3	0.9
Cement (1,000 t)	2,258	2,402	2,263	1,908	1,488	1235	198
Window glass (million m2)	8.7	9.3	10.4	8.8	6.9	5.6	1.6
Chemical fibers (1,000 t)	453	443	385	293	217	209	49
Cotton yarn (1,000 t)	50.5	50.5	44.9	35.2	13	9.7	1.8
Wool yarn (1,000 t)	40.2	34.8	30.3	28.2	22	11.8	3.6
Linen yarn (1,000 t)	30	24.4	27.2	20.8	15.1	16.1	4.8
Electricity (billion kwh)	39.5	38.7	37.6	33.4	31.4	24.9	7.1
Steel (1,000 t)	1,112	1,123	1,105	946	880	744	191
Tractors (1,000)	100.7	95.5	96.1	82.4	42.9	26.5	4.2
Forage harvesters (1,000)	9.5	8.3	5.5	4.3	1.4	1.1	0.2
Elevators (1,000)	14	12.6	8.7	3.9	2.6	1.9	0.5
Electric motors (1,000 kw)	3,319	2,841	1,316	1,430	573	513	105
Transformers (1,000 VA)	6,205	5,847	4,039	3,778	1,884	2493	358
Electric bulbs (1,000)	306	301	278	180	142	130	36
Motorcycles (1,000)	225	214	165	128	55	42	9
Bicycles (1,000)	846	815	724	603	385	271	61
Radio sets (1,000)	979	932	721	768	545	277	43
T.V. sets (1,000)	1,302	1,103	798	610	473	250	64
Refrigerators (1,000)	728	743	740	738	742	746	186
Cameras (1,000)	885	965	949	495	128	34	11

Source: Ministry of Statistics and Analysis.

Table 8.3 - Production and Consumption of Energy Resources

	1992	1993	1994	1995
Production				
Electricity (mln Kwh)	37,595	33,369	31,397	24,918
Natural gas (mln qm)	292	291	294	266
Crude Oil (thous tons)	2,000	2,005	2,000	1,932
Gasoline (thous tons)	2,222	1,687	1,744	1,849
Diesel (thous tons)	4,499	3,316	3,053	3,465
Heavy fuel oil (thous tons)	9,006	6,285	4,962	5,592
Import				
Electricity (mln Kwh)	9,909	9,610	7,764	10,066
Natural gas (mln qm)	17,978	16,305	14,297	13,531
Crude Oil (thous tons)	19,747	12,378	11,300	11,555
Gasoline (thous tons)	168	10	31	53
Diesel (thous tons)	33	17	117	24
Heavy fuel oil (thous tons)	635	920	614	36
Export				
Electricity (mln Kwh)	3,405	3,605	3,944	2,907
Natural gas (mln qm)	...	...	...	...
Crude Oil (thous tons)	1,058	284	250	200
Gasoline (thous tons)	317	117	720	551
Diesel (thous tons)	1,869	276	1,231	1,711
Heavy fuel oil (thous tons)	732	95	57	233
Change in stocks				
Natural gas (mln qm)	16	382	71	43
Crude Oil (thous tons)	18	183	-191	-25
Gasoline (thous tons)	162	-22	39	-82
Diesel (thous tons)	230	-18	27	27
Heavy fuel oil (thous tons)	118	-47	616	-217
Consumption				
Electricity (mln Kwh)	44,099	39,374	35,217	32,077
Industrial sector	22,524	18,355	14,993	13,383
Others	21,575	21,019	20,224	18,694
Natural gas (mln qm)	18,286	16,978	14,662	13,840
Production of heating and electricity	13,278	12,122	11,262	9,903
Others	5,008	4,856	3,400	3,937
Crude Oil (thous tons)	20,707	14,282	12,859	13,262
Gasoline (thous tons)	2,235	1,558	1,094	1,269
Diesel (thous tons)	2,893	3,039	1,966	1,805
Heavy fuel oil (thous tons)	9,027	7,063	6,135	5,178
Production of heating and electricity	7,434	5,714	5,113	4,238
Others	1,593	1,349	1,022	940
Losses in distribution 1/				
Electricity (mln Kwh)	4,125	4,047	3,837	3,636
Natural gas (mln qm)	102	103	126	139

1/ Included in consumption.
Source: Ministry of Statistics and Analysis.

Table 8.4 - Enterprise Profitability and Number of Loss-Making Enterprises

	1991	1992	1993	1994	1995	1996 QI
	(Profits in percent of costs)					
Industry	22.1	29.1	22.7	29.0	10.1	8.2
Of which:						
Power generation	22.8	21.3	-1.3	3.9	-0.8	7.4
Refineries	13.5	21.7	30.9	30.9	18.1	22.6
Ferrous metallurgy	17.4	62.2	31.1	38.6	8.0	10.3
Chemicals	46.5	45.2	39.1	40.2	13.9	6.8
Petrochemicals	28.2	23.4	22.9	14.6	1.7	7.9
Machine building	19.9	27.3	22.9	38.5	9.2	4.8
Wood and paper	31.9	34.6	33.1	40.7	16.9	12.7
Construction materials	21.2	21.7	16.4	17.9	11.4	-0.2
Light industry	31.0	36.6	35.4	43.6	11.7	8.4
Food industry	14.4	16.7	13.8	14.6	11.7	9.9
Agriculture	44.5	16.7	9.4	13.0	15.4	19.0
Kolkhozes	47.2	21.2	9.4	12.9	18.2	23.5
Sovkhozes	43.4	9.3	7.5	12.1	11.8	15.5
Transport	20.5	17.5	20.4	17.5	26.5	19.8
Communications	34.1	14.3	15.7	32.5	11.1	3.7
Construction	18.3	14.5	16.4	18.5	11.3	1.8
Trade and catering	27.5	17.2	24.4	20.5	-0.1	-2.6
Material supply amd sales	9.3	8.4	5.6	8.3	5.8	3.5
Procurement	5.6	12.0	9.7	22.1	17.8	22.6
	(Number of loss-making enterprises)					
Industry	40	10	42	46	192	442
Of which:						
Power generation	...	...	1	6	2	...
Refineries	...	...	...	...	...	...
Ferrous metallurgy	...	...	...	...	...	1
Chemicals	...	...	...	1	3	3
Petrochemicals	...	...	...	--	1	3
Machine building 1/	...	...	2	7	43	99
Wood and paper	...	...	...	--	18	33
Construction materials	...	...	7	18	26	55
Light industry	...	...	20	2	52	124
Food industry	...	...	4	8	27	82
Other	...	...	8	4	20	42
Agriculture	37	65	128	179	380	550
Kolkhozes	10	17	60	116	219	289
Sovkhozes	6	9	26	42	125	135
Transport	3	5	5	8	17	81
Construction	33	24	24	33	114	450
Trade and catering	11	42	50	121	529	642
Material supply amd sales	26	1	7	9	51	167

1/ Machine building & metalworking.
Source: Ministry of Statistics and Analysis.

Table 8.5 - Tariffs and Cost Coverage, January 1995–January 1996

	1-Jan-95			1-Jul-95			1-Oct-95			1-Jan-96		
	Tariff 1/	Tariff 2/	Coverage	Tariff 1/	Tariff 2/	Coverage	Tariff 1/	Tariff 2/	Coverage	Tariff 1/	Tariff 2/	Coverage
Rent	7.0	198.0	1.8	831	24,930	50.0	899	26,970	38.1	899	26,970	36.4
Heating	213.0	6,380.0	3.6	2,871	86,130	64.8	3,105	93,150	51.6	3,105	93,150	67.5
Water	6.0	163.0	2.0	290	7,830	32.0	314	8,478	30.0	314	8,478	28.1
Sewage	6.0	160.0	2.2	286	7,722	40.2	309	8,343	37.1	309	8,343	32.3
Hot water	638.0	1,914.0	8.8	8,612	25,835	54.4	9,314	27,942	43.3	9,314	27,942	56.7
Radio	800.0	800.0	64.8	1,300	1,300	70.0	1,300	1,300	70.0	1,300	1,300	75.0
Telephone	5,000.0	5,000.0	52.6	12,000	12,000	75.0	12,000	12,000	75.0	12,000	12,000	100.0
TV antenna	140.0	140.0	50.0	1,300	1,300	70.0	1,300	1,300	70.0	1,300	1,300	70.0
Gas	660.0	1,980.0	9.3	3,300	9,900	50.0	3,569	10,707	54.1	3,569	10,707	54.1
Electricity	70.0	10,530.0	25.5	280	48,000	84.2	280	48,000	72.9	280	48,000	72.9
Total												
Winter 3/		27,265.0	9.2		224,947	53.7		238,190	54.2		250,190	59.3
Summer 4/		20,885.0	17.2		138,817	52.5		145,040	54.5		157,040	58.4
Average		24,075.0	11.5		181,882	53.1		191,615	54.3		203,615	58.8
Memorandum												
Energy Utilities 5/		20,803.0	8.0		169,865	66.0		179,799	55.5		179,799	62.8

1/ Per square meter for rent and heating; per cubic meter for water and sewage; per person for hot water and gas; per kwh for electricity; and per household for radio, television, and TV antenna.

2/ The following assumptions are made to calculate rent and tariffs:

a) the area of a two bedroom apartment is 30 square meters; b) each person consumes 9 cubic meters of water and 50 kwh of electricity per month.

3/ Including all services.

4/ Excluding heating (housing).

5/ Including heating, hot water, electricity, and gas.

Source: Ministry of Housing and Communal Services.

Table 8.6 - Share of Total Exports in Production of Selected Industrial Products
(in percent)

	1992	1993	1994	1995	1996 Q1 E[1]
Metal-cutting machinery	51.3	51.8	42.8	81.5	62.2
Forge presses	8.1	19.8	27.9	...	...
Tractors	75.2	72.0	71.6	94.1	48.8
Trucks	66.9	68.2	69.9	73.4	68.2
Motorcycles	75.4	73.3	59.2	83.1	82.4
Refrigerators	84.8	70.9	71.9	67.6	64.3
Watches and clocks	61.3	75.0	75.1	66.1	52.8
Cameras	40.4	48.5	66.1	194.6	96.5
T.V. sets	54.6	52.2	59.8	66.3	37.0
Radios	54.8	54.8	49.5	28.7	38.5
Diesel fuel	28.2	8.3	40.3	49.4	54.2
Potassium fertilizers	54.4	83.5	86.4	92.8	80.4
Nitrogen fertilizers	17.2	39.8	7.4	111.0	64.4
Particle boards					
Wood fibers	25.5	44.4	58.0	59.6	48.3
Wood particles	7.6	9.0	14.0	45.8	21.6
Synthetic fibers	61.5	70.8	78.3	78.9	52.1
Cotton and cotton-type textiles	16.4	10.5	26.7	... [2]	... [2]
Silk and silk-type textiles					
(including synthetic)	35.9	34.2	29.5	... [2]	... [2]

1/ Data for 1996 Q1 represent sales from inventories. Inventories at the start of the
quarter were 37.5 thousand items, while production in the first quarter was
8.7 thousand items.

2/ Export is recorded in tons, production -- in meters, hence comparison is impossible.

Source: Ministry of Statistics and Analysis.

Table 9.1 - Consumer Price Indices

		1/95=		CPI Inflation (%)		Goods			
Year	Month	100	Total	Month	YoY	Total	Food	Non-food	Services
1990	Dec	0.004	100.0			100.0	100.0	100.0	100.0
1991	Jan	0.004	105.9	5.9		105.9	103.5	108.6	106.0
1992	Jan	0.026	640.1	158.6	505	667.0	607.8	732.0	429.8
1993	Jan	0.19	4,715	14.8	637	4,803	5,118	4,472	4,055
	Feb	0.23	5,645	19.7	486	5,705	5,755	5,659	5,215
	Mar	0.29	7,233	28.1	529	7,315	7,556	7,068	6,635
	Apr	0.37	9,026	24.8	576	9,113	9,699	8,498	8,410
	May	0.44	10,801	19.7	599	10,980	11,810	10,106	9,462
	Jun	0.55	13,636	26.2	692	13,888	15,678	11,985	11,746
	Jul	0.68	16,807	23.3	764	17,229	20,361	13,889	13,585
	Aug	0.85	21,028	25.1	893	21,637	26,504	16,441	16,364
	Sep	1.16	28,594	36.0	1,141	29,471	36,102	22,396	21,843
	Oct	1.67	41,333	44.5	1,493	42,188	50,813	32,987	34,870
	Nov	2.40	59,172	43.2	1,784	60,734	71,880	48,854	47,221
	Dec	3.49	86,096	45.5	1,997	88,805	103,364	73,305	65,193
1994	Jan	4.91	121,137	40.7	2,469	123,945	150,922	95,172	99,700
	Feb	5.82	143,741	18.7	2,446	147,928	181,046	112,598	111,405
	Mar	6.42	158,403	10.2	2,090	162,529	197,050	125,704	126,734
	Apr	8.25	203,674	28.6	2,156	208,248	254,530	157,118	169,380
	May	10.6	262,169	28.7	2,327	270,577	334,401	196,963	195,549
	Jun	12.7	313,397	19.5	2,198	325,531	395,228	250,714	215,339
	Jul	16.1	396,886	26.6	2,262	413,880	501,426	320,863	258,256
	Aug	24.7	608,982	53.4	2,796	633,940	800,276	428,802	406,236
	Sep	31.0	764,516	25.5	2,574	788,875	987,301	550,196	572,956
	Oct	38.9	960,920	25.7	2,225	989,092	1,217,539	729,284	742,092
	Nov	54.7	1,350,381	40.5	2,182	1,376,420	1,716,974	970,969	1,163,229
	Dec	71.8	1,773,321	31.3	1,959	1,807,652	2,282,889	1,220,799	1,526,041
1995	Jan	100.0	2,468,285	39.2	1,937	2,505,225	3,211,796	1,598,637	2,220,999
	Feb	133.7	3,299,357	33.7	2,195	3,357,002	4,337,531	2,077,109	2,893,962
	Mar	160.4	3,958,898	20.0	2,399	4,012,960	5,157,324	2,536,358	3,608,771
	Apr	183.7	4,530,959	14.5	2,126	4,408,236	5,565,784	2,979,459	5,776,560
	May	189.9	4,685,917	3.4	1,688	4,561,202	5,722,183	3,154,056	5,955,055
	Jun	194.7	4,804,471	2.5	1,433	4,688,004	5,841,204	3,368,531	6,024,729
	Jul	204.8	5,054,304	5.2	1,174	4,731,133	5,866,321	3,490,135	7,777,926
	Aug	211.0	5,203,406	3.0	755	4,896,723	6,026,472	3,753,990	7,823,815
	Sep	221.9	5,476,064	5.2	616	5,199,830	6,393,484	4,005,507	7,897,359
	Oct	229.5	5,663,345	3.4	489	5,393,264	6,612,780	4,213,393	8,053,727
	Nov	238.0	5,871,757	3.7	335	5,563,152	6,830,341	4,317,885	8,555,474
	Dec	247.3	6,099,581	3.9	244	5,790,128	7,145,220	4,380,494	8,805,294
1996	Jan	261.1	6,438,717	5.6	161	6,108,006	7,563,930	4,539,068	9,321,284
	Feb	271.5	6,696,266	4.0	103	6,353,548	7,889,179	4,654,361	9,681,086
	Mar	276.7	6,828,852	2.0	73	6,462,829	8,014,616	4,766,996	9,996,689
	Apr	280.9	6,932,651	1.5	53	6,547,492	8,112,395	4,851,372	10,245,607
	May	282.7	6,977,020	0.6	49	6,594,634	8,166,748	4,901,826	10,294,786
	Jun	289.1	7,136,793	2.3	49	6,758,181	8,387,250	4,952,805	10,494,505
	Jul	295.0	7,282,384	2.0	44	6,916,998	8,590,221	5,034,031	10,614,142
	Aug	298.9	7,377,055	1.3	42	6,986,812	8,670,839	5,101,019	10,844,180
	Sep	227.6	7,509,842	1.8	37	7,119,561	8,835,585	5,203,040	11,028,531
	Oct	192.2	7,607,470	1.3	34	7,226,355	8,959,283	5,307,101	11,028,531
	Nov	174.4	7,904,161	3.9	35	7,537,052	9,371,406	5,453,203	11,227,060
	Dec	177.8	8,330,986	5.4	37	...	...	...	...

Note: The CPI uses 1991 household expenditure weights and retail price data for 1991; 1992
  household expenditure weights for January 1992-March 1994; and from April 1994, 1993 weights are used.
Source: Ministry of Statistics and Analysis.

Table 9.2 - Producer Price Indices

Year	Month	Producer Price Index			PPI vs. CPI					
		12/91	PPI Inflation		CPI Index				CPI:PPI	
		= 100	Month	YoY	1990=100	12/91=100	MoM	Cumulative	Monthly
		PPI				CPI	CPI		
1990	Dec								
1991	Jan				106			-	
1992	Jan	482.5	382.5		640	259	158.6	1.87	2.41
1993	Jan	4,254.7	26.1	782	4,715	1,905	14.8	2.23	1.76
	Feb	5,317.5	25.0	775	5,645	2,281	19.7	2.33	1.27
	Mar	7,372.2	38.6	921	7,233	2,922	28.1	2.52	1.37
	Apr	9,005.9	22.2	895	9,026	3,647	24.8	2.47	0.90
	May	10,197.4	13.2	866	10,801	4,364	19.7	2.34	0.67
	Jun	11,545.5	13.2	877	13,636	5,509	26.2	2.10	0.50
	Jul	13,987.3	21.2	964	16,807	6,790	23.3	2.06	0.91
	Aug	17,596.0	25.8	1,120	21,028	8,496	25.1	2.07	1.03
	Sep	23,724.7	34.8	1,398	28,594	11,552	36.0	2.05	0.97
	Oct	37,010.6	56.0	1,705	41,333	16,699	44.5	2.22	1.26
	Nov	63,510.2	71.6	2,253	59,172	23,906	43.2	2.66	1.66
	Dec	81,521.7	28.4	2,316	86,096	34,783	45.5	2.34	0.62
1994	Jan	101,494.5	24.5	2,285	121,137	48,940	40.7	2.07	0.60
	Feb	119,144.3	17.4	2,141	143,741	58,072	18.7	2.05	0.93
	Mar	133,382.1	12.0	1,709	158,403	63,996	10.2	2.08	1.18
	Apr	182,666.8	37.0	1,928	203,674	82,286	28.6	2.22	1.29
	May	241,960.4	32.5	2,273	262,169	105,918	28.7	2.28	1.13
	Jun	295,264.3	22.0	2,457	313,397	126,615	19.5	2.33	1.13
	Jul	346,906.0	17.5	2,380	396,886	160,345	26.6	2.16	0.66
	Aug	494,410.4	42.5	2,710	608,982	246,033	53.4	2.01	0.80
	Sep	697,810.8	41.1	2,841	764,516	308,870	25.5	2.26	1.61
	Oct	988,239.7	41.6	2,570	960,920	388,219	25.7	2.55	1.62
	Nov	1,268,603.3	28.4	1,898	1,350,381	545,564	40.5	2.33	0.70
	Dec	1,603,387.7	26.4	1,867	1,773,321	716,435	31.3	2.24	0.84
1995	Jan	2,315,452.2	44.4	2,181	2,468,285	997,206	39.2	2.32	1.13
	Feb	2,622,018.1	13.2	2,101	3,299,357	1,332,966	33.7	1.97	0.39
	Mar	2,872,158.7	9.5	2,053	3,958,898	1,599,425	20.0	1.80	0.48
	Apr	3,089,006.6	7.6	1,591	4,530,959	1,830,542	14.5	1.69	0.53
	May	3,141,519.7	1.7	1,198	4,685,917	1,893,147	3.4	1.66	0.50
	Jun	3,181,102.9	1.3	977	4,804,471	1,941,044	2.5	1.64	0.51
	Jul	3,256,176.9	2.4	839	5,054,304	2,041,978	5.2	1.59	0.46
	Aug	3,423,870.0	5.2	593	5,203,406	2,102,216	3.0	1.63	1.76
	Sep	3,594,036.4	5.0	415	5,476,064	2,212,372	5.2	1.62	0.95
	Oct	3,668,792.3	2.1	271	5,663,345	2,288,035	3.4	1.60	0.61
	Nov	3,769,317.2	2.7	197	5,871,757	2,372,235	3.7	1.59	0.73
	Dec	3,852,242.2	2.2	140	6,099,581	2,464,278	3.9	1.56	0.57
1996	Jan	4,033,297.6	4.7	74	6,443,357	2,603,166	5.6	1.55	0.85
	Feb	4,042,170.9	0.2	54	6,701,092	2,707,293	4.0	1.49	0.05
	Mar	4,067,636.5	0.6	42	6,828,852	2,761,439	2.0	1.47	0.30
	Apr	4,135,972.8	1.7	34	6,932,651	2,802,860	1.5	1.48	1.13
	May	4,150,035.1	0.3	32	6,977,020	2,819,678	0.6	1.47	0.50
	Jun	4,266,236.1	2.8	34	7,136,793	2,884,530	2.3	1.48	1.22
	Jul	4,376,731.6	2.6	34	7,282,384	2,942,221	2.0	1.49	1.30
	Aug	4,513,339.8	3.9	33	7,377,259	2,980,470	1.3	1.51	0.33
	Sep	4,603,606.6	2.0	29	7,510,049	3,034,118	1.8	1.52	0.90
	Oct	4,686,471.5	1.8	28	7,607,680	3,073,562	1.3	1.52	0.72
	Nov	4,775,514.5	1.9	28	7,904,379	3,193,431	3.9	1.50	2.05
	Dec	4,861,473.7	1.8	27	8,331,216	3,365,876	5.4	1.44	3.00

Note: The CPI uses 1991 household expenditure weights and retail price data for 1991; 1992
household expenditure weights for January 1992-March 1994; and from April 1994, 1993 weights are used.

Source: Ministry of Statistics and Analysis.

Table 9.3 - Consumer and Producer Price Indices

Dec. Year	Consumer Price Index: 12/90 = 100							Producer Prices		
	Average			Goods			Services	12/91 = 100	Infl YoY	Average YoY
	Total	Inflation	YoY	Total	Food	Non-food				
1990	100	0		100	100	100	100			
1991	248	148		258	226	293	163	100		
1992	4,106	1,559	969	4,271	4,596	3,929	2,827	3,375	3,275	
1993	86,096	1,997	1,188	88,805	103,364	73,305	65,193	81,522	2,316	1,536
1994	1,772,813	1,959	2,222	1,807,652	2,282,889	1,220,799	1,526,041	1,603,388	867	2,171
1995	6,101,664	244	709	5,790,128	7,145,220	4,380,494	8,805,294	3,852,242	140	499

CPI	1987	1988	1989	1990	1991	1992	1993	1994	1995
90=100	88	92	96	100	248	4,106	86,096	1,772,813	6,101,664
87=100	100	105	109	114	281	4,667	97,845	2,014,748	6,934,354

Note: The CPI uses 1991 household expenditure weights and retail price data for 1991; 1992 household expenditure weights for January 1992-March 1994; and from April 1994, 1993 weights are used.

Source: Ministry of Statistics and Analysis.

Table 9.4 - Price and Wage Developments
(percentage change; period average unless otherwise indicated)

	1991	1992	1993	1994	1995 QI	1995 QII	1995 QIII	1995 QIV	1995 Year	1996 QI
Consumer prices	94	971	1,190	2,221	138	44	12	12	709	13
Change end of period	148	1,559	1,996	1,960	123	21	14	11	244	12
Goods	96	985	1,170	2,224	122	17	11	11	220	12
Food	88	1,054	1,415	2,374	126	13	9	12	213	12
Nonfood	102	922	918	1,918	108	33	19	99	259	9
Services	69	823	1,170	2,184	137	67	31	12	477	14
Industrial producer prices 1/	151	2,327	1,536	2,171	102	21	9	10	499	8
Change end of period	278	3,275	2,316	1,867	79	11	13	7	140	6
Industrial goods	234	4,343	2,450	1,848	63	12	14	4	115	4
Consumer goods	354	1,937	2,006	1,921	111	9	11	15	194	9
Minimum wage (end of period)	64	755	783	927	200				517	
Average monthly wage	101	838	1,107	1,504	115	62	15	9	669	8
Real wage 2/	0	-12.4	-18.1	-43.4					46	
Memorandum items:										
Average monthly wage (in rubel)	54	507	6,121	98,203	461,110	746,095	861,254	937,412	755,129	1,014,288
Minimum wage (in rubels, eop)	13	200	2,000	20,000	60,000	60,000	60,000	60,000	60,000	100,000
Real wage index 3/	54	47	44	31					29	

1/ Data for 1995 are based on a Laspeyres formula.
2/ Growth of annual average minimum wage.
3/ Based on average wage and inflation as measured by the Consumer Price Index (base: 1991=100).
Sources: Ministry of Statistics and Analysis; and IMF staff calculations.

Table 9.5 - Nominal and Real Exchange Rates
(January 1993=100)

	Exchange Rates		PPI Index	Real Exchange
	BYR/USD	Index		Rate Index
1992 Jan	11.0	19.7	13.6	69.1
Feb	12.6	22.5	20.4	90.5
Mar	12.7	22.7	24.4	107.4
Apr	13.3	23.8	28.3	118.9
May	12.3	21.9	32.8	149.7
Jun	12.0	21.4	36.5	170.7
Jul	12.7	22.7	41.3	181.8
Aug	13.8	24.6	44.9	182.5
Sep	19.3	34.5	48.9	141.6
Oct	23.9	42.7	55.0	128.9
Nov	29.1	52.0	66.6	128.2
Dec	33.1	59.1	87.1	147.3
1993 Jan	56	100	100	100
Feb	63	112	120	107
Mar	88	157	153	97
Apr	110	196	191	97
May	157	280	229	82
Jun	183	327	289	88
Jul	200	358	356	100
Aug	282	505	446	88
Sep	335	599	606	101
Oct	419	749	877	117
Nov	603	1,079	1,255	116
Dec	731	1,308	1,826	140
1994 Jan	680	1,217	2,569	211
Feb	772	1,381	3,049	221
Mar	1604	2,870	3,360	117
Apr	1917	3,429	4,320	126
May	2018	3,609	5,560	154
Jun	2633	4,710	6,646	141
Jul	2758	4,933	8,417	171
Aug	3260	5,832	12,915	221
Sep	4601	8,231	16,215	197
Oct	6577	11,766	20,380	173
Nov	7843	14,030	28,641	204
Dec	9666	17,292	37,611	218
1995 Jan	11551	20,664	52,350	253
Feb	11666	20,869	69,977	335
Mar	11643	20,828	83,965	403
Apr	11496	20,565	96,098	467
May	11501	20,574	99,385	483
Jun	11501	20,574	101,899	495
Jul	11507	20,585	107,198	521
Aug	11518	20,605	100,360	487
Sep	11511	20,592	116,143	564
Oct	11513	20,596	120,115	583
Nov	11505	20,581	124,535	605
Dec	11500	20,572	129,367	629
1996 Jan	11500	20,572	136,560	664
Feb	11500	20,572	142,023	690
Mar	11500	20,572	144,835	704
Apr	12037	21,533	147,036	683
May	12534	22,422	147,977	660
Jun	13310	23,810	151,366	636
Jul	13510	24,168	154,454	639
Aug	14272	25,531	104,890	411
Sept	14674	26,250	106,987	408
Oct	14930	26,708	108,913	408
Nov	15208	27,206	110,982	408
Dec	15380	27,513	112,980	411

Source: Ministry of Statistics.

Table 10.1 - Transformation of State Property

	1991	1992	1993	1994	1995	1996 Q1
	Number of enterprises transformed					
Total	61	189	239	641	466	44
Cumulative since 1991	61	250	489	1130	1596	1640
Republican property	19	32	140	184	53	0
Cumulative since 1991	19	51	191	375	428	428
Communal property	42	157	99	457	413	44
Cumulative since 1991	42	199	298	755	1168	1212
	Share in total number of enterprises to be transformed 1/					
Total	1.4	4.5	5.7	15.1	11.3	1
Cumulative since 1991	1.4	6.1	12.2	26.8	38.6	39.1
Republican property	0.4	0.7	3.2	4.2	1.2	
Cumulative since 1991	0.4	1.2	4.3	8.5	9.7	9.7
Communal property	1	3.8	2.5	10.9	10.1	1
Cumulative since 1991	1	4.9	7.9	18.3	28.9	29.4
	Assessed value as of January 1, 1994, in billions of 1993 Brub 2/					
Republican property	12.8	22.9	172.6	254.4	...	
Cumulative since 1991	12.8	35.7	208.3	462.7	...	
	Share in total assets of enterprises to be transformed 3/					
Republican property	0.3	0.5	3.8	5.6	...	
Cumulative since 1991	0.3	0.8	4.6	10.2	...	

Note: The authorities define transformation to include enterprises converted to joint stock companies where the Government owns all
  or most of the shares.

1/ As of January 1, 1994, 4,423 Republican enterprises and 4,114 communal enterprises (a total of 8,537 enterprises) were planned
  to be transformed.

2/ In billions of Belarussian rubles before currency reform to rubels. Figures for 1991-93 were increased by a factor of 4.105
  to account for the general revaluation of property in 1994.

3/ The total fixed assets value (gross) of state property to be transformed (in 1993 prices, balance sheet data) was
  Brub 4,538.9 billion as of January 1994.

  Source: Ministry of Management of State Property and Privatization.

Table 10.2 - **Number of Transformed Enterprises Distributed by Privatization Method**

	1991	1992	1993	1994	1995	1996 Q1
Total	61	189	239	641	466	44
Republican	19	32	140	184	53	--
Communal	42	157	99	457	413	44
Conversion to joint stock companies	3	4	71	217	259	7
Republican 1/	3	3	68	152	52	--
Communal	--	1	3	65	207	7
Buy-outs of leased enterprises	34	47	56	152	35	13
Republican	9	20	44	28	1	--
Communal	25	27	12	124	34	13
Auction 2/	--	--	41	164	139	21
Republican	--	--	7	--	--	--
Communal	--	--	34	164	139	21
Sell by competition 2/	11	50	47	96	32	3
Republican	1	--	11	3	--	--
Communal	10	50	36	93	32	3
Other	13	88	24	12	1	--
Republican	6	9	10	1	--	--
Communal	7	79	14	11	1	--

Sources: Ministry of Management of State Property and Privatization.

1/ Mainly conversion to joint-stock companies of Republican enterprises, where the shares later are sold (to be sold).

2/ A tender, unlike an auction, involves conditions on the purchase of enterprise.

Table 10.3.a - Number of Transformed Enterprises by Activity
(flow - new transformations during period)

	1991	1992	1993	1994	1995	1996 Q1
Total	61	189	239	641	466	44
Republican	19	32	140	184	53	--
Communal	42	157	99	457	413	44
Industry	23	35	69	63	17	--
Republican	12	23	68	58	15	--
Communal	11	12	1	5	2	--
Construction	7	9	30	43	5	--
Republican	5	4	28	40	3	--
Communal	2	5	2	3	2	--
Agro-processing	1	--	12	48	221	7
Republican	1	--	9	9	27	--
Communal	--	--	3	39	194	7
Transport	--	--	9	10	1	--
Republican	--	--	9	10	1	--
Communal	--	--	--	--	--	--
Service	6	71	43	138	30	6
Republican	1	4	1	24	--	--
Communal	5	67	42	114	30	6
Trade and catering	21	53	36	293	160	27
Republican	--	--	1	15	3	--
Communal	21	53	35	278	157	27
Other	3	21	40	46	32	4
Republican	--	1	24	28	4	--
Communal	3	20	16	18	28	4

Sources: Ministry of Management of State Property and Privatization.

Table 10.3.b - Number of Transformed Enterprises by Activity
(stock - cumulative totals)

	1991	1992	1993	1994	1995	1996 Q1
Total	61	250	489	1,130	1,596	1,640
Republican	19	51	191	375	428	428
Communal	42	199	298	755	1,168	1,212
Industry	23	58	127	190	207	207
Republican	12	35	103	161	176	176
Communal	11	23	24	29	31	31
Construction	7	16	46	89	94	94
Republican	5	9	37	77	80	80
Communal	2	7	9	12	14	14
Agro-processing	1	1	13	61	282	289
Republican	1	1	10	19	46	46
Communal	--	--	3	42	236	243
Transport	--	--	9	19	20	20
Republican	--	--	9	19	20	20
Communal	--	--	--	--	--	--
Service	6	77	120	258	288	294
Republican	1	5	6	30	30	30
Communal	5	72	114	228	258	264
Trade and catering	21	74	110	403	563	590
Republican	--	--	1	16	19	19
Communal	21	74	109	387	544	571
Other	3	24	64	110	142	146
Republican	--	1	25	53	57	57
Communal	3	23	39	57	85	89

Sources: Ministry of Management of State Property and Privatization.

Table 10.4 - *Employment in Transformed Enterprises*
(Thousands of employees)

	1991	1992	1993	1994	1995	1996 Q1
Total						
Increase during the period	23.3	47.2	128.1	141.6	74.5	1.7
Cumulative since 1991	23.3	70.5	198.5	340.2	414.6	416.3
Republican enterprises						
Increase during the period	18.0	30.4	125.2	115.0	31.1	--
Cumulative since 1991	18.0	48.3	173.6	288.5	319.7	319.7
Communal enterprises						
Increase during the period	5.3	16.8	2.8	26.7	43.3	1.7
Cumulative since 1991	5.3	22.1	24.9	51.6	94.9	96.6
Memorandum items:						
(In percent of total employment)						
Employment in enterprises						
transformed since 1991	0.5	1.4	4.6	8.5	11.3	11.4
Number of employees in						
transformed enterprises						
(Average number of employees)						
Republican	945	949	895	625	588	--
Communal	126	107	29	58	105	38

Sources: Ministry of Management of State Property and Privatization.

Table 10.5 - Housing Privatization

	1989-91	1992	1993	1994	1995
Number of apartments privatized during period (in thousands)	46.5	69.3	197.0	200.3	112.2
(in percent of total government and public owned housing) 1/	2.8	4.3	12.5	13.8	8.1
Cumulative number of apartments privatized (in thousands)	46.5	115.8	312.8	513.0	625.3
Number of square meters of housing privatized					
(in millions)	2.5	4.1	10.0	10.4	5.8
of which: Given free of charge	0.5	0.4	0.1	0.1	0.0
Cumulative	2.5	6.6	16.6	27.0	32.8
Average size of privatized apartments (in square meters)	55	59	51	52	52

1/ The total number of dwelling units that had been privatized since 1989 until 1995 corresponds to 35.9 percent of the total stock of government and public owned housing. Adding annual percentages will give a different result due to the expansion of the housing stock during this period.
Source: Ministry of Statistics and Analysis.

TECHNICAL ANNEXES

Technical Annexes

ANNEX A

Social Asset Divestiture by Enterprises And Local Government Finance

David Sewell

"Social Asset" Divestiture By Enterprises And Local Government Finance

David Sewell[1]

BACKGROUND

Firms in Belarus spend money on many functions classified as "social" in their enterprise accounting. Examples are housing for employees, summer camps for the children of employees, spas for employees, health and dental clinics on site and specialized medical and dental facilities off site, subsidized food, crèches and kinder-gartens, and vocational schools. In some localities firms also provide local infrastructure such as district heating, electricity, and water and sewer reticulation. Extensive provision of such local infrastructure may have been particularly common by state and collective farms.

It has long been asserted that the "divestiture" of such "social" functions is critical to improving the competitiveness of enterprises in transition economies. It might well be added that enterprise "divestiture" of such "social" functions is equally critical to appropriate functioning of governments in transition economies. Enterprises and governments should be responsible and accountable for different and distinct sets of functions. Achievement of these goals is impossible if enterprises share vague respon-sibilities for social functions and are repeatedly subject to pressures to provide such functions by means of unfunded government mandates. Obviously, such a system of financing social objectives is not transparent, allows both parties to evade hard budget constraints, and thereby obscures and dilutes accountability to enterprise owners and the electorate.

In transition economies, the state also has to consider whether it wishes to continue to directly fund some of these social functions if enterprises discontinue their funding. If government is to be involved in continued provision of these services, the appropriate level of government has to be chosen for the purpose and the function should be adequately funded. The objective of this paper is to examine these issues as they apply to Belarus and suggest appropriate policy actions.

The Russian Government was the first to ask the World Bank for assistance with respect to enterprise social asset divestiture in early 1994. Since then, the Bank has undertaken several loans in support of enterprise divestiture of functions such as housing, kindergartens, medical care, enterprise privatization and related social protection programs in Russia, Kazakhstan, and the Kyrgyz Republic. Staff Appraisal Reports for these loans are a rich source of information on this problem. In addition, an extensive published literature is being built up on the issue. Aggregate surveys of the problem have been undertaken for specific countries by authors within and outside the Bank,[2] and are complemented by in-depth surveys in particular fields such as kindergartens,[3] housing,[4] and asset divestiture in problem industries and regions.[5] We shall draw on this literature as appropriate in our own study of Belarus, and attempt to augment it in areas which, in our opinion, have not received as much attention, such as the implications for local government and the interactions of enterprise provision of these functions with the tax system.[6]

ANALYSIS OF ENTERPRISE SOCIAL SPENDING

Tables A.1-A.3 use enterprise statistics in Belarus to examine characteristics of spending on employee remuneration and "social development" and "social benefits" by type of benefit, size of firm, sector of the economy and region. In addition, but not shown in the tables, the relative size of enterprise spending on these fringe benefits was compared for the years 1994 and 1995. It was also reported to us that there are systematic differences in fringe benefits available to different occupations; some occupations such as teaching allegedly receive fewer fringe benefits. Our enterprise data did not allow us to examine such occupational differences, however.

There are measurement difficulties. Most importantly, data on some types of user cost recovery are incomplete, such as where fees are collected for the use of facilities such as kindergartens. This imparts a downward bias to comparisons over time, since user cost recovery has been increasing for housing and utilities as a result of government policy, and indeed is required as a condition of loans to Belarus by the IMF. A further factor impeding comparisons over time is that data on the important category of housing maintenance undertaken by enterprises was not collected in 1994.

With these qualifications in mind, four components of employee remuneration and enterprise spending on social functions are distinguished in Tables A.1-A.3: wages; other monetary payments to employees (such as bonuses and retirement allowances); enterprise spending on "social development" functions (primarily construction and maintenance of housing, infrastructure and facilities for sports, culture, and education); and other "social benefits" which consist of enterprise spending in kind (taking such forms as subsidized meals, transport fares, medicines, and so on). In Tables A.2 and A.3, we have aggregated firm spending on "social development" and "social benefits" to show a separate category of employee remuneration, namely non-monetary remuneration or fringe benefits.

Table A.1 gives a breakdown of the types of spending by firms on "social" functions or nonmonetary remuneration in 1995. Expenditures on social development made up 75 percent of the total, with this category of spending dominated in turn by expenditures on maintenance of housing, infrastructure and social facilities, which accounted for 53 percent of all nonmonetary remuneration of employees. Unfortunately, no breakdown of expenditures on construction by type of facility is available, but housing makes up the largest category of expenditures on maintenance of facilities, accounting for 14

Table A.1: Composition of Enterprise "Social" Expenditures, 1995

	Billions BYRs	Percent
Expenditures on Social Development	2,649,653	75
Construction of Facilities	609,512	17
Maintenance of Facilities	1,864,250	53
Health	267,135	8
Social Insurance	133,177	4
Sports	65,134	2
Education	294,840	8
Culture	88,289	2
Housing and Infrastructure	917,359	26
Housing	484,891	14
Infrastructure	432,468	12
Special Events	175,891	5
Health and Sports	100,442	3
Education and Culture	39,606	1
Expenditures on Social Benefits [a]	890,876	25
Total Expenditures on Social Development and Social Benefits	3,540,529	100

[a] Subsidies in kind to employees such as subsidized food, vouchers for transport, and so on.
Source: Ministry of Statistics, Republic of Belarus.

percent of total nonmonetary remuneration. It is also of interest that maintenance of infrastructure, such as repair of heating plants, made up a further 12 percent of total "social" spending by enterprises.

Finally, enterprise spending on "social benefits," or subsidies in kind which do not include construction, maintenance or financing of special events, made up 25 percent of all "social" expenditures by enterprises. These "social benefits" included subsidies for such things as commuting and food. The transportation subsidies were and are important in tight housing markets. The importance of food subsidies is seen in the

Table A.2: Composition of Employee Remuneration

By Size of Enterprise, 1995

Type of Remuneration	Highest Quartile % of Total	Second Highest Quartile % of Total	Third Highest Quartile % of Total	Bottom Quartile % of Total	Grand Total (%)
Wages	70%	81%	88%	96%	74%
Other Monetary Payments (Bonuses, etc.)	15%	12%	8%	2%	14%
Total Monetary Remuneration	**85%**	**93%**	**96%**	**98%**	**88%**
Expenditures for Social Development	11%	4%	2%	1%	9%
Expenditures on Social Benefits	4%	3%	2%	1%	3%
Total Non-monetary Remuneration	**15%**	**7%**	**4%**	**2%**	**12%**

By Sectors of the Economy, 1995

Type of Remuneration	Industry % of Total	Agriculture % of Total	Construction % of Total	Transport % of Total
Wages	69%	80%	78%	72%
Other Monetary Payments (Bonuses, etc.)	16%	10%	12%	11%
Total Monetary Remuneration	**85%**	**90%**	**90%**	**83%**
Expenditures for Social Development	11%	8%	7%	15%
Expenditures on Social Benefits	4%	2%	3%	2%
Total Non-monetary Remuneration	**15%**	**10%**	**10%**	**17%**

Note: Enterprises are ranked by size of total outlays from the largest to the smallest.
Source: Special compilation by the Ministry of Statistics, Republic of Belarus.

fact that food expenditures in 1995 accounted for 62 percent of consumer budgets in Belarus—ten times as much as the next largest category of consumer expenditure, which was clothing.

Enterprise provision of many of these social benefits in former Soviet Union countries has been observed to be superior in aggregate to those available from other sources.[7] To an outside observer, differences in provision of nonmonetary benefits are most evident by size of enterprise, however. The dental benefits provided by a large enterprise such as Belarus Railways greatly exceed both in quality and availability those

extended to the ordinary member of the public through state clinics.

Aggregate statistics support this observation that enterprise spending on fringe benefits is systematically correlated with size of firm. As can be seen in Table A.2, the quartile comprised of the largest firms spent more than 15 percent of their total outlays for employee remuneration on nonmonetary benefits in 1995, while the quartile of enterprises comprised of the smallest firms spent only 2 percent.

While there is often a substantial difference in costs of providing "social" services, depending on whether they are provided by enterprises or local governments, such differences in costs are not entirely attributable to differences in the quality of services provided. In fact, municipal cost structures may be lower in part simply because enterprise workers capture substantial rents as compared to their municipal colleagues. Several examples have been found in other CIS countries where municipal wage levels for those providing these services are a third less that those in the enterprise sector. [8]

The proportion of employee remuneration made up of fringe benefits is also shown in Table A.3 to be much greater in industry than in agriculture and construction, and even greater in transport than in industry. The apparent reason for the lower spending on fringe benefits in agriculture is greater rural availability of housing and home-grown food. Table A.3 shows that enterprise spending on social development, which is largely construction and maintenance of housing and infrastructure, and spending on social benefits, which is in part subsidies for food and meals, account for lower proportions of worker remuneration in agriculture than in other sectors. A possible explanation offered for the importance of fringe benefits in transport is the dominance of large enterprises in this industry as compared to, say, the more atomistic nature of much of the construction industry.

The provision of fringe benefits varies widely by oblasts, the principal regional subdivisions of Belarus. These differences, which are shown in Table A.3, are not great and may reflect underlying differences in the importance of agriculture and industry in the economies of these regions. Separately, it was also found that they were not consistent between 1994 and 1995.

Although not reported in Tables A.1-A.3, it was also found that expenditures by enterprises for fringe benefits in 1995 were one third or less of what they were as a proportion of employee compensation in 1994. We have noted that data were not collected for maintenance of housing and infrastructure in 1994, which made up the largest single category of enterprise social expenditures in 1995, accounting in the latter year for 26 percent of the total. Even without this component, however, enterprise "social" expenditures amounted to 35 percent of total employee compensation by firms in 1994. In 1995 by way of contrast, when maintenance expenditures were recorded and could be included in calculations of enterprise "social" expenditures, the latter amounted to 12 percent of total employee compensation.

Enterprise spending on construction of houses and infrastructure declined precipitously between 1994 and 1995; this category of spending in 1995 being less than 8 percent of what it was in 1994. Enterprise construction amounted to BYR 768 billion in 1994 and BYR 610 billion in 1995. Taking into account the fact that the producer price index rose more than tenfold from June 1994 to June 1995,[9] however, enterprise social construction in 1995 amounted to only BYR 61 billion in 1994 prices.

Table A.3: Composition of Employee Remuneration By Oblast, 1995 (% of Total)

	Brest	Vitebsk	Gomel	Grodno	Minsk City	Minsk Region	Mogilov	Grand Total
Wages	78%	76%	71%	78%	72%	72%	77%	74%
Other Monetary Payments to Employees	11%	11%	17%	12%	16%	13%	12%	14%
Expenditures for Social Development	8%	10%	10%	7%	9%	12%	8%	9%
Social Benefits for Employees	3%	3%	3%	3%	3%	3%	3%	3%
Non-monetary Remuneration	11%	13%	13%	10%	12%	15%	11%	12%

Source: Special compilation by the Ministry of Statistics, Republic of Belarus.

The decline in enterprise spending on fringe benefits in 1995 was also evident in our interviews; enterprises that were visited reported reductions in spending for some types of benefits, such as summer camps for children, by actively promoting purchases by non-employees and by insisting on greater cost-recovery from employee users. Many fringe benefits which continued to be offered by enterprises were being treated as stand-alone activities which were increasingly expected to pay for themselves.

As economic pressures on enterprises increased between 1994 and 1995, it is of interest that enterprises chose to reduce such employee fringe benefits by a greater proportion than direct monetary compensation to employees. Earlier research in Russia found that continued enterprise social provision cushioned the effects of sharp falls in real money wages in the process of transition.[10] Managers interviewed in Belarus, however, regarded many fringe benefits as poorly targeted or low priority forms of benefit which were obvious candidates for reduction or elimination in cost-cutting drives.

The overall decline in profitability of enterprises in recent years undoubtedly accounts for the decline in the provision of fringe benefits in Belarus between 1994 and 1995. The economic pressures on enterprises have had effects similar to the institution of hard budget constraints in other former command economies. One would expect the elimination of services of marginal value in these circumstances, and faced with such hard budget constraints, enterprises in other CIS economies have apparently stopped offering some or even most "social" services[11]

When the very survival of the enterprise is in question, it is also to be expected that new capital investments will be postponed and even maintenance of existing capital will be deferred if necessary. Similarly, construction of new housing for employees might be expected to cease along with investments in new plant and equipment, and maintenance of housing might suffer along with maintenance of plant and equipment. Such cuts in housing construction and maintenance are well documented in declining industries in other CIS states, such as in the deeply troubled coal industry in Russia.[12]

Other economic pressures on enterprises may have been more substantial in Belarus than in many CIS states in recent years, such as those imposed by unfunded mandates of government. In particular, pressures to maintain employment have led to overmanning by an estimated 40 percent, according to submissions to the Supreme Soviet of Belarus. With such pressures to assist in reaching unfunded governmental objectives, it is perhaps surprising that discretionary spending on items such as fringe benefits by Belarusian enterprises has not fallen even further.

COMPARISONS WITH PROVISION OF FRINGE BENEFITS IN OECD ECONOMIES

The relative size of enterprise spending on fringe benefits in Belarus is not necessarily that different from the practice in some market economies. Whereas fringe benefits amounted to 12 percent of total employee compensation in Belarus in 1995, in the United States nonwage payments voluntarily provided by employers were 10.1 percent of employee compensation the same year[13] On the other hand, the range in spending on nonwage benefits in all OECD countries appears to be quite substantial.[14] Practice also appears to vary substantially in the former command economies; for example, "social spending by enterprises" in Russia was 17 percent and 20 percent of the enterprise wage bill in 1993 and 1994 respectively.[15]

Such comparisons are of interest because of concerns as to whether voluntary enterprise spending on fringe benefits, together with mandatory wage taxes imposed to raise revenue and to pay for social protection programs, are so high that they adversely affect the "competitiveness" of enterprises in the former command economies. Evidence on the comparative burden of wage taxes in Belarus is presented in Appendix A. Wage taxes in Belarus do not appear to pose a problem for competitiveness. If fringe benefits are fungible with wages in Belarus, which is what our research strongly suggests, they are part of the normal functioning of a competitive labor market and do not adversely affect either the competitiveness of the enterprise nor the economy.

The types of spending on fringe benefits in Belarus and in the OECD economies are quite different, however. Whereas firms in Belarus spend primarily on housing, clinics, kindergartens and subsidies in kind, voluntary employer spending on nonwage benefits in the U.S., for instance, is primarily on pensions and insurance, including health, life, and supplemental unemployment insurance.

A further substantial difference is in the methods of provision. Western firms "outsource" provision of these benefits; by hiring other companies to provide them. In Belarus, firms engage directly in a variety of heterogeneous

activities which are extraneous to their core business activities in order to provide fringe benefits. It is distinctly curious to see producers of television sets and heavy construction equipment running farms to produce food and vegetables, to mention two examples from our interviews. One suspects that the result of this is an inefficient diversion of management time from the core activities of the enterprise. This practice of not hiring specialist enterprises to provide these services was attributed to the need to ensure reliable sources of supply in the former command economy. We may expect such vertical integration in production of fringe benefits to decrease as alternative sources of supply become available in the transition to a market economy.

REASONS FOR ENTERPRISE SPENDING ON SOCIAL ASSETS

The reasons for enterprise provision of most of these social assets provide clues to their appropriate treatment in public policy.

Many previous studies have emphasized the importance of non-economic objectives in provision of these fringe benefits. When their opinions have been canvassed, for instance, over half of Russian enterprise managers have cited their social responsibilities as being an important reason for their continued provision of fringe benefits.[16] This study parts company with the emphasis in much of the previous literature not only on the social significance of these fringe benefits but also on the significance of non-economic reasons for their provision.[17] Simple explanations based on the economics of enterprises and economic behavior of employers and employees are quite successful in predicting enterprise provision of fringe benefits and might be preferred on that basis.

A market economist may well wonder why many of these "social" benefits were provided by enterprises and need to be provided by governments. These are not classic "public goods," in the sense that they are not collectively consumed and non-rival in use. There are also few "externalities" attached to much of this expenditure, or advantages that are not captured by households or individuals who benefit directly from them. Examples are housing, summer camps

for children, spas, sports clubs, vocational schooling and subsidized canteen meals. We should also note that employees are expected to contribute user fees to many of these activities from which they benefit, such as for use of kindergartens, thus explicitly recognizing that these services confer private benefits. We therefore conclude that much of what is called "social" spending by enterprises was merely a convention of socialist enterprise accounting, and that there is little that is "social" about it. Enterprise spending on such fringe benefits may simply be regarded as part of the wage bargain with employees. An implication is that reductions in spending on many of these fringe benefits merely represent reductions in the real wage level and have no wider social significance.

This is not to deny the obvious—that there are social concerns with respect to the supply of public goods aspects of services such as kindergartens and public health; that the firm was regarded as an extension of the state in supplying these goods in the former command economy; and that whatever means of providing these services eventually evolves in Belarus, their supply in the period of transition needs attention. With respect to kindergartens, it should also be noted that the final two years of enrollment are in fact the beginning years of schooling, since primary schooling in FSU countries begins at the age of seven years.[18] This would argue for public financing of kindergartens by similar means to that used for schooling.

If there is little that is "social" about many of these goods and services, however, one might ask why they were provided by enterprises in the first place and why do they continue to be provided by enterprises. A primary reason for their provision by enterprises was that wages were centrally fixed in the former command economy and such controls have continued into the period of transition. Until 1995, for example, enterprises in Belarus were subject to global caps on the wage bill which, if exceeded, led to tax penalties. But enterprises could compete for labor by the provision of fringe benefits and such competition was a rational economic response to the general scarcity of labor in the old command economy.[19] Such motivations were evident in enterprise provision of benefits such as kindergartens.[20] It was especially important, however, for enterprises to compete for labor by providing housing, which was the largest form of in-kind payment.[21] Some other subsidies in kind, such as for transportation, also originated in this need to supply housing; commuting subsidies were offered in an effort to offset the effects of tight local housing markets by drawing in labor from wider areas.

We inferred above that the breakdown of worker pay between money wages and fringe benefits should ordinarily be of no interest to public policy, if there is no bias in public treatment of the two types of remuneration. In these circumstances, the composition of remuneration is strictly a matter between employer and employee. In fact, however, public policy does not provide a level playing field in treatment of fringe benefits and wages in Belarus. Whatever the historical origin of enterprise provision of nonmonetary benefits, their continued provision appears to owe much to their tax treatment.

Strategic objectives in all tax systems involve balancing goals of raising revenue, equitable treatment of individuals, efficiency in the allocation of resources, and incentives for the supply of particular goods and services. With respect to equity, a fundamental principle underlying an income tax is that all income from whatever source should be taxed similarly.[22] Efficiency concerns dictate similar equality in treatment of different sources of income, so that resources are not wasted on avoidance activities to minimize tax liability or on enforcement efforts to counter such avoidance.[23] It is not unusual, however, to find some types of fringe benefits receiving preferential tax treatment to encourage their provision. In the United States, for instance, employer-provided health insurance premiums are deductible business expenses in the calculation of corporate income taxes, are not taxable as personal income in the hands of the beneficiary, and are not included in the wage tax base for the payroll tax.

There is, in fact, a close relationship between the sizes of tax rates on income and the extent to which nontaxable benefits are offered to employees. Recent econometric evidence suggests that lowering income tax rates substantially reduces the demand for nontaxable benefits in the U.S..[24]

Belarus is no exception to this relationship between tax rates and the extent to which nontaxable benefits are extended to employees except that all fringe benefits in Belarus are deductible before enterprise profit taxes are calculated.[25] All non-wage fringe benefits are excluded from the payroll tax base, however, and such taxes amount to 46 percent of payrolls. On the side of personal income taxation, moreover, the principal nonmonetary form of income, that from housing services which have been substantially provided by employers, is tax-free to the recipient—whether such housing is actually built by employers or acquired by means of monetary subsidies from employers. Other types of financial and non-financial benefits for workers receive less favorable but still advantageous tax treatment. They are theoretically subject to tax if they exceed 30 and 20 minimum monthly wages, respectively, or just under 3 and 2 months salary for the average worker.[26] Enforcement of the latter provision appears to be ineffective, however.[27] In total, this tax treatment constitutes a powerful incentive to both employers and employees to substitute nontaxable benefits for wages.

Not unnaturally, both state-owned enterprises and firms in the newly emerging private sector respond to these incentives in the tax system to supply nontaxable benefits to employees. Newly emerging enterprises also build housing for their employees, for instance. Some of the new private enterprises are able to exploit possibilities for tax avoidance in non-taxation of certain types of income in ways that may be difficult for state-owned enterprises to emulate, however.[28]

It has been reported elsewhere that workers in some transition countries have opted for preservation of these nonmonetary benefits instead of receiving wage hikes; the bias in tax treatment described above may suffice to explain why. Great care has to be taken in giving tax incentives for some of these services, however, with housing being a pertinent example. Most citizens of Belarus pay nothing for rent in the sense of paying for the capital costs of housing, since the latter has been provided by enterprises or the state. The term that is frequently translated as rent—in Russian *oplata za zhil'e*—is simply a payment for routine operation (including all utility charges) and maintenance. This explains in large part why families in Belarus spend so little on housing in comparison to families in OECD countries. Rent and utilities accounted for only 4.4 percent of family expenditures in Belarus in 1995, less, it might be noted, than the share of family budgets spent on clothing (6.3 percent) or even alcohol and tobacco (4.9 percent).[29] By way of contrast, the median share of consumer expenditures on housing and utilities in 23 OECD countries recently surveyed was 19 percent (in Switzerland).[30] The virtual exemption of such a large sector of the economy from the tax base in Belarus requires that tax rates be raised substantially on remaining activities to obtain given revenue goals and supplies a potent incentive to seek preferential tax treatment for other "worthy" activities. It might be objected, of course, that owner-occupied housing in many OECD economies is also known for receiving preferential tax treatment, taking such forms as exemption of returns and the deductibility of

debt-finance from income taxation. Recent research challenges the conventional wisdom that owner equity in housing is a lightly taxed asset in OECD countries, however.[31]

It is of interest that the Russian Government has recently acted to make fringe benefits taxable in calculation of the payroll tax base for social insurance programs. Although it fell short of what was needed, a decree issued in January 1996 expanded the payroll tax base in Russia to include non-wage worker compensation in the form of fringe benefits and payments in kind. The Government of Belarus might well consider following the example of the Russian Government in broadening the base subject to payroll taxation. The incentive to substitute nontaxable fringe benefits for money wages is even higher in Belarus than in Russia as a result of payroll tax burdens to finance social insurance and related programs. Such payroll taxes amount to 46 percent of wages in Belarus, as opposed to 39 percent in Russia.

While pressure to provide "tax expenditures," or favored tax treatment for particular activities, exists in all economies, there are methods of controlling such pressure. "Base broadening" by elimination of tax incentives permits revenue goals to be obtained with lower overall tax rates, and has become synonymous with "tax reform" in many OECD economies in recent years. We saw above that reduction in overall tax rates leads to a reduction in demands for nontaxable fringe benefits. More selective incentives can also be substituted for blanket exemptions. An example might be to eliminate tax deductibility for enterprise expenditure on kindergartens but allow daycare expenditures to be deductible from personal income taxes paid by employees. Individuals might also be required to declare an extensive list of fringe benefits as taxable income—Canada, for instance, goes so far as to declare frequent flyer points as taxable income for recipients! Alternatively, enterprises may not be permitted to reduce their tax liability by providing some fringe benefits. Australia is one country which has recently tightened up on such corporate tax deductibility for fringe benefits.

We hasten to add that none of these policy options is intended simply to increase overall tax revenues. The primary objective of these base-broadening exercises is to share a given tax burden more equitably and efficiently over all sources of income.

PRIORITY PROBLEM AREAS: UTILITIES, HOUSING AND CRÈCHES/KINDERGARTENS

Governmental attention in Belarus is currently focused on the problems of enterprise divestiture of utilities, housing and crèches/kindergartens.

The concern with utilities simply reflects an interest in ensuring continuity of supply where enterprises are failing or are reluctant to continue supplying community services because of arrears in payment. Problems with cost recovery for utilities in Belarus appear to have come mostly from low cost recovery from households. According to a letter from the former Minister of Industry to the Council of Ministers in December 1995, arrears for heat supplied to residential areas in December 1995 amounted to over 34 billion rubels, but were not consequential for enterprises, government departments or other "budgetary" organizations.[32]

As we saw above, the final two years of kindergarten in Belarus are the beginning years of schooling, since primary schooling in the FSU countries begins at the age of 7 years. This would argue for financing of these final years of kindergarten by means similar to those used for schooling. Further, expenditures on kindergartens in part represent spending on "custodial" care such as daycare or crèches. Although kindergarten enrollment has fallen with declining birthrates, its use for custodial purposes has increased as a share of total enrollment. Owing to recent economic difficulties, more mothers appear to have chosen early return to the labor force after childbirth.[33] Finally, kindergartens are part and parcel of the problem of enterprise divestiture of housing. When enterprises created housing estates, kindergartens were included in the yards of the apartment blocks and so were a joint cost with housing.

Enterprise divestiture of housing remains clearly the most substantial adjustment to be made in the system in view of its importance to consumer budgets, and an understanding of the issues involved requires an understanding of how housing was formerly provided and financed, and what changes have recently taken place in this respect. We should note that privatization of housing is proceeding in Belarus, but this does not affect the analysis. Nor are the problems associated with divestiture of housing restricted to enterprises.[34]

We should note first that housing is a liability and not an asset of enterprises. Indeed, it is somewhat of a misnomer to speak of enterprises "divesting" themselves of this "asset." Housing never was an asset that was available for disposition by the enterprises which built it. Once housing had been allocated to employees (all but the contract workers), it was at the disposition of the employee. The occupants could not be evicted by the enterprise because they changed employers and they could hold this housing after they retired from the enterprise. They could even swap apartments with other families. Contract workers were the exception, but even they had the same rights to dispose of housing if they lived in it for 10 years.

Whereas the connection between enterprise-provided housing and employment in an enterprise became increasingly remote with the passage of time, enterprises were still left with the burden of maintaining the apartments they constructed—a burden they wanted someone else to assume. Interestingly enough, the process of enterprises ridding themselves of their housing responsibilities started before transition; enterprise housing was being transferred to local executive councils in the early 1980's.

The view set out above that enterprise-produced housing is not considered to be an asset of the enterprise is supported by Russian practice in privatization. There, enterprises to be privatized are not allowed to include housing, utility networks supporting housing located outside enterprise property, or maintenance activities in their charter capital.[35]

Housing nevertheless remains critical to efficient allocation of resources and growth. It has been estimated, for example, that a quarter of all unemployment in 1992 in Poland was due to limitations on labor mobility caused by lack of housing.[36] Public policy therefore should be concerned with continuity in the supply of housing in the transition to a market economy.

FUTURE GOVERNMENTAL RESPONSIBILITY FOR AND FINANCING OF DIVESTED SERVICES

Divested Services: Whose Responsibility?

Which level of government should assume responsibility for those social functions being divested by enterprises that might continue to be supported by the state? The assumption in most of the literature on enterprise divestiture of "social" assets in the former Soviet Union is that government provision of these services should be undertaken by local governments. The question as to whether this is the appropriate level of government to undertake these functions is seldom if ever raised, and needs to be examined more closely. It is obviously appropriate for local governments to be responsible for local infrastructure such as roads, district heating and water and sewer reticulation. Many of the benefits from these functions are strictly local in effect.

Responsibilities for other social services appear to have been assigned to different levels of government in the past on the basis of complexity of the services involved. Thus local governments have been responsible for basic education in the primary schools and for local health clinics, while higher and more specialized levels of education and medical care were responsibilities of the national government. In view of their previous responsibilities, local governments may be the logical level of government in the transition economies to undertake some social functions being divested by enterprises. For example, kindergartens would seem to be a logical responsibility for local governments, given that they are now responsible for primary school education.

While not common, there are legitimate questions as to whether "people" services such as health or education are appropriate local responsibilities. It is not apparent, for instance, that externalities in health or education which lead to government intervention in provision of these services are primarily local in nature.

The suitability of services for decentralized provision may also differ among CIS states. The amount of decentralization appropriate for Russia with its 11 time zones, numerous ethnic groups and population of 150 million, for instance, may not be appropriate for Belarus with its more compact area, and homogeneous ethnic composition, and population of only 10 million. The period of transition may provide an opportunity for Belarus to reconsider the assignment of responsibilities between levels of government. One smaller CIS state, Armenia, has, in fact, reassigned responsibilities for education to the center.

Whatever level of government is assigned responsibility for social services that are divested by enterprises, the means of financing these services need to be adequate to perform the function. In this respect, some observers have viewed the actual process of assigning "divested social functions" to subnational governments as a form of buck-passing by central governments, in that the responsibilities have been transferred without assignment of adequate revenue sources.[37]

Another problem with the question of what level of government should be responsible for these functions in Belarus is that neither the allocation of functions between levels of government, nor the financing of regional (oblast) and district (rayon) governments suggests that there really are fully autonomous local governments in Belarus. Meaningful local government requires some autonomy in its functions and financing. Although local and regional executive council members are elected in Belarus, these subnational levels of government are, in other respects, simply lower level branch offices of the central of government. They raise little revenue themselves and often appear to function as mere agents for the delivery of services such as health and education; the parameters of providing such services are set by the central government. In these regards, Belarus is typical of many countries in transition.

Responsibility for vs. Delivery of Divested Services

We should note that it is the *responsibility* for functions that is in question here, and not their actual provision. Actual delivery of these functions can be accomplished by a number of alternative organizations, including private contractors, non-governmental organizations, and even other levels of government under contract. Citizens of Belarus might be surprised by some of these alternatives. For example, fire services are provided entirely by voluntary organizations in Chile, and municipal and provincial police services are often provided by means of contracts with the federal police force in Canada. Nor is enterprise provision of these services simply a matter of replacing state-owned enterprises with private enterprises; as has been repeatedly shown, it is the presence of competition and not simply state ownership that leads to efficient provision of these services.[38]

LOCAL GOVERNMENT FINANCE: PROBLEMS AND POSSIBLE SOLUTIONS

If some of these "social" functions are to be divested by firms but continue as a governmental responsibility, it follows that they have to be acceptably financed. Existing sources of financing may not be satisfactory for this purpose. Alternative sources of finance include increased cost recovery from users. Where this is not appropriate, financing could be sought from the local or the central governments. If local governments are to be used as agents of the central government in delivering services, appropriate means of transfers have to be devised for this purpose. Partial or bridge financing by enterprises might also be requested to ease the problems of divestiture.

Sources of Local Government Finance and Trends Over Time

Table A.4 indicates the sources of budget revenues for subnational governments and their changes over recent years. As will be described below, some subnational functions are also financed by extrabudgetary funds. Table A.4 reveals what appears to be a striking increase in centralization of government in Belarus in recent years—in the period from 1992 to 1996, the share of total budget revenues allocated to subnational governments decreased from 70 percent to 48 percent. The primary sources of local government revenues are shown to be revenue sharing with the central government and direct subsidies from the central government. The share of explicit central government subsidies in local budget revenues has been growing rapidly in importance, from 1.4 percent in 1992 to 24 percent in 1996.

Table A.4 also confirms that there is little independent local government financing in Belarus—as compared to other countries. As a proportion of local government revenues in Belarus, Table A.4 shows that local taxes accounted for the puny share of only 0.6 percent in 1995 and are projected to account for only 0.4 percent in 1996.

The so-called local taxes that regional and district governments are permitted to levy are for the most part minor "service" fees such as license fees for dogs or parking charges, although local governments do have the right to levy "sin" taxes on tobacco and alcohol. With the exception of the sin taxes, these taxes which have been assigned to local governments are not real revenue raising instruments.

Local governments were originally given wider scope to impose local taxes. Khankevich (p.19) observes that "when the existing taxation system was introduced local authorities were granted the right to impose within their jurisdictions local taxes, duties and levies without legislative restrictions as to their number, composition and maximum amount." This experiment led to complaints by enterprises about tax-grabs by local authorities. As a result, the taxes that local governments could impose on enterprises were restricted in 1993 and a ceiling was imposed on their total burden. They are not allowed to exceed more than 5 percent of a firm's disposable profit or 3 percent of its added value.

The central government acted correctly in restricting the ability of local governments to impose some types of taxes. For efficiency reasons, most tax policy specialists support restrictions on the ability of local governments to impose corporate taxes, for instance, so that local governments cannot "export" the burden of their actions to non-residents.

Weaknesses of Revenue Sharing: Rural Local Governments and Stability of Transfers

As Table A.4 indicates, revenue sharing is the principal method of financing subnational governments in Belarus by budgetary revenues. Table A.5 indicates 1996 sharing arrangements for each major tax. Revenue sharing is intended to be a form of untied transfer payment, in which the central government shares some of the taxes it collects with local governments according to the "derivation" principle, or the area of origin (or collection) of central government taxes. In revenue sharing arrangements, local governments have no control over the base and rate structure of the tax and are not responsible to taxpayers for funds obtained. A serious problem with revenue sharing based on the derivation principle is that it yields more resources to the wealthier regions and

makes inter-regional income imbalances worse. This reflects patterns of production and the fact that most taxation in Belarus is based on the source or location of production, rather than the residence of the taxpayer or the destination of goods taxed.[39] Revenue sharing arrangements accordingly reflect these concentrations in the location of output in Belarus.

We can illustrate this generic defect of revenue sharing by examining the case of agriculture and by extension agricultural districts in Belarus. Because it regards agriculture as a particularly troubled sector, the Government of Belarus has made significant efforts to lower this sector's tax burden. As a result, while the share of GDP arising from agriculture was 11 percent in 1995, the sector accounted for only 5 percent of total tax and extrabudgetary fund revenues.[40] Ironically, such favorable tax treatment for agricultural producers penalizes subnational governments in agricultural areas, because 75 percent of subnational government revenues are derived from revenue sharing on the basis of taxes collected within the subnational jurisdictions.

Revenue sharing in Belarus has another shortcoming. The distribution of revenue sharing is decided annually in Belarus by means of the State Budget Law. It would obviously be desirable for subnational governments to have more stability in their revenues for planning purposes. Transfer arrangements for longer

Table A.4: Sources of Subnational Government Revenues and Share of Subnational Government Revenues in the Central Government Budget

	1992 (%)	1993 (%)	1994 (%)	1995 (%)	1996 (%)
Total subnational revenues	100.0	100.0	100.0	100.0	100.0
•National taxes entirely allocated to subnational governments	52.7	43.4	50.5	52.5	31.0
•National taxes shared with central government	45.9	53.9	46.6	24.3	44.4
•Central government subsidies	1.4	2.7	2.9	22.6	24.2
•Local taxes and duties				0.6	0.4
Share of local revenues in budget of the central government	70	60	56	55	48

Source: Khankevich, "The Taxation System in the Republic of Belarus," p.41.

periods of time exist in market economies. In Canada, for instance, federal-provincial transfer arrangements are renewed by federal legislation every 5 years, and changes within the period require notification and in some instances compensation.

Extrabudgetary Funds

We noted above that subnational governments have received a rapidly decreasing share over time of budget revenues in Belarus. Belarus has, however, made increasing use of the device of "earmarked" or "extrabudgetary" funds to finance critical governmental needs. While all taxes and contributions were equal to 50 percent of GDP in 1995, extrabudgetary funds amounted to 19 percent of GDP, or 38 percent of all taxes and contributions. Even more extraordinary, such earmarked funds are scheduled to increase to 56 percent of government receipts in 1996, so that more government revenues will accrue from off-budget than from on-budget sources![41]

This extrabudgetary financing method has been adopted to support operating and maintenance costs of kindergartens and housing, which as we have seen are two of the principal "social assets" of enterprises that are increasingly being divested to local governments. Two extrabudgetary funds were instituted in May 1992 and December 1993 for kindergartens and housing respectively. In the case of housing, 0.5 percent of enterprise revenues have to be devoted to maintenance of housing. If not spent directly by the enterprise, payment of an equivalent amount of enterprise revenues has to be made to the local executive councils for support of housing. The burden of this levy on the turnover of enterprises is substantial. Further, the required rate of earmarking revenue is arbitrary and has little to do with the costs of maintaining housing. (Complaints about the burden of this earmarked tax led to its rate being reduced from 1 percent of enterprise revenues in 1995 to 0.5 percent for 1996.)

Funding for the operations and maintenance costs of local kindergartens is also promoted by an extrabudgetary fund, but one levied on after-tax profits. Local executive councils are permitted to raise this levy at a rate

Table A.5: 1996 Revenue Sharing in Belarus Share of National Taxes Allocated to Central and Subnational Budgets

Tax	Central Govt. Budget (%)	Local Budget (%)
VAT	50	50
Profit tax	60	40
Excise	70	30
Personal Income Tax		100
Real Estate Tax		
• Central Government Property	100	
• Subnational Government Property		100
Severance Tax		100
Tax on Potassium and Rock Salt Extraction	50	50
Land Tax		
• Within cities	40	60
• Outside cities	25	75
Chernobyl Tax	100	
State Duty	100	
Timber Tax		100
Fire Team Maintenance Duty	100	
Duty on the right to use public roads	100	

Source: Khankevich, "The Taxation System in the Republic of Belarus," p.39.

varying from 1 percent to 5 percent of the after-tax profits of enterprises. (Minsk City levies a 5 percent tax). Again, the tax is only collected if enterprises do not spend the specified amount directly on their own kindergartens. This source of financing obviously varies with the profitability of firms.

It is widely acknowledged that the use of extrabudgetary funds, or the "earmarking" of revenues for specified purposes, should be restricted to those instances where there is a strong benefit connection between the expenditure financed and the revenue raised—that is, when the latter is basically a user charge for rationale—where the activities concerned redistribute income, for example. All other prospective public programs where there is no benefit rationale should receive general fund financing and should compete on the same terms for these limited public funds within a common budgetary framework. It is therefore cause for concern that 56 percent of all government receipts in Belarus are currently flowing into extrabudgetary funds. By these standards, too, housing maintenance and kindergartens are not appropriately financed as benefit taxes by the extrabudgetary funds levied on enterprises in Belarus. The financing of these major fringe benefits is redistributional. In the case of both housing and kindergartens, enterprises are footing the bill for activities which benefit only subsets of their employees and which also benefit many non-employees. As we have seen, for instance, those now living in housing built and maintained by enterprises often have no past or present connection with the enterprise.

POTENTIAL SOURCES OF FINANCE

User Cost Recovery

Appropriate financing for local utilities requires full cost recovery from users. Low levels of cost recovery for housing and utilities were a matter of deliberate redistributional policy in the Soviet Union, and low-priced energy helped to make this policy possible. This policy proved difficult for the authorities in Belarus to change. As late as 1994, the cost recovery rate for all housing maintenance and utilities was only about 10 percent, and was as low as 4 percent for heating and 2 percent for housing maintenance and water. The cost recovery rate for electricity was significantly higher than for most utilities, but was still only 25 percent.

These cost recovery rates were unsustainable once Belarus no longer had access to low-priced energy. In 1995, the government pursued a policy of increasing housing and utility cost recovery ratios with determination. As a result, household cost recovery ratios were raised to 50 percent for household maintenance, 65 percent for heating, 54 percent for water and 84 percent for electricity.

An important step towards increasing user cost recovery for household utility services is to meter individual apartment usage, since this enables the household to control its own usage. In the former Soviet Union, electricity usage was the only household utility which was individually metered—which may also account for the fact that it had the highest cost recovery rate. Belarus has taken an important step towards increasing user cost recovery for other utilities with a government initiative to encourage additional metering for household water supply.[42] Metering of water supply to households has yet to be adopted in many other member states of the former Soviet Union. Unfortunately, it would seem to be impractical to meter individual household usage of heat in many of Belarus' Soviet era apartment buildings. Installation of individual metering for apartments would necessitate complete replacement of the plumbing systems in these buildings.

It is enigmatic to an outsider that property owners and residents in Belarus actually continue to receive subsidies for housing maintenance, particularly where housing is being privatized. The principle that is applied is that if one type of housing occupant gets a subsidy, all housing occupants benefit from the same subsidy regardless of whether the housing is enterprise, state or privately owned. Housing maintenance services are an obvious case where user cost recovery principles should be applied—the resident of Grodno should not be expected to pay for maintenance of housing which has been privatized in Minsk, for instance.

Objections to user cost recovery for housing and utilities often rest on assumptions that users in transition economies will not be able to afford the price levels entailed, given their current reduced incomes. Such arguments ignore the fact that shortfalls in cost recovery are now being paid for somehow—by taxpayers, including those who do not use these utilities, or by "inflation taxes" arising from printing money to finance government deficits. Cost recovery from users leads to savings which can be applied to reducing these taxes or government deficits.

It is, in fact, counterproductive to subsidize aggregate utility use for distributional reasons—better-off people benefit more from such subsidies since consumption normally rises with income.[43] Belarus appears to be no exception to this rule. The 1995 Household Budget Survey shows that average monthly spending on rent and utilities rose from 57,000 rubels per family member in the lowest quintile of the income distribution to 67,000 rubels in the highest income quintile.[44] The Government of Belarus is attempting to deal with income distributional problems arising from housing and utilities payments in a more appropriate manner than by subsidizing all users. Low-income households receive housing allowances if payments exceed 15 percent of household income. This approach targets assistance to families in greater need, and would also seem to be appropriate for dealing with distributional considerations which arise in provision of services other than housing and utilities, such as daycare.

Property and Real Estate Taxes

Property and real estate taxes are appropriate means for financing municipal services to property, such as street lighting and road maintenance. Indeed, Appendix B indicates that property taxes are the principal form of autonomous finance of local governments in OECD countries. Keen (p. 4) notes that property taxes accounted for 5.5 percent of all OECD governmental revenues in 1992 and only 2.7 percent of total revenues in Belarus in 1995, or less than half of their comparative importance in OECD countries. Belarus needs a more useful form of property or real estate tax than the present land use tax, which in 1995 cost more to collect than it raised in revenue![45] Fortunately, reform of this tax is being considered by the Task Forces examining tax reform in Belarus in 1996.

Appropriate Forms of Central Transfers to Local Governments in Belarus

It is clear that local governments will not be able to finance municipal services from their own revenues until appropriate tax instruments

such as a reformed property tax are put in place. Indeed, there will always be a case for transfers to enable poorer local governments to provide critical services in a manner similar to that in better-off localities. To achieve this objective, some systematic form of "equalization" of local revenues is needed in Belarus. (The argument for such transfers is separate from that for personal transfers such as low-income supplements or unemployment insurance). While the Government of Belarus recognizes this need, it deals with it currently in ad hoc ways—by subsidies which differ by locality, and by changing the local share in revenues assigned to oblasts. For instance, the share of lower-income oblasts in VAT revenue is higher than that permitted to the city of Minsk (which has the status of an oblast). These local revenue shares have been changed several times in an attempt to benefit low-income regions.

The most thoughtful approaches to these intergovernmental transfers involve formula financing for transfers from central to local governments, where the criteria for the transfer is determined in advance by legislation. Formula financing of transfers to local government makes possible greater stability, certainty and openness in these payments. Because this formula financing is systematic and open, it avoids implications that some kind of political slush fund is involved and reduces the interminable bargaining that was (and continues to be) a feature of inter-regional distribution in the former Soviet Union and many of its successor states.

Equalization schemes in many countries compensate for differences in local revenue-raising capacity, and sometimes compensate for local cost differences in supplying services.[46] Such equalization payments are unconditional with respect to uses of the funds.

"Conditional" grants are also used if higher levels of government wish to ensure that local governments supply specific services such as teaching Belarusian in schools) or to ensure that specific levels of service are provided (usually minimum levels of service). Such grants give general guidance to local governments providing the service with respect to the objectives of the donor government, but do not lead to the latter micro-managing the service.[47]

The Government of Belarus should consider adoption of such formula financing. Since officials in the Ministries of Economy and Finance are interested both in formula approaches to equalization and in conditional grants from the republican to subnational governments, the World Bank might well consider arranging courses for officials in Belarus on such approaches to intergovernmental financing.

Continued Partial Financing or Bridge Financing of Services by Enterprises

Some incentives already exist for enterprises to share the burden in transferring physical assets to local governments. Thus local executive councils have the right not to accept housing or kindergartens divested by enterprises, if they are not in "satisfactory" condition. While it is presumed that local governments would be obliged to accept most of these assets if an enterprise failed, some kindergartens are known to have been closed by enterprises rather than turned over to local governments.

Perhaps more use might be made of continued enterprise contributions to aid divestiture. An example might be drawn from the case of educational institutions where human capital is being created which is to some extent specific to the enterprise. One large enterprise interviewed in Minsk, for instance, had just divested a trade school to the local authorities, but will continue to hire many of the graduates. The local authorities would seem to have a good case for asking for some continued support from the enterprise for such schooling.

CONCLUSION

In Belarus as in other former command economies, divestiture of "social assets" is seen as a necessary process in the transformation of enterprises so that they can function appropriately in a market economy. An important public policy problem in transition economies is widely considered to be that of maintaining the supply of these services after enterprise divestiture.

The present study finds that the term "social assets" is a misnomer for just about all enterprise activities described under this heading in Belarus, most of which are simply fringe benefits that are part of the wage bargain with the employee. Provision of these fringe benefits was a rational response by enterprises to shortages of labor and constraints on wage offers in the old command economy, firms in market economies have responded similarly to such economic incentives to provide fringe benefits. The favorable tax treatment of fringe benefits explains much of their continued importance, both in Belarus and elsewhere.

These fringe benefits were cut by at least two-thirds as a proportion of employee remuneration between 1994 and 1995 in Belarus. The economic downturn in this period contributed to the relative decline in payment of these benefits, particularly those involving capital expenditures such as housing construction and maintenance. The relative decline in fringe benefit payments may not have been so great had enterprises not been required to fulfill a number of costly unfunded government mandates, such as that of maintaining employment at levels estimated by some to amount to overmanning equal to 40 percent of the labor force. In effect, enterprises may have cut fringe benefit payments to pay for these unfunded mandates.

Larger enterprises were found to provide more of these fringe benefits than other firms and the quality of enterprise provision of these services is generally considered to be superior to comparable services provided by government. Research in other CIS countries has found that some enterprises collect substantial rents in providing these fringe benefits, however, thus inflating costs compared to government provision.

It is eminently debatable whether most of these fringe benefits should receive continued public subsidy or preferential tax treatment. There is a strong case for some government funding of the public health and kindergarten services being divested by enterprises. Enterprise divestiture of public subsidy or preferential tax treatment. There is a strong case for some government funding of the public health and kindergarten services being divested by enterprises. Enterprise divestiture of public utility services and housing is also a cause for concern during transition. As much as a quarter of total unemployment in transition economies has been attributed to the lack of labor mobility caused by unavailability of housing.

Those services which enterprises are divesting but which should be retained as government functions are often assumed to be the appropriate responsibility of local governments. Local infrastructure is clearly an appropriate local government responsibility; the reasons for assigning services such as education and health to local governments are more debatable.

Financing arrangements have not kept pace with the reassignment of functions to subnational governments, nor with performance of their existing functions—the subnational share of total government revenues declined from 70 percent in 1992 to 48 percent in 1996. Special extrabudgetary funds have been created to finance local government operation of kindergartens and housing maintenance.

There are other problems with existing means of financing local governments. A principal difficulty with revenue sharing, which accounts for 75 percent of subnational government revenues, is that it yields more resources to wealthier regions and makes inter-regional imbalances worse. Tax breaks to agriculture have also reduced revenue sharing with rural local governments. There is no close link between beneficiaries and payments which would justify the use of the present extrabudgetary funds for housing maintenance and kindergartens. Too much use, in fact, is now made of extrabudgetary funds in Belarus—their revenues now exceed those on budget so that programs on the budget are not competing on a level playing field for more than half of public resources. Finally, true subnational taxes—those whose base and rate structure are determined by subnational governments and for which the latter are responsible to their own electorates—raise insignificant amounts of revenue.

The financing of local utility services is most appropriately accomplished by user cost recovery, with any resulting income distributional problems being addressed by direct income support measures, such as the housing allowance that the Government of Belarus has instituted. Belarus also needs effective real estate taxes to finance local government services to property; the existing land use tax has been a nuisance tax, in that it costs more to administer than it raises in revenues. Where transfers to local governments are required, formula financing is suggested. Such formula financing is appropriate for both unconditional grants to low-income local governments and conditional grants to support specific objectives such as maintaining minimum national standards in services delivered by local governments.

APPENDIX A

The Relative Burden of Wage Taxes in Belarus, the OECD and European Union

The argument that wage taxes in the former command economies levied to finance social protection programs such as pensions and unemployment compensation are so great as to threaten the "competitiveness" of enterprises is frequently encountered. Payroll taxes account for 46 percent of payrolls in Belarus. The Social Protection Fund is financed by a 35 percent payroll tax, the Employment Fund is financed by a further 1 percent payroll tax and an additional 10 percent tax on payroll is levied to pay for measures to ameliorate the effects of the Chernobyl nuclear disaster. Social security levies in many CIS countries such as Russia account for slightly smaller total shares of payrolls, but even payroll taxes in the range of 35 percent to 40 percent in many Eastern European countries arouse concern because of possible adverse effects on enterprise and national competitiveness.[48]

A good case can be made, however, that these payroll taxes are not substantially larger than similar taxes in many Western industrial countries. Furthermore, payroll taxes may be a suitable method of financing appropriately designed social security programs.

The importance of payroll and social security taxes as a source of revenues in Belarus can be compared with European and OECD practice. Keen (p.4) reports that social security and payroll taxes accounted for 26.3 percent of revenues in Belarus in 1992, 25.9 percent of revenues of OECD member countries, and 29.3 percent of revenues in European Union countries.

The greater use made of payroll taxes by European countries is of interest from the point of view of the competitiveness hypothesis, as is the size of the effective tax rate on earnings in many of these countries. In a 1996 article, Kesselman compares effective tax rates on earnings for OECD countries. He finds that, "at earnings of USD 20,000 (noted as being near the average earnings rate in most OECD countries considered), the total average effective payroll tax rate exceeds 35 percent in 8 of the 20 countries tabulated; it exceeds 45 percent in Belgium, France, Greece and Italy."[49]

What might also be taken into account is the finding in the present study that payroll is only part of worker remuneration in Belarus because the "social benefits" provided by enterprises are not taxed as part of payroll, or indeed as personal income. We found that such fringe benefits amounted to 35 percent and 12 percent of wages and salaries in 1994 and 1995 respectively. Consequently, the "effective" (as opposed to nominal) wage tax would have amounted to only 30 percent of worker remuneration in 1994 ($.46*.65=.30$) and 40 percent of worker remuneration in 1995 ($.46*.88=.40$). The relevance of this calculation of effective payroll tax rates is shown by the recent decision of the Government of Russia to expand the payroll tax to include non-wage worker compensation, as indicated in a decree of January 1996.

It is also relevant to include income taxes in comparisons of tax burdens on wages. The personal income tax is almost exclusively a tax on wages and salaries in Belarus, is levied on a narrow base because of non-taxation of fringe benefits, and does not assume the importance as a revenue source that it does in OECD countries. Lumping the personal income tax together with payroll and social security taxes in his 1996 inquiry, Keen (p.6) finds that these three taxes account for 32 percent of tax revenue in Belarus compared to 55 percent of tax revenue in both the European Union and OECD countries. The differences in relation to GDP are not as marked but are still substantial. Keen finds that the three taxes account for about 16 percent of GDP in Belarus and about 21 percent in the European Union and OECD countries.

Finally, tax specialists who have considered the question do not view payroll taxes as an inappropriate means of financing social security programs. Kesselman concludes for example that,

> Payroll taxes in general are a relatively efficient form of taxation in the long run, at least compared with taxes on income or capital. They can also be simple and low-cost to operate for both governments and taxpayers. When tied to benefits

in a well-designed program of social security, payroll taxes offer the additional advantage of posing minimal distortions to labor and other economic behaviors. This potential is unlike most other forms of taxation, which have unavoidable efficiency costs.[50]

In one respect, Kesselman's conclusion suggests that our inquiry into the effects of wage taxes in the former command economies has been literally one-sided. A comprehensive assessment of the impact of wage taxes in these countries would also need to take into account the benefits obtained from the social insurance programs financed by these wage taxes.

APPENDIX B

Autonomous Sources of Revenue for OECD Local Governments: Property vs. Income Taxes

Where the application of direct user charges are impractical, forms of the property tax have been the traditional source of much local government finance in many parts of the world. In terms of OECD usage, the property tax is the primary (and often the only) local government tax in the Netherlands and the English-speaking countries—Australia, Canada, the United States, Ireland, New Zealand and the United Kingdom. Income taxes are more important as a source of local government revenues in other European countries and Japan. In his recent survey of OECD practice for the Bank, McMillan notes that out of 24 countries, local governments in 20 countries have property taxes and in 17 have income taxes.

One has to be careful, however, to ensure that local income taxes are not simply revenue sharing arrangements, where local governments have no control over the base and rate structure of the tax and are not responsible to taxpayers for funds obtained. As McMillan and Bird and Slack observe, a number of revenue sharing arrangements of this type are recorded in OECD statistics as local income taxes.[51]

Table A.6 shows that if one excludes income taxes identified by McMillan as revenue sharing (in Austria, Germany, Norway and Spain), revenues from property taxes exceeded revenues from local income taxes in the OECD in 1990 by 4.5 percent (USD 283 billion as opposed to USD 271 billion).

Table A.6: Comparative Importance of Local Income and Property Taxes, Selected OECD Countries, 1990

Country	Income Tax	Property Tax	GDP	Income Tax	Property Tax
	As Percentage of GDP			(USD Million)	
Australia	-	1.1	296,300	-	3,259
Austria	[2.0]	0.4	157,380	[3,148]	630
Canada	-	2.8	570,150	-	15,964
Switzerland	4.7	0.7	224,850	10,568	1,574
U.S.A.	0.2	2.9	5,392,200	10,784	156,374
Belgium	1.6	-	192,390	3,078	-
Denmark	14.4	1.1	130,960	18,858	1,441
Finland	10.9	0.1	137,250	14,960	137
France	0.5	1.5	1,190,780	5,954	17,862
Germany	[2.7]	0.6	1,498,210	[40,452]	8,989
Iceland	4.5	1.2		-	-
Ireland	-	1.0	42,500	-	425
Italy	0.7	-	1,090,750	7,635	-
Japan	5.3	1.9	2,942,890	155,973	55,915
Netherlands	-	0.8	279,150	-	2,233
New Zealand	-	1.9	42,760	-	812
Norway	[9.0]	0.9	105,830	[9,525]	952
Portugal	0.4	0.8	56,820	227	455
Spain	[0.8]	2.0	491,240	[3,930]	9,825
Sweden	17.9	-	228,110	40,832	-
Turkey	1.8	0.1	96,500	1, 737	97
United Kingdom	-	0.6	975,150	-	5,851
Total				270,607	282,794

NOTE: Income taxes for countries whose rates are indicated in brackets were treated as revenue sharing and not included in the calculations.
Sources: World Development Report, 1992 and McMillan, Table A.5.

Notes

1. This document was produced as part of the author's responsibility in the 1996 Belarus Country Economic Memorandum Mission headed by John Hansen. I wish to thank Elena Klochan, Nikolai Lisai and Konstantin Senyut of the World Bank's Resident Mission in Minsk, and John Hansen and Yuliya Merkulova for assistance in preparing this report. I have also benefited from specific comments from Jorge Martinez-Vasquez and Richard Bird, and from extensive discussions at the Bank with Lev Freinkman and Philip O'Keefe, both of whom are engaged in operations work associated with this issue.

2. See Simon Commander and Richard Jackman, "Providing Social Benefits in Russia: Redefining the Roles of Firms and Government." Policy Research Working Paper 1184, Economic Development Institute, The World Bank, 1993; Simon Commander and Une Lee with Andrei Tolstopiatenko, "Social Benefits and the Russian Industrial Firm," Joint Conference of the World Bank and the Ministry of Economy of the Russian Federation, *Russia: Economic Policy and Enterprise Restructuring*, June 1995; Lev M. Freinkman and Irina Starodubrovskaya, "Restructuring of Enterprise Social Assets in Russia," Policy Research Working Paper 1635, The World Bank, August 1966; Jorge Martinez-Vasquez, "The Challenge of Expenditure-Assignment Reform in Russia," *Journal of Environment and Planning,* Vol. 12, 1994, pp. 277-292; Mark E. Schaffer, Richard Jackman, Gaspar Fajth and Judit Lakatos, Martin Rein, Irina Tratch and Andreas Woergoetter, "Round table on 'Divestiture of Social Services from State-Owned Enterprises,' " *Economics of Transition*, Vol. 3 (2), 1995.

3. See for instance Jeni Klugman, Sheila Marnie, John Micklewright and Philip O'Keefe, "Enterprise Divestiture of Kindergartens and Childcare Arrangements in Central Asia," in Jane Falkingham, Jeni Klugman, Sheila Marnie and John Micklewright (eds), *Household Welfare in Central Asia,* (Macmillan, UK, forthcoming 1996).

4. See Robert M. Buckley and Eugene M. Gorenko, "Unwinding the Socialist Wage Package: The Role of Housing in Russia," PADCO Working Paper, Dec. 1995; "Russian Enterprise Housing Divestiture," Urban Institute Research Paper, 1995.

5. Vladimir Lexin, Alexander Shvetsov, and Lev Freinkman. "Regionalnuye kollizii funktsionirovaniya sotsialnukh obyektov" (Regional conflicts in operating social assets) in *Rossiisky Economicheski Jurnal (Russian Economic Journal),* 1996, Issue 8, pp. 62-72.

6. I have used the following sources for information on the tax system in Belarus: Mick Keen, "Tax Reform in Belarus: Preliminary Report on Economic Aspects," EU Tacis, April 1996; and L. A. Khankevich, "The Taxation System in the Republic of Belarus," EC4C1, June 1996.

7. "Enterprise kindergartens were considered to be superior in quality to municipal facilities, and these differentials appear to have persisted: 1994 data for Kazakhstan show per child expenditures in enterprise kindergartens to be twice that in those run by the Ministry of Education." Klugman et al., "Enterprise Divestiture of Kindergartens and Childcare Arrangements in Central Asia," pp. 3-4. In another 1995 study for the Bank by ADB Associates, it was estimated that adoption of municipal standards would reduce total kindergarten costs in the Kyrgyz Republic by 20 percent. Cited in Freinkman and Starodubrovskaya, "Restructuring of Enterprise Social Assets in Russia," p.24.

8. ADB Associates found that enterprise kindergarten teachers' salaries in the Kyrgyz Republic were 10 percent to 50 percent higher than those of municipal kindergarten teachers (cited in Freinkman and Starodubrovskaya, "Restructuring of Enterprise Social Assets in Russia," p.24). Lexin et al. (p.65) report that municipal service workers (for example, in housing maintenance) received wages that were 30 percent to 40 percent less than those of equivalent employees of Russian coal companies.

9. Setting the producer price index for June 1994 to equal 100, the June 1995 value of the index was 1078.

10. See Commander and Lee with Tolstopiatenko, "Social Benefits and the Russian Industrial Firm," p.i.

11. Freinkman and Starodubrovskaya state that with the imposition of hard budget constraints in The Kyrgyz Republic, "most enterprise non-housing social facilities were simply closed." See "Restructuring of Enterprise Social Assets in Russia," p.8.

12. Lexin et al. (p. 67) report that "in the three years preceding housing divestiture, coal associations' actual expenditure on housing decreased almost twofold in real terms due to the deterioration of the mines' financial performance."

13. *Survey of Current Business*, May 1996, Table 1.14, p.10.

14. By way of contrast, Schaffer cites "costs of social provision" in a 1988 survey of West European industry varying from 1.4 percent to 12.0 percent of total labor costs in different countries, but still concludes that "employees in Western firms receive social benefits from their employers which are about as costly in relative terms" as those in transition countries (Schaffer, *Economics of Transition Round Table*, p.248).

15. Freinkman and Starodubrovskaya, "Restructuring of Enterprise Social Assets in Russia," p.7.

16. Commander and Lee with Tolstopiatenko, "Russia: Economic Policy and Economic Restructuring," p.4.

17. The studies by Schaffer in the *Economics of Transition Roundtable* and Martinez-Vasquez, "The Challenge of Expenditure-Assignment Reform in Russia," indicate similar skepticism about the importance of non-economic motives in provision of these fringe benefits.

18. Klugman et al observe that "kindergartens did indeed have a developmental role in the Soviet Union and primary school curricula assumed that children already had basic literacy and counting skills." See "Enterprise Divestiture of Kindergartens and Childcare Arrangements in Central Asia," p.3.

19. Interestingly enough, provision of important fringe benefits such as employer-provided health insurance has similar origins in the United States. "Employer provided health insurance was encouraged by the 1942 Stabilization Act, which placed limits on wage increases but allowed employers to offer insurance plans to their employees," (Jonathan Gruber and James Poterba, "Tax Subsidies to Employer-Provided Health Insurance," *NBER Working Papers* No. 5147, June 1995, p.5 fn. 3).

20. "..enterprise provision of kindergartens ...furthered state policy of attaching employees to their place of work to discourage unplanned turnover. Enterprise managers were willing agents in this respect, as they had little autonomy in setting money wages, and used noncash benefits, such as subsidized kindergartens, to attract and retain workers." Klugman et al., "Enterprise Divestiture of Kindergartens and Childcare Arrangements in Central Asia," p.3.

21. "In all socialist countries, enterprise housing production programs were a key means of gaining access to new housing...enterprises which produced significant amounts of housing were seen as attractive employers. Employment with such firms provided a way to jump the waiting list for housing provided by the state." Buckley and Gorenko, "Unwinding the Socialist Wage Package: The Role of Housing in Russia," p 1.

22. The underlying principle is that of *horizontal equity*, meaning that likes should be treated alike.

23. The significant costs of such anti-avoidance activity are illustrated by the estimate that as much as one-half of the U.S. Tax Code before 1986 (the year of substantial tax reform) was devoted to limiting the extent to which taxpayers could take advantage of the lower tax rate applied to income in the form of long-term capital gains. See Charles E. McLure, Jr., cited in Economic Council Of Canada, *The Taxation of Savings and Investment*, (Ottawa, Ont.: Minister of Supply and Services, 1987), p.9.

24. Stephen A. Woodbury and Daniel S. Hamermesh find that .".wages and [nontaxable] benefits are highly substitutable and that the demand for benefits is price elastic. Changes in income taxes induce a change in the relative price of benefits and wages that in these samples generates substantial substitution between wages and nonwage compensation." Their estimates suggest that cuts in average marginal tax rates of 3-6 percent in the mid-1980s in the United States reduced the share of nontaxable benefits in total compensation by one-half percentage point (from a hypothetical 19 percent to 18.5 percent). "Taxes, Fringe Benefits and Faculty," *The Review of Economics and Statistics*, Vol. LXXIV, May 1992, No. 2, pp. 294-295.

25. The exception is that grants or loans to employees for housing are only exempt up to 10 percent of after-tax profit of enterprises.

26. In June 1996, the minimum monthly wage was equal to BYR 100,000. The average salary in March 1996 was BYR 1,066,600.

27. Khankevich, in "The Taxation System in the Republic of Belarus," (p.18) comments that "even though legislation says that income tax should be paid on any form of income, in this case it is possible to calculate the tax amount but not actually collect it."

28. Because interest income is untaxed, for instance, it has been common practice for banks to pay their employees in part in the form of interest income on deposits that the banks contribute to the accounts of their employees'.

29. *Expenditures and Income of the Population in Belarus: 1995*, Table II.1. Ministry of Statistics and Analysis, Republic of Belarus, Minsk 1996.

30. Charles Yuji Horioka, "Japan's Consumption and Saving in International Perspective," in *Economic Development and Cultural Change*, vol. 42, no. 2, Jan., 1994, Table 4, p.304.

31. "...it is striking that, contrary to popular belief, these rates [effective tax rates for house purchase financed by equity] taking into account all relevant taxes are *not* generally low compared to other assets, particularly in the case of zero inflation." OECD, *Taxation and Household Saving*, (Paris: OECD, 1994), p. 110.

32. Letter to the Cabinet of Ministers from Minister V.I. Kurenkov, December 15, 1995.

33. Minsk City officials informed us that of 90,000 children in 500 kindergartens that the city was operating, some 10,000 were less than 3 years old. Such crèches were only introduced at the beginning of 1994, when the economic situation worsened. Previously, mothers stayed on paid maternity leave until children were three years old.

34. Disposition of employer constructed housing has also been a problem for government departments (other budgetary organizations, in the nomenclature employed in Belarus). Much housing formerly owned by the Ministry of Defense, for example, was turned over to local authorities in Minsk in 1994/1995.

35. Freinkman and Starodubrovskaya, "Restructuring of Enterprise Social Assets in Russia," p. 9.

36. Fabrizio Coricelli, Krysztof Hagemejer and Krysztof Rybinski, "Poland," in Simon Commander and Fabrizio Coricelli (eds), *Unemployment, Restructuring, and the Labor Market in Eastern Europe and Russia*, EDI Development Studies, Washington, DC., The World Bank, 1995, p. 74.

37. See for instance Jorge Martinez-Vasquez, "The challenge of expenditure-assignment reform in Russia," *Journal of Environment and Planning*, 1994, Vol. 12, pp. 277-292; Christine I. Wallich, "Russia's Dilemma," in *Russia and the Challenge of Fiscal Federalism*, a World Bank Regional and Sectoral Study, ed. Christine I. Wallich, 1994, pp. 38-43.

38. According to one examination specific to the efficient supply of local government services, "most of the efficiency gains from contracting out have resulted from an increased scope for competition rather than from the fact that the service was provided by a private contractor." Harry Kitchen, *Efficient Delivery of Local Government Services*, Discussion paper No. 93-15.

School of Policy Studies, Queen's University, Kingston, Ont., Canada, 1993, p.22.

In the context of Belarus, we note that Presidential Ukase No 351 of 4 September 1995 simply *orders* the reduction of housing maintenance expenditures by 10-20 percent by the introduction of "contracts." These contracts do not reduce housing maintenance costs by encouraging competitive provision of communal services.

39. Personal income taxes, as well as wage taxes to finance social insurance programs, are deducted by the employer at source in Belarus, whereas the personal income tax is often based on rules applying where people live (rather than where they work) in OECD countries. Profit taxes are similarly collected on the basis of where corporate headquarters are located in Belarus, and property taxes are naturally origin-based taxes. Under GATT rules, the destination principle is normally applied in taxation of goods traded internationally, so that tax rates are determined by the jurisdiction in which the goods are purchased. In the case of Belarus, the VAT is based on the source of production although there is a lack of coherence in the principles applied to taxing international trade. As a result, most Belarus taxation is source or origin based, as opposed to residence or destination based, and tax-sharing arrangements reflect concentration in the location of production by region and hence produce disparities in regional revenues.

40. See Khankevich, "The Taxation System in the Republic of Belarus," p. 16. By way of contrast, industry accounted for 26 percent of GDP and 47 percent of tax and extrabudgetary fund revenues.

41. All data in this paragraph are taken from Khankevich, "The Taxation System in the Republic of Belarus," p.11.

42. The program was launched on 7 June 1994 by a decree of the Cabinet of Ministers, and consists of metering for both individual apartments and apartment blocks. Although apartment meter installation was subsidized by 75 percent in 1995 and by 50 percent in 1996, the subsidy is scheduled to be reduced to 25 percent.

43. For an explanation and graphical illustrations of this point, see the *World Development Report, 1994* (Washington, DC, The World Bank, 1994), p 81.

44. *Expenditures and Income of the Population in Belarus: 1995*, Table II.2E. Ministry of Statistics and Analysis, Republic of Belarus, Minsk 1996.

45. The conventional definition of a "nuisance tax" is that it costs more to levy than it raises in revenue.

46. Equalization schemes based on fiscal capacity usually calculate the per capita revenue-raising capacity of all taxes in different regions and redistribute revenues to achieve some target of relative per capita fiscal capacity in all regions. Such programs may consist of *direct* redistribution between regions, as in Germany, Switzerland and Denmark, or *indirect* redistribution as in Canada, where equalization schemes for provincial revenues are a constitutional responsibility of the federal government.

47. Conditional grants have also been recommended for use in Russia. For a more detailed description of this type of transfer, see Annex 4, "Conditional Grants: International Experience" in World Bank Country Study, *Fiscal Management in the Russian Federation,* 1996, pp. 141-145.

48. Commander and Lee with Tolstopiatenko found that "payroll taxes and deductions comprise up to 40 percent of the wage bill" for a large sample of Russian industrial firms in 1994. See *Social Benefits and the Russian Industrial Firm*, p.3. Current *employer* contribution tax rates for social insurance in Russia appear to be 38.1 percent of payroll, with *employees* paying 1 percent of gross salary to the pension fund (information from Mark Sundberg, World Bank, EC3C2, 20 October, 1996). Kesselman reports *employer* contribution rates for Russia which were 1 percent lower in 1993. See Jonathan R. Kesselman, "Payroll Taxes Around the World: Concepts ana Practice," *Canadian Tax Journal* 1996, Vol. 44, No 1, p.78.

49. *Ibid*, p.78.

50. Jonathan R. Kesselman, "Payroll Taxes in the Finance of Social Security," *Canadian Public Policy*, vol. 22 (June 1966), p.174.

51. McMillan observes that "where property taxes prevail, rates are locally established. In contrast, local income tax revenues are typically shared revenues not determined by local authorities. Denmark and Sweden are exceptions demonstrating the viability of true local income taxes." Melville L. McMillan, "A Local Perspective on Fiscal Federalism: Practices, Experiences and Lessons from Developed Countries," World Bank (PRDPE) 1995, (p. S-1). Bird and Slack observe that "the property tax has the clear advantage from a political and accountability perspective that it is, as a rule at least, in part a locally designed and locally-implemented tax...Potentially more productive alternative "local" taxes on income and sales in most countries do not have this advantage because not only the design and administration but even the rates of these taxes are almost always determined by central, not local, authorities." Richard M. Bird and Enid Slack, "Financing Local Government in OECD Countries: The Role of Local Taxes and User Charges," in J. Owens and G. Panella eds., *Local Government: An International Perspective*, (Amsterdam: North-Holland, 1991), p. 90.

BIBLIOGRAPHY

Belarus, Ministry of Statistics and Analysis. 1996. *Expenditures and Income of the Population in Belarus: 1995*. Minsk.

Bird, Richard M. and Enid Slack. 1991. "Financing Local Government in OECD Countries: The Role of Local Taxes and User Charges." In J. Owens and G. Panella eds., *Local Government: An International Perspective*. Amsterdam: North-Holland.

Buckley, Robert M. and Eugene M. Gorenko. 1995 (Dec.). "Unwinding the Socialist Wage Package: The Role of Housing in Russia." World Bank: Washington, D.C..

Commander, Simon and Richard Jackman. 1993. "Providing Social Benefits in Russia: Redefining the Roles of Firms and Government." Policy Research Working Paper 1184, World Bank: Washington, D.C..

_____ and Une Lee with Andrei Tolstopiatenko. 1995. "Social Benefits and the Russian Industrial Firm." In *Russia: Economic Policy and Enterprise Restructuring*. Joint Conference of the World Bank and the Ministry of Economy of the Russian Federation.

Coricelli, Fabrizio, Krysztof Hagemejer and Krysztof Rybinski. 1995. "Poland." In Simon Commander and Fabrizio Coricelli (eds), *Unemployment, Restructuring, and the Labor Market in Eastern Europe and Russia*. EDI Development Studies. Washington, DC, The World Bank.

Economic Council of Canada. 1987. *The Taxation of Savings and Investment*. Ottawa, Ontario: Minister of Supply and Services Canada.

Freinkman, Lev M. and Irina Starodubrovskaya. 1996. "Restructuring of Enterprise Social Assets in Russia," Policy Research Working Paper 1635, World Bankf: Washington, D.C..

Gruber Jonathan and James Poterba. 1995 (June). "Tax Subsidies to Employer-Provided Health Insurance," NBER Working Paper No. 5147.

Horioka, Charles Yuji. 1994 (January). "Japan's Consumption and Saving in International Perspective." *Economic Development and Cultural Change*, 42 (2).

Keen, Mick. 1996 (April). "Tax Reform in Belarus: Preliminary Report on Economic Aspects." EU-Tacis.

Kesselman, Jonathan R. 1996 (May) "Payroll Taxes Around the World: Concepts and Practice." *Canadian Tax Journal* 44 (1): 59-84.

_____. 1996 (June). "Payroll Taxes in the Finance of Social Security." *Canadian Public Policy*. 22: 162-179.

Khankevich, L.A. 1996 (June). "The Taxation System in the Republic of Belarus." World Bank: Washington, D.C..

Kitchen, Harry. 1993. *Efficient Delivery of Local Government Services*. School of Policy Studies Discussion Paper No. 93-15. Kingston, Ontario: Queen's University.

Klugman, Jeni, Sheila Marnie, John Micklewright and Philip O'Keefe. 1996 (forthcoming). "Enterprise Divestiture of Kindergartens and Childcare Arrangements in Central Asia." In Jane Falkingham, Jeni Klugman, Sheila Marnie and John Micklewright (eds), *Household Welfare in Central Asia*. Macmillan, U.K.

Lexin, Vladimir, Alexander Shvetsov, and Lev Freinkman. 1996. "Regionalnuye kollizii funktsionirovaniya sotsialnukh obyektov" ("Regional conflicts in operating social assets") in *Rossiisky Economicheski Jurnal (Russian Economic Journal)*, 1996, Issue 8, pp. 62-72.

Martinez-Vasquez, Jorge. 1994. "The Challenge of Expenditure-Assignment Reform in Russia," *Journal of Environment and Planning*. 12: 277-292.

McMillan, Melville L. 1995. *A Local Perspective on Fiscal Federalism: Practices, Experiences and Lessons from Developed Countries*. World Bank (PRDPE).

Schaffer Mark E., Richard Jackman, Gaspar Fajth and Judit Lakatos, Martin Rein, Irina Tratch and Andreas Woergoetter. 1995. "Round table on 'Divestiture of Social Services from State-Owned Enterprises." *Economics of Transition*. 3 (2): 247-266.

Urban Institute. 1995. "Russian Enterprise Housing Divestiture." Urban Institute Research Paper.

Wallich, Christine I. 1994. "Russia's Dilemma." In Christine I. Wallich ed., *Russia and the Challenge of Fiscal Federalism*. Washington, DC: World Bank Regional and Sectoral Study: 1-18.

Woodbury, Stephen A. and Daniel S. Hamermesh. 1992 (May). "Taxes, Fringe Benefits and Faculty", *The Review of Economics and Statistics*. LXXIV (2): 287-296.

World Bank. 1994. *World Development Report, 1994*. New York: Oxford University Press.

_____. 1996. "Conditional Grants: International Experience." Annex 4, World Bank Country Study. *Fiscal Management in the Russian Federation*: 141-145

ANNEX B

Agro-Industry Sector Review
Sudhee Sen Gupta

Agroindustry Sector Review

Sudhee Sen Gupta

Some initial progress in reforming the agribusiness sector has been made at the national level by reducing, and in some cases removing, administrative controls over pricing, processing, procurement and distribution. Most prices have been liberalized. Vertical administrative linkages have been removed at the supply, processing and distribution enterprises, and many enterprises in the sector have been corporatized and a few also privatized. The stated objective of completing the corporatization process in agroindustry by 1996, is also a step in the right direction.

However, these accomplishments at the national level are still incomplete and are being undermined at the regional or oblast level, with local administrations and their agriculture departments moving in to re-assert the controls that had appeared to have been removed at the national level. Even though most prices have been liberalized, some remaining floor and indicative prices are often enforced by regional authorities as mandatory prices. Although the extent of the interventions vary from region to region, these interventions severely limit the flexibility of enterprises in the sector to follow independent courses of action that might maximize efficiency and resource generation for the enterprise. As a result, dependence of the enterprises on outside resources (for example, on-budget and off-budget support) increase, and management finds justification for being less self reliant and less self sufficient.

Urgent measures are thus needed to loosen the hold of the regional administrations and their agriculture departments over enterprises in the sector. The only way to effectively achieve this is to transfer the ownership of these enterprises out of the hands of the regional administrations into private hands. Such a transition would also require that the MoAF and its regional counterparts, the Oblselchozprods, as well as the regional executive councils, shed most of their business administration functions and retain only their public administration functions. In order for a fair market system to emerge, potential monopoly situations would also need to

be adequately addressed; consideration should also be given to removing other potential barriers to competition that exist.

These issues are discussed below by first providing a brief outline of the structure and organization of the sector, followed by a review of the progress in the reform process, a discussion of the issues that still face the sector, and finally some recommendations for the Government to consider.

STRUCTURE AND ORGANIZATION

One helpful way to review the structure and organization of the agroindustry sector is to look at the sequence of the agribusiness chain. The agribusiness chain goes from input supplies to agricultural production to processing to wholesale and retail distribution, and includes functions such as procurement and financing. The following discussion is limited to supply of

Table B.1: Agricultural Machinery

	Units in Field	Annual Purchases (Units)	Hectares per Unit
Combine Harvesters			
1990	30,301	3,013	183
1995	22,506	42	224
% Change (95/90)	-26%	-99%	+22%
Fodder Harvesters			
1990	9,258	1,040	600
1995	8,871	98	568
% Change (95/90)	-4%	-91%	-5%
Tractors			
1990	113,385	9,085	49
1995	97,417	401	52
% Change (95/90)	-14%	-96%	+6%

Source: Ministry of Statistics.

inputs, procurement of agricultural products, processing and distribution.

Input Supply

The bulk of agricultural machinery in the country is supplied by an organization called Agrosnab. At the republican level this organization is subordinate to the MoAF. There are also oblast and regional level Agrosnabs which used to report to the republican Agrosnab but are now subordinated to the oblast and regional authorities. These organizations sell agricultural machinery to farms and provide a variety of services including construction, repair and maintenance. Selected data on machine populations and trends are provided in Table B.1. The data in this table seem to indicate that while purchases have fallen in all categories, the smallest decline has been in fodder harvesters. About 60 percent of the existing machines in this category, however, are worn out. The investment level may therefore partly reflect an effort to correct this problem. On the other hand, this probably indicates a very serious level of deterioration in the categories where even less investment has taken place. This could be due to support the government may have provided to prop up the meat and dairy subsector in which Belarus had historically specialized.

There is a parallel organization called Agrotechnic which also provides technical services to farms. Fertilizers and chemicals are supplied by a similar organization called Agrochemia (subordinate to the MoAF) which also has its counterparts at the oblast and regional levels. These counterparts also report to the oblast and regional authorities now. In addition to fertilizer sales this organization also provides application services for fertilizers and chemicals.

Producers

Agricultural production is done by state and collective farms as well as by private farmers, including on private household plots. Most of the state farms have been converted into collective farms, which now number 2,400; only one hundred of the largest state farms remain. There are now about 3,100 private farmsteads with 0.5 percent share of farmed land, accounting for 1

percent of the farm output. However, these household farms concentrate mostly on potatoes, vegetables and some livestock. It is worth noting, as shown in Table B.2, that production has increased in potatoes and vegetables, while for grains and sugar beets, which still are produced mainly by the state and collective farms, production has fallen. Belarusian agriculture specialized in meat and dairy products in the FSU and these commodities still account for a substantial portion (51 percent) of agricultural output. These commodities are more capital intensive, and private producers have not been able to compensate for the fall in collective and state production.

Processing

Food processors used to be administratively organized into four groups: (a) meat and dairy (including meat, poultry and milk processing); (b) fruits and vegetables (including canning, juices, jams and jellies); (c) food and beverages (including items such as sugar, cookies and confectionery, vegetable oils and margarine, wine, beer, vodka and cognac, soft drinks, etc.); and (d) the bread complex (including grain elevators, flour and feed mills, and bakeries). In Belarus all of these groups have been absorbed into the MoAF. Details on the number of enterprises, output trends, and employment are provided in Tables B.3, B.4, and B.5.

Procurement

There are three major groups involved in the procurement of agricultural produce. Food processors, the government (for state procurement), and Belcoopsoyuz, the national union of cooperative societies.

- *Food Processors*. While a major share of procurement of agricultural produce was delivered to the food processors through allocations and quotas under the state order system, presently most processors procure on their own, although they have to submit their requirement forecasts to the regional executive councils for agriculture. The share of procurement of food processors has declined significantly

Table B.2: Production of Staple Crops

Crop Item	1990	1993	1994	1995	1995/ 1990 (%)
Grain (Th. tons)	7,035	7,508	6,095	5,502	78
% State & Collective Farms	99	94	94	93	
Sugar Beets (Th. tons)	1,479	1,569	1,078	1,172	79
% State & Collective Farms	100	99	99	99	
Potatoes (Th. tons)	8,590	11,644	8,241	9,504	111
% State & Collective Farms	46	25	15	13	
Vegetables (Th. tons)	749	1,098	1,029	1,031	138
% State & Collective Farms	67	27	24	23	
Livestock & Poultry (Th. tons)	1,758	1,242	1,138	995	57
% State & Collective Farms	87	82	80	76	
Milk (Th. tons)	7,457	5,584	5,510	5,070	68
% State & Collective Farms	76	65	64	60	

Source: Ministry of Statistics.

Table B.3: Number of Agro-Processing Enterprises by Form of Ownership
(As of Dec. 1994)

	Total	Republican	Municipal	Joint Stock Co.	Other	Bel-Co-op
Meat	47	1	25	1	20	20
Dairy	122	1	107	8	6	-
Fruit & Vegetables	63	-	40	-	23	23
Flour & Cereal	14	12	-	2	-	-
Bakeries	86	19	-	-	67	67
Other	124	52	54	9	9	1
Total	456	85	226	20	125	111

Source: Ministry of Statistics.

Table B.4: 1994 Agro-Processing Output by Form of Ownership
(billions of BYR at 1994 Prices)

Item	Total	Republican	Municipal	Joint Stock Co.	Other	Bel-Co-op
Meat	1,040	6	948	46	40	40
Dairy	801	3	601	88	108	-
Fruit & Vegetables	169	-	101	-	68	68
Flour & Cereal	495	404	-	91	-	-
Bakeries	416	285	-	-	131	131
Other	1,144	533	250	217	144	-
Total	4,065	1232	1900	442	491	240

Source: Ministry of Statistics.

Table B.5: *Agro-Processing Employment by Form of Ownership*
(As of Dec. 1994)

	Total	Republican	Municipal	Joint Stock Co.	Other	*of which* Bel-Co-op
Meat	20,978	209	17,773	1,071	1,925	1,925
Dairy	21,392	93	16,589	2,272	2,438	0.0
Fruit & Vegetables	9,757	-	6,068	-	3,689	3,689
Flour & Cereal	5,909	5,191	-	718	-	-
Bakeries	20,845	12,461	-	-	8,384	8,384
Other	25,290	9,712	8,748	4,475	2,355	88
Total	104,171	27,666	49,178	8,536	18,791	14,086

Source: Ministry of Statistics.

Table B.6: *Market Share of Retail Sales*

Periods	Retail Trade Turnover Billions Rubles	Market Share of State Trade (%)	Market Share of Belcoopsoyuz (%)	Market Share of Other[a] (%)	Market Share of Food (%)
1990	18	66	33.5	0	44
1991	33	66	33.5	1	45
1992	286	46	33.4	21	50
1993	3,804	50	27.9	22	56
1994	6,928	48	21.9	28	60
1995	38,161	46	20	34	61
1996 - I	11,845	46	19	35	70
1996 - II[b]	14,226	44	19	37	70
1996 - III	18,000	43	20	38	63

[a] Mostly private retailers.
[b] 1996 II & III Fore*cast from Ministry of Statistics.*
Source: Ministry of Statistics.

in recent times due to low utilization levels of plant capacity caused by lack of demand and working capital. Among the processors, one major group is the bread complex, which procures most of the grain in the country.

- *Belcoopsoyuz* was the second largest procurer of agricultural produce, and through its 118 regional procurement offices and 1,400 procurement points around the country, it accounted for a significant share of agricultural procurement. For example, it procured 26 percent of all potatoes, 19 percent of all vegetables, 35 percent of all fruits, and its 134 bakeries baked 30 percent of all the bread in the country. While its present procurement levels have declined significantly, it is still a major factor in the rural marketplace.

- *State Procurement.* The share of state procurement has declined significantly in recent years and is now limited to seven items: grain (31 percent of output), meat (56 percent) and dairy (49 percent), fruits and vegetables (10 percent), sugar beets (60 percent), rapeseed (62 percent), and flax fiber (98 percent). Grain is procured for state stocks, spirits production, and food supplies for budget organizations. Similarly, meat, dairy, fruits and vegetables are procured for supplies to budget organizations such as hospitals and the military. For sugar beets, rapeseed and flax, state procurement is a way of financing the procurement of these items by the processors and distributors.

A fairly large portion of the output of fruits and vegetables (potatoes, in particular) is grown on family plots. While some of these are sold in the open market, most are consumed by households as a way of supplementing income. Several private traders have also begun to emerge, but their share of overall procurement is still relatively small.

Distribution

As in procurement, distribution is also dominated at the wholesale level by three organizations—the former warehouse enterprises of the Ministry of Trade, Belcoopsoyuz, and the MoAF. The former warehouse enterprises of the Ministry of Trade have large central and regional warehouses devoted to the distribution of meat and dairy through 8 large cold storage warehouses (6 in the oblast centers and 2 in Minsk), as well as the distribution of general food products through 8 large terminal warehouses (6 in the oblasts and 2 in Minsk) which handle items such as drinks, confectionery, sugar, canned goods, spices, and liquor. Belcoopsoyuz is also a major player in wholesale distribution, although its target markets are primarily in the rural areas. It has 107 general warehouses and 26 larger terminal warehouses. It also has 227 smaller cold storage warehouses.

The MoAF warehouses generally handle fruits and vegetables, although much of the consumption and (private) retail trade in this and other commodities is now by-passing the wholesale stage and going straight to the consumer.

In retail distribution, Belcoopsoyuz still dominates in the rural areas, particularly in the remote ones. It has several thousand food stores in rural areas including 470 mobile stores which serve the remote areas. It also has markets at each of the oblast centers and six in Minsk, as well as another 186 markets at the rayon level. The retail outlets of the Ministry of Trade, however, have been largely corporatized or privatized. These outlets and the retail stores of Belcoopsoyuz are beginning to see some competition from private retail operators. With the emergence of private retailers, the market shares of the state and the cooperative union have declined significantly (see Table B.6); Belcoopsoyuz now accounts for only 20 percent of retail distribution in the country. Table B.6 also shows that food now occupies a much larger share of retail purchases.

PROGRESS IN THE REFORM PROCESS

Prices

Since 1992, prices have been steadily liberalized for most products. (see Tables B.7a-B.7c). With the exceptions of oil produced in Belarus, petrochemicals based on Belarusian oil, power, natural and liquefied natural gas, certain communal services, transport, communications, and to a limited extent vodka, prices on most products are said to be legally free. In cases of production determined to be a monopoly, there remain some margin controls, and prices and changes in prices have to be declared and registered with the Pricing Committee. Prices also have to be declared for one type of bread, milk with 2-3 percent fat, and potash fertilizer. There are some margin limits and floor prices set for meat (5 percent) and milk (8 percent). Floor prices are also set for some export products such

Table B.7a: *Remaining Price Controls*
(As of 1995)

		Belarus Price	World Price
Oil & Oil produced locally		$90/ton	$118/ton
Diesel Fuel			
	For Industry	$0.121/Liter	$0.83/Liter
	For Population	$0.123/Liter	(Avg. Europe)
Electricity			
	For Industry	$0.038/kwh	$0.08/kwh
	For Population	$0.010/kwh	(Avg. for Europe)
Natural Gas			
	For Industry	$72/mcm	$87/mcm
	For Population	$19/mcm	

Source: State Committee for Pricing and Staff Estimates.

Table B.7b: *Prices for State Procurement*
(As of December 1995)

	Belarus Price	World Price
Sugar Beets	$34/ton	n.a.
Grain	$65/ton	$121/ton
Potatoes	$39/ton	$178/ton
Vegetables (Typical Basket)	$227/ton	$598/ton (Winter Fresh)

Source: State Committee for Pricing and Staff Estimates.

Table B.7c: *Other Prices*

Indicative (floor) Prices include:
Timber, Hides, Flax & Flax fiber, Leather, Powdered Milk, Casein, Pork & Beef on bone, Dark rye bread, Fertilizer.

Declared Prices on Monopolies
These have margin ceilings and have to be registered with the Pricing Committee. There are also margin ceilings on processed Milk (8%) and Meat (5%).

Source: State Committee for Pricing.

as hides, flax, fiber, leather, powder milk, casein, and pork and beef on the bone.

The Council of Ministers has since reviewed these controls and adopted the policy of indicative rather than mandatory prices. Thus the floor prices would be set at world prices, but if the enterprise cannot sell at these prices it could sell for less and no economic sanctions would apply. There are some indicative prices also set for state procurement, for example for sugar beets, grain, beans, and vegetable oil products. These indicative prices are mainly used to calculate the advances that are provided for state procurement. It is expected these indicative prices will have been changed to market prices by August 1996. Other than the above, all prices are free by law.

Production and Distribution

There has also been significant progress in removing state control over production, procurement and distribution. The state order system has been abolished and production quotas have been removed. The Ministry of Agriculture, which enterprises make deals and sign contracts for the season's procurement and delivery. In many cases, agricultural procurement is now being done through direct dealings between processors, traders and the agricultural producers. By a recent decree of the President, all agro-processing enterprises have to be corporatized by the end of 1996.

Most of the vertical structures in distribution have been dismantled. For example the former warehouse enterprises of the Ministry of Trade are no longer controlled by the Ministry but rather are owned by and report to the regional authorities. As mentioned before, most of the retail outlets in the country (nearly 74 percent) have been converted to joint stock companies or privatized, and many of the processors deal directly with these stores. The monolithic input suppliers of the past have also been dismantled, and the regional Agrosnabs and Agrochemias no longer report to their republican counterparts. In fact, the republican Agrosnabs have diversified into other areas of business and often compete with their regional units for the farmer's business. There is emerging private activity in imported fertilizer supply, which now accounts for about 15 percent of consumption, and about 40 percent of imported consumption. This private sector activity in chemicals and fertilizer uses the infrastructure of the regional agrochemias on a rental basis.

Ownership

There has also been a significant reorganization of the ownership structure among organs and levels of government · in the agroindustry sector. Tables B.3 and B.4 show that flour and cereal production is primarily concentrated at the republican level, while the control of bakeries is shared between the republican authorities and Belcoopsoyuz. On the other hand, meat and dairy processing is concentrated at the regional level, while fruit and vegetable processing is shared between regional ownership and Belcoopsoyuz.

The privatization program essentially came to a halt sometime in 1993, and very little progress has been made since then. Out of a total of about 456 agro-processing enterprises, about

20 have been converted to joint stock companies (accounting for eleven percent of total agro-processing output) and about twelve are leased companies. While another 111 belong to Belcoopsoyuz and are therefore technically private, these only account for about six percent of total agro-processing output.

MAJOR ISSUES FACING THE SECTOR

Regional Price Controls

In spite of the lack of legal grounds to impose price controls, many regional executive councils (Oblastpolkoms) have aggressively sought to enforce price and administrative controls over the agribusiness enterprises operating in their oblasts. In spite of regulations preventing the oblast administrations from setting prices, and instances where these authorities have been taken to court for violating these regulations, the regional executive councils, through moral suasion, administrative harassment and other means often seek to prevent market prices from emerging. Indicative and floor prices are sometimes enforced by regional authorities as fixed prices deemed necessary in the best social interests of their communities. Since such enforcement is illegal, the regional executive council often resorts to verbal communications over the telephone and other means to exert these controls.

While conceived with good intentions and even though limited, the price interventions that remain can often have detrimental side effects. Anomalies often appear and disincentives are created. For example, one farmer had to sell raw milk to the processor at an indicative price of BYR 1,700 per liter, while the open market price was BYR 4,000 per liter. A dairy plant on the other hand was unable to compete with imported butter as its cost at this price of milk was USD 2.7 per kilogram—the same as the price of imported butter. The plant therefore had no margin for processing costs or profits. The dairy plant felt that the imported butter was subsidized.[1]

Another example where price supports might have been detrimental is in cattle breeding, where price interventions, most recently floor prices, might have contributed to the impaired competitiveness of the sector. Floor prices for cattle in the face of soft demand may have, among other things,[2] contributed to a sharp fall in sales of cattle and poultry at the expense of preserving headcounts. This has contributed to increased feed-to-weight ratios which in turn have further undermined the cost competitiveness of the sector (Table B.8)

Measures are thus needed to ensure that the state's laws on price liberalization are respected. Options that might be considered include information programs to educate enterprise managers as to their rights under the law and procedural mechanisms to seek recourse in case of violations. However, unless ownership changes, the internal pressures exerted on management to enforce price behavior and exert operational control will not be eliminated.

Table B.8: Cattle Breeding Statistics

	1990	*1995*	*% Change (95/90)*
Sales (Th. Tons Live wt)			
Cattle & Poultry	1758	995	-43%
Headcount			
Cattle (Th.)	6975	5054	-28%
Hogs (Th.)	5051	3895	-23%
Poultry (Mln.)	51	40	-22%
Feed/Wt			
Cattle	12.43	16.04	+29%
Hogs	6.89	8.54	+24%
Poultry	n.a.	n.a.	n.a.

Source: Ministry of Economy.

Administrative Controls

Because the ownership of assets in the agribusiness sector has been largely relegated to regional authorities, and because agro-processing enterprises under regional subordination account for almost 50 percent of output (Table B.4), the regional authorities appear to be moving in to resume the price and administrative controls that have been relinquished at the national level.[3]

The regional executive councils also exert administrative controls over procurement and distribution of agricultural products, and in many cases over the day-to-day operations of agribusiness enterprises. In some regions, the regional executive council requires the processors to submit demand requirements and production plans for the season, and then translates these into production assignments (notifications) which are provided to the farmers before planting. In some cases, production quotas are allocated to processors in the region, for example, to dairies, so that plant loading can be uniform. This reduces the opportunity of competition between these dairies. In some cases, interference by the executive council in trivial day to day operational activities has also been reported. However, the influence that the regional authorities exert or try to exert varies significantly between regions with some regions being more control-oriented than others.

As long as the ownership of property in the sector remains in the hands of government (in this case the regional governments), and the management of the agribusiness enterprises reports to the executive councils, it is unlikely that enterprises will have the autonomy and motivation required to make the transition to a more efficient and profit-oriented operation. It is thus critical to accelerate the divestiture of ownership from government to private hands. There appeared to be significant support for this at the enterprise level, even though this was not the case at the ministerial or regional level.

Shortage of Working Capital

There is also a severe working capital shortage being reported by enterprises at all levels of the agribusiness chain. While the cost and lack of credit due to macroeconomic stabilization measures are seen as barriers to a solution to this problem, the roots of the problem can be traced to other factors as well. Closer inspection of the working capital problem reveals that payment arrears by state-owned wholesale and distribution enterprises (as well as temporary payment delays) which reduce the real value of eventual proceeds are also major contributors to the working capital problem. These payment arrears can be traced to (a) the lack of recourse mechanisms for state-owned suppliers to enforce collection on state-owned customers, (b) a lack of demand ascribed to greater demand for imported goods; and (c) the mismatch between price and consumer income levels.

Again, unless the state-owned distribution enterprises are privatized, they cannot be adequately subjected to collection processes and the financial discipline that these processes bring. State-owned enterprises, albeit regional ones in this case, can seldom foreclose on other state owned enterprises. The issue of import competition, while a positive trend, is presently subject to certain distortions that might need to be addressed. The complaint often heard is that in spite of inferior quality and higher prices, consumers still prefer imports due to better packaging. It is likely that in some cases, the price premium for the packaging and the related quality differential perceived would be much higher if the exchange rates had kept up with inflation. As to the mismatch between prices and incomes, there may be some validity to this issue. Prices for many if not most food items are approaching world levels while consumer incomes remain a fraction of that. This is also evidenced by the larger share of food in retail purchases (Table B.6).

However, incomes in the case of Belarus can only increase through investment and fuller utilization of human resources and of the significant existing capital stock. Since, for reasons of macroeconomic stability, internal credit expansion is not an option, significant reliance would need to be placed on foreign investment in order to restructure the existing productive capacity to increase income levels and regain previous standards of living. This again would require a demonstrated willingness on the part of the government to privatize and create a healthy private sector environment in order to attract this investment.

Once the required structural changes are in place and privatization in the agribusiness sector starts to gather momentum, some immediate initial infusion of working capital would be essential to restart the sector. A financial sector would also need to be in place to serve the normal credit needs of the privatized enterprises in the sector with adequate financial intermediation. This might require significant external financial as well as consultative support. Without this the privatization process and the public commitment to it is likely to falter.

Fiscal Burden

In the meantime, agriculture and to some extent agroindustry continue to consume significant fiscal resources. This burden is both direct (on budget), as well as indirect, (off budget). There also appear to be parallel fiscal activities being conducted by branch ministries such as the Ministry of Agriculture.

Direct budget support to agriculture has amounted to BYR 3.1 trillion in 1996, including BYR 808 billion in local budget subsidies to collective farms for procurement of equipment and inputs (mineral fertilizers, elite seeds, cattle, etc.). Extrabudgetary financing amounts to BYR 2.2 trillion, including BYR 0.4 trillion for leasing of agricultural equipment. As a result, in 1996 the total amount of public support to agriculture can be estimated at BYR 5.3 trillion.

In addition to off-budget support accountable through the Ministry of Finance, there are other funds which are mobilized and spent by ministries such as the Ministry of Agriculture, thus, by-passing the Ministry of Finance. While fully aware of the process, The Ministry of Finance appears not to have any record of these fiscal transactions. Examples of these transactions are the Centralized Investment Fund and the Research and Development Fund. These funds are mobilized by levying upon the industry sector 15 percent of the depreciation, and 1 percent of prime cost for the former, and 1 percent of revenue for the latter. The proceeds are then provided as a subsidy to the agriculture sector. It was not clear if these contributions or levies were voluntary or mandatory. The exact figures for these support programs were not readily confirmed but were informally estimated by various sources to be BYR 1-2 trillion.

The total fiscal burden of the sector would thus be at least BYR 8-9 trillion or about 7 percent of GDP.

Potential Monopolies

Once privatization begins to progress and economic activity increases, the structural configuration of the agribusiness system in Belarus may give rise to certain monopoly situations which would need to be addressed. The major areas where this could occur are in the cold storage warehouses, grain elevators, and organizations such as the Belcoopsoyuz.

As mentioned before, the cold storage capacity of the country is concentrated in 8 large regional cold storage warehouses. Once privatized, these could begin to exert a strong monopolistic influence on the market. Safeguards would need to be in place to reduce the potential for market manipulation by these entities. The cold storage facilities were previously used to maintain buffer stocks to seasonally balance the supply and demand for meat and dairy products. Although currently these warehouses are under-utilized due to the shortage of working capital, and most of the trading bypasses them, upon privatization they could provide their owners significant leverage over local production, supply, and prices. One option might be to limit the owners of these facilities to only renting space and not using these facilities to store their own products. Another alternative would be to sell the

cold storage warehouses in portions or modules to different owners who could then compete with one another. As additional or alternative capacity is built these restrictions could be relaxed.

Grain elevators also pose a significant monopoly (i.e., monopsony or more appropriately, oligopolistic) threat. Generally each region is served by a few large elevator facilities which procure, dry and store the grain. Because most farms do not have their own storage and drying capabilities, they are captive to these grain elevators enterprises. The republican authorities, who presently own all but 2 of the largest of these facilities, can use this power over farmers to enforce price and delivery norms that are set for flour and bread products. The activities of these elevators would have to be closely monitored and regulated in order to assure the producers a fair and competitive market for their output. Again as on-farm storage and drying facilities emerge, these regulations could be relaxed and eventually eliminated.

The Belcoopsoyuz could also emerge as a major monopoly in the agribusiness chain. This organization owns a significant share of the agribusiness infrastructure in the rural areas. As mentioned before, they own a significant number and share of the cold storage and warehouse facilities in the rural areas. They also have 10 large trucking enterprises comprising 11,000 vehicles, and presently operate over 13,000 retail outlets in the rural areas.[4] While in the other republics of the FSU the coop unions have essentially lost a major portion of their market share due to financial difficulties and competition from emerging private traders, in Belarus the coop union appears to be very much intact. Some restructuring and dismantling of this organization might thus be needed in order to reduce its potential monopoly threat as the economy strengthens.

Although the Agrosnab organization has been a potential monopoly threat in other republics of the FSU, the dismantling of its vertical structure and the incipient competition between the regional and national level Agrosnabs significantly reduce this threat. One issue to address however, is the subsidized state financing being made available to it for leasing operations. These funds, as long as they are continued, should be made available to all vendors of agricultural machinery, and the allocation role for these funds should be removed from the Agrosnab organization.

SUMMARY OF RECOMMENDATIONS

- All remaining price interventions should be gradually phased out as soon as possible.

- The laws and regulations providing for liberalized production and pricing should be better enforced at the regional level so as to prevent the regional authorities from re-exerting controls that have already been eliminated under the law.

- The corporatization goals for the agroindustry sector as set by the presidential decree should be met, and all agroindustry enterprises should be corporatized by the end of 1996.

- The privatization process should be accelerated for agroindustry enterprises in order to:

  - remove regional administrative controls on enterprises;
  - ensure a true hard budget constraint on these enterprises; and
    - improve output and efficiency.

- Parallel fiscal or quasi-fiscal activities should be closely reviewed by the government to assess their macroeconomic implications; at a very minimum these activities, if continued, should be transparent and accountable.

- As the economy gathers strength, potential monopoly situations should be examined more closely and appropriate action taken if needed. In this context the following organizations need close monitoring:

  - cold storage warehouses
  - grain elevator complexes
  - Belcoopsoyuz

Financial support for agricultural inputs, such as leasing of farm machinery, should be distributed on an arms length basis so that all purveyors have equal access.

Table B.9: State Budget Allocation for the Ministry of Agriculture
(*in BYR Billions*)

Items	1994	1995	1996
Budget organizations	25.4	157.1	261
Repair of irrigation systems	7.2	87.8	117.8
Lime & applications	38.4	174.0	478.8
Capital investments	11.2	45.3	104.0
Priority programs	158.6	909.4	1,408.4
Private farm support	13.2	44.2	80.0
Soft loans	8.65	45.7	0.0
State Subsidies	50.214	13.0	4.7
Miscellaneous	12.2	560.2	1,077.7
Price compensation	125.7	0.0	0.0
Road construction & maintenance	0.0	119.0	0.0
Total	**450.9**	**2,155.7**	**3,533.2**

Source: Ministry of Finance.

Table B.10: Fiscal Burden

Budget support for agriculture sector (not counting loans)	= BYR 1.758 trillion
Republican off-budget support	= BYR 2.6 trillion
Loans from budget	= BYR 1.2 trillion
Guaranteed bank loans	= n.a.

Note: Above tables do not include off-budget support from the oblasts or the Ministry of Agriculture.
Source: Ministry of Finance.

Table B.11: State Financing of Inputs

Off-budget funding for leasing of Farm Machinery	= BYR 1.2 trillion
Off-budget financing of Fertilizer purchases:	
Republican Support:	= BYR 794 billion
Oblast Support:	= BYR 1.2 trillion (estimate)

Note: Above tables do not include off-budget support from the oblasts or the Ministry of Agriculture.
Source: Ministry of Finance.

Notes

1 Interviews with a collective farm and a dairy plant.

2 For example, the effects of increased real exchange rates on exports. One collective farm visited exported cattle to Poland for a profit at $600/ton before 1995, but today it loses money even at $800/ton.

3 The administrative structure at the oblast level is somewhat complex. First, there is the regional executive council (oblast plodkom) which is part of the oblast government, and then there is the Oblastselchosprod which is the oblast counterpart, and previously a branch of the Ministry of Agriculture. The enterprise reports directly to the former, and indirectly to the latter on policy and technical issues. In addition, there is the management association for the enterprise's commodity group which straddles the two administrative organs and to which the enterprise also reports. This results in significant opportunity for command and control tactics and also provides the opportunity for conflicting directives.

4 This figure excludes restaurants and other public catering facilities.

ANNEX C

The Sustainability of External Debt
Sergei Shatalov

The Sustainability Of External Debt

Sergei Shatalov

From 1992 to 1995, external debts accumulated rapidly in Belarus. At the end of 1995, the country's external public debt stood at USD 1.95 billion.[1] Of this total, 24 percent was owed to Russia; bilateral OECD creditors held 49 percent (including both official lending and officially guaranteed export credits). Multilaterals, including the IMF, held 27 percent.

FSU Debt

Belarus was one of the first CIS countries to sign the "zero option" agreement with Russia (on July 20, 1992).[2] Under the zero option agreements, Russia assumed full responsibility for external assets and liabilities of the FSU. This was confirmed on April 2, 1993 in a special statement made by the Russian Government at the Paris Club meeting. Belarus, therefore, has no liabilities arising from the external borrowing of the Soviet Union.[3]

New Borrowing

Borrowing was undertaken in 1992-1995 both by the central Government and by enterprises, with the latter contracting debt both with and without the government guarantee. The amount of non-guaranteed enterprise debt is estimated by the Belarusian MOF at about 19 percent of the total debt outstanding at end-1995. It is very important to note that even when enterprises contract external debt without the explicit payment guarantee of the central Government, the creditors consider this debt as public, because all borrowers remain in public ownership. Since the start of sovereign borrowing in 1992, the Government of Belarus was displaying a commendable realism, monitoring enterprise debt on an equal footing with the debt of the central Government.

If only the public external debt proper (including external debts of public enterprises) were taken into account, the creditworthiness indicators would be comfortably low. The debt service ratio in 1995 was less than 5 percent. (20 percent is often quoted as a level above which the

country's liquidity position may become stressed.) The debt-to-GNP ratio stood at 21 percent in 1995. (For this ratio, the "sustainability threshold" is widely considered to be 50 percent). At the same time, external indebtedness has grown rapidly during 1992-1995, with most of the debt contracted on non-concessional terms. The latter is reflected in the high ratio of the present value of debt to its nominal value, which stood at 81 percent at the end of 1994 and implied a grant element of less than 20 percent.

The reasons for this rapid accumulation of debt become evident once the *overall liability position* of Belarus is examined. In addition to almost USD 2 billion in public debt owed by the central Government and public enterprises, the latter at end-1995 also had *payment arrears* totaling USD 679 million for energy imports from Russia, with another USD 253 million in penalties for these overdue payments. The total external liabilities of Belarus at end-1995 thus stood at USD 2.88 billion, equivalent to 31 percent of GDP. Russia's share in Belarus' total liabilities was also much higher at 49 percent (compared to 24 percent for the public debt only).

The inclusion of enterprise cross-border arrears in the debt sustainability analysis is of critical importance, due to the *pattern of transformation of enterprise payment arrears into long-term public debt*. This is a region-wide pattern, which is sometimes called "involuntary lending" and is caused by the interdependence of CIS economies, and in particular by the dependence of other CIS states on gas and oil imports from Russia and Turkmenistan.

Belarus was luckier than many other FSU states, since in the early 1990s its energy import prices were rising more slowly. However, Belarus' economy was adjusting to this terms-of-trade shock much more slowly than many of its neighbors, and the Government was unwilling to pass higher energy prices on the consumers. Consumers continued to run up huge arrears on payments to Beltransgas and Beltopgas, the two main energy importers, which in turn accumulated large trade arrears to the Russian exporter, RAO Gazprom by early 1993. Smaller amounts of arrears were accumulated by importers of other CIS goods.

On June 30, 1993 Russia and Belarus signed an agreement that consolidated all enterprise arrears into long-term public debt of USD 385.4 million. Similar bilateral consolidation agreements were made between all CIS republics, but in a unique exception to the usual CIS practice, debt consolidation for Belarus was granted on concessional terms (zero interest rate, maturity of 14 years and a grace period of 7 years). The consolidation loan for Belarus was denominated in U.S. dollars, but at the same time the agreement allowed debt servicing in kind. In 1993-1994, two new Russian trade credits were granted to Belarus that added another USD 84.6 million to its external debt.[4]

Belarus also accumulated external debt to non-CIS creditors. Much of the debt contracted in 1992-1993 from bilateral creditors (in particular, Germany) was on market terms. The *central Government's* repayment record vis-à-vis the OECD countries remains impeccable, but the *enterprises* have run up modest arrears on their hard-currency debts. These arrears are estimated by the Ministry of Finance at USD 15 million at March 31, 1996. Belarus' long-term ability to carry external debt on commercial terms in the environment of slow growth and slow reforms may be less than certain.

Adjustment to the intra-FSU terms-of-trade shock remained very insufficient over 1994-1995, as there was no improvement in the collection of arrears owed by domestic consumers, and trade arrears to Russia continued to accumulate as well. By December 31, 1995 arrears to Russia reached USD 654 million; another USD 262 million was owed in penalties on overdue gas payments. On the other side, long-term debt to Russia did not represent a serious liquidity constraint in 1994-1995, since only small interest payments were falling due (about USD 1 million as reported under the Debt Reporting System). Belarus has no arrears on its public debt to Russia.

To prevent another transformation of payment arrears into public debt, Belarus entered into bilateral negotiations with Russia, and on February 27, 1996 the two sides signed an Intergovernmental Agreement on the Mutual Settlement of Claims. The agreement sets the mutual claims of the two sides as follows:[5]

1. Russian claims on Belarus:

   a) Belarus' long-term public debt in the amount of USD 470 million; and

   b) enterprise gas arrears and penalties for late gas payments in the amount of about USD 900 million (the exact amount to be agreed upon by the two sides).

2. Belarus claims on Russia:

   a) claims of Belarusian enterprises on Russian Vneshekonombank (VEB), arising from the freezing of their accounts in VEB in 1991, of about USD 200 million;

   b) liabilities of the Russian Government arising from the transfer of fissile material to Russia (in the amount to be agreed upon by the two sides);

   c) claims related to the environmental damage inflicted in the process of withdrawing Russian strategic troops from Belarusian territory (amount to be agreed upon).

The amount of Belarusian claims under 2(b) and 2(c) combined is estimated by Belarusian authorities at about USD 1 billion. These detailed numbers are currently being reviewed by the two sides. Until the reconciliation of debt data, it is impossible to determine whether this Agreement will eliminate all of Belarus' liabilities to Russia, including the gas arrears, or whether there will remain a debtor balance that will be transformed into long-term debt (like in 1993). It is clear, however, that the Agreement would substantially reduce the total liabilities of Belarus' public sector to Russia. Further work is required to evaluate the implications of this Agreement on the debt prospects of Belarus.

The Agreement's implementation mechanism remains to be clarified as well. It is proposed that the two Ministries of Finance would issue and exchange promissory notes which would then will be canceled. However, it is also envisaged that part of these notes will be passed by the Russian Government to Gasprom as a form of clearance of gas arrears owed to it by Belarus, and that the latter would then be able to convert these claims into equity on the territory of Belarus. It is useful to evaluate the likelihood and the macroeconomic and fiscal implications of such debt-for-equity programs.

Notes

1 Not to be confused with the agreement signed with Russia on February 27, 1996, on the mutual settlement of debt claims, which is also called the "zero variant."

2 Zero option agreement of 1992 did not include the 1992 disbursements on the territory of Belarus under loans signed by the last Soviet Government, in the amount of USD 131.4 million. The legal status of this debt is not clear; there has been no communication between the two Governments regarding it since 1994. Belarusian authorities believe that Russia will not be able to insist on its repayment.

3 The original commitment amounts for these credits were RUR 70 billion and RUR 150 billion. The first one was utilized in full; under the second one, only about RUR 110 billion was disbursed. To minimize the creditor's exchange rate risk, the stock of debt outstanding was fixed in dollars, with the ruble amount of individual drawings under these loans converted into dollars at the ruble/dollar rate fixed on the day of each drawing.

4 The text of this agreement is not available to the World Bank. It is summarized here on the basis of discussions with officials from Belarus MOF.

ANNEX D

Macroeconomic Projection Framework
Yuri Sobolev

RMSM-X:
A Flow-of-Funds Framework for Modeling Economic Policy Options

Yuri Sobolev

MODEL STRUCTURE

The model used to develop the macroeconomic scenarios presented in this report is based on a flow-of-funds framework that relies on a fundamental accounting identity—expenditures on consumption, public and private investments, and net exports (exports minus imports) must be equal to gross domestic product at market prices. In addition, the model incorporates budget constraints for each of the following sectors: (a) the public sector, defined as the central government; (b) the financial sector, defined as the monetary system consisting of the central bank and commercial banks; (c) the "private" sector, defined as a residual domestic sector;[1] and (d) the foreign sector or the rest of the world, which is defined as the balance of payments viewed from outside the country. The budget constraints require that the total sources (or revenues) for each sector equal the sector's total uses (or expenditures), and that a use in one sector be a source of funds in another sector.

The model distinguishes between current and capital transactions.[2] Each of the sectoral budget equations is expressed as current or capital sources and uses of funds. The difference between current income and current expenditure is savings, which in turn are a capital source of funds. Investment and capital transfers represent capital uses of funds.

Besides the four budget equations for each sector (current and capital sources and uses of funds), the model incorporates four market-clearing conditions for financial assets. These conditions require that the supply of broad money, domestic credit, government domestic borrowing from the private sector, and foreign loans be equal to the demand. Broad money consists of currency in circulation, demand deposits, and time deposits.[3] Foreign loans are available to all domestic sectors, that is, to the government, private, and monetary sectors.

Borrowing from abroad is determined by the balance of payments requirement. The amounts likely to be disbursed by foreign lenders from existing loans as well as from expected commitments to the central government are specified in the debt module of the model. The input data on the external debt flows and stocks are taken from the World Bank Debt Reporting System, which provides the stock of existing debt and projections of disbursement and repayment flows based on this stock. New loan commitments are entered based on the amount of borrowing considered possible from each source (official international financial institutions, bilateral official creditors, commercial lenders, and so on). The model then computes the streams of gross and net disbursements, as well as debt service flows, for each creditor. Any additional foreign capital required to close the balance of payments financing gap is assumed to be provided by a "marginal" (or residual) lender. This "gapfill" loan is calculated and assigned in the present version of the model to the private sector rather than the public sector because the maximum borrowing thought to be possible by the public sector is reflected in the input data for the model. This gapfilling credit is assumed to come from foreign commercial banks. Hence the terms and conditions of the gapfill loan are set to be equal to the terms and conditions of a regular loan from commercial bank creditors.

GENERAL ASSUMPTIONS

Assumed values for the following variables are entered directly into the model: (a) GDP growth rates by sector; (b) inflation per annum (GDP deflator); (c) gross domestic investment and foreign direct investment as shares of GDP; (d) foreign portfolio investment as a percentage of foreign direct investment; (e) government consumption and government investment as shares of GDP; (f) direct taxes as a percentage of GDP at factor costs; (g) monetary sector credit to the public sector as a percentage of government budget deficit; and (h) broad money velocity. The values assigned to these variables take into account the values for corresponding indicators from countries of similar size and level of development that have already established market-based economies.

The rate of growth of exports of goods and non-factor services is jointly determined by the following external sector parameters: (a) elasticity of manufactured goods exports with respect to the real exchange rate;[4] (b) foreign income growth rate and foreign elasticity of demand for domestic exports with respect to foreign income; and (c) assumed export growth rates for primary goods and non-factor services. The rate of growth of imports of goods and non-factor services is determined by: (a) elasticities of imports with respect to the real exchange rate and GDP; and (b) elasticity of capital goods imports with respect to gross domestic investment. The values of the above parameters are chosen within the range of their empirical plausibility and result in total export growth rates that are similar to those of middle-income economies. The current account deficit is limited to about 6 percent of GDP, thus helping assure a sustainable external debt service position.

The price indices of the country's exports and imports, which are not differentiated by product, are given exogenously based on the Manufactured Unit Value (MUV) index (which is equivalent to world inflation).[5] This series is provided by the World Bank's Commodity and Policy Analysis Unit. The model calculates the price index of consumption goods (CPI).

The nominal exchange rate path is determined by specifying the rate of devaluation. The model then calculates the path of the real exchange rate by linking the nominal exchange rate with the GDP deflator and the MUV index.[6] Devaluations of 100 and 50 percent in 1997 and 1998 respectively are assumed in order to bring the real exchange rate more or less in line with fundamentals. These can be broadly defined as determined by productivity growth in the traded goods sector and domestic inflation; these factors plus historical trends in trade balances and movements in external reserves indicate the rate needed to establish a competitive, sustainable balance-of-payments position. The real exchange rate is assumed to appreciate back to its 1995 level in the latter years of the model as the result of future productivity gains.

SOLUTION PROCEDURE

The solution procedure starts with the goods market. The paths of real GDP, gross domestic investment, government consumption and investment, and total exports and imports are calculated as specified functions of the user-supplied parameters. Private consumption and investment, which are the residual variables, are determined through the goods market identity: private consumption equals GDP at market prices minus net exports minus gross domestic investment minus government consumption; and private investment equals gross domestic investment minus government investment.

The change in money stock is determined through the quantity theory of money equation, which says that nominal money stock equals GDP in constant (base year) prices times GDP deflator divided by the velocity of broad money. The value of total banking system credit is calculated as the residual stock on the monetary sector accounts. Since the value of the public sector credit from the banking system is specified exogenously as a percentage of nominal GDP, banking system credit to the private sector and hence the flow of private credit can also be determined.

The change in the country's foreign indebtedness—the gapfill loan charged to the private sector—is the residual value needed to close the foreign sector identity after allowing for all non-debt and short-term capital flows, and changes in the stock of foreign exchange reserves. Net private sector borrowing from abroad is thus calculated as the difference between total net capital inflow and net capital inflows to the public and monetary sectors. Hence, the value of the gapfill loan is also known.

Notes

1   State-owned enterprises are thus defined as belonging to the private sector. It is implicitly assumed that privatization would be implemented, that the role of government significantly reduced, and that enterprises still in the public sector would be subjected to hard budget constraints as recommended in this report, thus leading them to behave like private sector entities. That would make the definition of the private sector more meaningful.

2   For example, a tax payment would be a current transaction. Borrowing, which creates a financial asset for the lender and a financial liability for the borrower, would be a capital transaction.

3   The private sector holds currency and deposits. Credit is extended to government as well as to the private sector.

4   Defined as the ratio of the percentage change in manufactured goods exports to a one percent change in the real exchange rate, reflecting the fact that a competitive real exchange rate that compensates for domestic inflation in excess of that in trading partner countries is vital to the success of exports.

5   Except for the price of energy imported from Russia in the first three years of the projection period. It is assumed that the Russian energy price charged to Belarus will converge to that prevailing in the world market as soon as in 1998. Starting in 1999 the imported energy price will be determined by the MUV index.

6   The real exchange rate index produced by the model is bilateral with respect to the U.S. dollar, and does not represent a trade-weighted multilateral index.

ANNEX E

Purchasing Power Parities
John Hansen

Purchasing Power Parities

John Hansen

Although purchasing power parity PPP rates can be difficult to calculate and interpret, the concept is really very simple. It says that, once overall price levels in different countries have been converted to a common currency, the national average price levels should be equal—the *Law of One Price*. If prices are not equal, traders will make a profit by purchasing goods in countries where they are cheaper and selling them where they are more expensive. In theory, this arbitrage will continue until prices have been equalized. According to the Law of One Price, if the current exchange rate does not make the prices equal, the exchange rate is either overvalued or undervalued. The prices of individual goods may of course vary, and research indicates that prices converge slowly and *imperfectly,* but if one takes the average national prices, as is done when calculating the consumer price index, for example, the price levels should be similar if the exchange rates are correct, according to the purchasing power parity principle.[1]

The PPP concept has been made popular and easy to understand by *The Economist's* annual publication in recent years of a "Big Mac Index" (BMI). *The Economist* uses the price of the Big Mac hamburger sandwich that is sold in McDonalds restaurants around the world as a proxy for the national price levels in each country. The Big Mac is a reasonably good indicator for this purpose because (a) it is a homogenous product across countries, and (b) it has a high domestic content. These prices are used to calculate a PPP exchange rate that would make this hamburger cost the same in dollars as it costs in the United States. This PPP exchange rate is then compared with the market exchange rate. If the PPP rate is higher, the currency is overvalued with respect to the dollar. If the PPP rate is lower, the currency is undervalued. For example, in August 1995, the yen/dollar exchange rate was JPY 97 per U.S. dollar. However, to make a Big Mac in Japan cost the same as in the

U.S., an exchange rate of JPY 169 per U.S. dollar would have been needed. Since the number of yen required to purchase a dollar was higher at the PPP rate than at the market rate, the market rate overvalued the yen in PPP terms—by nearly 75 percent.[2] The tendency of market rates to converge with PPP rates is seen in the developments since then in the yen/dollar exchange rate. By April 1997, the market rate had moved to 126 yen per dollar, very close to the Big Mac PPP rate of 121 yen per dollar.

Much of the empirical work on PPP rates in the current century has been designed to find out why market and PPP exchange rates do not converge as theory says they should. The literature on this topic, which has been ably summarized by Rogoff (1996), and empirical research done for the present report reveal the following factors of special relevance. First, the prices of goods that are not traded internationally are not subject to arbitrage. The prices of such "non-traded" goods will gradually converge with international prices, but much less quickly than those for traded goods. For example, the cost of most non-traded goods depends heavily on wage costs, but the wages for workers producing non-traded goods and services such as restaurant meals will not rise towards international levels until the demand for labor to produce traded goods pushes up wages in the non-traded sector by attracting workers into the production of traded goods and services. Second, economies in transition by definition have not yet established well-functioning markets, and this increases the share of goods that are not subject to arbitrage. For example, market imperfections such as noncompetitive exchange rates, protective tariffs, and poorly-developed international marketing common in these countries restrict the growth of exports, leaving more goods in the non-traded category and thus not subject to the direct trading and arbitrage that leads to international price convergence. Third, countries that are relatively wealthy have usually attained this status because much broader range of products as indicated by their Hirschman/Hirfindahl export concentration ratio, which reflects the degree to which a country's export earnings depend on a narrow or a broad range of export products.[3] As a result of the improved functioning of markets that comes with development, the international convergence of prices, and thus of the MER and PPP, tends to increase as countries become richer.

Fourth, as suggested by Balassa and Samuelson some 30 years ago, average price levels in lower income countries tend to be lower because labor productivity is lower in these countries, and because these countries tend to have a higher share of low value, non-traded, labor-based goods in their total production basket. With a larger share of these non-traded goods that are not subject to arbitrage, prices in poorer and less-reformed countries will not have converged with world prices as fully as prices in richer countries. Figures E.1 and E.2 help demonstrate these points.

Figure E.1 shows the relatively high degree of correlation among FSU and CEE countries between (a) the degree of transition, as measured by the Liberalization Index used in the World Bank's 1996 *World Development Report*, on the horizontal axis and (b) the convergence of prices on the vertical axis as measured by the ratio of the PPP and MER rates. The FSU/CEE economies that have not liberalized tend to have a PPP rate that is only 10 to 20 percent of the way towards convergence with the market rate. Those that are further advanced in establishing a market economy tend to have a PPP rate that is perhaps 50 percent towards convergence with the market rate.

Figure E.2 helps explain why the maximum convergence is still only 60 percent rather than close to 100 percent for the FSU/CEE countries shown in Figure E.1. Figure E.2 shows the degree of price convergence for a much broader group of countries ranging in income levels from Nigeria and Kenya, which have 1990 per capita incomes equal to about 5 percent of U.S. levels, up to the United States. This graph clearly demonstrates the increasing convergence

Figure E.1: Prices converge as the level of liberalization increases.

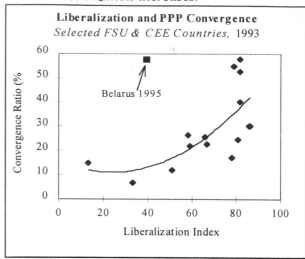

to world price levels (with prices in the U.S. as the numeraire) as per capita incomes rise.

The implications of these graphs for Belarus are that, given its liberalization index in 1995 (49 percent) and its low per capita income relative to that in the U.S. (about 8 percent), the price convergence ratio as indicated by the ratio of

the PPP exchange rate to the market exchange rate, should be about 20 percent, not almost 40 percent as it is now. The overvalued market

Figure. E.2: Prices converge with world levels as countries grow richer.

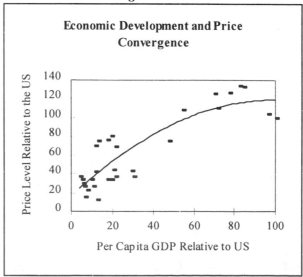

exchange rate is too close to the PPP rate to provide the margin of competitiveness that domestic producers need to overcome the handicaps of an economic system that is inadequately liberalized and where per capita incomes are still far below those in the industrialized countries.

Notes

1   Choosing a good with high local content like a hamburger in a restaurant avoids the problem that, as the percentage of imported content increases, the price converges with the price determined by the dollar price and the market exchange rate. For example, assuming no differences due to transportation, taxes, or profit margins, the domestic price of a gallon of imported gasoline converted to dollars at the market exchange rate would be the same as the dollar price of the gasoline in the U.S. because the domestic price is determined by the dollar price and the market exchange rate. Thus a PPP exchange rate based on the domestic price of gasoline would be very similar to the market exchange rate —and this is exactly the result found in both Belarus and Ukraine

2   The fact that Japan simultaneously had a trade surplus indicates that PPP rates must be interpreted with caution and must be used as only one of several indicators when determining the appropriate valuation of an exchange rate. The apparent explanation for the simultaneous overvaluation of the yen and a balance of payments surplus is that, among industrialized countries where full price convergence has already taken place, a country that has a large balance of payments surplus needs to maintain an overvalued exchange rate to bring the balance of payments back into equilibrium.

3   The World Bank. *From Plan to Market: World Development Report 1996* (WDR 1996), pp. 192 and 226.

Sources

The World Bank. 1996. *From Plan to Market: World Development Report 1996.* New York: Oxford University Press.

OECD. 1996. *Transition Brief.* (1/96). Paris.

Rogoff, Kenneth. 1996. "The Purchasing Power Parity Puzzle," *Journal of Economic Literature,* vol. XXXIV (June 1996), pp. 647-668.

The Economist. "Economics Focus: Buy Hard with a Vengeance," August 26, 1995, p. 66, and "Big MacCurrencies: Can hamburgers provide hot tips about exchange rates?" April 12, 1997, p. 71.

Transition. "Purchasing Power Parities," 7(3-4), March-April 1996, p. 19.

Distributors of World Bank Publications

Prices and credit terms vary from country to country. Consult your local distributor before placing an order.

ARGENTINA
Oficina del Libro Internacional
Av. Cordoba 1877
1120 Buenos Aires
Tel: (54 1) 815-8354
Fax: (54 1) 815-8156

AUSTRALIA, FIJI, PAPUA NEW GUINEA, SOLOMON ISLANDS, VANUATU, AND WESTERN SAMOA
D.A. Information Services
648 Whitehorse Road
Mitcham 3132
Victoria
Tel: (61) 3 9210 7777
Fax: (61) 3 9210 7788
E-mail: service@dadirect.com.au
URL: http://www.dadirect.com.au

AUSTRIA
Gerold and Co.
Weihburggasse 26
A-1011 Wien
Tel: (43 1) 512-47-31-0
Fax: (43 1) 512-47-31-29
URL: http://www.gerold.co/at.online

BANGLADESH
Micro Industries Development
Assistance Society (MIDAS)
House 5, Road 16
Dhanmondi R/Area
Dhaka 1209
Tel: (880 2) 326427
Fax: (880 2) 811188

BELGIUM
Jean De Lannoy
Av. du Roi 202
1060 Brussels
Tel: (32 2) 538-5169
Fax: (32 2) 538-0841

BRAZIL
Publicações Tecnicas Internacionais Ltda.
Rua Peixoto Gomide, 209
01409 Sao Paulo, SP.
Tel: (55 11) 259-6644
Fax: (55 11) 258-6990
E-mail: postmaster@pti.uol.br
URL: http://www.uol.br

CANADA
Renouf Publishing Co. Ltd.
5369 Canotek Road
Ottawa, Ontario K1J 9J3
Tel: (613) 745-2665
Fax: (613) 745-7660
E-mail: order.dept@renoufbooks.com
URL: http://www.renoufbooks.com

CHINA
China Financial & Economic
Publishing House
8, Da Fo Si Dong Jie
Beijing
Tel: (86 10) 6333-8257
Fax: (86 10) 6401-7365

COLOMBIA
Infoenlace Ltda.
Carrera 6 No. 51-21
Apartado Aereo 34270
Santafé de Bogotá, D.C.
Tel: (57 1) 285-2798
Fax: (57 1) 285-2798

COTE D'IVOIRE
Center d'Edition et de Diffusion Africaines
(CEDA)
04 B.P. 541
Abidjan 04
Tel: (225) 24 6510; 24 6511
Fax: (225) 25 0567

CYPRUS
Center for Applied Research
Cyprus College
6, Diogenes Street, Engomi
P.O. Box 2006
Nicosia
Tel: (357 2) 44-1730
Fax: (357 2) 46-2051

CZECH REPUBLIC
National Information Center
prodejna, Konviktská 5
CS – 113 57 Prague 1
Tel: (42 2) 2422-9433
Fax: (42 2) 2422-1484
URL: http://www.nis.cz/

DENMARK
SamfundsLitteratur
Rosenoerns Allé 11
DK-1970 Frederiksberg C
Tel: (45 31) 351942
Fax: (45 31) 357822

ECUADOR
Libri Mundi
Libreria Internacional
P.O. Box 17-01-3029
Juan Leon Mera 851
Quito
Tel: (593 2) 521-606; (593 2) 544-185
Fax: (593 2) 504-209
E-mail: librimu1@librimundi.com.ec
E-mail: librimu2@librimundi.com.ec

EGYPT, ARAB REPUBLIC OF
Al Ahram Distribution Agency
Al Galaa Street
Cairo
Tel: (20 2) 578-6083
Fax: (20 2) 578-6833

The Middle East Observer
41, Sherif Street
Cairo
Tel: (20 2) 393-9732
Fax: (20 2) 393-9732

FINLAND
Akateeminen Kirjakauppa
P.O. Box 128
FIN-00101 Helsinki
Tel: (358 0) 121 4418
Fax: (358 0) 121-4435
E-mail: akatilaus@stockmann.fi
URL: http://www.akateeminen.com/

FRANCE
World Bank Publications
66, avenue d'Iéna
75116 Paris
Tel: (33 1) 40-69-30-56/57
Fax: (33 1) 40-69-30-68

GERMANY
UNO-Verlag
Poppelsdorfer Allee 55
53115 Bonn
Tel: (49 228) 212940
Fax: (49 228) 217492

GREECE
Papasotiriou S.A.
35, Stournara Str.
106 82 Athens
Tel: (30 1) 364-1826
Fax: (30 1) 364-8254

HAITI
Culture Diffusion
5, Rue Capois
C.P. 257
Port-au-Prince
Tel: (509 1) 3 9260

HONG KONG, MACAO
Asia 2000 Ltd.
Sales & Circulation Department
Seabird House, unit 1101-02
22-28 Wyndham Street, Central
Hong Kong
Tel: (852) 2530-1409
Fax: (852) 2526-1107
E-mail: sales@asia2000.com.hk
URL: http://www.asia2000.com.hk

HUNGARY
Euro Info Service
Margitszgeti Europa Haz
H-1138 Budapest
Tel: (36 1) 111 6061
Fax: (36 1) 302 5035
E-mail: euroinfo@mail.matav.hu

INDIA
Allied Publishers Ltd.
751 Mount Road
Madras - 600 002
Tel: (91 44) 852-3938
Fax: (91 44) 852-0649

INDONESIA
Pt. Indira Limited
Jalan Borobudur 20
P.O. Box 181
Jakarta 10320
Tel: (62 21) 390-4290
Fax: (62 21) 421-4289

IRAN
Ketab Sara Co. Publishers
Khaled Eslamboli Ave., 6th Street
Kusheh Delafrooz No. 8
P.O. Box 15745-733
Tehran
Tel: (98 21) 8717819; 8716104
Fax: (98 21) 8712479
E-mail: ketab-sara@neda.net.ir

IRELAND
Government Supplies Agency
Oifig an tSoláthair
4-5 Harcourt Road
Dublin 2
Tel: (353 1) 661-3111
Fax: (353 1) 475-2670

ISRAEL
Yozmot Literature Ltd.
P.O. Box 56055
3 Yohanan Hasandlar Street
Tel Aviv 61560
Tel: (972 3) 5285-397
Fax: (972 3) 5285-397

R.O.Y. International
PO Box 13056
Tel Aviv 61130
Tel: (972 3) 5461423
Fax: (972 3) 5461442
E-mail: royil@netvision.net.il

Palestinian Authority/Middle East
Index Information Services
P.O.B. 19502 Jerusalem
Tel: (972 2) 6271219
Fax: (972 2) 6271634

ITALY
Licosa Commissionaria Sansoni SPA
Via Duca Di Calabria, 1/1
Casella Postale 552
50125 Firenze
Tel: (55) 645-415
Fax: (55) 641-257
E-mail: licosa@ftbcc.it
Url: http://www.ftbcc.it/licosa

JAMAICA
Ian Randle Publishers Ltd.
206 Old Hope Road, Kingston 6
Tel: 809-927-2085
Fax: 809-977-0243
E-mail: irpl@colis.com

JAPAN
Eastern Book Service
3-13 Hongo 3-chome, Bunkyo-ku
Tokyo 113
Tel: (81 3) 3818-0861
Fax: (81 3) 3818-0864
E-mail: orders@svt-ebs.co.jp
URL: http://www.bekkoame.or.jp/~svt-ebs

KENYA
Africa Book Service (E.A.) Ltd.
Quaran House, Mfangano Street
P.O. Box 45245
Nairobi
Tel: (254 2) 223 641
Fax: (254 2) 330 272

KOREA, REPUBLIC OF
Daejon Trading Co. Ltd.
P.O. Box 34, Youida, 706 Seoun Bldg
44-6 Youido-Dong, Yeongchengo-Ku
Seoul
Tel: (82 2) 785-1631/4
Fax: (82 2) 784-0315

MALAYSIA
University of Malaya Cooperative
Bookshop, Limited
P.O. Box 1127
Jalan Pantai Baru
59700 Kuala Lumpur
Tel: (60 3) 756-5000
Fax: (60 3) 755-4424

MEXICO
INFOTEC
Av. San Fernando No. 37
Col. Toriello Guerra
14050 Mexico, D.F.
Tel: (52 5) 624-2800
Fax: (52 5) 624-2822
E-mail: infotec@rtn.net.mx
URL: http://rtn.net.mx

NEPAL
Everest Media International Services (P) Ltd.
GPO Box 5443
Kathmandu
Tel: (977 1) 472 152
Fax: (977 1) 224 431

NETHERLANDS
De Lindeboom/InOr-Publikaties
P.O. Box 202, 7480 AE Haaksbergen
Tel: (31 53) 574-0004
Fax: (31 53) 572-9296
E-mail: lindeboo@worldonline.nl
URL: http://www.worldonline.nl/~lindeboo

NEW ZEALAND
EBSCO NZ Ltd.
Private Mail Bag 99914
New Market
Auckland
Tel: (64 9) 524-8119
Fax: (64 9) 524-8067

NIGERIA
University Press Limited
Three Crowns Building Jericho
Private Mail Bag 5095
Ibadan
Tel: (234 22) 41-1356
Fax: (234 22) 41-2056

NORWAY
NIC Info A/S
Book Department, Postboks 6512 Etterstad
N-0606 Oslo
Tel: (47 22) 97-4500
Fax: (47 22) 97-4545

PAKISTAN
Mirza Book Agency
65, Shahrah-e-Quaid-e-Azam
Lahore 54000
Tel: (92 42) 735 3601
Fax: (92 42) 576 3714

Oxford University Press
5 Bangalore Town
Sharae Faisal
PO Box 13033
Karachi-75350
Tel: (92 21) 446307
Fax: (92 21) 4547640
E-mail: oup@oup.khi.erum.com.pk

Pak Book Corporation
Aziz Chambers 21, Queen's Road
Lahore
Tel: (92 42) 636 3222; 636 0885
Fax: (92 42) 636 2328
E-mail: pbc@brain.net.pk

PERU
Editorial Desarrollo SA
Apartado 3824, Lima 1
Tel: (51 14) 285380
Fax: (51 14) 286628

PHILIPPINES
International Booksource Center Inc.
1127-A Antipolo St, Barangay, Venezuela
Makati City
Tel: (63 2) 896 6501; 6505; 6507
Fax: (63 2) 896 1741

POLAND
International Publishing Service
Ul. Piekna 31/37
00-677 Warzawa
Tel: (48 2) 628-6089
Fax: (48 2) 621-7255
E-mail: books%ips@ikp.atm.com.pl
URL: http://www.ipscg.waw.pl/ips/export/

PORTUGAL
Livraria Portugal
Apartado 2681, Rua Do Carmo 70-74
1200 Lisbon
Tel: (1) 347-4982
Fax: (1) 347-0264

ROMANIA
Compani De Librari Bucuresti S.A.
Str. Lipscani no. 26, sector 3
Bucharest
Tel: (40 1) 613 9645
Fax: (40 1) 312 4000

RUSSIAN FEDERATION
Isdatelstvo <Ves Mir>
9a, Lolpachniy Pereulok
Moscow 101831
Tel: (7 095) 917 87 49
Fax: (7 095) 917 92 59

SINGAPORE, TAIWAN, MYANMAR, BRUNEI
Asahgate Publishing Asia Pacific Pte. Ltd.
41 Kallang Pudding Road #04-03
Golden Wheel Building
Singapore 349316
Tel: (65) 741-5166
Fax: (65) 742-9356
E-mail: ashgate@asianconnect.com

SLOVENIA
Gospodarski Vestnik Publishing Group
Dunajska cesta 5
1000 Ljubljana
Tel: (386 61) 133 83 47; 132 12 30
Fax: (386 61) 133 80 30
E-mail: repansekj@gvestnik.si

SOUTH AFRICA, BOTSWANA
International Subscription Service
P.O. Box 41095
Craighall
Johannesburg 2024
Tel: (27 11) 880-1448
Fax: (27 11) 880-6248
E-mail: iss@is.co.za

Oxford University Press
P.O. Box 1141
Cape Town 8000

SPAIN
Mundi-Prensa Libros, S.A.
Castello 37
28001 Madrid
Tel: (34 1) 431-3399
Fax: (34 1) 575-3998
E-mail: libreria@mundiprensa.es
URL: http://www.mundiprensa.es/

Mundi-Prensa Barcelona
Consell de Cent, 391
08009 Barcelona
Tel: (34 3) 488-3492
Fax: (34 3) 487-7659
E-mail: barcelona@mundiprensa.es

SRI LANKA, THE MALDIVES
Lake House Bookshop
100, Sir Chittampalam Gardiner Mawatha
Colombo 2
Tel: (94 1) 32105
Fax: (94 1) 432104
E-mail: LHL@sri.lanka.net

SWEDEN
Wennergren-Williams AB
P.O. Box 1305
S-171 25 Solna
Tel: (46 8) 705-97-50
Fax: (46 8) 27-00-71
E-mail: mail@wwi.se

SWITZERLAND
Librairie Payot Service Institutionnel
Côtes-de-Montbenon 30
1002 Lausanne
Tel: (41 21) 341-3229
Fax: (41 21) 341-3235

ADECO Van Diermen EditionsTechniques
Ch. de Lacuez 41
CH1807 Blonay
Tel: (41 21) 943 2673
Fax: (41 21) 943 3605

TANZANIA
Oxford University Press
Maktaba Street, PO Box 5299
Dar es Salaam
Tel: (255 51) 29209
Fax: (255 51) 46822

THAILAND
Central Books Distribution
306 Silom Road
Bangkok 10500
Tel: (66 2) 235-5400
Fax: (66 2) 237-8321

TRINIDAD & TOBAGO, AND THE CARRIBBEAN
Systematics Studies Unit
9 Watts Street
Curepe
Trinidad, West Indies
Tel: (809) 662-5654
Fax: (809) 662-5654
E-mail: tobe@trinidad.net

UGANDA
Gustro Ltd.
PO Box 9997, Madhvani Building
Plot 16/4 Jinja Rd.
Kampala
Tel: (256 41) 254 763
Fax: (256 41) 251 468

UNITED KINGDOM
Microinfo Ltd.
P.O. Box 3, Alton, Hampshire GU34 2PG
England
Tel: (44 1420) 86848
Fax: (44 1420) 89889
E-mail: wbank@ukminfo.demon.co.uk
URL: http://www.microinfo.co.uk

VENEZUELA
Tecni-Ciencia Libros, S.A.
Centro Cuidad Comercial Tamanco
Nivel C2, Caracas
Tel: (58 2) 959 5547; 5035; 0016
Fax: (58 2) 959 5636

ZAMBIA
University Bookshop, University of Zambia
Great East Road Campus
P.O. Box 32379
Lusaka
Tel: (260 1) 252 576
Fax: (260 1) 253 952

ZIMBABWE
Longman Zimbabwe (Pvt.) Ltd.
Tourle Road, Ardbennie
P.O. Box ST125
Southerton
Harare
Tel: (263 4) 6216617-
Fax: (263 4) 621670